For Chris,
my favorite
Teen-ager—whose research
contributed
this book

Fritz [signature]

The Search for Structure

The Search for Structure

A Report on American Youth Today

Francis A. J. Ianni

THE FREE PRESS
A Division of Macmillan, Inc.
NEW YORK

Collier Macmillan Publishers
LONDON

The Free Press
A Division of Macmillan, Inc.
866 Third Avenue, New York, N.Y. 10022

Collier Macmillan Canada, Inc.

Printed in the United States of America

printing number

1 2 3 4 5 6 7 8 9 10

Library of Congress Cataloging-in-Publication Data

Ianni, Francis A. J.
    The search for structure.

    Bibliography: p.
    Includes index.
    1. Teenagers—United States.   2. Youth—United States.
3. United States—Social conditions—1945–
I. Title.
HQ796.I223   1989   305.2'35'0973   88-30945
ISBN 0-02-915360-3

For Tom James and Art Singer

Contents

Preface and Acknowledgments   ix

1. Growing Up in America   1

2. Peer Worlds and Adolescent Development   22

3. "Home is Where We Start From"   55

4. From Home to School   103

5. After School: Youth In and Out of the Labor Market   140

6. Pathways to Crime   184

7. Tell Me Who I Am   224

8. The Search for Structure and the Caring Community   260

Notes   285

Bibliography   317

Index   327

Preface and Acknowledgments

The descriptions and analyses of teenage life in ten communities which are presented in this book are my gleanings from a program of research which began in September of 1973 and continued through June of 1985. The first study examined how school cultures developed and how they comparatively affected adolescents in three high schools: one urban, one suburban, one rural. After a separate study analyzing how desegregation altered the social system of the urban school, we then moved beyond the three high schools initially studied into their communities. In the first phase of this research, which began in 1979 and was completed in 1982, we followed students out into the community to observe their interactions in various social settings in the community. We also interviewed these students and the peers and adults in their lives to discern how what is experienced in these settings relates teenagers and their communities to each other. Over the next three years, in seven additional communities, we did comparison studies including a close examination of the mediating and mentoring role of adults in adolescent social networks.

Although I was the project director and principal investigator in each of these studies, a number of colleagues and an even larger number of graduate students were directly involved in finding what we sought and refining what we learned. Professors William Dalton, Hope Jensen Leichter, and Hervé Varenne, all then associated with the Horace Mann–Lincoln Institute at Teachers College, Columbia University, directed teams of graduate student field researchers in the initial study of three high schools, as did Margaret Terry Orr, presently at the Academy for Educational Development, and Elizabeth

Reuss-Ianni, research director of the Institute for Social Analysis, in later periods of the research. Howard Becker, MacArthur Professor of Sociology at Northwestern University, was the principal research consultant throughout the project. The following graduate students were field research assistants in the various communities during some period of the research: Carol Ascher, Patricia Caesar, Simon Chow, the late Peter Clute, Shelley Goldman, John Halbreich, Samuel Henry, Paul Jennings, Suma Kurien, Melanie Lewis, John Mavros, Margaret Terry Orr, Edward Reynolds, Rodney Riffle, George Sanchez, Dora Schriro, Mercer Sullivan, and Claudia Ulbright. Nine of these students have written doctoral dissertations based on their work in the research program. Other teams of graduate students surveyed the popular and scientific literature on adolescents as well as policy and program materials at the federal and local levels and interviewed writers and policy specialists. Craig Calhoun, Peter Gibbon, Ann Marie Isaacs, Mary Ellen James, Wamboi Karunde, Gibran Majdalany, Margaret Terry Orr, Elizabeth Reuss-Ianni, and Stephanie Shipman researched and wrote the literature and policy reviews.

In writing this book I have drawn from all of these studies, but the major analyses were developed in the three studies which took place between 1979 and 1985. I have also drawn some data from my work during 1976 and 1977 in the Safe Schools Study carried out by the National Institute of Education and a study of dropouts Elizabeth Reuss-Ianni and I did for a school district in a southern city in 1984. Where I have used data or analyses from these studies, I have specifically identified them as such. Support for the research program came from a variety of sources, and I want to thank each for making the research program possible. The initial study of three high schools was supported by the Ford Foundation, and the desegregation study by the National Institute of Education. I am particularly grateful to the Spencer Foundation for three grants and continuing support over the period of six years during which most of the research reported here was carried out.

I would also like to express my appreciation to:

The Rockefeller Foundation for the opportunity to spend time as a Resident Scholar at their center in Bellagio, Italy, to work on the manuscript. Roberto and Gianna Celli, who direct the center, were particularly helpful during that time.

Laura Wolff of The Free Press, who consistently provided insights and firm but fair criticisms which helped shaped as well as improve the manuscript. Gibran Majdalany, my assistant at Teachers College, Columbia University, who organized the checking and word processing of the manuscript by me and a number of others, including Marilyn Breeze, Virginia Roach, and Vasiliki Tsigas.

The students in my social organization and field and clinical research seminars at Teachers College and the interns in my supervision seminars at St. Luke's Hospital Center, listened patiently and responded to ideas and formulations as they developed.

My colleagues at the New York Psychoanalytic Institute, particularly Aaron Esman, M.D., and in the Department of Psychiatry at St. Luke's, particularly the late Adam Muns, for help and advice in the research process.

Most profoundly, I am grateful to the many parents, youth professionals, and teenagers in the different communities whose cooperation made the research possible.

1

Growing Up in America

The lives of adolescents hold a fascination for all of us. We have an enduring faith that the future of our world rests with the young, and so we look to this period of life more than any other for an evaluation of current society and the probable social future. As adults we assign to these younger members of society the role and the responsibility both to carry on our accumulated knowledge and to learn from our mistakes. Much more than childhood or even early adulthood, adolescence is viewed as a period of promise and preparation, and yet it is also seen as a time of special problems. As the vehicle for a troubled transition from childhood to adult status, it sets the stage for many of the most dramatic social and psychological problems in American society. In fact, it may well be that it is the drama of the problems associated with it that makes us so particularly aware of the adolescent passage.

A variety of social problems identify adolescence as a statistical and social fact. Juvenile delinquency has increased almost threefold since World War II. Recurrent evidence of drug and alcohol abuse inevitably centers on adolescents as individuals or in groups. Despite the legalization of abortion, teenage pregnancy rates have been higher in the United States than in most industrialized and even some unindustrialized nations. These are the compelling social facts, yet they tell us little or nothing about the inner experience of adolescence: feelings about society and its future, about education, sex, and work. Neither can we document statistically the psychic and societal costs of youthful alienation from major social institutions such as the school, or the psychological and social tragedies behind adolescent suicide.

The drama of these social facts also supplies the forms, the symbols, and the colors by which popular culture produces a group portrait of what most if not all American adolescents are like. In the media and popular press American adolescents have been portrayed in a number of different ways in each decade since World War II. In the 1950s, a period of relative peace and prosperity, most were shown as clean-cut, materialistic conformists, indifferent to political and social issues. To liven things up, a few were "greasers," "beatniks," "rebels without a cause." In the 1960s, a decade characterized by the war in Vietnam, urban riots, and political assassinations, teenagers became angry, assertive, hedonistic, idealistic, and antimaterialistic. Then in the 1970s, disillusioned by the failure of the activism and reforms of the sixties and by an oversupply of would-be professionals, youth again became grade-grubbing, apathetic, and conservative, the young adult "yuppies" of the 1980s. Only the hedonism was left from the 1960s. Still another picture began to emerge in the eighties, when, plagued by ever-expanding and deepening concern about problems of physical and mental health, sexual and social conduct, and various forms of abuse of self and others among young people, we began to see and hear this cohort of adolescents described as "the New Lost Generation." Despite the conformity in behavior and style assumed in such collective characterizations, there has always been considerable controversy in both professional and public arenas over "the adolescent problem," who is responsible for it, and what can and should be done about it.

In March 1987 four teenagers, two boys aged eighteen and nineteen and two sisters aged sixteen and seventeen, brought national attention to a northern New Jersey community, Bergenfield, when they committed suicide in a pact that bound them together in death as they had been by the shared problems of their short but troubled lives. All of them had experienced problems with their families, and one of the boys had seen his father kill himself a few years earlier. The two girls were having a problem adjusting to their mother's remarriage and the stepfather and his children who now became part of their household. Both males and the older of the sisters had dropped out of school and had been joined by the younger sister when she was suspended and showed little inclination to return to school. All had also been part of a troubled and troublesome peer group known as The Burnouts, addicted to punk fashion and heavy-metal music. The two young men had been only intermittently employed, and there were indications of frequent drug and alcohol use by the group and their friends. They were, said the local police chief, "pain-in-the-ass-type kids" who were "going nowhere fast."[1]

The tragedy shook the community in which these young people had lived and died. Parents and teenage peers alike turned their anger on the schools, which, they said, had offered little or no help for their problems. The dramatic death pact drew wide media coverage and shocked the nation, particularly when it was followed shortly afterward by the "copycat" suicide of two teenage girls in a midwestern town. Like the New Jersey teenagers, they had died from the exhaust fumes of a car left running in a garage. Their lives had been as tragically similar to those of the four earlier suicides as was their means of escape. The two girls, one nineteen and the other seventeen, were inseparable friends who had dropped out of school and were unemployed. The older girl had seen her marriage fail and twice had miscarried. Friends of the girls said that sometimes the pair drank a good deal, beginning early in the morning.[2] When their bodies were found, the older girl had her album of wedding pictures and the younger was holding a rose and her toy stuffed walrus.

The aftermath of these teenage suicides produced a series of controversies throughout the country as well as in Bergenfield itself. Who was responsible for the uneasy lives and early deaths of these young people? No one seemed to agree. For some it was uncaring families who neglected their children and did not heed their calls for help; for others it was an insensitive and ineffective school system which had failed these adolescents at risk. Many saw it as yet another example of the power of the peer group to influence and pressure its members to conform to self-destructive behavior; teenagers in Bergenfield laid the responsibility on the schools and berated the media for intruding on their lives. Even the experts on teenage suicide could not agree on whether the media exposure had added to the problem, planting the thought of suicide in young minds throughout the country.

The experts seem just as confused about the *good* things they discover about adolescents. Hoang Nhu Tran, whose family escaped from Vietnam when Saigon fell, arrived in the United States at the age of nine and settled in a Colorado trailer park along with his family. Thirteen years later he was class valedictorian at the United States Air Force Academy and a Rhodes scholar. In between, his family had moved out of the trailer camp to be near the area's best junior high school when he entered the seventh grade; later they moved again to be near the best high school. Was the young man's success the product of the good schools? Could it be that he was molded by his father, who had been a South Vietnamese Army major and who explained his son's success by saying "You have to bend the bamboo when it is young"?[3] Here again the experts disagree. Some see this as an example of the single-minded dedication of the Asian-American family to help their children capture the American Dream. Others trace it back to Asia and the Confucian values of family and education. Some even see it as the result of "genetic differences" in the rate at which Asian and white children mature.[4] How can we account for the brilliant success of this young immigrant, and how do we explain the tragic lives of the Bergenfield teenagers? Were these different outcomes the result of differences in their families, in the friends they made, or in the schools they attended, or was there some inherent difference in the youngsters themselves?

For over a decade, spanning the 1970s and 1980s, my associates and I observed and interviewed adolescents in ten communities throughout the United States in order to examine and hopefully to help resolve some of these controversies. We observed how teenagers behave and interact with each other and with adults in peer groups, in families, in schools, in the workplace, in juvenile detention facilities, and in mental health settings. Our observations of thousands of adolescents allowed us to determine how the variety of social environments—the family, the school, the peer group—in these communities work, sometimes together but more frequently in competition or even in open conflict with each other, to define and structure the transition from childhood to adulthood. At first we selected three communities for study: one urban inner-city polyethnic area, one affluent suburban residential community outside that city, and one rural area, a northeastern farming community presently undergoing some gentrification as the result of the introduction of a major corporate headquarters nearby. As the research progressed we decided to include more sites, both to add some diversity to our samples of adolescents and to give us some basis for comparison. In each case I first contacted the local school authorities, all of whom I had met previously, and worked through them to gain access to the community.

We selected another major metropolitan inner-city area with considerable ethnic diversity to expand what we knew about adolescents in urban areas. Three more sites were in the same large county political unit in a southern state but differed significantly, since one is an affluent resort-retirement city, one a migrant worker community, and the third a fishing village which has become a major drug-importing center. The other communities were a small mining town in the Southwest, a planned community which was intended to have a mixed racial and socioeconomic structure, and a small city in the mid-Atlantic region which was undergoing racial and ethnic change. We also wanted to get some idea of how institutionalized adolescents relate to the new environments which envelop and isolate them from the familiar social contexts of their home communities. Therefore, we observed and interviewed in two adolescent psychiatric facilities and in one juvenile detention center, all in the same city.

We began our observations in each community in the local high school or middle school, where graduate students, who were usually in their early twenties and had specific roles in the schools, would meet and interact with students. Some of these graduate student field researchers were working as teachers' assistants or interns; one spent a semester as a student attending a full schedule of classes in one of the high schools; others were in less structured roles, simply "hanging out" with groups of students in the schools or in nearby gathering places.[5] We could not, and did not, systematically sample youngsters for observation and interviewing. Rather, after meeting one youngster we developed a "snowball" sample, meeting other youngsters through him and eventually the adults with whom they came in contact. It is impossible to give an exact enumeration of how many students we observed over the more than ten years, but we have over thirty-five hundred names of teenagers and over four hundred adults in our field notes. These names, by the way, as well as the names of the communities we studied, were always recorded as pseudonyms to ensure confidentiality. I have used the same pseudonyms in this book.

As we met more and more teenagers and became accepted, our observations and interviews followed the students out of the school and into their homes, neighborhoods, peer groups and gangs, workplaces, and anywhere else the naturalistic observations led us. In every community, for example, we rode in patrol cars with police runaway or juvenile units or, in rural areas, with sheriff's deputies. When we rode with runaway units in an urban area, we observed and interviewed the runaways and the police. We also interviewed the directors and other personnel of the detention centers or the halfway houses where the teenagers were taken. Wherever possible, we interviewed their parents and peers as well. We interviewed the youth professionals who worked with these same adolescents to look for the linkages among these professionals and their agencies. For example, in investigating a community's programs and policies for dealing with juvenile justice problems, we interviewed school and community criminal justice personnel, and obtained information on how juvenile justice problems were identified and treated, what linkages the school system had established with other community resources such as families and voluntary agencies, and how the existing policies came into being.

Since we wanted to determine how community norms are related to the individual values of teenagers and with what tensions or accommodations between inner and outer experience, I conducted intensive psychodynamic interviews with a sample of adolescents from each community as we were gathering the observational data. These adolescents were either referred by the fieldworkers or were selected by me as a result of my own contacts in the community. They were racially, ethnically, and socioeconomically representative of the communities we worked in, about evenly divided between males and females, and ranged in age from eleven to twenty years of age, with fifteen being the median age. I saw each of the 311 adolescents I interviewed for five sessions each lasting fifty minutes to an hour. I used a relatively unstructured approach in an attempt to penetrate the thoughts, emotions, and meanings underlying the behavior we were observing. The interviews followed a protocol in which I introduced a topic area for discussion and then allowed the adolescent to associate to that topic, intervening whenever I needed explanation or the individual needed redirection.[6]

As the research proceeded we continuously compared and combined all the pertinent material from the field observations and interviews with both teenagers and adults, the psychodynamic interviews, and the literature and policy sources, so that we were analyzing the data from the outset of the research. We analyzed the data from each of the communities first and then did comparative analyses across communities. It was in this comparative process that we began to identify the major themes which seemed to connect or explain what we had amassed. At the same time we also verified our insights and analyses by re-interviewing significant adults in social agencies, schools, families, and other community settings to describe our findings and get their reactions. In all ten communities I also conducted a series of group discussion-interviews in which I met with a number of classes (during regularly scheduled class time and usually without the teacher present) in high schools and middle or junior high schools to describe our findings and obtain feedback from the students.[7] From the outset of this program of research, our basic questions have always been, "What are the codes of rules which structure and organize the transition from child to adult status in the social contexts of actual communities, and how do the adolescents in these communities internalize and learn to use or abuse these rules?" This book is a report on the answers we found when we compared the inner-city, suburban, and rural teenagers we observed and interviewed in peer groups, in their homes, in schools, at work, and in the other social settings of their communities.

While most people tend to talk about adolescence as if it were one unified period in the life course, teenagers more often experience it as a number of more or less synchronized periods, each structured by the various socializing environments, such as the family, the peer group, the workplace, the media, or the criminal justice system. We found that in most of the communities we studied, different rules and roles emerge from each of the different institutions, and differentiating among them is a difficult process which requires an understanding of societal and personal agendas. Unfortunately—particularly in those communities where the family and the school are in opposition, where the workplace proclaims its inability to hire youngsters who are neither motivated by their families nor made literate by the schools, and where the criminal justice system cannot turn to these institutions for support because it sees each of these institutions as antagonistic— the adolescent is left to rationalize these competing and sometimes conflicting ideologies for himself or herself. Conflict and confusion must occur when the home, the school, the workplace, and other social institutions present different standards of adulthood and different means of attaining it. Proclaiming a minimum age of twenty-one for legal use of alcohol, for example, means that in some states a youth cannot drink for a period of three years after being considered old enough to vote, drive, or, if a male, be drafted into the armed services. It also means that an individual cannot drink until five years after being able to marry in some states and until seven years after being eligible for trial as an adult for felonies which carry the death penalty. While our society is raising the age of the legal attainment of adulthood for some activities, we are at the same time lowering it for others, and we continue to think of and treat adolescents as members of a distinctive and age-graded caste despite all we know about individual differences in maturation and development.

While there has been some blurring of both the boundaries of socially defined life periods and the age-appropriate behaviors associated with them in the latter half of the twentieth century, adolescence as an age-grade has been expanded rather than diminished. At one end, we have come to recognize the transformational period of "early adolescence" (ten to thirteen years of age), when the social and biological changes that mark child-into-adult development begin to occur. At the other end, a new life period identified as "youth" (about ages sixteen through twenty-four), no longer adolescent but not yet quite adult, has emerged as post–high school education has expanded and as marriage and career choices have been delayed while various life styles and options are exploited.

The variability of the demarcation of the end of the adolescent period by a variety of legal standards for adult competence is also true of the traditional transitions into adulthood. Such turning points as completing one's formal education, obtaining full-time employment (still primarily for males), and then settling down into marriage and parenthood now come earlier for some youths but later for others than they did in the past. As recently as the first half of the twentieth century, these events were scheduled to happen at roughly the same time in the life span, collectively confirming adult status and responsibilities. Each of these transitions, however, has become independent of the others as some individuals extend their education until their late twenties or beyond, others drop out of school in their teens to get a job or have babies, and the age of marriage has been pushed back.

If there is confusion about which individual and social changes signal the end of adolescence, there is general agreement that it is the onset of puberty which marks its beginning. Puberty is affected by environmental factors—as reflected in the four-year drop in the age of its onset over the last century—and it produces internal and external changes that impinge on human behavior. The changes that puberty ushers in are always subject to social influence as well as interpretation.[8] Most importantly, puberty changes how the new adolescent thinks about her body, self, and relationships with others.

While some of the confusion and much of the public storm and stress over adolescence can be attributed to media overexposure of youth and their problems, the confusion and concern does in fact grow out of a number of age-old controversies in science as well as in society which are still unresolved. Probably the oldest and most fundamental of these questions is the relative importance of internal, genetic factors and external, environmental forces in the development, character, and even existence of a life-course stage called "adolescence." While at first glance this seems to be just a restatement of the heredity versus environment conundrum, there are a number of unresolved and still-contested issues which complicate and confound any definitive resolution. For most of this century our inability to resolve these issues, as much as anything that teenagers themselves have done or not done, is what has produced so much uncertainty about the adolescent period.

When G. Stanley Hall first focused attention on adolescence in America in the early 1900s, he did so with a firmly fixed biogenetic faith in Lamarckianism and the theory of recapitulation. Throughout his wide-ranging and encyclopedic two-volume *Adolescence,* Hall promulgated the principle that the individual's behavior unfolds through a series of age-specific patterns built into the organism with the immutability that characterized the Darwinian evolutionist certainty of his time. While he gave some attention to environmental influences as factors which stimulate, modify, and support growth, he insisted that the human psyche, like the human physique, was genetically preprogrammed to "recapitulate," or retrace, the stages of the evolution of the species. Adolescence, which began with puberty, was one of these stages of individual human development. Hall reasoned that since the recapitulatory processes weakened as growth came to an end and "the second birth" of adulthood approached, hereditary influence diminished and adolescents were more subject to cultural and social as well as physical pressures from the environment. It was Hall who used the phrase "storm and stress" to describe what he saw as a transitional stage of vulnerability to emotional disturbance which accounted for youthful inconsistency and conflict in this period of life. An impressive array of scholars and scientists reaffirmed this epigenetic, or stage theory, approach to defining and describing adolescence, although there have been differing perspectives and emphases.[9]

It was Erik Erikson's projection of the instinctual adolescent conflict, which other psychoanalytic writers had seen as a result of puberty, outside the teenager and into the social world which was to become most influential in describing how adolescents come to view or identify themselves. Erikson proposed a series of eight age-related stages, each of which presents a particular bi-polar conflict in the human life cycle.[10] The goal for the individual is to proceed sequentially through each stage by resolving its characteristic social as well as emotional conflict. If the conflict is worked out, a new trait is success-fully incorporated into the ego. If it is left unresolved, a negative trait is incorporated, with dysfunctional consequences for further devel-opment and possibly for mental and social health as well. The task of adolescence is the resolution of the conflict between identity clarifica-tion and identity confusion.

While the various stage approaches differ in perspective and in the role they assign to environmental influences, they are related by the shared assumption that the organism progresses through a finite set of developmental stages, each stage being dependent upon the successful completion of prior stages. On the other side of the argument, however, are those who dispute the primacy of internal forces, instead portraying social and cultural influences as determining the character of, if not creating, adolescence. This movement originated in the great public as well as scientific debates in the 1920s and 1930s over nature versus nurture and the widely read accounts of the ventures by anthropologists and sociologists into contemporary American cities as well as the primitive cultural world. It was in the period after World War II, however, that the focus on adolescence as a social construction rather than an internally produced life stage developed.[11]

Since that time the inconsistencies, contradictions, and rapid trans-formations in values and attitudes resulting from technological and social change have increasingly been associated with adolescent turmoil and the problems of youth. Some see a conflict between the confusion of social change and the biological constancy of problems of sexual expression as the critical factor in creating an adolescent trauma.[12] Others indict industrialization, the emergence of insensitive bureaucra-cies and complex organizations, the growth of technology, or political turmoil.[13] Still others complain of the lack of integration of culture, the rapidity of social change, or the uncertain future, linking these with current social behavior and problems for adolescents.[14] These crises, singly or in concert, are viewed as plaguing American adoles-cence with problems of socialization and role identification, crippling the achievement of identity and self-esteem. Here adolescents are seen as the victims of society, and it is social forces, not biological susceptibility, which make adolescence a shaky and often risky pas-sage. This, in turn, leads to a form of conflict or crisis between the adolescent and society. This view moves the conflict from inside the adolescent into the outside world with which the individual must con-tend. Edgar Friedenberg, for example, maintained that the adolescent is frequently "the victim of hostile social processes" and is often "goaded into hostile action" by these same social processes, which he does not comprehend.[15] Adolescents, individually and collectively, also came to be described as isolated and often alienated from the world of adult work, a society unto themselves.

This new emphasis on the social power and uniqueness of the adolescent peer group began to appear after World War II when sociologists focused attention on the effects of industrialization as inevitably diminishing the socialization functions of the family and the school. Denied informed familial guidance and the protection of kinship in this changing world, youth sought intimacy and direction in the fellowship of peers. The peer group became part of a new institutional environment, the basic unit of a separate social system more persuasive to youth than family or school and increasingly independent of adult authority and control. Talcott Parsons, for example, declared that adolescents were forced to look to each other to develop their own social codes because of a manifest lack of adult guidance as well as the conflicting expectations of adult society.[16] Fellow sociologist David Riesman insisted that youth were becoming "other-directed" and that the family was "merely a part of a wider social environment to which [the youth] early becomes attentive."[17] Neither parents nor teachers acted as prototypes for adulthood; youth found their models in the abstract and fantasized images present in films and on television.

The conceptualization of a unique and separatist adolescent society emerged most distinctly in sociologist James Coleman's study of peer behavior in high schools during the late 1950s.[18] Coleman asked teenagers in high schools to select the most popular students and to explain why they should be considered popular. The characteristics they cited were not good grades or industriousness or any of the other school and adult valued features which Coleman had anticipated. Instead girls tended to choose good personalities, good looks, being well-dressed, and having a good reputation. The only characteristic they mentioned which could be associated with parental values was being born into the right family. Boys were not very different in their preferences, listing good personality, good reputation, being an athlete, and adding good looks before listing good grades. It was this orientation to current concerns and relationships to peers rather than any reference back to family or to any future goals which led Coleman to proclaim the existence of an "adolescent society," a separate and distinct social system. Like any society, this one had its own values, its own norms, and hence its own culture or at least subculture, and over the next decade widely publicized notions of a "generation gap" and a "counterculture" linked the local peer group into a national youth culture in the popular perception as well as in much of the literature on teenagers.[19] Adolescents supposedly looked to this collective cultural consciousness—broadcast nationally through the lyrics and beat of rock-and-roll music and made increasingly visible as television spread throughout the country—rather than to parents or local community norms for support and guidance. Within this counterculture, youth everywhere became, in Coleman's description, "inward looking," with a "psychic attachment to others their own age." A "press toward autonomy" produced a deviation from adult norms manifest "in a high regard for youth who successfully challenged adults, or who act autonomously of adults."[20]

When the forces of social change moved out of the home and into industrialized society, the new discontinuities also moved adolescent turmoil—Hall's "storm and stress" and the Freudians' psychic conflict—into that outside world. It was Erik Erikson's apt and timely capturing of the painful crisis in identity we all suffer in an impersonal industrial society, but which is most critical in the adolescent's conflict in seeking an integrated rather than diffuse identity, that provided the psychological support necessary to validate the existence of an adolescent society. In times of rapid social change and diminishing faith in the old role models, wrote Erikson, the teenage peer group (and the youth culture which sustains it) provide the "ideal prototypes of the day."[21] More dramatic validation came in a series of social upheavals involving youth: the draft protests of the Vietnam era, the uprisings in colleges and universities, and other incidents and behaviors which brought public attention to a media-hyped "rebellious youth subculture" that seemed in open and hostile opposition to adult values and attitudes. By the mid-1970s Coleman could report that the youth culture had become even more self-conscious and stood in even sharper contradistinction to adult society: "Youth now see themselves more as a specific group with specific interests than in earlier times."[22]

The creation of the notion of a youth culture did more than supply an explanation for the mounting social problems of teenagers who moved out of childhood in the decades after World War II. It moved both the source of the crises and the hopes and means for their resolution out of the hands of the local community, and the parents and other adults who were closest to the teenager's daily life, into a more national and distant arena. If the problems were national, then national strategies and resources were required to combat them and local options and the authority structure which could empower these options were powerless. Lost in this nationalization was the fact that communities differ, just as the families within them and teenagers themselves differ along a variety of dimensions. As we moved from community to community during the decade in which we conducted our research, we found that the diversity among communities persisted over time. Although certain specific problems surfaced or intensified in every community (for example, dropouts, child abuse, fear of AIDS), each community responded to them differently. We also found that families and the other adult institutions which organize the social structure of communities continue to play a major role along with teenagers in determining the nature and the outcomes of the adolescent experience. To focus only on the teenagers is to get a distorted picture of the adolescent experience, to miss the significance of how and why most teenagers look to adults for guidance in shaping a secure and successful transition from child to adult.

There are a number of emerging theoretical approaches to adolescence, such as social cognition and social learning theories and a life-course developmental perspective, which do combine elements of developmental and social perspectives.[23] Sparked by increasing evidence of genetic influences on personality in general and the role of puberty as a social plus biological marker in particular, conflicts between the inner-development and social-development traditions have become muted. Yet the tension between deterministic models which give greater emphasis to either internal developmental or external socialization perspectives on adolescence continues, and the resulting controversies that remain have not always been productive for science or for society. In one perspective we are told that the basic social competencies are developed in essentially familial interaction in childhood and then modified and extended by other social contexts: peer groups, the school, work settings, etc. The second perspective assumes that specific skills or competencies are more or less independently developed in each of the institutional contexts as a response to the demands of that system, and the individual adolescent is left with the task of integrating all the demands into a coherent system of values.

The conflict between developmental and social perspectives is of more than academic interest, since how we define and describe adolescence determines our social policies and remedies for dealing with it. Employers, teachers, and policemen who claim to be unable to do anything constructive with adolescents because the environments of their early childhood did not provide a secure basis for learning, job readiness, or constructive social behavior are drawing explanatory evidence from the epigenetic theoretical model. When, on the other hand, they propose training or remediation programs for youth, they insist that it is within their own social context that remediation and the development of the specific social learning required must take place. In each of the communities we studied, we found that there is already a good deal of information available to parents and professionals on both environmental and developmental aspects of adolescent behavior in specific contexts such as the school, the family, and the criminal justice system, but very little about how behavior is organized and structured by the interdependence of the diverse parts of the adolescent's social world.

What has been lost in this controversy between developmental and social models is an understanding of the continuing interplay between individual minds and life situations and the collective forces of all of the community's agents of socialization. Lost with it—as we have argued about whether adolescence is a matter of inner biological change or the result of changes in the larger society which produce a break in life's continuity—is the fact that socialization does not take place in some abstract "society"; it results from children's life experiences as they grow up in the smaller contexts of communities and their families, peer groups, schools, and other social institutions. More importantly, from the perspective I want to develop in this book, we have seldom stopped to take account of the differences which may result from the pattern of relationships existing among the socializing agencies in the community. Instead we have more frequently considered the effects of one institution which is time-dominant (such as the family in infancy or the school or peer groups in adolescence), or we have looked at the effects of supposedly extracommunity influences (such as the media or a youth culture). As a result we have failed to look empirically at the interactive effects of differing definitions of the child-into-adult transformation provided by the family, the school, the workplace, and other social institutions, and the resulting tension between inner and outer worlds of experience.

In the research done by my colleagues and myself, a different perspective on the relationship between the web of social institutions and individual lives of adolescents emerges. When we compared the ten communities we looked at, it became clear that each exhibits some variation of a synergistic association rather than a sequential trajectory or an independent, situational pattern of relationships among institutional contexts in the lives of adolescents. How the various social contexts of a community are integrated in terms of the continuity and congruence of their values, norms, and rules, rather than the individual impact of any single institution, emerges in our analyses as the most important determinant of how adolescence will be experienced and with what results. It follows that all American adolescents are not alike, different communities can and do develop different kinds of adolescents, and diversity among adolescents—even within the same community—can be as great as it is among adults. It is the local community and the more intimate social contexts of the community, rather than some generic and immutable developmental or social process, which have the major role in establishing the character and the impact of the adolescent transformation. Rather than debating the relative roles of biological versus environmental controls over developing skills and social competencies in adolescence, the question is how they interact—in each community—to produce cultural age norms and the social meaning of adolescence. A number of interactive biological and social factors make puberty and the early adolescent period it ushers in a time of trouble for society if not for the individual adolescent. Parents, for example, often have considerable difficulty adjusting to the new sexuality and their own concerns about relating to the child-becoming-an-adult. Peter Blos and other psychoanalytic theorists have seen this emergence of sexual impulses as a major problem in intrafamilial relations, necessitating individuation or distancing.[24] There are also changed relationships with both younger and older siblings as a result of the new sexuality and the status it confers. The result of all this is often an increase in the level of conflict within the family as parents, the adolescent, and his siblings react and readjust. The importance of the fact of puberty to this turmoil is underscored by research findings which indicate that adolescent–parent conflict is often triggered by the arrival of puberty, and if puberty comes early or late, so does the onset of the family quarrels.[25]

The other biologically determined characteristic that is socially defined during adolescence is gender. Historically, we always saw adolescence as preparing males and females for different roles in society. For males it was traditionally a period of preparation for a life of work as well as for parenthood, while females were prepared for homemaking and child care. Consequently the tasks of adolescence, as well as the encouragement of a host of attitudes and behaviors— such as dependence or independence, achievement motivation, and interest in events outside the home—were gender-bound. New life styles for women which include careers with or without having families at the same time should have changed all that. Research and observation, however, both suggest that the importance of gender in the interaction of puberty and culture is resistant to rapid change.[26]

The biological characteristics of adolescence provide the raw material from which societies and communities seek to mold their newborn into adult members. It is important to remember, however, that questions of cohort size and composition, the number of adolescents in relation to the number of children and of adults, and their geographic distribution also condition the course as well as the complexity of the task. Alternating periods of "baby booms" and "baby busts" since World War II have had repercussions throughout the life course of each cohort. In the two decades following that war, there was a dramatic increase in births, and the 75 million children, 50 percent more than in the previous generation, caused a wave rather than a ripple to move through all aspects of American life as they matured and aged. In the mid-1960s, however, birthrates began to decline, but then stabilized in the 1980s, so that the generation born between 1965 and 1984 is about 11 percent smaller than its booming predecessor.

The most obvious effect of these swings in cohort size is on the sheer number of children who will be entering puberty and becoming adolescents. There are, however, a variety of attendant social and economic effects of cohort size as well. The baby boom generation, for example, swelled and eventually overflowed the existing schools, and new facilities were extensively and rapidly built and staffed. This surge through the educational system first affected the elementary, then the secondary schools and had dramatic effects on college and eventually even professional school enrollments. When the birthrate declined so did the number of potential students, and what had been a massive school building and staffing program became one of school closings and staff reductions. Faced with a shrinking job market, the number of young people choosing education as a career declined, causing teacher shortages once again. Similar effects were felt in the labor market, health care, criminal justice, and other institutional sectors of society.

Births are not the only avenue for population growth. Immigration rates, illegal as well as legal, can have, and at various times in our history have had, major effects on the size and heterogeneity of American society. Internal migration has a direct effect on the size and composition of regions and communities throughout the country. It also has indirect effects on the national society as economic, political, and even social balances of power and influence shift to follow population concentrations. Since the 1970s, immigration has once again become a major source of new membership in American society, and in this new wave of immigrants Central American, West Indian, and Asian émigrés predominate. Immigrants, of course, show the same variability as other Americans, but they do contribute some important special effects to the character of adolescent cohorts. Language, and the logic and values contained in it, becomes more diverse, adding a new (or at least more complex) dimension to communication between these adolescents and traditional institutional sectors as well as within adolescent peer groups. When new immigrants arrive in late childhood or as adolescents, their prior life experiences are different from those of their native born and nurtured age-mates. Education, health care, and other developmental histories can be startlingly different and present additional problems to be worked through in the adolescent transformation.

As the number of young people in our aging society has been declining, the relative number of minority children has increased and they constitute larger and larger proportions of those entering the adolescent years. The number of black adolescents is declining but not as rapidly as the number of whites, and so they are becoming a proportionately higher percentage of the adolescent population. There have been similar increases in the proportion of Hispanic and Asian youth, but this is in part due to actual increases in number as a result of immigration.[27] The effects of this increasing proportion of minority group youngsters in the adolescent cohorts of the last two decades of the century are dramatic, and ruling out any unlikely changes in immigration or mortality rates, will continue to be so. Given the relationship between ethnicity and socioeconomic status which still prevails in America, more and more adolescents will experience the social ills resulting from minority group membership, such as lower levels of educational attainment, higher unemployment and arrest rates, poverty, and higher fertility.

These effects of the changing minority status of the adolescent population will be differentially felt in various regions of the country, and in cities more than in suburban areas. States differ in the relative number of youth in their populations as a result of the proportionate numbers of childbearing and pre- and post-childbearing persons in their populations. Also there are distinct differences by region in the settlement patterns of minority and majority members of society. Black youths are overrepresented in the South, while there are relatively larger populations of Hispanics in the Southwest and Florida, and a disproportionate number of Asians live on the West Coast. While a slightly higher proportion of all young people tend to live in metropolitan areas, minority group youngsters are especially concentrated in cities. The majority of black adolescents live in central-city areas, and they are glaringly underrepresented in suburban populations and, outside of the South, in rural areas as well. While Hispanics and Asians are not as dramatically concentrated in inner-city areas, they are much more so than white youth.

The interaction of these demographic trends with individual characteristics such as age, pubertal status, and gender is played out in each of the social institutional sectors of communities and in the lives of adolescents as they anticipate major life events and begin thinking about jobs, marriage, and parenthood. Social trends as well as population characteristics change and present new, or at least different, challenges to young people's developing skills. As recently as the 1950s and 1960s, for example, the developmental path for girls was predicated on a future in which the turning points would be marriage and childbearing. Communities organized their institutions to direct and facilitate this developmental role for females. A series of social changes altered all of that. Soaring divorce rates forced occupationally unprepared mothers to become family breadwinners and to assume other roles traditionally served by the male head of household. The women's movement, which, if not a result of this crisis was at least contemporaneous with it, also led to major changes in the social meaning of adolescence for girls and to new perspectives for the major social institutions. Schools and the labor market were the most obvious settings for such changes, but over time other institutional sectors such as the criminal justice system, the media, social agencies, religion, and even families themselves had to adjust to this shift in perspectives. These new ways of living and thinking about life inevitably began to have an effect on childbearing rates and childrearing practices.

The campaign for gender equity is one example of a number of cultural and technological changes in society which have biosocial implications for adolescence. While such trends may be national or regional in origin and impact, it is through the local community—with its web of social institutions and the system of rewards for conformity and penalties for deviance—that they intersect with the lives of adolescents.

There are other unique experiences and characteristics, chance events and life contingencies, which combine with the various differences among adolescents to insure that there is no universal developmental path into and throughout adolescence. Adolescence can be a very different experience for the physically or mentally handicapped, for example. The death of a parent before or during adolescence has a profound effect on growing up, and, as I frequently heard in interviews with surviving children, on how the youngster perceives the probable course of life events. Moving from one community to another, or even to another neighborhood within the same community, requires a process of readjustment to expectations of peers as well as adults in the new social contexts. Sometimes children or adolescents come in contact with religious or ideological systems which reorient their feelings and attitudes about life and society. It is such events and their individual and social meaning—and not simply the passage of time—which schedule the traditional transitions in the life course.

The fluidity of such developmental patterns denies the insistent claim of stage theorists that adolescence is a fixed and largely predetermined period which comes to an abrupt end with adulthood. From the legacy of Hall's concern with the "storm and stress" of the pubertal transformation and the psychoanalytic concerns with the internal and external conflicts it creates, the notion of an inevitably troubled transition has been modified, but not expunged from the public consciousness. Generally, we still expect most adolescents to be in turmoil, moody, ill at ease with their developing bodies and selves, and uncertain of how to interpret and deal with their new body images and sexuality. However, the recent work of Anne Petersen and her associates confirming the earlier studies of psychiatrist Daniel Offer—as well as what we learned from our own observations and interviews—indicates that most adolescents enter and eventually complete the transition without significant emotional and social problems.[28]

The variations in life styles and social scripts which result from community differences as well as perceptions of age, sex, and race also raise questions about how pervasive and widespread the massive external social forces are in shaping the lives of all adolescents wherever and however they live. Looking and listening to the variations in adolescent life in the social settings of the ten communities we studied demonstrated, among other things, that the relationships among individual development, communities, and the cultural age norms which define adolescence are just as complex and influential for the individual teenager as they are for the society at large.

The interactionist perspective on adolescence that underlies this book was arrived at after over a decade of research. How best to go about organizing and reporting these years of inquiry, the thousands of pages of field notes and hundreds of hours of interviewing, and my own developing and changing awareness of how communities imprint their adolescents?

While both field ethnography and clinical psychoanalysis cherish unbiased exploration, there was an emerging focus to our interactionist inquiry. We began our observations and interviews in the everyday life of the *individual* social institutions of communities, but we soon discovered that the harmony and accord among the institutions and what their adolescent members heard from them *in concert* was what scored the adolescent experience. Music results from the interaction of the notes, and the congeniality or discord of the arrangement can lead to harmony or discord in the listeners. In the chapters that follow, I want to look at ensembles of institutional settings rather than solo performers, beginning with the adolescent peer group and the family and then adding voices from other institutional sectors and from individual adolescents as well, to describe how communities compose and orchestrate the adolescent transformation. Some of what we heard was harmonious and consonant. But some of it was dissonant, often because of the inexperience of the adolescent players themselves as much as the way in which the institutions conducted their performance.

In *The Interpretation of Dreams* Freud observes that "if a few bars of music are played and someone comments that it is from Mozart's *Figaro* (as happens in *Don Giovanni*) a number of recollections are roused in me all at once, none of which can enter my consciousness singly at the first moment."[29] And so it was in our research. Understanding came from listening to the youngsters themselves and in chorus with adults in the variety of institutions in a number of communities over time. What seemed dissonant in one setting often took on a new harmony as we began to piece it together with what was happening in other parts of adolescents' lives. In some places the disharmony among the institutional settings was the dominant theme for many of the youngsters in that community, and in others one institution seemed to offer a sanctuary for some but not all adolescents. Over the ten years of the study I also saw enough change or potential for change in adolescent development to convince me that the first task for all of us is to keep the music playing.

2

Peer Worlds
and Adolescent
Development

M ost teenagers are usually seen in a group with their peers or, if alone, are thinking or talking about each other and about being with each other. Most enjoy spending time together in each other's homes or just hanging out together wherever they can. They go to school and the movies together, go to the same stores to buy clothes or hamburgers, and when they get older, drive around to places where they know they will see and be seen by each other. Some work in the same location or go to music lessons or martial arts classes together. Others congregate in street gangs or roam suburban shopping malls, sometimes forming roving bands and acting boisterously. Even when they are not gathering somewhere, they talk to each other on the telephone about what they have just done or are planning to do together. How and why do they join together with such enthusiasm to share sorrow and anxiety as well as exuberance and joy? And why do they often seem so much alike?

One reason why teenagers seem so similar is that they are all undergoing the same transition, giving up the freedoms of childhood, learning the new roles they will take as adult members of society, experiencing the same uncertainties about what adult life will be like, and wondering and worrying about whether they will fail or succeed when it is their time to contribute. All of this uncertainty is easier to bear if it can be shared with friends and age-mates who are going through this same transition, and peer groups offer the reciprocity, supportive companionship, and social feedback out of which friendship circles grow. Like any group of people required to depend on each other, they develop norms, work out roles, even develop their own special language to express what is happening to them and how they feel about it. Even when they remember their own adolescence, adults still tend to classify teenagers and the groups they form in terms of the similarities which emerge from the commonality of the tasks of the transition. They forget that the variability of adult identities is in large measure a product of the very different life paths upon which they embarked as teenagers.

The teenagers in the ten communities we studied were actually as different from each other as adults are. The variation went beyond individual differences in biological predisposition or temperament or some critical life experience, such as the loss of a parent. Teenagers live in poverty or affluence or someplace in between, come from broken or intact families, attend good or bad schools, and encounter very different role models in the communities in which they live. Adolescent development takes place within a specific community as the individual teenager's internal resources are nurtured or stifled by the opportunities available. Just as teenagers differ depending on where and how they live, so do the peer groups they form.

In adolescence the peer group shares the day with the family and the school, and the interrelationships among these institutions are at the heart of both the developmental gains and the stresses of the child-to-adult transformation. Far from being isolated in their peer groups, it is in the dynamics of the interacting social network of adults and teenagers that lives are shaped, individual teenagers classified and judged, and future careers found or lost.

But that is not the whole story. Some fundamental issues still remain: How do different types of communities and the social environments of the teenagers' daily life shape and influence their peer worlds? Which of these various social environments are most influential in the lives of adolescents? How much freedom does the adolescent have to choose among possible social worlds and among roles within them? Where do adolescents look to find social models to follow? Comparing two of the communities we studied illustrates the possible variations among communities and provides a background for looking at how these environments can influence the peer groups teenagers form, which in turn help to shape individual development.

SOUTHSIDE

Southside has all of the ingredients for the social problems and personal tragedies we associate with adolescence. It is one of a number of urban inner-city areas of a major eastern metropolis; it is multiethnic, poor, bounded by massive public housing projects and squalid aging tenements, and it seems to have always been that way. Generations of European immigrants have lived here and struggled to leave in pursuit of the American Dream, only to be displaced by new migrant groups in an unending process of ethnic succession. Now the process seems to be accelerating, and over one-quarter of a million people live out their lives within this two-square-mile area as Chinese and Hispanic immigrants crowd in next to the remaining European émigrés.

There is Little Italy, an area of deteriorating tenements which the Italians took over from the Irish and Jewish immigrants who preceded them. There are still enough Italian families left to maintain some semblance of community, but most have already left for other sections of the city or for the suburbs. What has been left behind are the newly renovated and prospering Italian food stores, restaurants, and specialty shops, now catering less to the Italian colony than to affluent "uptowners" looking to relive holidays in Italy and tourists who flock to the restaurants and the several streets of food stalls that appear for each religious *festa*. But Little Italy is being compressed between rapidly expanding Hispanic neighborhoods to the north and an exploding Chinatown to the south. The few old Italian families still there will tell you that it is only a matter of time before the Chinese buy them all out.

Chinatown's expansion is trackable as the open air markets shift to Chinese groceries and the restaurants and stores replace their old signs with new ones in Chinese characters. The area's immigrants from Hong Kong, mainland China, and Taiwan come, settle, and run their business enterprises as families. Puerto Ricans and Dominicans are the largest of the Hispanic groups, but there are also Cubans, although their major settlements are elsewhere in the city, and some smaller groups of South and Central Americans. Southern blacks, earlier migrants to the area, have been joined in recent decades by West Indians and even a few Africans. There are pockets of Ukrainians, an enclave of old Jewish families left over from the time when immigrant Eastern European Jews predominated, a small gay community, and even some yuppies who have renovated apartment-lofts. But mostly, the people who live here are still poor families struggling at the bottom of the ladder of social mobility.

There are also business establishments in Southside. Not the fancy uptown stores or the major corporate and financial high-rises further downtown, but the kinds of ethnic goods and products markets, discount stores, mom-and-pop grocery stores, pizza parlors and delicatessens, candy and soda stores, and pharmacies that serve local residents and those who come warily into the area in search of bargains. Outsiders also come in looking for the major product of the underground economy of Southside: the drugs which are readily available on street corners or in tenement hallways. There are also schools and medical clinics, social agencies and centers, drug rehabilitation centers, and a variety of programs for the elderly as well as for the young—and, of course, there are the police. Most of the professionals who staff these programs and services do not live in Southside, but commute from other parts of the city or from the suburbs, where their youngsters are reared and socialized, quite apart from the Southside children and youth who are their students, clients, patients, or caseloads.

Polyethnic diversity further isolates families and children within Southside, since the pattern of settlement there remains one of ethnic neighborhoods. Each of these enclaves has a cultural focus, often heard in the language spoken in neighborhood life and visible in the patterns of family organization and childrearing. Youngsters are born, or accompany migrating families, into these ethnic neighborhoods and grow up in the family structures, childhood groups and gangs, and schools associated with them. It is the local high school which eventually serves to bring the teenage children of all of these diverse groups together. The school is quite large, even by urban standards: forty-five hundred students. Blacks, Chinese, and Hispanics in roughly equivalent proportions account for about 80 percent of the student body, with the remaining 20 percent being an ''other'' category containing a variety of white groups and some small number of non-Chinese Asians. The majority of teachers and administrators, however, are white, and only a small percentage are from the minority groups which predominate among their students.

The result of this diversification is an obvious pattern of conflict in relationships. Peer interaction in such a situation also becomes conflictual. Clothing, as well as styles of walking and talking, are ethnically identified and often exaggerated to make the point. The most frequent type of interaction both within and between peer groups, for example, is a highly structured way of talking and teasing which becomes almost a ritual means of expressing hostility. A further result of this ethnic diversification is that there is no homogeneous pattern of association which relates all youth to each other. The pattern of peer organization is one of gangs, cliques, or "crews," which symbolize and display this diversity. The Chinese youth gangs, for example, are closely associated with adult society in Chinatown and reflect the familial system there. Such gangs are highly structured, often based on family ties, homogeneous in terms of provincial origin in China, and serve some important economic functions in the community. Some of the gangs are involved in a number of illegal activities related to the adult "Tong" criminal groups in Chinatown. Black and Hispanic gangs, on the other hand, seem less related to economic functions and serve other needs frequently related to reputation, recognition, and the development of an identity.

SHEFFIELD

The town of Sheffield is a small, affluent suburb near the city where Southside is located, and, in fact, many of the male heads-of-household who live there commute daily into the business district which is just downtown from Southside's slums. Sheffield is not a newly developed suburb; it is actually an old town by American standards, dating to pre-Revolutionary days. Not only did George Washington sleep here, he had his headquarters in the town for some time while he planned an attack on what is now Southside. Today Sheffield still has a small-town flavor: its streets lined with tall, arching trees, its houses still mostly wooden structures painted in the more subdued shades of an earlier era, and its large lawns with abundant, well-manicured shrubbery. Like Southside, Sheffield is a little more than two square miles in area, but fewer than ten thousand people live here.

If the texture of Southside is tangible in its ethnic diversity, it is the homogeneity of the people and of their life styles which one feels immediately in Sheffield. There are, of course, differences, such as those of religion or politics—there are Congregational, Episcopal, Methodist, Presbyterian, and two Roman Catholic churches, and there are Democrats as well as Republicans—but these distinctions have nowhere near the visibility or power of the ethnic differences which divide Southside. There are virtually no black or Hispanic families, and although a few affluent Japanese families have moved into town in recent years, visible ethnic differentiation is as alien as social class segmentation in Sheffield. Families are just as important in the enculturation of children in Sheffield as they are in Southside. But similarity rather than diversity characterizes childrearing and family organization here because parents have such similar social and cultural backgrounds.

Much of the peer association and the socialization environment is parent-organized and parent-directed. Parents are active in school committees and in organizing sports and other extracurricular (they would say "co-curricular") activities at the school. The churches as well as the school have a variety of family activities ranging from family outings to youth clubs with parent advisers. These family-centered groups not only share a common culture and values, but have the same goals, the same objectives for their children, and the same standards for measuring progress toward them. The family's future orientation as well as its present life style centers heavily on preparing youngsters for college and careers. Sheffield's parents and the community institutions which they have developed encourage a pattern of competitive relationship in respect to those goals which is immediately evident even in the elementary and junior high schools. The schools, which reflect community and hence family expectations, are structured to encourage that competitive spirit not only in sports but in academic and social life as well. Mothers in Sheffield will tell you that the two things you never ask a mother over midmorning coffee or at a cocktail party are her husband's salary and her children's S.A.T. scores.

Like Southside, Sheffield has only one high school, but unlike the urban inner-city area, its nine hundred students are not differentiated by ethnicity, social class, or even religion. There are, however, some distinctions made among students in the school, establishing categories such as "jocks," "the Braintrust," and "freaks" to indicate life styles which are competitive but not conflictual. Clearly, however, and unlike in Southside, these distinctions are based on the adolescent's own personality, habits, or reputation in the school and have little or no relationship to the social reality outside the school. Peer groups tend to be quite small, and the most common form of interaction is with a small and noncompetitive group of "best friends." Students are also differentiated by a complex system of ability grouping in the schools, and teachers and administrators complain that some parents threaten to send their children to private schools if they are not placed in honors courses.

At the heart of American communities there exists an interrelated set of environments which make social life work. People and the groups they form empower these environments, which teach, train, and nurture children as they grope toward adult status. It is in these collectives, or what Emile Durkheim called "little aggregations," that adolescents seek and find both personal selves and public identities.[1] The differences between growing up in Southside and in Sheffield entail more than the contrast between urban poverty and suburban affluence. They are differences in the many ways the daily life of the adolescent is structured by relationships, beginning in the family and reaching out into the other social environments of the community. It is in the intimacy of kinship and friendship that the process of growth, exploration, and identity formation begins. One of the indications of the growth of social competence is movement from the childhood play group to the teenage peer group, which is expected to ease adolescents out of dependent childhood, through a relatively dependent adolescence, to an independent adulthood.

The family's role is to bring children into the world and see them through childhood. The behavior-setting role of the peer group begins when children's games bring them together to share a lore and language frequently known only to them.[2] Such early groupings of age-related youngsters, however, are always anchored in the home and the neighborhood, and even when a child starts in school, she returns to or, more frequently, remains within that same cultural community. The peer group provides a means of beginning to separate from parents and move into the larger society outside the home. This process begins when children go off to school and are subjected to a new set of institutional expectations. As well, they meet significant adults other than parents and kin, and peers other than siblings or playmates. Peer interaction plays a major role in the social development of adolescents by presenting a different perspective on the social world. But like families, peer groups are human inventions, and they show the same diversity by region, community, and social class. When adolescent peer groups are portrayed as a separate social system or subculture with loosened ties to adult society or even in opposition to it, the continuing importance of these variations and of adults as role models in adolescent development are incorrectly denied.

As teenagers grow older and spend more time with each other, their peer groups become social environments in themselves; they are institutional settings for adolescent social development just as families or the school are, and their influence on adolescents is considerable.[3] They are also quite different from these more traditional and recognized institutions. Peer groups do not have their own physical structures, such as homes or school buildings. Lacking their own territory, they must congregate in the space of one or the other institutions, such as the home or the school, or they must find some neutral and usually temporary space to meet outside the scrutiny of adults. Nor do peer groups have the legal status and protection these other social institutions enjoy. They form and interact, particularly in the early teens, at the sufferance of one or more of the adult institutions. But social institutions are not always place-bound, nor do they require governmental recognition or sanction to influence their adherents. Institutions are the major rallying points through which cultures and communities seek to attain their shared values and to serve the functions necessary for continuity. What becomes institutionalized in this process is a pattern of behaviors, a set of attitudes, a system of reciprocal relationships which are believed to be effective in maximizing some of these shared social goals.[4] While the institutions of a community may be competitive or, as in Southside, conflicting, they are interdependent and thus cannot long survive as independent social environments. The peer group, often described as serving to emancipate adolescents from the adult community, is no less subject to these same constraints. As a result, adolescent peer groups share their influence over their members with the adult institutions of a community and cannot be invoked to fully explain teenage behavior or misbehavior or to suggest that all teenagers are pretty much the same no matter where and how they live.

While the adolescent peer groups we saw and interviewed in each of the communities we studied were not all the same, there were certain characteristics and feelings they all shared. One was that "just being together" was the most important reason virtually all of them reported for wanting to spend time with each other: "Just being together with other kids is what makes my day for me." Most of them described "understanding each other" as what they felt they gained in peer association, and they specified a variety of dimensions of this feeling. Many saw it as the result of "being the same age," "wanting the same things," or "wanting to help each other." A few talked about "going through the same changes," or "facing the same problems." Another set of attributes frequently mentioned as distinguishing peer relationships was the sense of freedom, the lack of constraint, the possibilities of spontaneity, the openness which was possible with peers: "You can be yourself," "You can talk about what you want," or "You can joke or fool around." There were also less frequent but still significant responses such as "Nobody tells you what to do" or "You get away from teachers and parents," which we heard more frequently when we interviewed teenagers in groups than when we spoke with them alone. Being together with other peers was also described as being with people who tell you things about yourself "that they really feel even if it gets you mad."

Being together was not, however, the same as "doing things together." Whenever we asked what teenagers did together we got the same response many parents report: "Nothing much, we just hang out together." When we asked teenagers to tell us what they did when they "just hung out," they described talking, gossiping, relaxing, joking, looking for excitement or adventure, "goofing off," or any number of activities that required interaction but not a specific focus or purpose. They also reported that they did things together such as going to the movies or watching television, playing sports or games, taking drugs or drinking alcohol, dating or having sex, studying or working. Sometimes being together led to doing things together, but more frequently the two were seen as belonging to separate and distinct times spent with peers in a day or during the week. Being together was important even if there was nothing specific to do together.

There were also differences among and within peer groups in each community. Some groups were quite large and fluid, changing with some frequency as new families moved in and out of neighborhoods or communities, while others were smaller and their members were in much closer and more frequent contact. What we considered a peer group was any group of youngsters of about the same age whose interactive association with each other provided a stable framework for interpersonal relationships, support, and self-evaluation. The group could be as large as all of the teenagers in a small community, all of whom knew each other and saw each other almost every day, or it could be as small and self-contained as a street gang whose members all lived on the same block in a large city. It could be all boys or all girls of a certain age-grade or it could include both. What made it a peer group was that the teenager found a place within the wider network of age-mates in this particular group.

In every community some youngsters were more involved with peers than others. Most but by no means all youngsters interact with a number of peers in a variety of settings, and over time relationships with peers come to take up more and more of their time. Some, however, remain closely bound to their parents, siblings, or extended family networks by personal or parental choice or both. Some stay close to their neighborhoods and have the same circle of peer associates and stable relationships throughout adolescence and even into adulthood. Others change peer groups frequently, either as a result of families moving from one community or one neighborhood to another or as a result of their own changing interests or activities. There are a few teenagers in every community who are always on the margins of peer groups and feel isolated, unwanted, and alone, and we even met a very few who said that they preferred to be alone.

Within peer groups different members relate and interact with each other in different ways. Two or more members of the group might have particularly close relationships based on common interests, which may or may not be shared with most of the other members of the group. The peer group might, for example, share an interest in heavy-metal music, but within that general interest two or more members may appreciate it more or less or have some favorite performers. On the other hand, the small subgroup may be interested in cars but share other interests or alliances with the larger peer group. Some members of peer groups relate to each other more than to other members because of shared levels of competence or talent in some activity or field such as music, art, sports, or academic subjects. Most frequently, however, selectivity within the general sociability of peer relationships is based upon "liking each other" and being close friends who share more with each other than with other members.

There are also less positive emotions and associations within peer groups in every community which help to account for the considerable anxiety which we found such groups can generate in their membership. Relationships between or among members can be competitive or even hostile, full of antagonism and anger which can and sometimes does lead to confrontations or even violence. One member might take a particular dislike to, or even feel enmity for, another at some time or even over a longer period of time, but remain in the group because there are others the individual wants to be with or because it is the only peer group available. There are also factions within the peer groups, just as there are in any other group. Feelings and judgments about particular members or the collective itself also change over time. Sometimes tension and anxiety generated within the group or induced by circumstances outside the group break it up or split it into other groups. We saw and heard about members joining and leaving particular peer groups for a variety of reasons. Nevertheless, peers and the groups they form in each community become increasingly important social units over the course of the teen years. But even within the peer group, the effects of the community on both its form and membership are obvious in the differences between the peer associations available to youngsters in Southside as contrasted to Sheffield.

Josie Delgado is sixteen years old and has lived in Southside ever since her family moved here from the Dominican Republic when she was seven. She is the youngest of ten children, and lives alone with her mother in a three-room apartment although several married siblings live in the same tenement building or nearby in the same neighborhood. Up before 7:00 A.M. on school days, Josie begins her day early. She dresses, applies some makeup (usually eyeliner), and eats breakfast in time to meet a girlfriend or two and walk to school by 8:30. Most of her girlfriends are also Dominican.

Arriving at school a few minutes early, she smokes a cigarette with her friends outside the school in a location where other Dominican students hang out. Nobody has ever said that she or other Dominicans have to congregate here, just as no one has ever said they all have to live on the same block or in the same building. But ethnicity, not wealth or talent or even interests, is the primary source of social identity in Southside, where it structures peer group formation in the school just as surely as it does residence.

The ethnic diversity which has always divided Southside surfaces in different areas of the community's life. Intense struggles over access to political power, particularly since the antipoverty programs of the 1960s, surface again and again, and the factionalism hampers political effectiveness in competing with other sections of the city for limited resources. People who live here complain that police protection, health services, and the education provided their children are of poorer quality than those provided elsewhere in the city. Even in the collection of garbage, they say, the municipal government does far less here than in more affluent and politically powerful neighborhoods. The residents of those neighborhoods, of course, say that Southside's ethnic poor create these problems for themselves. In any case, Southside's minority groups are left to fight among themselves for a share of both local decision-making power and outside resources. Inevitably, this divisiveness affects other areas of neighborhood life. Gangs of adolescents and youths defend various areas of turf and occasionally collide. Struggles over scarce housing are often enacted in ethnic terms, especially as Chinatown spills out of its boundaries and as gentrification increases property values in the area. Josie's family has moved seven times in the nine years they have lived in this country, but always within the same three-block area of Southside.

Ethnic conflict is not inevitable, however. There have been issues which bring the people of Southside together, such as when they successfully fought against a new expressway which would have further fragmented the area and worsened pollution. But for Josie, as for her family, language, residence, and perhaps even preference all combine to make her peer group and close associates—male as well as female—mostly Hispanic, usually Dominican. Her neighborhood is largely peopled by Puerto Ricans, and even within it she and her family cleave to other Dominicans. She attends what is for all intents and purposes a segregated high school, one where students select friends to whom they are bonded by language, culture, and ethnicity. Segregation is not the official policy of the school, and many of the teachers and administrators try to combat it, but it happens anyway.

There really is not much open conflict among the various ethnic and racial groups which come together in the school—at least not any more than happens within the various groups themselves. One reason for this, however, seems to be an informal but strictly adhered to pattern of territoriality for each of the various groups: even the restaurant where Josie eats lunch is "closed" to the white and Chinese students, who go to their own lunch spots to eat. Josie does have non-Dominican, even non-Hispanic, friends she has made at the school, but they are individual acquaintances of hers and are not part of the peer group with whom she attends classes and spends most of her time. She never sees any of them outside of the school.

If you arrive at the school early in the morning, just before classes start, you will see a large number of students milling around, particularly in front of the two main entrances. You can also observe how the students group themselves in a pattern which is always the same. The black students predominate on the north side of the school, probably because many of them come from uptown and get off the public transportation on that side. They then congregate at the northwest corner of the building and inside the doorways down the street westward. The long side of the school on the west is the side most sheltered from the wind and the sun, and here you can find a variety of students, but it is the Hispanics who predominate. The few white and Chinese students who hang out before and during the school day can be found on the south side of the school. The white students come mostly from the high-rise apartments to the east, next to the river; the Chinese arrive here by walking directly across from Chinatown, a few blocks to the west.

Bruce Megan moved to Sheffield when he was eleven years old and his father was transferred to the area by the multinational corporation for which he works as a middle-level executive. He grew up in another suburban area outside of Detroit, which he describes as very much like Sheffield, "only colder." He describes his first experiences in Sheffield as a process of "finding the right keys to unlock the social doors." His mother, who was a schoolteacher in Michigan, could not find a teaching position in Sheffield and chose not to seek one outside the community, fearing that this might detract from the time she could spend on overseeing the education and development of Bruce and his two younger sisters. Bruce remembers that both his mother and father—but mostly his mother—encouraged him to make friends as soon as possible so that the family's integration into the community could be facilitated by contact with other families: "It wasn't so much that she was a joiner; it's just that we learned in Michigan that families were important for feeling part of what was going on." He also recalls that one of their neighbors had always been described as "a childless couple" and never seemed to quite fit in with the families with kids.

One of the reasons his family had moved to Sheffield—a reason given by most of the parents we spoke with there—is that "it's a great place to raise children." The schools are considered first-rate, and almost all the high school's graduates get into good colleges or even major universities. Sheffield is also a place where the cultural diversity and conflicts which seem so plentiful in Southside just do not exist. Not only do all of the families seem to have similar social backgrounds and aspirations for themselves and their children, but the cultural insularity leaves little opportunity for distractions from what is a commonly agreed upon pattern of providing a protective environment for children and adolescents. If some people would consider Southside a jungle in which youngsters must learn early how to survive, Sheffield is a greenhouse where kids can be nurtured and cultivated in a sheltered environment.

"Breaking into" Sheffield, however, was not all that easy. Bruce found that by early adolescence there was already an established pattern of relationships which seemed to be based on "best friends" and on coming into contact with a variety of social activities that bind groups of best friends together. Bruce made his first friends as part of the Youth Fellowship at the church which he attended with his family but found it difficult to make friends in his middle school. He was considered a good student and didn't have any problems with the school or with other students, but for the first two or three years he was "pretty much alone and struggling to keep up in school."

In high school Bruce joined the soccer team and made a number of friends as a result. Two, Carl and Drew, became particularly close— possibly, he surmises, because they were from the same section of town he lived in and because their parents became friends with his parents through "booster" meetings for the soccer team. What seemed most important to him was that all of the parents in his neighborhood knew who was whose best friend and what patterns of relationship existed among friendship groups; consequently there were many places where parents could "relax when the kids were there because they knew that some adult they trusted would keep an eye on them."

Both Bruce and Josie are members of peer groups of teenagers who live in the same neighborhood, come from the same kinds of families, go to the same school, and also share other involvements in the communities in which they live. Their peer associations are not random choices, but are influenced by the families in which they grew up and the communities in which they live. They are also influenced by the schools they attend and how the school relates to the family and the community. The school provides a new locus and a new social network within which teenagers can seek help, support, and feedback within some stable group of like-minded peers who understand and share those needs. What the peer group provides is a new arena in which the developing adolescent can try out ways of meeting the newly emerging social needs which result from physical, emotional, and cognitive changes he is undergoing.

Two such social needs seemed to be most important in the peer groups we observed and interviewed. One was to share the wonder as well as the confusion which these changes can provoke with others who are also experiencing them. In interview after interview most teenagers, particularly in the early teens and among the few ten- or eleven-year-olds we interviewed, used the term "sharing" to describe their interactions with peers. Sometimes, particularly in early adolescence, it was an activity which was shared: "Jackie and I first met when we were both on the Little League team" or "We were all in dance class together." Later, shared interests seemed to bring teenagers together: "I got interested in riding and now all of my friends are at the stable" or "The guys I hang out with are all into karate." But sometimes friendship just seemed to happen because of some shared sense of wanting to be together: "I knew him since we were kids, but we didn't become friends until we met again in junior high school and then it just clicked." Sharing in this sense meant more than just common experience, however; it seemed to represent a new way of relating without the hierarchical controls of parents or the parent-constrained relationships with siblings. This new relationship was usually described as "having a friend." The friendships we observed and heard about were particularly intense among early adolescents, probably because they were a new experience and required some new social learning and working out. But in my interviews I also heard about the conflicts and guilt this new self-awareness and self–other awareness can produce and how even friendships continued to relate teenagers to their families.

One area of conflict reaches back into the family. Parents, and to a lesser extent older siblings, are instrumental in the process of establishing friendships. Parents can encourage or discourage the movement outside the family and into friendships. In Sheffield, for example, youngsters sometimes complained that their parents pressured them to have friends—almost, it seems, pushing the child out of the nest early. In Southside I seldom heard this complaint but did hear frequent assertions that parents did not understand what friends are. This was particularly true among Hispanic and Chinese adolescents and is, I believe, related to the importance of kinship and family values in these groups. Conflict over an adolescent's choice of friends occurred not only with parents, but, to a lesser extent, with older siblings.

In both Southside and Sheffield parents would complain about the friends the adolescent had chosen, but the focus of the objections differed in the two communities. In Southside the concern was with present behavior, the most frequent complaint being that the friend or group would get the teenager into trouble. The prohibition was usually issued as a stop order, forbidding the teenager to see the person or associate with the group. In Sheffield, however, the objections were to the future consequences of not choosing the proper friendships now, and became particularly pressing as college careers came closer. In Sheffield the attempt to control friendship choices was more frequently one which directed the teenager to a different friend or friendship circle than it was an outright injunction against any further contact. There were frequent examples of Sheffield parents selecting or trying to influence the selection of their children's friends. A parent might, for example, ask why the teenager wasn't friendly with some particular person whose characteristics or family background were deemed to be potentially beneficial to the child.

These continuing family contributions to adolescent peer and friendship selection and development are potentially problematic for families as well as for teenagers. A previous harmony worked out over the years in family relationships either facilitates the movement to friends and peer group formation or makes it guilt-laden and hostile. In either case, the interdependence of family and peer groups in adolescent social development is apparent.

The other area of conflict in the movement from family to peers is part of the dynamics of peer groups themselves. Friendships and wider peer associations serve to recast the adolescent's self-image in new and often unfamiliar mirrors. Self-awareness in this new evaluative reference group can and often does result in an embarrassed self-consciousness: "I can't seem to get my feet to do what I want them to" or "I thought I would die when she called on me to read." As a result, a number of new sources of social anxiety emerge. One is the fear of social rejection. We are, for better or worse, our parents' children, not through choice but as a result of birth. Since we choose our friends, there is the new anxiety that comes from the mutuality of the choice process and the possibility of rejection. The real or imagined physical, social, or personality characteristics being rejected can become particularly painful elements of negative self-awareness during adolescence.

Getting used to a new body and the enhanced sexuality that comes with it was difficult for boys as well as girls in both Southside and Sheffield and in the other communities we studied as well. But there were differences both by gender and by place of residence. Some of the awkwardness and heightened self-awareness that physical change engenders was related to comparing one's body and the tempo of the changes to that of age-mates. But there were differences between Southside and Sheffield, particularly among girls, in how these differences were dealt with and resolved. In Sheffield we found that girls showed greater concern than boys about comparative growth rates, a finding similar to what others have reported to be true nationally.[5] Sexual maturation and the bodily changes it produced were an unwelcome signal of a changing social role for a thirteen-year-old girl in Sheffield:

> Sometimes I talk to my friend Millie about how we're getting older and changing, and we talk about other girls and how they are changing, too. Some of them are changing faster than I am, but some aren't. I never talk to them about it, but you can see. Millie and I are about the same and I'm glad, because I don't know what I would do if I was changing faster than her. I want us to stay the same with each other.

Girls in Southside mature sexually and socially sooner than their age-mates in Sheffield, and, outwardly at least, seem to be much more comfortable with their new sexuality. Teasing comments about body changes and sexual interest were found to be much more common among teenage girls in Southside than they were in Sheffield, and this difference continued throughout the teen years. While some commentators see this precocity as a factor in the higher rates of teenage pregnancy in urban inner-city areas, it also has the more positive effect of making the psychosexual transition a less secretive and hence an often less troubled one. As I will discuss later, sexuality and sexual awareness are necessary but far from the only factors involved in teen pregnancy.

In both Southside and Sheffield evidences of physical growth and pubescent sexuality were more welcome (even looked forward to) among boys than among girls.[6] We also found less difference between boys in Southside and those in Sheffield, although the inner-city teenagers reported becoming sexually active at an earlier age, and, like the girls there, talked about sexuality and sexual experience earlier and more frequently than we heard among younger teenage boys in the suburbs. There was also much more "cutting," or teasing, about comparative sexual development and experience in Southside than in Sheffield. By the later teen years, however, this sexual teasing, and the boasting mention of real or imagined sexual partners which often accompanied it, tended to diminish in Southside but increased in Sheffield.

While these differences between the suburban and urban inner-city teenagers had their most immediate effects in peer group interaction, they had their origins in the adult community as well as in the peer group. Parents in both Southside and Sheffield showed greater concern for the developing sexuality of their daughters than their sons. It would begin at about the time of puberty or even before, when, as one sixteen-year-old Sheffield girl said, "My father would give my mother a nervous look whenever I tried to sit on his lap, and my mother would say something dumb like I was too big to do that now." In addition to the self-doubt created in the teenagers, this new social distance is also problematic for fathers, who must find new ways to relate. But the new sexuality of the female following puberty is seen as a special vulnerability by many members of the community in both Sheffield and Southside. Teenagers saw this in the stricter rules and more stringent curfews imposed on girls in both communities. Mothers we spoke with in Sheffield worried that sexual experimentation could lead to unwanted pregnancy, and while they were concerned about schooling and career consequences for their boys as well as their girls, it was always the girl, they usually added, who paid the highest price. In Southside mothers warned their daughters that all men, including teenage boys, were out to get "it" any way and from anyone they could, and that marriage and the protection of a husband was the only sure safeguard to escape "getting into trouble."

While newly emerging sexuality and changing bodies are a major source of anxiety for teenagers, they are not the only source. Popularity, the social feedback which results from patterns of choice and preferences in peer interaction and response, is another source. One factor is the heightened self-awareness—mentioned earlier—as the teenager seeks to fit into the peer group and to be accepted by other members. Another factor is the conformity that is required for acceptance. We found in our research that both self-awareness and conformity were frequent bases for conflict with parents, friends, and siblings. In many of the interviews the issue of conformity was a distinctive area of conflict and even expressed concern for adolescents, particularly in the early teens but in later years as well. Here again, while conformity to perceived peer norms was important in each community, we found some differences by age, gender, and residence.

Conformity needs among peers, and the conflicts with parents which resulted, were both particularly obvious during early adolescence in every community. It is during this period of adolescence that conformity to the family begins to give way—accompanied by various degrees of resistance from parents in different communities—to conformity to the peer group. Parents in Sheffield were still influential in deciding both the group membership and the social activities of their early adolescent youngsters. These early teenage children acquiesced to the parent-defined conformity, but not without some resistance. One twelve-year-old girl, for example, describes how parents still organize and control out-of-school social contacts with peers and also gives some indication of wanting to make some decisions for herself:

The kids in my school are just beginning to have parties. Last year I think we had about eight during the year. They are all pretty much alike. My parents had one for me and I invited a lot of people from my class. My mother and I talked over who should come and I know she talked to my father and that he told her she shouldn't be so concerned about having the same number of boys as girls.

My party was on a Saturday night in November, just after Halloween. We had the party in our basement rec room. We bought popcorn, potato chips, pretzels, and lots of soda, and my mother and one of her friends made Sloppy Joes on Saturday afternoon. The kids started coming about 7:30, and my mother would meet their mother or father, whoever brought them, and after all the kids arrived my parents went upstairs for the rest of the evening.

Some of the kids brought their own records and we played music and talked. My older sister and my kid brother came down to the rec room once or twice and I asked my mother to stop them, and she told them that it was my party and they should not be teasing me about it. My mother brought the Sloppy Joes down around 9:30 and we also had cake.

Then the other kids' parents began arriving to pick them up. Parents would come to the front door and talk to my parents for awhile, and my mother would come downstairs and say "Janie, your mother and father are here" and then Janie would leave, and by 11:00 everybody was gone except Debbie and Marissa [the respondent's "best friends"], whose parents stayed afterward and had coffee and cake with my parents. . . .

Every party last year and the parties I've been to so far this year have been just like mine except sometimes they have pizza. I told my mother I wanted pizza for the party, but she said Sloppy Joes were easier and that the kids would enjoy them more. Parents give the parties and help you to decide who to invite. I guess it's good to have them help, but it's not as much fun as if we could decide for ourselves who to invite.

By early adolescence many youngsters in Southside have already begun to form peer groups, which introduce them into a world of peer interaction and conforming behavior that is outside direct parental control. Often such groups have already begun to move away from the family and to establish a social system of their own, but even these remain in the local community and membership is jealously restricted to, and even protective of, the immediate neighborhood. Parents, and other adult figures such as older siblings, relatives, and the local adult community, are still important in setting limits to what the peer group becomes and does, but, unlike in Sheffield, it is the peer group rather than the family which defines and controls conformity because so much of the teenager's time is spent outside the home.

Most of the neighborhoods in Southside have younger street gangs, some of which are allied with the gangs of their older brothers and all of which stay pretty close to their home base. Membership can begin as early as nine or ten years of age and continues until a youngster joins one of the older groups, moves out of the neighborhood, or simply matures out of gang life. The gangs' names—"The Little Devils," "The Bad Little Boys," "Young Ghost Shadows"—represent their juvenile status and their need to present fearsome images for self-protection. They do, however, become involved in delinquent and even criminal activity.

John Maldonato, for example, belonged to The Little Devils from the time he was ten until his family moved out of Southside when he was thirteen. His older brother had also been a member, and when John was eight or nine he began hanging out on the periphery of the gang and slowly became involved in whatever they were doing. Sometimes they would go into other neighborhoods and steal things from parked cars, from bums or drunks who were asleep or passed out, or from stores; sometimes they would just hang out or play stick ball. Did his parents know and approve of his being in the gang? His parents knew who the kids were that he was hanging out with; they were the other kids in the neighborhood, and where else would he go to find friends? Some of the members of The Little Devils were known for getting into trouble with the police, in school, or even with their parents—or they had older brothers or parents who themselves had bad reputations. Sometimes John's mother would tell him that he would get into trouble by being with the gang ("You walk with a cripple and you learn how to limp"), but as long as he didn't get into any real trouble they didn't say very much about it.

Our study of these new ventures into the different social world that comes with puberty presented abundant evidence that the unfamiliar roles demanded of early adolescents were sufficient to heighten anxiety for them in every community. We noticed, however, that shyness and reticence disappeared much sooner in Southside than in Sheffield—because, we concluded, of the greater familiarity with varied situations which characterizes urban living and the earlier emancipation of city youngsters from parental surveillance. In both communities the need to conform was greater among females than among males in the peer groups of early adolescence. Girls in both communities said that they did not want to appear different from age-mates. They also expressed more concern than boys about what gender mates felt about them, showing more sensitivity and empathy but more envy and jealousy as well. But the way they expressed these feelings differed.

In Sheffield the concern for the opinions of peers was comparative and competitive: "I know she thinks that her parents are better than mine." Southsiders were more defensive, often almost belligerent: "She's always giving me looks like I'm dirt." The most frequent type of interaction both within and between groups of Southside peers was the "snap session," in which a highly structured way of talking and teasing becomes an almost ritual means of expressing hostility. Over the course of the teen years, these differences between the competitive norms which were part of growing up in Sheffield and the conflict which was a daily experience of the same process in Southside became more important than gender. Older teenage girls—and to a lesser extent older boys—in Sheffield, most of whom were getting ready to leave the community to go to college, showed less concern about conformity than did their younger brothers and sisters. In Southside, however, the older male youth became subject to much more intense peer pressure than they had been in early adolescence since few would leave the community. The neighborhood-based youth gang and its strict, pervasive code of conduct is one indication of how important and interconnected conformity pressures can become for males. Many of the girls in Southside had already married by the late teens and had new families to look to, as well as to look after, and conformity to peers was replaced by family obligations.

While conformity was an issue in every community, it was not an important one for all teenagers. Sometimes this was because teenagers' parents consciously isolated them from youngsters who were not kin, as was the case with the Chinese whose children worked with them from an early age. At other times it was because a teenager had a special relationship with some adult or adult group, as when some Sheffield adolescents spent all of their free time with a swimming coach preparing for competitions, or with tutors getting ready for college entrance exams. Often, however, a teenager just seemed to have outgrown the need to conform, or, in some cases, to have always been invulnerable to it. Conforming behavior was explained by the need to be popular, to be accepted, and to fit in with peers. But as self-awareness increased, there were also strivings toward autonomy, some sense of individualism, some escape from conformity, and the need for affiliations outside the peer group. Some of this was expressed in terms of new relationships with parents, but most frequently it centered on the wider world outside the immediate social environment. These "escape plans" could relate to occupational plans, to educational futures, to travel, to any number of future states, but always seemed to describe a need to separate from the intensity and immediacy of the peer group.

Peer groups introduce adolescents to new or at least newly defined roles in the community. But these roles always grow out of and eventually fit into other institutional environments. For example, adolescents first learn their basic sex roles, what it is to be a male or a female, in the family and then they expand that knowledge and learn the interactive aspects of the role in the peer group. In school and in other social environments they also come in contact with peers from families or even communities different from their own, who demonstrate other possible selves than those to which they were directed in childhood. They also take on the social role of "adolescent," which makes them no longer children and changes the community's expectations of them, as they are constantly reminded by adult caretakers. They are, in effect, newly emerging and developing persons, still creatures of their past, heavily involved in exploring the present, and working to develop a future. Novelist Mary McCarthy describes this new birth as an adolescent in the opening sentence of *How I Grew,* the autobiography of her own adolescence: "I was born as a mind during 1925, my bodily birth having taken place in 1912."[7]

The peer group is often described as the major social setting within which the teenager seeks to find an identity to make this transition from the childhood past to the adult future. In our interviews we discovered that the adolescent's ability to "find" an identity was limited by the degree to which a community presents a consistent, believable set of role models of what a teenager (or categories of teenagers) should be like in order to consolidate a valued adult identity. Often one community constrains individual identity achievement—how the individual sees himself—by assigning him to a particular social category. Thus, key elements of identity are assigned to a teenager on the basis of characteristics such as race or ethnicity, social class, physical appearance, religion, life style—which are shared, or perceived to be, by the members of a particular peer group. Ethnicity, for example, can have a major influence on peer relations and on possible selves or identities in Southside. According to a high school student in that community:

> Everybody is known by his race in this [high] school. You're either black, Chinese, or Hispanic, and the rest of us get known by who we hang out with. I hang around mostly with other Italian guys and we get called "Guidos," which usually means that you come from Little Italy, but girls who go out with Guidos are called Guidos too, even if they aren't Italian. When the Italians won the world soccer championship, we put up a sign "Guidos are Number 1."

In our suburban and rural samples, ethnicity was less all-encompassing. In these communities Italian-American adolescents were identified as such primarily in situations when, for example, Italian foods or organized crime were discussed and someone would say "Ask Rossi, he's Italian." Such ethnic comments seemed to create little concern about identification for the youngster, unless, as was the case with Hispanics, blacks, Mexicans, and Native Americans in some of our sites, there were sufficient numbers to form an identifiable minority. But other individual characteristics besides race or ethnicity can "place" youngsters in social categories which limit choice of identity and predispose peer group selection. A Sheffield student explained:

> I really did not have much trouble deciding who my friends would be when I came to Sheffield High. Our family is Pentecostal and I belonged to the youth league at our church since I was ten years old. When I came to the high school I went around with the kids I met through the youth league because I knew them and it was easy to be with them. There is another reason, though. I got a lot

of teasing about being a "Jesus freak" from some of the other kids, and even one of the teachers called on me one day when we were discussing school prayer. She didn't actually say anything like "Mattie, you should have an opinion on this because you're so religious," but I was sure that everybody else in the class felt that she was calling on me for that reason.

The differences between the communities we studied led us to question the reality of a homogeneous national youth culture which could intervene between the local community's social institutions and the children or teenagers they raise. What the media said teenagers in general do or do not do and what the media defined as "in" or "out" did not have nearly as much influence on the youngsters we studied as did their closest friends and local peers as well as parents and other significant adults. We were just as convinced that the local peer group itself is not an isolated subsociety. Peer groups are necessary and effective social evaluation arenas which do exert powerful influences on their teenage members, often causing considerable anxiety and stress. But these groups grow out of and continue to be related to the adult institutions which sanction them, and they are as short-lived as they are ad hoc. While they do provide a locus for peer interaction and permit group as well as individual questioning of adult standards and values, few teens can or ever do completely reject these standards and values.[8] To some extent this results from the continued dependence of teenagers on adults, but there are also more positive reasons for the continued intermeshing of teenage peer groups and the adult community.

Most teenage peer groups we encountered in every community were closely associated with significant adults and institutional settings, and even with adult ideological or religious systems which first brought the group together and, in most cases, continued to provide both a setting and a rationale for continuing association. In Sheffield the setting could be the neighborhood of families, the elementary or middle school in that neighborhood, the high school (as the locale of athletic activities, clubs, or even classes), the church (as the locale of youth groups), and so on. Where else could teenagers first meet and where else could they go to continue relationships? Parental control over Sheffield's teenagers is a clear indication of how the adult authority structure organizes and controls the day-to-day lives of its adolescents, who have no space in which to congregate freely. Sheffield offers one of the clearest examples of just how intermeshed the settings, values, and norms of peer groups are with the local adult community.

It might seem that pathways for self-exploration available to adolescents are as diverse as the wide variety of cultural alternatives in the ethnic crazy quilt which is the social fabric of Southside. But in fact, despite the anonymity we ascribe to urban centers such as Southside, how and where teenagers met and associated was just as dependent on adults there as it was in Sheffield. Like Josie, most teenagers in Southside were limited in their friendship choices to members of their own racial or ethnic group and social class because of both family residence and de facto segregation within the schools. These social structural constraints on freedom of choice in group membership limited the opportunities for the exploration and extension of self in the ethnic diversity of Southside just as surely as they did in the more socially and culturally homogenized environment of Sheffield. The absence in Southside of many of the cultural and recreational programs available in the more affluent social world of Sheffield also limited the kinds of groups formed and the social feedback received from them.

Because of the differences between the two communities, there were some noticeable differences in the character and structure of the peer groups developed in each. In Sheffield, for example, the relatively small size of the adolescent population and the close control of the small community over youthful behavior limited peer networks to a few close friends. While Southside is geographically the same size as Sheffield, its much greater density and diversity of population means youth there come into daily contact with a much larger number of teenagers. Not only are peer networks larger in Southside, the friendship groups which form within them are also larger. One reason is that there are more possible friends to choose from. Southside's youngsters also spend more time at an earlier age outside the direct supervision of adults, so that peer interaction tends to come earlier and allows for a wider range of contact. In addition, because of the need for protection from the greater level of risk in the urban inner city, a wider circle of close friends for support and protection becomes prudent if not essential.

Both Sheffield and Southside have worked out a form of peer group association which fits the community's particular expectations for teenagers. While the patterns may differ, each works for the community which developed it. Both serve to usher most youngsters in each community through the teen years without appreciable turmoil or rebellion. The vast majority of the teenagers we observed and interviewed were well aware of both adult and peer influences in their lives. There was no question in their minds or ours that both served as referees for doubts about present and future and that they could distinguish between them.

It should not be supposed, however, that the influence of local adult institutions on teenagers is a one-way street. Teenagers also learn how to influence their families, as explained by a Sheffield adolescent:

> My parents, particularly my mother, wanted me to go to her college and join her sorority too, and so I applied there. I went there with her and it seemed like a nice enough place, but Charlene—she's my best friend—had decided that she wanted to go to Brinkley, and we wanted to go together. We both started to work on my mother, and my mother agreed that we could all go out and look at it, and she and my father and Charlene and her parents all drove over together. I was accepted at both schools and my mother tried to influence me to go to her college. What finally convinced her was that Charlene was accepted also [at Brinkley], and my father said that it would be nice to have friends with me from Sheffield at college.

In a community such as Sheffield, there is little question about whether one will or will not go to college. If Charlene had suggested that they should not go to college but take a year off to travel or perhaps to go to some occupational training program, the preeminence of the parental authority would probably have overruled the influence of one girl on her peer and of the two girls on their families. Influence can work in either of two ways: by providing information which leads one to accept someone else's attitudes, beliefs, and opinions as one's own or by leading one to seek social approval and avoid rejection.[9] Adult influences on teenagers, which are largely of the former type, are long-standing, reaching back into childhood, and, while they might be challenged, continue to shape the basic values that have been instilled in early life. The peer influence we observed, on the other hand, tended to be of the latter type, dependent upon the individual's need for social approval, and usually lasting only so long as the teenager was a member of or continued to accept the norms of the peer group. The peer influences did not become internalized with the same salience and persistence as adult-mediated influences and usually did not conflict with the values expressed by adult caretakers. It was the individual teenager's willingness and perhaps even need to conform, particularly in the early years, rather than any consciously articulated group pressure which had the greatest impact in the groups we observed.[10]

Nevertheless, youth culture or teenage peer groups are often blamed when a new social problem involving adolescents emerges. Yet despite continuing professional and popular assumptions that adolescents look to themselves and progressively look away from the influences of the adult community, we found significant congruence between the world views of teenagers and the adults in their lives. This congruence means that the problems of adolescents are as much ours as they are theirs and cannot be explained away by indicting teenagers themselves or the youth culture we say they invented.

Teenage suicide, for example, is often linked to the depressive effects of youth culture and peer pressure on adolescents' emotions. The occasional group suicide among adolescent friends and the evidence of so-called copycat incidents following media reporting of teen suicides, such as those in Bergenfield, add to the belief that peer pressure is most influential. A more careful examination of the national trends in suicide rates and what factors seem involved links adolescent suicide directly to adult society and casts some doubt on just how much youth culture is implicated. The suicide rate among youths increased 50 percent between 1950 and the mid-1980s, reaching 12.4 per 100,000 in 1979 (about the same rate as homicide but only about half the rate for death by accident among youth) and remained fairly stable after that.[11] The progressive increases in the suicide rate did not seem to respond to factors such as economic boom or bust or fluctuations in drug use, which were believed responsible for shifts in the youth culture. Rather, the increases in teen suicides were clearly associated with increases in the number of youth in the population.[12] Demographers and others have cited increased competition for desirable adult roles in society and also point out that large birth cohorts experience high suicide rates at all age levels.[13] There are also similar demographic differences in the frequency of suicide among teenagers and adults: As is true in the adult population, adolescent males are three times more likely than females to commit suicide, and blacks only half as likely to do so.

Most people who have studied suicide among adolescents attribute its causes to factors in the general (as contrasted to teenage) culture:

increasingly strong pressures to compete and attain success, as well as the breakdown of the American family, the loss of a sense of community, and the resultant anomic sense of loneliness in American society.[14] A number of studies have traced youthful suicide back to problems in a child's experience in a broken home.[15] Others cite the loss of a parent, or parental rejection or hostility to the child and the resentment which can result.[16] And some researchers even more directly indict the ambivalance of parents who want the child but shy away from caring and emotional involvement with him; sexual abuse, particularly when it involves incest, has also been implicated in teenage suicides.[17]

Our own experience with suicide among the youth we observed was not extensive, but I did hear a good deal about it during the interviews. The material always came up in association with personal feelings and daydreams, reported suicides in the media, and actual or attempted suicides among peers. In these instances there was frequent mention of peer groups but not much about any nihilistic adolescent culture or heavy-metal music influences or pressures. The death or loss of a friend or even an acquaintance at school most frequently led to thoughts or concerns about mortality, but in the few cases where suicide was involved, there was a clear pattern of identifying with the victim. Far more frequently I heard thoughts about suicide in association with conflicts or disruptions in family relationships, particularly with parental attitudes and behaviors.

One frequent pattern of association directly linked parental indication of strong disapproval, or parental withdrawal (real or imagined) of love or caring. Not infrequently, parental pressures to do better in school or "shape up" produced an imagined acting-out of running away or even suicide in a thinly masked appeal for the return of the unconditional love of childhood. As was true for each of the four members in the Bergenfield suicide pact, multiple indications of failure—at home, in the school, in the community—reinforce the feelings of rejection and increase the pressures, causing teenagers to feel they have nowhere to turn for acceptance and support except to each other. My interviews also showed a pattern of suicidal thoughts arising in response to interpersonal problems between the parents: arguments, family violence, and threats of or actual movements toward separation or divorce. There were also a few cases where it seemed clear that thoughts about suicide were engendered by a form of separation anxiety: overwhelming fear of growing up, separating from parents and family, and going out on one's own to establish a new, independent identity.

Our society has, I believe, made the adolescent peer group the scapegoat for some of our own sins, both those we commit ourselves and those sins teenagers learn from us. The use and abuse of drugs, alcohol, and tobacco were all adult problems first and became teenage problems only after we introduced youngsters to them as indicators of an adult life style. Other adult-proclaimed youth problems such as unemployment and delinquent behavior follow the same demographic and cyclical patterns among youth as they do among adults. And some, such as poor nutritional and other health habits, are first learned as an inheritance of family living.[18]

Reasserting the continuing importance of parents and other significant adults in adolescent development does not negate the crucial role of peer groups in relationships with a community's social environments. What we concluded after years of observing and interviewing in each of the communities is that peer groups are the primary means by which teenagers share and validate personal and social growth as they expand their everyday experiences into the community beyond the family. The opportunities that peer groups provide youngsters to experiment with more egalitarian relationships, and the new patterns of self-representation involved, are a sometimes painful but necessary preparation for adult social relations.[19] As part of this process, adolescents learn from their own mistakes and those of their age-mates. Peer groups allow adolescents to explore new relationships outside the boundaries of kinship and to test and further develop self-knowledge and self-esteem as well as to resolve self-doubts. Teenagers also learn to evaluate critically what others say without having to question idealized parents.

But my research also concluded that peer groups are empowered and legitimated by the adult social institutions of the communities in which they develop and are a functional part of that social system rather than simply youth-driven collectives attempting to escape from adult society. Just as the peer group moves children from the orienting family into which they are born to a family in which they will become the parent generation, it also moves them from the adult society in which they have grown up to one in which they will be the adult authorities. Throughout this transition, adults remain influential and valued members of adolescent social networks. The notion that "peer group influence" is a generic process unresponsive to the community in which such groups are formed demeans the considerable influence which adults, particularly parents, have as mentors during adolescence.

It is now widely accepted that a "good enough environment" is a major determinant of success in moving from the relative passivity of infancy to the beginnings of social responsiveness in early childhood; it is just as important to provide a "good enough" transitional world through which adolescents can continue to progress to the social interdependence of adulthood.[20] If parents and other significant adults fail to meet teenagers' needs, they will turn to peer groups in some other social setting for support. My experience has been that the adolescent does not seek to escape—indeed can never be free of—the people who inhabit his childhood world. What occurs instead is that he finds transitional relationships and adult mediators to link that world to a number of new spheres as he moves into the larger society.

Varying parental and community strategies for adolescent development, chance encounters and unique experiences, and the motivation, determination, and personal belief systems of teenagers themselves make for a variety of patterns of growing up in America. This does not deny that peer groups are, in fact, a primary social group in the lives of teenagers which has become institutionalized in modern society, with the common interests and shared experiences, frequent social contact and reduced social distance, empathy, trust, and mutuality characteristic of all primary groups. But a peer group is not a spontaneously created or independent social group in the community; it is a collective which is contrived by the other, more established social institutions that organize and continue to monitor the social networks out of which peer groups are formed.

We did not find many indications of strong, active resistance to the community-derived standards and expectations of behavior on the part of teenage individuals or groups so long as there was general agreement among the community adult institutions on what teenagers were supposed (or not supposed) to be and do. As teenagers mature, they also seek to move away from the normative pressures of the adult community. But in our experience there was far more congruence than conflict among the world views of parents, other adults, and adolescent children. Most adolescent peer groups are closely tied to the views expressed by their families. These two primary groups more often complement than compete with each other; each socializes the other. Children are socialized by their parents, but as they become teenagers and gain more experience in the world outside the family they bring what they have learned back to the family, where parents as well as siblings share in the knowledge. While we found some elements of parent–child conflict in families, and teacher–student disagreement in schools, most teenagers continue to move into adult life and become integrated into the social fabric of their communities— and, indeed, into the mainstream of American society—under the guidance of parents and other adults. In fact, in peer-structured support groups as well as in the adult developed and mediated peer support networks in adolescent drug rehabilitation, mental health, and runaway programs, as well as in the Scout troops, church youth groups, and schools we observed, it was adult-proclaimed values which teenagers quoted to peers when attempting to influence beliefs and behaviors. We much more frequently heard a teenager preface some comment to a peer with "My mom says" than with any attributions to youth culture heroes or pundits. Therefore, we conclude that the development of an adolescent's identity and self-concept is a dynamic interplay between imitating parental models, showing sensitivity to peer influences, and striving as an individual for independence.

In all of the communities we studied, youths and adults expressed and exhibited age-appropriate versions of what is a common community culture. The relationships between peer pressures and adult pressures are much too complex to consider the effects of either individually in the social life styles of adolescents in the community. Adding to that complexity is the fact that both the family and the peer group are part of the same community of social institutions and interact with them singly and together. Family and community, for example, combine to provide the dominant influences of socioeconomic status in childhood and adolescence. Poverty backgrounds impose many of the major hardships of development on adolescents through differential participation in the social and cultural functions of other social institutions. Such youngsters are most likely to have learning disabilities and diminished educational achievement. They are also more likely to drop out of school earlier, to experience teenage pregnancy and early parenthood, to become involved in criminal and delinquent acts and to be arrested and incarcerated, to be unemployed, and, when they are able to find employment, to continue their working lives at the lowest levels of the labor force. The lives of their more affluent peers are quite different but have some problems as well. The pressures to excel and to do better than the kids next door are strong in suburbia.[21] We witnessed the stressful effects of such parental and community pressure in many of the suburban schools in which we observed and

interviewed. We also saw these effects in other areas of social life
such as sports: early adolescents, for example, practicing four to five
hours every day to fulfill a parental dream that their offspring become
superstar athletes and bring an Olympic gold medal home to the community. Even poverty and affluence, however, are not completely deterministic of the character and outcome of the adolescent years for all
of the individuals they touch.

Peer groups also provide an informal support group which can
provide access to a vast new set of opportunities for peer counseling
and peer tutoring in which both the helper and the helped benefit
from the exchange. A variety of youngsters-helping-youngsters programs are already in place in various communities (most are school-
based small groups or one-to-one tutorial programs). Some schools,
in response to suicide pacts such as the one in Bergenfield, are setting
up peer networks which work with adult counselors to watch for
signs of potential suicide and to offer help and care. Similar approaches
are aimed at curbing drunken driving or preventing or intervening in
drug abuse. Others, like the Yale Child Study Center's Primary Prevention School Program, are more broadly based intervention programs
which stress academic competence and help as well. There were a
few youngsters in every community who were able to deal by themselves with the problems which can beset teenagers. Such youngsters
seemed to possess such personal resilience that the most condemning
of environments was unable to hold them down. These "invulnerable
children," as they have come to be called, have been discovered in
a wide variety of adverse and high-risk environments ranging from
extreme poverty to schizophrenic and drug- and alcohol-abusing families. But they are the exception rather than the rule, and no one
seems quite sure of the source of their inner strength.[22] In the vast
majority of the cases, however, there was almost always some relationship with a supportive group of peers and adults in a church group,
the school, or some other community social agency. Once we accept
the ability of the local peer group to mediate external influences and
the importance of having caring adults as part of youth social networks,
it should be possible to help teenagers develop peer group structures
which enhance cognitive and social development.

But while these constructive uses of adult-mediated peer groups
are a creative meshing of adult concerns and the more relevant daily
access which youngsters have to each other, they are largely dependent
on adults and their continuing involvement for both initiation and

survival. The more spontaneous, informal groups which youngsters negotiate for themselves lack the continuity of the adult social institutions and respond to changes in the agendas of these institutions rather than to their own agendas or to extracommunity forces. Changes in the structure and functioning of the American family, for example, can have important effects on the influence of peer groups. Less adult supervision time as more women enter the labor market leads to more teenage time spent with peers and greater dependence on peer-defined cultural, social, and behavioral norms. It also means less time for the loving support of parents which all children need, even when they do not seem to be asking for it. Like all of us, teenagers cast about for this love, and for help and guidance wherever they can find it. Understanding how communities can and sometimes do provide these benefits for teenagers and how the peer group mediates in orienting its members to accept or reject such help requires determining how youth, as members of such groups, relate to each of the social contexts which make up a community's adult authority structure. The consolidation of identity begins in a stable integration among the family, the peer group, the school, and, eventually, all the social environments in the life path. The family, however, is where it all starts, and that seems the right place to begin to look at the influences on the lives of adolescents which develop in and among the social environments found in all communities.

3

"Home is Where We Start From"

In a posthumous collection of his essays entitled *Home is Where We Start From,* the late British psychoanalyst D. W. Winnicott makes the point that the family, and the individual child's experiences within that particular family, orient him to all the other human groupings, which grow wider and wider until they reach the level of the society.[1] Families are no less a product of this same widening circle of influence as they mediate the development of the child through adolescence. If the social environments which make up the extrafamilial world and the voices within them are in harmony, and if the family is aligned with and participates in that accord, the developmental process of relating past to future during adolescence can be a smooth transition. When, on the other hand, there is dissonance in the relationship between the family and the other institutional sectors, adolescents are faced with the task of choosing between family and other perspectives on the future as well as the present: a multiplicity which impedes the development of a holistic sense of self. The growing child's perception of accord or discord in these environments is also first experienced in the family, and it is here that the emotional tone of how the child defines the emerging self begins.[2] Even when the peer group becomes a central influence, the basic social structure of the self—established in the family—continues to shape the interaction between the adolescent and the external world of the community.

Families also provide continuity for society as well as for their children. Generational inheritance of social position and roles is a continuing fact in American society. The correlation between fathers' and sons' occupational attainment has remained stable in recent decades.[3] And size of family, education of parents, and other family-determined identifications, such as race and rural or urban origin, are still influential factors in the level of educational attainment. In 1982, writing with a group of his associates about schools, the same James Coleman who twenty years earlier was so influential in the discovery of an adolescent society and the youth culture concluded that

> if studies of school achievement have shown one thing, it is the importance of the family. And school achievement is only one element in the process of becoming an adult; the family's contribution to other elements is even more important. If an early withdrawal of family attention, interest, and involvement is to become the fate of an increasing fraction of our youth, it can be expected to have especially serious consequences.[4]

The head start the family has in the socialization and enculturation of children gives it an enormous influence not only in childhood but throughout the life course. But its role in shaping and directing the lives of adolescents is by no means the same everywhere. Family environments differ, even within the same cultural and social milieu, because each family is a dynamic collection of individual personalities whose interaction changes as individual members change. Furthermore, the experiences of different children even within the same families are not identical. Different children have different relationships with parents and siblings and experience those relationships differently. While we speak of "family life" as if it is a common experience shared among all of its members, each experiences it differently. No two children have the same relationship with their parents, and, indeed, the child's relationship with each parent differs as well. Experientially, there are as many "families" within a family as there are children; while much is shared, each child and each parent contributes and experiences the family from an individual perspective.

Still, most teenagers at every age and almost all of the early adolescent boys and girls I interviewed seemed to find the major source for their emotional support within their families. Well over 90 percent of *all* the teenagers studied in every community reported that their relationships with their parents were good and that they were pleased with what they considered to be the parents' good characteristics.[5] But we found that in every community, if not in every family, there were problems of communication and understanding, disputes over discipline, even examples of physical as well as emotional abuse, flowing in both directions between parents and their children and among siblings as well.

Patterns of communication and of discipline and control varied among families and were also subject to interpersonal as well as cultural differences. There were areas and incidents of disagreement, discord, and conflict which usually grew out of the day-to-day encounters of living together. But as children became adolescents and as they proceeded toward adulthood, the conflicts centered more and more around issues of freedom and responsibility.[6] As adolescence advanced, issues of freedom and responsibility moved into the outside world along with the teenager's new ventures outside the family. Dating, clothing, curfews, and the choice of friends seemed to join rather than replace the family-centered hassles of childhood.

In Sheffield, and in other suburban areas we studied, more than current issues and behavior are at stake. We found that as teenagers move closer to adulthood, conflicts over the long-term effects of current behavior or misbehavior increase. Families in Sheffield, for example, start very early to emphasize the importance of education and diligent effort to children as early as the elementary years. In the high school years, however, there is a more constant and concerted pressure for success in schooling, more concern with industriousness, the work ethic, and the use of leisure time, and more pressure for adherence to the norms and laws of the community—always with an eye to the future. As Bruce Megan of Sheffield said:

I couldn't tell you when it started, but all of my life I knew I was going to be going off to college someday. I don't think my father ever said "Bruce, you're going to go to college someday" or even, you know, put catalogues in front of me or told me horror stories about what would happen if I didn't go. He never really said much to me about what I'm going to be either, like he never said I couldn't be a professional football player or join the marines or the Peace Corps. He and my mom never once said to me "You have to do so-and-so" or "Parents know best." But I knew that they wanted me to hang out with the right crowd in school and that when I started dating Marcia Allen they were impressed with the fact that her father is a doctor. In fact, the only time I can remember my father actually telling me I couldn't do something was when we all decided to shave our hair off the summer after sophomore year and he said it would be a dumb-ass thing to do because it wouldn't grow back in time for the next school year. Now that I'm trying to choose a college he and my mom both tell me that I can pick where I want to go but that I should go to the best possible place and what did I think about such and such a place.

Communications from parents to youngsters in Sheffield tend to be more subtle than direct, but the message comes across for most teenagers who live there. Parents also focus their influence and control on educational preparation for future careers, and, while manifestly respecting and even encouraging the spirit of individualism, they circumscribe it to insure that it is put to use in preparing for a socially and economically acceptable future. Clothing styles, friendships, dating, how one spends one's time, and even "attitude" can produce hassles with parents, but even exchanges and injunctions about these topics are invariably framed in terms of long-range effects on school and career. Bruce and others we talked to feel and, at some level, recognize how pervasive the pressure for success is among Sheffield's parents. A few rebel, but most internalize the drive over time because they get the same message from the school, other community environments, and peers as well.

Spending time with Josie Delgado's family in Southside reveals a much less subtle and much more direct approach to communication and discipline, but also a greater concern for the here-and-now effects of behavior than for the future. Josie doesn't see her father very much but says that whenever he is around he is very pointed in asking her (and her mother) about how she is behaving. He also admonishes her about "getting into trouble." He doesn't just mean getting into trouble with the law or even in school; "trouble" seems to be a generic term to cover anything that might diminish her reputation, bring disgrace or ridicule on her family, and, most importantly, says Josie, give the impression that he cannot control his children even though he is separated from their mother. He seems far less concerned about the behavior of his older, married daughters because they are, after all, now some other man's responsibility. Josie's father seldom hits her, although her mother sometimes will when she fails to carry out some household chore or disobeys some rule the mother has laid down. Instead, Josie's father will yell at her, often calling her names

and telling her that he has "heard things" about her in the neighborhood. Josie usually yells back, telling him (with something between
mockery and bitterness) that he should pay more attention to his own
reputation in the neighborhood and in the family and get off her
back.

The different approaches to communication and discipline in the two
families are not solely a result of class or ethnic differences. Another
important element is how supportive each family is of the expectations
of the social world outside the family and how they orient their children
to that outside world and to what their likely destiny might be out
there. In Sheffield, for example, the institutional world of the community and the other contexts such as the school, churches, or even the
criminal justice system are in compliance with family values and
concerns. Parents can and do plot a steady course for their children
through long and arduous educational preparation in order for them
to achieve an occupation and life style similar to their own. Family
discipline is gentle but consistent in seeing this goal as the most
important determinant of adolescence, which is essentially a period
in which one prepares to go to college. The adolescents themselves
seldom resist or even question this inevitability. Most youngsters in
Sheffield and in similar communities we studied would tell you that
they accept the pressures from their parents because they know that
"it's for my own good" and that parents really want to see them
"get ahead." Getting ahead, Bruce's friend Drew once told me, means
"using your head" and being everything you can be. His father keeps
telling him, he says, that he can't leave him any fortune or any future
other than what he works for now.
  This confluence of values and expectations removes a good deal
of uncertainty from the attitudes of Sheffield's adolescents about how
much control they have over their own futures. Their concerns about
individual control of their destinies are primarily competitive in terms
of how well they will do, rather than conflictual in terms of what
they will be. Another result of this extension of family values out
into the community is that in Sheffield the community *is* the family,
and adolescents experience it that way. Like the other suburban areas
we studied, Sheffield is child-centered, and all of its resources are
directed to advancing the lives of its children as extensions of the
family. There is little or no discrepancy between the private world
of the family and the public preoccupations of the community. Bruce

once commented that he feels that Sheffield is "like one big family" and that his friends' parents were just as involved in his future as his own. They had the same expectations for him and would just as readily point out what he should be doing to advance that future as his mother or father. His church youth group, his teachers at school, even the occasional contacts he had with the local police, always reinforced those expectations. Bruce always talked about "mortgaging my future" whenever he told us about some situation in which he felt he had messed up. Communities like Sheffield mold their teenagers into a particular kind of person and start most of them off along well-prepared routes to college and careers. Much of this process involves reinforcing those particular behaviors at home, and in other community environments such as the school, which will help them on their way. Parents also apply sanctions, ranging from signs of displeasure or scolding to "grounding" or other forms of restricting the teenager's freedom of choice or action; on rare occasions, even physical punishment is resorted to. Day-to-day life proceeds as a series of compromises in which parents and their children influence each other's behavior, but in the long run the parents decide and their children come to accept how their behavior is judged in the pursuit of what become shared values.

In Southside, on the other hand, the family functions as the community. While Bruce can count on the community to meet his identity needs in growing up, Josie has only her family to depend on. Josie's parents have values and expectations for her just as surely as Bruce's family does for him. There is a strong and visible feeling of mutual support and love, and, despite the occasional conflicts, a sense of solidarity. But it must often be expressed as a joint stand against a hostile and largely unfamiliar world outside Josie's immediate family and beyond the confines of the extended family in the local Dominican community. Josie and her family agree that her teachers, with a few exceptions, don't really believe in her ability or power to shape a future. If Bruce's parents, real and proxy, are his guides as he ventures out into the community and beyond, just the opposite seems true for Josie. It is she who introduces her family to the ideas and possibilities of American society: "I get so mad sometimes when my mother won't do anything she isn't used to from back home. I tell her, 'Try it, Mommy, you'll like it.'" Her sisters encourage her to succeed in school and to go on "to make something of herself," indicating by the phraseology itself the fact that she must do it alone.

Josie's family includes a number of relatives of both parents as well as her siblings and their families. She is close to all of them but particularly to her sisters. None of them have gone beyond high school, and their early marriages and parenthood have extended Josie's family even further. Much of the family's social life is spent within that family in a round of weddings, baptisms, and funerals, as well as social visiting. It is this extended network of kin, rather than non-family co-ethnic neighbors, which operates as Josie's community even when they are not together at some event or ceremony. She is constantly under their surveillance, and they will report back to her mother, father, or sisters if they observe some misdeed or hear some gossip about her which could besmirch the family honor. But, although she often complains about being spied on by relatives, Josie finds what security she has within this family community. She says that there is no problem, big or small, that she could not share with them and get understanding and acceptance. Josie also talks to her sisters (more than she does to her parents) about what her future will be and how much control she has over it. In general, however, the support she receives from her family is limited to making life as secure and emotionally rewarding as limited resources permit in the present. The family often cautions her not to aim too high. The heights they have in mind—college, a career, and then perhaps a family—are the expected futures of virtually all children in Sheffield. For Josie, living at the margin of American society, they are a longed-for dream over which she feels she has little control; she must hope for some combination of "luck" and interested outsiders to see her through.

These cultural scripts of family life in the urban inner city as contrasted to suburbia do more than simply set the stage for how adolescent social life will be acted out in the community; they also help to establish the growing child's first perspectives on social reality. They intrude into the family and have an effect on much of the interaction which takes place within as well as between families. In Sheffield and other suburban communities, families in the small area of the neighborhood interact as a mini-community. Visits back and forth among neighbors and the mutual exchange of goods and services, such as borrowing tools or household equipment or baby-sitting, bind families into an identifiable community within the larger community. Bruce's parents are friends of his friend Drew's parents. Bruce and Drew spend considerable amounts of time in each other's homes, know and interact with each other's parents, brothers, and sisters.

One result of this expanded family experience is that it allows the growing child to see a variety of different family configurations and environments: large families and small families, some more permissive and some less so; different husband–wife and parent–child relationships and resultant child identities. Another result is that the smaller community offers a source for role models larger and more diverse than the family but smaller and more intimate than the total community.

For Josie, however, and for most of the youngsters we met and interviewed in Southside and other urban inner-city areas, there is no expanded family experience beyond her own extended family. She catches glimpses of and hears comments (mostly complaints) and gossip about the family life of her friends, but her own family is not involved in this exchange and has never met most of her friends' parents even though they live nearby. She, and most of the other urban inner-city teenagers in our study, live in what are essentially isolated families, physically but not socially close to their neighbors—often afraid of others who are not somehow related to the family. Josie's friends are friends she has made outside the family; their parents are not her parents' friends, nor are their siblings friends of her sisters. What little time she spends in the crowded apartments in which her friends live is usually when their parents are not there. She knows and can tell you a good deal about the brothers and sisters of her friends who are there when she is, but virtually nothing about the parents or how they interact with their children and each other. Other than the family life of her sisters and the relatives she visits with her family, her only idea of other possible family structures or environments is what she sees on television. Her school, which has over four thousand students, is much too large and too impersonal for her to identify with and so she identifies with other Hispanic, mostly Dominican, teenagers. She does not, however, enjoy the consequent identity as a Dominican: "I'm here in America; what do I know from an island ten thousand miles away?" When you ask Josie who she is, she smirks and says, "I'm my mommy's little girl." Paradoxically, the very diversity of Southside condemns her and teenagers like her to rely primarily on the limits of her family and its traditions and values for the early prototypes for identification and social learning.

In every community, whether rural, urban, or suburban, we found that much of how teenagers come to think about themselves—who and what they are, and their feelings about self-worth or self-deficiencies—is first established in, and continues to be dependent on, their families. In turn, the family's self-concept is affected by *its* sense of belonging in the community.

A critical aspect of family influence on children and teenagers is the relationship between the parents: both the relative role of each spouse in parenting and the stability of the marriage.[7] Society tends to talk about parenting as if it is a unitary influence, but in the families we observed there were considerable differences between parents and how they related to their children.[8] Some of these were the result of personality differences between the parents: a more or less dominant father, a caring or indifferent mother, and so on. Other differences resulted from the effects of varied life circumstances: a father or mother who worked long hours or was away from home a great deal or was chronically ill during the formative years of childhood and adolescence; both or neither of the parents working for a period of time; chronic unemployment; being on welfare. Separations, divorce, the death of one or both parents, the remarriage of a divorced parent—all of these affect parenting and provide a more or less stable home base for children as they approach and complete the teenage years. Most of these are experiences which burden and trouble numbers of teenagers in every community. There were some patterns of parenting, however, which we found to be more characteristic of some types of communities and which were clearly linked to the culture of that community.

In every community we studied, almost all teenagers generally expressed positive feelings toward both parents but saw their mothers as more understanding and influential in their lives.[9] Similarly, while they said that they learned a lot from both parents, most—both boys and girls but particularly girls—said that they would go to their mothers to discuss any "personal" problem they encountered or felt. The reasons given, however, differed. Boys everywhere reported that their fathers might become angry or show disappointment in them, as did girls in both rural and urban inner-city areas. Girls in suburban areas considered their fathers insensitive and aloof or complained that they did not have enough time for them. While this preference for mothers was true in each community, there was a clear difference between urban inner-city centers such as Southside and suburban areas like Sheffield. In the urban areas, we found a greater turning toward fathers (even those who did not live at home) for advice and problem solving by boys as they grew older than was true in the suburban areas. They would still maintain that they got more understanding from the mother, but many boys, regardless of race or ethnicity, actively sought out paternal help and advice as they grew older. Another aspect of our research offers some additional insight into this increasing bond between fathers and sons.

While most studies of the emancipation of teenagers conclude that there is a gradual but steady decline in parental control from early adolescence to young adulthood, our findings differed somewhat.[10] We did find that there was an overall decline in parental control as children matured into the older teen years. In Sheffield and other suburbs, however, there was often a perceptible increase in certain kinds of parental monitoring and pressure of older teens—particularly for boys but for girls as well. This was expressed in a number of ways. One common example was increased parental concern over schooling and grades, with clear emphasis on the proximity of getting into college and starting a career. Some parents would push older teens to seek part-time or summer employment to "learn what it is going to be like to work." Often, however, the pressure was expressed as a fear that now the kids were old enough to get into "serious trouble" over drugs, alcohol, or sexual relationships. The specific nature of the trouble changed as national attention was focused on one or the other of these problems, whether or not there was evidence that they were major problems in the specific community. The net effect of this redirection of control served to restrict autonomy and to lengthen or prolong adolescence in these communities. Curfews, for example, would be extended or made more restrictive depending on how well a teenager was doing in school. Rewards were given for doing well in school or on college entrance examinations. Parental promises to give a teenager an automobile as a reward for high school graduation, or for not smoking or using drugs until a certain age (usually twenty-one in our experience), were not uncommon.

In our urban inner-city sites, we saw a very different pattern of diminishing parental controls, which indicated an early emancipation and assumption of maturity. Parental controls began to diminish by the midteen years for both boys and girls, but autonomy came particularly early for boys, and by late adolescence the boys were already considered adults. One reason was that, unlike sixteen- and seventeen-year-old boys in the suburbs, much more of the urban inner-city youth's time was spent outside the home working or "on the street." Many parents I spoke with expressed a feeling that there was little they could do to control these boys' behavior outside the home where they now spent so little of their time. This was frequently expressed as "What can I do? He's a man now." It was at this stage of developing social maturity that the older males sought and often found a new relationship with their father, bonding with him in the adult male social world of the community. For girls there was a greater awareness of both the need and the possibility of continuing control, largely because they spent more of their time at home. As boys turned into men at an early age, they were expected to become more autonomous from the family than girls, who were viewed as more dependent. In addition, girls were considered more vulnerable than boys because they could get into sexual "trouble," a more serious blight on the family's honor than whatever trouble boys might get into. Hopefully, they would soon be married and then they would be "somebody else's problem." But even inner-city girls became emancipated sooner than their suburban counterparts. Inner-city parents let go earlier and adolescence became ever more foreshortened over the decade of our observations. By the late teen years inner-city youth were already seen by their families as young adults—often in conflict with the other social institutions, which persisted in seeing them and treating them as older children.

While congruence among the social environments is essential to a coherent sense of self, time and continuity in those environments are also important to develop a feeling of belonging and consolidate an integrated identity. When families move, children and adolescents experience disconnections as well as the need to make new connections. The developmental problem of changing communities is not just that residential mobility requires adjustment to new social settings such as schools or neighborhoods. It is the confusion, sometimes even anguish, of having to learn how to evaluate new and possibly different social feedback which seems to cause the greatest difficulty.

When children and adolescents are exposed to changing social environments and to a variety of behavioral expectations, they have a greater chance to encounter or perceive inconsistency than if they get feedback from a more limited array of social contexts. Part of knowing who they are is a function of how their families relate to other settings. Where the father works, where the family goes to church, who the neighbors are, what relatives live nearby, as well as what schools the children attend, work interactively to orient the growing child to the community environment. Not only the settings but the people who live, learn, work, and worship in them become familiar. Moving from one community to another community, and to a new set of places and people and the interactions among them, increases the probability of problems in self-definition and identity consolidation. This may very well be a more traumatic experience for teenagers than for younger children, who have not had as much time to become engaged with peers, hobbies, athletic activities, and other involvements outside the family—including, possibly, new or developing romances.

Parents are influenced by their neighbors, by their church, and by other institutions and pass these influences on to their children. Teenagers who move, therefore, are moving away from a whole web of institutional environments. All this requires readjustment, and the readjustment may be different for different members of the family. An interview with an older teenager, whose family had moved to Newtown, another of the communities we studied, illustrates this point.

NEWTOWN

Newtown is a planned community, conceived and created by a developer in the early 1960s as a series of neighborhood "villages" on a 15,000-acre tract of rural land which is now home to about 60,000 people. Found midway between two large cities, Newtown has many adult citizens who work in one of them, but it also is home to a developing series of research, business, and even some light manufacturing establishments. The plan was that people of all ethnic and socioeconomic backgrounds would settle in the diversified but contiguous village-neighborhoods. The planners, augmented by consultant social scientists and educators, were concerned about the malaise of the modern city, where the schools, the churches, and the social activities are all separated from each other; they felt that the village-neighborhoods would serve to "bring people together." Each of the villages, which is made up of about three neighborhoods, has about seven hundred dwelling units, which range from federally subsidized rental units to custom homes worth upward of half a million dollars.

Every village has a community center, its own schools, and retail businesses such as a supermarket, a pharmacy, and a gasoline station, but the geographical and transactional center of Newtown is its huge shopping mall, a two-level series of shops and department stores complemented by trees and fountains—a major gathering place for its youth. We spent a good deal of time in the mall talking to adolescents about life in Newtown and what it was like to be a teenager there. One of the things we asked was what it was like growing up in a place where there were seldom any relatives or extended families nearby, since many of the teenagers had been born somewhere else before their families moved to Newtown.

The following conversation took place with a teenager who had originally lived in California:

INTERVIEWER: How long has your family lived in Newtown?

TEENAGER: Let's see, I came here when I was twelve, so we've been here about seven years. Actually, my family has been here a little longer than that because when my father was transferred I stayed on with my grandparents to finish out the school year. I didn't want to come here—I didn't want to leave my friends and my school and go to a strange new place, new kids, a new school. It's funny, my younger brother who is five years younger than I am didn't mind at all. I think I would have been willing to stay with my grandparents to not have to move and face a whole different world that I would have to work myself into.

INTERVIEWER: How different is it here in Newtown?

TEENAGER: We had moved once before, and it was difficult for me then too, but this time it was really different. My parents had all of these brochures that the Newtown people put out to tell you how great it's going to be and how everybody is together—all one big family. They even had a movie that showed the people doing things together, and I should have realized then that all the kids in the movie were young kids, five, six, maybe ten years old, but there were no teenagers and no old people either. I don't think they ever thought that there might be teenagers who didn't go off to college or that people would get older. I kept thinking that it was like Disneyland; they were going to make the great American Dream come true; everybody was going to feel a part of the village center they lived in and everybody would share that part of their lives. You know, we would all have the same values and the same beliefs, and while we might all be different colors or go to different churches, we would all be Newtowners first. It was like being a Newtowner was more important than being a Jones or being a Smith.

INTERVIEWER: And did it work out that way?

TEENAGER: Oh, I don't know; it's hard to say. I think it did work out for some kids. It did for my brother; he made his friends here, and since he is still in the village school, he sees all of them every day in school and in the neighborhood. It didn't work for me because I was older when we moved and I came here with the idea that it wouldn't be very long until I was going off to college, and I didn't want to spend too much time and talent finding new friends and winning over the teachers. I had already begun to know who I was, what I thought about myself, and how other people saw me. I didn't want to test that anymore in a place where I didn't have roots and didn't have time or interest in planting any. I think that was true for a lot of the kids my age who moved here. You know from Day One that you are not going to be staying here as part of the place and so you find your place outside it. Coming here to the mall is one way of saying that the village center is too small and you want to bust out and find a bigger world.

INTERVIEWER: Is it different for parents?

TEENAGER: I think so, at least to the extent that they don't want to make waves and be different because they are going to stay here and raise other kids. They still want me to be more successful than the neighbors' kids, and they bragged on me when I made the dean's list this year, but my mother still gets nervous and embarrassed if her azalea bushes bloom before the other ones in the neighborhood.

The Newtown youth's parents were, of course, the same parents he had known in California, but in a sense the family was not the same family because not only the community settings, but how they interacted with each other and how the family related to each and all of them, were different. A teenager, this young man was quite upset by the move and the need to adjust to this new pattern of relationships; he said he would rather have stayed in California with his grandparents and finished school there with his former schoolmates before he went off to college. His younger brother, however, had less difficulty because, as the older brother explained, he had more time to settle in before having to leave for college. This sense of loss of a former home and a familiar community of social settings was expressed by many of the teenagers in Newtown and Sheffield, who moved with some frequency because of their fathers' careers.

Josie, on the other hand, whose family had moved seven times in the eleven years they had lived in Southside, was much less disturbed by the moves because they were all within the same community, and the extended family, the schools, and other life settings she knew were all still there. Largely self-contained and little involved with others in the community, her family simply changed apartments.

But even when children remain in the same community throughout adolescence, there is not always an interactive community of workplaces, social services, and other settings which can work with the family to define and demonstrate the values, beliefs, and behaviors necessary to proceed through adolescence to adulthood. Paradoxically, we found this to be a particular problem in the rural areas, where family ties seemed to be strongest. Possibly because the family was so central in rural life and because of the strong value placed on independence, combined with a suspicion of "outsiders," other institutions were kept at a distance. More probably, it was because the isolation of the communities meant that social services and their related environments, found in urban and even most suburban communities, were usually socially and emotionally as well as geographically distant.

GREEN VALLEY

Green Valley, one of the two rural sites we studied, is a small community of about seven hundred families. A local economy based on family dairy farms and orchards and the business and service infrastructure to support these activities has always been the local way of life. Actually, there really is no community here in the sense of a settled area. It is the location of the consolidated high school in the small town of Green Valley, drawing students from ten separate communities covering a fifty-square-mile radius, which makes it a central focus in the lives of the area's children and adolescents. The daily interaction of the family, the peer group, the school, and work (for those who can find it) is structured by the social as well as geographic isolation which seem to dominate so much of daily life in and around Green Valley. There are churches, a Grange, a 4-H Club, a Future Farmers of America hall, and a two-man (one is part-time) police department, but all of the other social, juvenile justice, and employment services are forty miles away in the county seat.

Family and school are the only institutional sectors available, and they combine to organize most of the teenager's social world. (Churches are, and pride themselves in being, family centered and controlled.) Even peer social activities require being old enough to drive to some school function or to one of the large shopping malls or into the county seat in the hopes of being anonymous and able to get served in a bar. Since there is a curfew for teenagers, the possession of "wheels" as a means of getting out of town becomes an important landmark in adolescence. The close relationship between family and community carries over into the school, where youth are identified and categorized by their community of origin. "Everybody knows," for example, that kids from Orchardville are hell raisers and most of the smarter students come from Wrightstown. However, the influx of "commuter types," as a result of the recent establishment of a number of corporate headquarters nearby, seems to be changing the mix of students, and a pattern of identifying youngsters similar to what we found in Sheffield is emerging. But, while the children of the more affluent local residents who commute to jobs outside the local economy are also like Sheffield's adolescents in having college and career as assured futures, the future is much more distant for the children of the poorer "old" families who are part of the local economy. Futures for them are almost always someplace else. One seventeen-year-old boy, whose parents were both born and reared in the Green Valley area, told us:

> My family has always lived in Green Valley and so I have a lot of relatives here. . . . Everybody here knows you and they think of you as part of your family. Even in school teachers will tell me about my cousin so-and-so who was a good student, and I always feel that they don't think of me as a person but as part of a family. It's going to be very hard for me when I graduate because I don't want to live around here anymore, but my parents are already talking about my settling down here.

Jill, another seventeen-year-old, said that she and her friends in Green Valley know everything and everybody in the area. "Whenever we go out we know that there aren't that many places to go around here, so one or the other of us tries to arrange to be with somebody who has a car. None of us can drive yet, and so that means some guy who has a car. Then we drive into Pottersville or even into Powhatan [the county seat] and hit some of the bars where they don't know us and don't ask for our IDs." She went on to explain that "you have to have access to wheels" because "there just isn't anything to do in Green Valley; whenever anyone asks where we're from we usually don't tell them we're from Green Valley."

Green Valley is like Southside in that the family is a community unto itself. Even the school responds directly to family values; at one time there were five "faculty couples," husband and wife teams teaching in the high school. But unlike the urban center, the family role here is not dictated by conflict with other social environments; there simply are no other environments available—literally no place to escape the scrutiny of kith and kin. In Green Valley escape plots start early, as one fourteen-year-old girl told us:

> All I'm waiting for is to get my driver's license, graduate from high school, and get away from here. I have this daydream over and over again where I get a car, drive up to the school, yell out "Lloyd sucks!" [Mr. Lloyd is a teacher in the school who has strong community ties there], and then drive off into that big world out there.

Emancipation from the home community and separation from the family are issues which teenagers face everywhere and respond to in different ways. Most of the youth I interviewed felt comfortable at home, enjoyed their parents and family, and did not look forward to leaving them someday. A surprising number felt that their parents were preparing to eventually push them out and expressed resentment at parental injunctions such as "Wait until you see what it's like when you're out on your own." Some few, however, couldn't wait to get away from a family life which they considered empty or meaningless; a parent who was abusive; a family beset by crisis, such as divorce or the death of a parent; or a problem with a new stepfamily. We found all of these problems—which cause about one million teenagers throughout the country to run away from their families every year—present in some families in every community, but there were characteristic differences among types of communities in the relative number of teenagers who decided to flee or to stay home, and their reasons for the decision.

There were not very many cases of running away—leaving home without parental approval—in suburban communities such as Newtown or Sheffield. What few cases we heard about were usually short-term, episodic, mostly overnight ventures to the home of a relative or friend. Usually these followed some conflict with parents over discipline or a problem in school, and the impulsive flight was meant to escape from or punish the parents. It was not unusual for a parent (usually the mother) of the family to which the teenager fled for sanctuary to call the refugee's parents (again, usually the mother) and say that Billie or Betsy was there and could stay overnight to give things a chance to simmer down. In some few cases teenagers did actually leave the community, usually soon after having moved there from another community and in most cases to go back to stay with a friend or relative they missed. One of the county sheriff's deputies who serve as the police force for Newtown, for example, said: "We don't get calls about runaways from Newtown like we do from outside in the county itself. Once in a while a couple of kids will go into the city and stay over and then not come back for a few days because they're afraid to catch hell, but mostly they take care of their own there."

Running away from home in Southside, which was much more common there and in similar communities we studied than it was in the suburbs, also seldom involved leaving the community, but there the flight was to the street rather than to some friend's or relative's house or to some other community. Teenage runaways in Southside leave home to be with their peers. They are no less escapees from a chaotic family life or from some trauma, but the insularity of family life in the inner city means that there are no family friends to take them in even if they could manage to stretch their meager resources to feed and shelter someone else's child. Some do go to stay with relatives, but most simply move out and become street people, usually remaining in the same neighborhood or a similar one a short subway ride away. Some few of those we met did manage to find work, but most went underground to support themselves as best they could, frequently through petty crime, begging, drug trafficking, prostitution, or any of the other illicit opportunities available there. Few willingly leave Southside, or some similar nearby community in the city— perhaps because the world outside that community is alien, possibly because life in the city is all they can imagine.

For many youngsters in Green Valley, leaving the community as the inevitable ending for adolescence is all that they can imagine. Except for the few who can remain on the family farm, growing up means finding a job someplace else. For most, a job is just that— not the career that suburban youth will leave to pursue, but any job that is available, and jobs are not easy to come by in or even near

Green Valley. We heard much more about running away (as an accomplished fact, in realistic future plans, and in escape fantasies) in Green Valley and other rural communities than in any other type of community. State police investigators we talked with said that the pattern of running away starts early and that kids run "as far away as they can get" each time. "Far away" is not just measured in miles; it also means that they seek out communities which are very different from Green Valley. They go to the cities, which they imagine can offer the excitement and the opportunities they can't find in Green Valley. Some come back, usually defeated in the search, only to run away again after a short time. Others get lost somewhere in their search for a responsive community and either cannot or will not come back home.

Not all teenagers who leave home are runaways. Most of the adolescents of both Southside and Green Valley who make their plans to escape the impoverished environments of their childhood when they become older are doing so with parental support. In many cases they will take with them the identities they developed in their home communities as a basis for renegotiating identity when they establish new intimate relationships and start a new family. Runaways, on the other hand, often have fragile or even absent identities in the families and communities from which they are running, and those they pick up on the streets are often as full of stress and pain and as disorienting as the street life they lead.[11] Even on the streets where they seek escape and anonymity, however, they also look for some form of bonding, some sense of group structure which they lacked at home, to fight off the loneliness and depression that haunt so many of them.

Marly, for example, came to the metropolis which includes Southside from a medium-sized city in the Midwest when she was fourteen years old and has been living on and off the streets for the last three years. Her parents were divorced when she was nine years old and her father was given custody because, she says, "My mother was more interested in her new boyfriend than she was in me." In and out of shelters and halfway houses, she lives by selling herself or anything she can shoplift or steal, and sometimes resorts to begging ("I hate it; it reminds me of always having to ask my father for money whenever I wanted to do anything or go anywhere"). She has, she tells me, started her own "street family," which consists of herself, another seventeen-year-old named Dolly, who ran away from New England, and Pete, a sixteen-year-old who left his family in another part of the city when he was fifteen. Actually, she says, he had only lived with his family off and on from the time he was eleven, when he first ran away and returned six times in one year. Like Marly, Dolly and Pete are in and out of prostitution. Pete also shoots heroin and more recently has become addicted to crack. He "knows" that he has AIDS, he insists, because if he didn't get infected from the needles he shared with other teenage junkies then he surely picked it up hustling in the gay bars.

Society tends to think of the runaway as a Huckleberry Finn character seeking adventure or advancement in a wider world, or as a more grown-up version of the youngster who leaves home after a disagreement or row with parents only to return after a few hours or days. During our research we heard and saw a very different pattern of decision making leading to teenage flight. The decision to flee may indeed have come as the result of some specific precipitating event like divorce, residential mobility, or the death of a parent, but the flight usually had a long-standing emotional history. Regardless of the community, some form of parent–adolescent conflict was present in the pre-flight family backgrounds of almost all of the teenage runaways I interviewed, even those from communities like Green Valley, where youngsters were fleeing the community as much as if not more than the family. These teenage runaways spoke of deep and long-standing differences with their parents and even with siblings which went back into childhood and resulted in a process of gradual family disengagement, rather than some one-time spontaneous decision to leave. The reasons we heard for leaving home were similar to what other research suggests: poor communication with parents,[12] excessive discipline or controls,[13] sexual and physical abuse or harassment,[14] criticism of one's behavior or friends,[15] and a feeling of being rejected or unloved at home.[16] What was striking was the sense of deprivation and depression with which the young people spoke of the absence or loss of love and affection in childhood: "They didn't want me around, so I left; why should I stay?"

We encountered a number of cases of sexual abuse of mostly female, but also some male, runaways by parents (usually the father), again often reaching back into early adolescence or before. Prostitution, either occasional or as a life style, was a common occurrence among the runaways with incest or other sexual victimization in their pre-flight family histories. One interpretation of the dynamics of incest is that the child victim develops a feeling that the sexual favors demanded by the father can be a means of paying for love and care.[17] The prevalence of a history of incest and other forms of sexual abuse which we found among runaway prostitutes suggests that the lessons learned at home may be acted out on the street. It also is a negative example of the importance of the family as the first source of sexual information as well as identity.

Most of the teenagers we met, however, experienced a stable and progressive movement toward adulthood under the guidance of their families. This guidance is the first step in providing congruence and continuity for the adolescent transition and in developing the attachments which produce positive social bonds. The other social settings in the community, in turn, depend on the family to provide that first step as well as to continue to monitor compliance with community social norms throughout adolescence. The workplace, for example, hopes to receive workers from homes which have modeled and taught the importance of work as a major adult task and, hopefully, have even instilled good work habits. Schools, particularly, have always based their programs on the expectation that the children they are sent will have had sufficient social experience at home to move easily into the school "family." The popularity of the "family" analogue is not just symbolic, since the traditional model of school organization is derivative from that of the traditional stereotype of the family. Discipline and resource allocation are the prerogatives of the father-figure principal, while it is the teacher-mother who deals with growth and learning for the student-child.

There are, however, clear and potentially troublesome social indications that the "traditional" American family, which has been the model upon which notions of childrearing and adolescent development have been based, is disappearing as a result of changing patterns of marriage, divorce, childbearing, and parenting; since the mid-1980s less than one-fourth of our families have had the traditional structure of a father, mother, and children living together, and about three-fifths of all children born can now expect to live at least part of their lives in single-parent families.[18] Quite apart from the social and emotional problems which any one of the current crises in beginning and maintaining families suggests, children and adolescents today and in the future will be raised in a variety of family configurations. Most will go through childhood and adolescence with the same two parents, but some will begin childhood in a two-parent family and then complete adolescence with only the mother or father present.

Others will begin life with one set of parents and then experience a new father or mother, and still others will grow to maturity in an alternating two-parent, then one-parent, household.

Additional problems of adjustment will come from the creation of "blended families," in which remarried parents bring their children from previous marriages into the new family, making for new stepbrothers and stepsisters as well as new child–parent relationships. In addition to the social and emotional problems such new relationships may present, such changes also can mean new and perhaps conflicting perspectives of parenting, changes in the socioeconomic status of the family, and new inconsistencies in the role models presented by parents. Inevitably they must also place new demands on the other community social institutions for different and perhaps even new roles in that community's script for adolescence.

We found considerable diversity among the various communities not only in the structure of families but in how teenagers responded to changing patterns in those families. By far the greatest number of single-parent families we encountered in the decade of the study were in Southside and other urban inner-city areas; probably as many as three-fourths of the youngsters we worked with came from single-parent homes and almost all were living with their mothers. In most cases the father had abandoned the family (or never married the mother) or was present only part of the time. Such homes were most frequent among black and Hispanic adolescents and least frequent among the Asian-Americans in these communities. They were also infrequent in Sheffield and Newtown, although over the decade their frequency tended to increase, just as divorces did over that same period. There were more cases of divorced and remarried parents among the teenagers we interviewed in Newtown than in Sheffield because, we concluded, Newtown, as a new and developing community, tended to attract more "second families," who came there to get away from the communities they had lived in prior to the divorce. In Green Valley and other rural areas there were also frequent cases of missing fathers, not as much so as in the urban inner city, but with sufficient frequency among the "old families" that "not having a man around to straighten out the kids" was a frequent reason cited by criminal justice and social service professionals in the county seat whenever we asked about delinquency, teen pregnancy, or running away. And the patterns of family desertion by adult males in Green Valley and Southside were similar to those we found among youthful runaways in the two communities: in Southside the males remained in the same community, often in the same neighborhood, while in Green Valley they much more frequently left the community.

Along with these different family patterns, we found very different feelings expressed by youth in the various communities about family break-ups. In Southside and other urban inner-city areas and among the poorer families in Green Valley as well, teens expressed much less concern about family disruptions. However, in Sheffield and similar communities, including the more affluent commuter families in Green Valley, actual, impending, or even imagined separation and divorce, or the death or job transfer of a parent, was a prominent feature of concerns about the future. One obvious reason for this difference is that broken families are the norm in Southside but fairly unusual in Sheffield. Southside youngsters usually could relate their own experiences to those of their friends or older siblings, whereas in Sheffield teenagers from single-parent homes reported that they were teased about it by peers. In Southside the extended family—grandmothers, various uncles and aunts, older sisters and brothers, even godparents—forms a kinship network which makes the absence of particular members more tolerable. Josie Delgado, for example, who doesn't see her father very often, fondly calls her mother's brother "Poppy," and he will often stand in for her real father when a male parental presence is required. It would be a mistake, however, to assume that even in Southside there are not some deeper psychic wounds left from the abandonment. In more than a few cases I heard from Southside youths that they had been reluctant to move to a new apartment when the father abandoned the family, because, after all, the old home was where he would come back to if he ever chose to return to them.

Inevitably, the changes which are taking place in the American family will add to the already considerable diversity of family environments which adolescents experience. But we found that some of these social changes in families have already begun to affect the adolescent experience. Delayed marriage and other social changes leading to the extension of adolescence seem to have led to the prolongation of conflicts between parents and teenagers.[19] While we heard about "hassles," the stressors and problems all adolescents have with a variety of adult authority figures as well as with their parents, older adolescents more frequently talked about open hostility and fantasized "escaping" from parental controls. Our traditional expections for adolescent development are predicated on the assumption of a stable family environment, and we have yet to adjust this expectancy to new forms and configurations of family life. These new arrangements affect adolescents both in their development in their orienting families and in how they go about developing their own new procreative families.

Despite the taboos which have hindered family as well as public discussion, teenage sexuality has always been a major issue for communities as well as parents. The centrality of sexuality to the emergence and unfolding of adolescence would be sufficient reason in itself for such heightened, if largely hidden, attention. But, once again, it was the widespread discovery of another "teenage problem"—the sharp increases in the number of teenagers who became pregnant in and following the 1970s—which made teen sexuality a public issue. Like most other problems which afflict youth, teen pregnancy has frequently been blamed on the excesses in youth culture (combined with the greater freedom accorded by the sexual revolution). Yet the issues of teenage sexuality and contraception, and the sharp rise in carried-to-term pregnancies by teenage mothers, are separable, and each is linked to adult society rather than being simply an aberration of teenage behavior. The general relaxation of taboos which led to the sexual revolution, frequently described as the cultural force behind the increases in teen pregnancy, is not a phenomenon restricted to youth or a youth culture. Neither has it had the same acceptance and hence the same effects in every community. Those areas which we studied varied considerably in openness about sexual behavior, but in each case similar variations characterized values about adult versus adolescent sexual behavior, and these values were also shared by both groups. While the availability of and knowledge about birth control techniques has led to a reduction in pregnancies among adult women, teenagers have not shown a similar decline despite increasing emphasis on sex education and family-planning services.[20] These educational approaches, however, like the schools which provide them, are under the authority and control of the local community and its values. Toward the end of our research we were beginning to observe some greater emphasis on AIDS education programs and on the use of condoms for health rather than birth control purposes. Here again local sensitivities, and especially parental resistances, were what determined if such information could or could not be given.

We did not do a controlled study of the actual incidence of teen pregnancy in the various communities, but we heard about teenage girls becoming pregnant most frequently in urban inner cities such as Southside, less frequently in rural areas such as Green Valley, and least frequently in suburban areas such as Sheffield and Newtown. These differences coincide with what has generally been reported elsewhere about the effects of marriage age, the age of first pregnancy, income levels, and educational attainment on both the incidence of teen pregnancy and abortion decisions in various types of communities.[21] What we can report from our own findings is that there were important differences in what happened when a girl did become pregnant and had to decide whom to tell and what to do about it.

Parents in Sheffield described teenage pregnancy as a tragedy in terms of preparation for adult life and careers, even in those very few cases where the pregnant teenager was or soon planned to be married. Becoming pregnant too early in Sheffield was treated as a personal failure, a lien placed on future life chances. In Southside, on the other hand, becoming pregnant was considered another form of the pervasive problem of "trouble" which many youngsters get into, and its present rather than future implications were what we heard being considered. For example, a teenage girl in a Southside social agency's career workshop brought up the topic of how well some people respond to being supervised and taking directions. One girl said she had a problem with being supervised, so she felt it would be best for her if she could own a small business or something of the sort one day. She remarked, "I really want something of my own," and a response was shouted back at her in a chorus of "Have a baby!" However, from the small-group conversations that followed, as well as in other "rap group" discussions, it was clear that these girls were in some conflict about what pregnancy would do to their present lives. On the one hand it would establish them as women among their peers, but on the other it would bring them into conflict with their families, who would no longer see them as dependent daughters. (One of the counselors, commenting later on the "Have a baby" response in the workshop, said that the families of these girls still continue to see careers and motherhood as inimical alternative life styles. When a girl becomes pregnant, as they see it, she has in effect already made a life decision to settle down and raise a family. The counselor also said that the girls' boyfriends encourage them to get pregnant; they consider it really "macho" to impregnate a girl and go around bragging about how many girls they have "knocked up.")

In interviews with pregnant teenagers or teen mothers, however, influence from peers was usually said to be a minor factor, and many of the young women we spoke with said that their friends had not been influential in developing situations or attitudes which led to the pregnancy. Neither did they consult with their friends about the possibility of having an abortion—something that many of the youngsters we met in Southside tend to reject in favor of having the child. Paradoxically, from our discussions with some young unwed mothers as well as with some adults who work with pregnant teenagers, it seems that having a baby is often seen as a means of achieving social status and even admiration rather than just condemnation from significant adults. Not just the family, but other adults in the community, were said to have a dual attitude toward teen pregnancy. For example, in one southern city we were looking at dropout problems in a minority area. Over 40 percent of the female dropouts from junior or senior high schools whom we located and interviewed either had left school because of pregnancy or had one or more children at home. In one of the junior high schools, there were 16 pregnancies among the approximately 175 female students in one academic year, and 8 of these students were in the seventh grade. When we talked with these adolescent mothers or mothers-to-be and when we were able to talk to their families, some of the adult influences which implicate the home but also the school in encouraging teen pregnancy became apparent. For example, we were told that being *pregnant* might be looked upon with disapproval by teachers, relatives, or other adults in the community, but once the baby is born, the young mother suddenly experiences acclaim, attention, and pride of accomplishment. Those same adults who had cast reproving glances at the pregnant teenager now rush to hold and lavish attention on the baby. Additionally, the young girl has something that is hers, that loves her and looks up to her. All of this is in contrast to the lack of status and attention bestowed on the youngster by an educational system that values accomplishments the youngster may never have achieved and may believe she never *will* achieve: good grades, class leadership, or skill in sports. She may, in effect, have already decided that her future role is to be a mother, and so she adopts that identity early. Here again, however, the long-term deficits eventually overcome the immediate rewards.

Girls who drop out of school have larger families, higher rates of divorce and separation, and even more restricted access to the labor market than do most women.[22]

In America—more so than in most other countries—the problem of teen pregnancy is inseparable in the public perception from the problem of unwed mothers.[23] And associated with this aspect of teen pregnancy is the question of the relative rights of parents and the pregnant teenagers to decide on the outcome of the pregnancy. Prior to the Supreme Court decision which led to the liberalization of abortion laws, the relative unavailability of illegal abortions and the requirements for obtaining a therapeutic abortion meant that parental involvement, whether supportive or condemning, was inevitable. Now, with the relative inexpensiveness and availability of abortion, terminating a pregnancy without parental consent or knowledge is quite possible for teenagers. Considering that parent–child communication about sex has not increased significantly as a result of the sexual revolution,[24] we might expect pregnant teenagers to choose to exclude their parents from the decision.

This was not the case among those teenagers in our study who sought abortion. Most, particularly in the urban inner-city areas and especially among Hispanics, not only confided in but sought the permission of their parents prior to having an abortion. Often excluded from any role in the decision, though, was the teenage father and his family. However, in those cases where the pregnancy was not interrupted, we found, contrary to what the job counselor had told us about macho indifference to paternal responsibility, that many young fathers did become actively involved in the support of the child even if they did not marry the mother. Here again, we found that this was particularly true in the urban minority communities we studied. Mercer Sullivan found in a subsequent study that contrary to popular belief, minority adolescent fathers have strong feelings of paternity.[25] These young fathers contribute to the support of their children by a variety of means, including, in some cases, income from criminal activity.

We found a different pattern in Sheffield. Telling one's parent there was an admission of failure, and that was a particularly difficult thing for Sheffield's youngsters to accept. So, if they did become pregnant they first told the teenage father, who was just as concerned with his parents' disapproval of how he was ruining his life, or they would confide in the small group of "best friends" and try to take care of the problem themselves. It was only when these efforts failed that they confessed to their parents.

The changes in the families in which adolescents grow up are clearly affecting the sexual, marital, and childbearing behavior of the adolescents themselves, and, in turn, their relationships with parents. Since the 1970s the age of marriage has been increasingly delayed, first extending adolescence and then leading to the social construction of the new life period we call "youth." While most of the reduction in teenage marriage has been true of females, who have always been a disproportionately higher percentage of married teenagers since they married at a younger age than males, there has been a similar reduction in the number of teenage males who marry. These same reduced rates of marriage are also taking place among youth even as the number of both males and females who marry before age twenty-four declines. The number of teenage women (and those in their twenties as well) who give birth has declined dramatically, over 50 percent since 1960, due in large measure to the availability of abortion. About half of all teenage pregnancies are terminated by abortion. But the number of out-of-wedlock births among teenagers has shown an equally dramatic increase, accounting for about half of all births to teenagers.[26] The age at which such births occur is declining as well, with the number of births to women under fifteen increasing.[27]

To some extent this is due to the reduction in the marriage rate among teenagers, but it seems also to represent a desire to bear children rather than terminate the pregnancy.[28] Some explanation for this may be found in the characteristics of those females who are most likely to experience teen pregnancy. While black female adolescents have always been at higher risk of early pregnancy than their white counterparts, race is not the major discriminator among pregnant teenagers. Teenage pregnancy rates for black females have recently been declining, while the rate for white females has been increasing. From what we saw over the ten-year period, we concluded that the reason for this was that much of the remedial and educational work on the problem has been targeted on black teenagers and seems to be having some effect. Poverty, and the impoverished social and emotional as well as educational and economic opportunities it metes out to adolescents, are clearly implicated. Regardless of race, teenage pregnancy is directly correlated with family income: between three and four times as many disadvantaged females become unwed mothers in their teens.[29]

Teenage mothers and fathers, like runaways, share a common problem of role confusion which begins in the family and which continues when they move out into the larger community. Other research evidence supports our conclusion that pregnancy and maternity in adolescence may be as much (if not more) connected to working out relational problems within the family as it is to precocious sexual activity. David Youngs, of the Johns Hopkins Center for Social Studies in Human Reproduction, indicates that girls may pick pregnancy rather than drugs or alcohol as a means of resolving family problems, splitting off from the mother, replacing the father as an object of affection, or searching for identity.[30] Virginia Abernethy reported similar findings in her study, and, interestingly, in terms of our findings about the multiinstitutional base of adolescent social problems, she cites the school as the best resource for dealing with such problems, but criticizes educators for evading their responsibility.[31] There is still some debate about whether girls suffer more from family disruption and tensions than boys, but little doubt that stresses in family life can and do confound the development of sexual identity. Also still at issue is how much of that confusion stems from the developing sexual impulses and awareness of the adolescent and the need to control them in the family, and how much stems from the problems of changing social characteristics of families and sexual roles in society. What, for example, is the effect of fathers' absences on the sexual identification of boys and of girls, and on how those roles merge with other social roles in the developing identity of adolescents? And, when new forms of family living do not provide the congruence and continuity necessary for a stable adolescent transition, where can teenagers turn for help?

The answer to these questions resides somewhere in the relationship between the family and the other social environments and significant adults in the community, and, to a lesser extent, among adolescents themselves. There has been considerable concern over the problems of "latchkey" children, who care for themselves in the time between their return home from school and the return of their single-income or dual-income parents from work. The absence of adult supervision leaves them vulnerable to a variety of potential problems, ranging from being victimized to getting themselves into some form of mischief or even serious trouble. We saw such children in each of the communities, and their plight is as real in Sheffield (where it's a new one) as it is in Southside (where it has long existed). The potential for victimization and getting into trouble is enough to worry about, but there are other problems, too, which result from the absence of adult guidance as well as protection and supervision.

While the patterns of family living and crowded residential space in the urban inner city have long put children out on the street at an early age, many suburban youngsters we talked to have not yet become used to early emancipation. Over the ten-year period of the study we saw many more teenagers who were in two-income or even single-parent working mother families than when we first began the study. Most of those we talked to were made uncomfortable by working mothers or absent fathers, complained that there was nothing to do, and frequently expressed resentment at being abandoned by parents. Even where the school had developed new after-hours programs to accommodate these children, the resentment did not go away. Youngsters would complain that they had been in school all day and the last thing they wanted to see was their tenth-grade social studies teacher, who was giving after-school chess lessons and organizing a tournament, or their gym teacher, who was supervising an aerobics program. Teachers were no less pleased at becoming what they called "baby-sitters for the no-longer-idle rich" or replacements for "working mothers in pursuit of a second Jaguar sedan." What we saw develop was the emergence of new forms of peer group organization, sullen and often disruptive bands of youngsters involuntarily liberated from parental guidance and supervision for several hours a day. To some extent, these peer groups are the suburban equivalents of the urban street gangs, and in both cases the reasons why they are on the street have as much to do with why they are not at home as with any need on the part of teenagers to be with age-mates.

As I indicated earlier in describing peer groups, we found that as teenagers grow older, most of them spend more and more time outside the home with friends, going to school, working, and participating as individuals in any number of activities. While "just being together" or "hanging out"—rather than doing things together—is sufficient reason for wanting to spend time with age-mates, we found that just the opposite is true of time spent at home. Teenagers in every community said that they enjoyed doing things with their families but that just being there was "boring," "a drag," or "the worst part of the day." Having to do household chores, caring for a younger sibling, and doing homework were also frequently mentioned as part of home life which teenagers did not enjoy. Yet when they described the things they did enjoy, most teenagers included one or more activities they shared with their families. In Sheffield it was family trips or vacations or going to athletic or cultural events together; in Southside it was watching particular television shows, visiting relatives, in some cases going to religious programs or services. In Green Valley watching television, family trips, and religious programs and services were most frequently mentioned. These enjoyed activities tended to be cited less frequently as the teenagers grew older, but they were still mentioned by many older teenagers, particularly urban inner-city girls.

One obvious conclusion from this is that peer groups have a distinct advantage over the home in that, like childhood play groups, there is nothing you have to do in them but try to enjoy yourself. In addition, having to do things like chores and homework is always a potential source of conflict with parents since it cuts into the leisure time which could be spent with peers. But while adolescents reported a preference for "doing something" with their families, we also frequently heard adolescents in each community report that they enjoyed just being able to talk with parents or to seek their advice. In early adolescence the preferred parent was primarily the mother: "I love to go shopping with my mom because we get a chance to talk a lot," "When I get really upset I go to my mother and she usually can make things seem better," or "My mother is always there for me." By late adolescence boys were turning to fathers for advice: "I prefer to go to the soccer matches with my dad because he really knows the teams and players," "My dad helps me with my car and I like to hear him talk about how he built his own 'hot rod,'" or "I talked to my father about finding a part-time job and he said O.K." In each case, what seemed to make these exchanges important to the youngsters was that they were *seeking* the advice or guidance, not just getting it unsolicited.

One of the myths perpetuated in the notion of a separatist youth culture is that it is created by what Coleman dubbed "a press toward autonomy" among youth, a self-conscious striving to be with those of their own kind and free of all adult supervision.[32] Such was not the case for many teenagers I interviewed, for whom the price of freedom was often loneliness and a sense of isolation from the adult world. Our observations of, and interviews with, teenage peer groups did indeed confirm the progressive movement from parental to peer models for the validation of day-to-day social learning as teenagers mirror and evaluate their behavior and attitudes by examining those of peers.[33] In the in-depth interviews, I also heard a number of examples of the idealization of other adolescents, which has frequently been reported to characterize teenage peer relationships, together with a devaluation of adults in general and parents in particular.[34] Among early adolescents in each of the communities, for example, fantasies and even descriptions of everyday life frequently related to feelings and actual experiences shared with age-mates which were in real or imagined opposition to parental values. But by middle adolescence, and impressively by late adolescence—particularly when I interviewed teenagers in groups—I found considerable evidence of the turning to adults for information, validation, and guidance about the future. Parents continued to be the major source for most teenagers. Another frequent source was relatives—grandparents, an uncle or aunt, even an older sibling—and sometimes neighbors or the parents of friends. Frequently, however, such adults were professionals (teachers, counselors, social agency or youth workers, for example) in a social setting in which the adolescent was striving to develop social competence.

To some extent this turning to adults may have been a manifestation of the increasing concern for educational and career futures, or even a search for a replacement for a devalued parent. But often it was also a self-conscious turning to adults for new ideals and values to defend against anxieties resulting from the adolescent's social marginality. The valued—sometimes even idealized—adults protect the adolescent from being alone in the new adult world outside the home. They have always been described as role models for adolescent imitation, and the idealized descriptions of them that we heard from youth underscore this interpretation. But there was also considerable evidence in the interview materials (particularly when I was able to interview several members of the same peer group associated with a particular organizational or institutional setting) that such adults are more than simply passive behavioral models whom adolescents can emulate. They are really active transitional agents ushering the teenager into the behavioral and social world of a particular institutional domain.[35] In many ways they seem to be the informal equivalents in our society of the *sensei* in Japanese culture, who challenge adolescents in the development of character and social competence. Who are these adults in American society, and how do they relate to adolescents? We found that apart from those who are relatives or neighbors, they are part of a growing network of professionals in each of the adult institutions that specialize in youth-related services in communities.

In Sheffield this type of mentor was often the coach of a sports team, the minister or priest in charge of a youth group, or some other local figure—usually, but not always, under thirty—who worked closely with adolescents. His role was to mediate between teenagers and the local community. In Southside the mentor was usually a social agency or school-related professional, again under thirty, who came from outside the adolescents' localized community and mediated between them and that outside world. What is important here is not just the role of the individual adult as a "significant other," but the search on the part of adolescents for a model or mentor who could guide them in seeking an identity within some supportive social structure. We heard and saw examples of this search in each community as youth sought to emulate valued teachers, coaches, social agency personnel, and others. Parents were also aware of this and commented on the influence, often positively ("Coach Szabo is fantastic with the kids; they all want to grow up to be just like him" or "Father Bragoni understands how kids feel and they really relate to him") but sometimes with disapproval or resentment ("I didn't send my daughter to private school for her to hear her teacher talk about joining the Peace Corps"). While such mentoring roles were available in every community, they served different functions in relation to the community and the family in different places. In Sheffield mentoring usually meant helping the adolescent and his family adjust to the inevitable loss of a sense of community which takes place with going off to college. In Green Valley and Southside it was more frequently a case of helping the adolescent to escape from the family and community to a wider world of opportunity. But in all three communities, and in the others we studied as well, most teenagers actively sought rather than avoided or ignored mentoring and mediating adult help.

Many of the professionals who provide help to teenagers work out of their communities' social or "voluntary" agencies. Many of these organizations, particularly in the urban areas, had a long, intense association with charity and welfare functions in situations where the family or other social institutions such as the school were unwilling or unable to provide necessary help.[36] Many were, in their initial formulation, religiously or socially motivated collectives of well-to-do citizens who volunteered time and money to work with poor and less fortunate fellow-citizens to alleviate various social problems.

Now, with the role of the extended family diminished, and with the form and function of the nuclear family moving ever farther away from the ideal model we have always proposed for child and adolescent development, community-based social agencies have taken on an increased importance for youth. A new institutional sector has been created—turning from individual giving toward community, corporate, and governmental subsidies as a basis of support and replacing charity with advocacy. In that advocacy, the child has often been championed in opposition to other social institutions including the family.[37] The range of professionals in this new sector who work with youth problems must be considered as potential sources of social learning for adolescents, whether they act *in loco parentis* or simply as adult transitional figures in adolescent identity formation. Here again the differences we found in the *pattern* of relationships among the social settings within which teenagers develop—and particularly the relationships between the family and community organizations—were more important than the individual role of any agency or individual.

Comparing the social agency networks in Southside, Sheffield, and Green Valley illustrates the very different forms of community social organization in each of these communities and, hence, why it is necessary to consider local rather than national strategies for dealing with adolescent social problems. In Southside as in other urban areas we studied, the agencies are oriented toward replacing those social institutions—the family, the school, the workplace, and the criminal justice system—which are perceived to have failed. Social agencies become an institutional sector in themselves, and, particularly in recent years—as a result of both their proliferation and reductions in federal funds for their programs—competitive with each other.

What seemed most important about the role of the social agency network in Southside was that it seeks to mediate between, or even replace, other institutions such as the school, the family, and the criminal justice system. To some extent, these attempts on the part of the social agencies result from the perceived inadequacy of the other, traditional contexts as behavior guides for youth. There is also, however, the development of a strong sense of advocacy for these social agencies' youthful clients in opposition to the traditional institutions. This advocacy becomes reinforced as a social agency argues the urgency of its clients' needs in the media as well as to government funding agencies and foundations. There is also (at least in the agencies in which we observed and interviewed) an extension of that advocacy to seek aggressively for new sources of funding, and, as a result, to focus on—and thereby help to identify and publicize—"current crisis areas'' for youth, in much the same way as voluntary organizations seek a new disease to attack and raise funds for as soon as they have successfully produced a cure for the health problem they originally were organized to combat. This is not to suggest, in either case, that remediation is not the motive force of the mission, but rather to indicate that one of the major sources of conflict among existing social institutions lies in their strong ethic of advocacy and in their competition with each other, particularly when federal, state, and local funds for their programs become scarce.

Each agency is likely to point to the "endemic" problems of the major social institutions in Southside and to portray teenagers as the most troubled and immediate victims and society as the eventual loser. In Southside the social agency is a distinct social environment for adolescents, and for many of them a "social agency culture" replaces the school and even the family as the source for significant adult transitional figures, major value orientations, and models of possible selves. This can (and, in our experience, sometimes did) lead to conflict for adolescents as they try to rationalize the conflicting identity images they see at home, in the school, and in that agency culture.

The homogeneity of Sheffield is reproduced in the intimacy of the relationships between the family and what is essentially its own network of social agencies. The agencies are closely joined with the major social institutions such as the family, the church, and the school, and rely heavily on competitive sports and recreational activities. They exist as a result of parental wishes and continue only so long as they conform to, rather than try to change, the community's ideal of what a good teenager should be. The result of this locally based, family-directed, church-related, school-associated network of activities for youngsters is that social agencies here are an interconnected but unobtrusive part of the community. As a result, the social life of youngsters is highly organized and integrated, if still competitive. One teenage girl commented when I seemed surprised at how much of her time was organized for her: "That's the way Sheffield is— always something to do, someplace to go, something to see, some new thing you have to learn. Sometimes I wonder what it would be like to live in a place where you have to find things to do yourself."

In rural Green Valley, what few social agencies exist are extensions of the local families, and so are limited to what they feel is necessary for family rather than individual development. The social differentiation which has resulted from the influx of more affluent "commuter type" families presents an additional strain, since the more traditional citizens, who control the agencies, adjust the programs to their own vision of what the community's teenagers need. Adolescent social, health, and juvenile justice services and the professionals who can introduce youngsters into these external environments are a long distance away and available only for emergency calls. This isolation, combined with the absence of a ready job market, is what makes for the strong movement toward withdrawal from the community on the part of youngsters once they are ready to leave their families. What social agencies there are in the county that have jurisdiction over teenage problems feel the other side of that isolation and say that they are not active in Green Valley because they are unwelcome outsiders there. The social services professional in charge of the youth division in the county seat, for example, told us she remembered a Green Valley girl who was caught shoplifting in one of the nearby malls. Once the police had turned her over to the youth division (she was a minor), they tried to contact the authorities in Green Valley, since the charges were being dropped and they wanted to put her in some kind of supervision. "We made some visits to Green Valley, but it just wasn't possible to establish any relationship with the police there. They said that in order to help her they would have to alter her whole family situation and maybe we should just turn her over to one of the local groups like the 4-H or the Grange."

Social agencies everywhere, however, do have a role to play in the functioning of a community's institutions and hence in the way these institutions are integrated, which in turn affects the developing identities of children and teenagers. Looking at how some specific social agency programs operate in Southside, Sheffield, and Green Valley provides some insights into how they perceive their mission in relation to their teenage clients. It also indicates how they define their responsibility to work with or to replace the other community institutions and how this can confuse or facilitate their clients' other roles as student, worker, or family member.

Southside's social agencies are as diverse as the people there and as numerous. We encountered a number of these different types of agencies, one of the most common being the settlement house, which traces its origins back to the time when the various waves of European immigrants came to the United States. Many settlement houses now receive federal, state, or city funding as well as money from foundations. The youth professionals who operate these programs are not usually volunteers, but part of a rapidly growing association that has considerable influence on youth policy as well as teenagers themselves. Agency staff and directors are part of a semibureaucratic, hierarchically organized career development system. These professionals move frequently from agency to agency. They specialize in the adolescent years and quite frequently remain associated with a particular problem area. One important development for minority adolescents seeking believable adult transitional figures is the increasing number of black, Hispanic, and Asian-American agency professionals who are competing with the more senior Jewish and Italian professionals (who in turn had replaced even earlier immigrants) for leadership roles.

There are also less comprehensive and more problem-oriented social agencies which target specific problems or crises and aim their efforts at remediation, job development, juvenile justice diversion or prevention programs, drug-related problems, and teenage pregnancy. Here funding comes primarily from governmental sources, and there is continuing tension and competition over its availability. Most social agencies in Southside have always been socially as well as financially based outside of its culture of poverty.

As a result they must find someplace to intervene in that culture if they are to alleviate it. This has always meant intervening in the family. Their original role of serving as "surrogate families" to the children of European immigrants has been extended to include Hispanic and black youngsters. One agency director told us that "we become surrogate parents; some kids are here every day. The important thing is to hook them; once you do, you can deal with them. It is very important to get them attached to someone in the program." Later she talked about the competition among agencies for "recruits" and how some kids (and adults as well) will become "agency hoppers" moving from one program to another.

A number of the settlement houses also maintain residential homes for the youngsters who have left or been pushed out of their own families. In a residential group home established in Southside by one social agency, every resident teenager is given a probationary period to see if he fits into "the family." The home director (called "Big Mamma" by the kids) explained that "we have incentives that we call AIM (Achievement in Me), and we give the guys money for extra chores (25 cents for taking out the garbage) or if they tutor younger kids, and they also get weekly allowances (a minimum of $1.50) and activity money ($4.00) each week to go to the movies, for example, and $2.00 transportation money. Our purpose here is to help them to grow up." Later she said that most of the youngsters go on to jobs working in the same agency when they reach eighteen years of age, which represents "graduation," since funding for the teenagers stops at that age.

Regardless of who staffs and directs such programs, however, the self-defined function of these agencies continues to be to intervene in, or even replace, the role of the family or the school in the developmental lives of children and adolescents. The Educating Connection, for example, sees its responsibility as helping Southside's adolescents to establish clear-cut educational goals. There are, they point out, no such plans for the youngsters in this community. In the high schools there are limited amounts of work, and this work is usually nonproductive. Schools in general operate on a system of rewards and punishments, with grades being used as the punishments—which is not conducive to good learning. A staff member complained that the agency's year-to-year funding creates serious problems. "How can you train kids in a short time with a program that's funded for less than a year when you have to undo the damage that schools have done to them for such a long time?" In another interview, the director of a federally funded work program told us that it prepares Southside's older adolescents for the General Education Diploma and teaches clerical skills. In order to get into the program, a youth has to have been out of school for at least six months, since "if they are not out of school for that long, then we would become a magnet for school counselors and they would just kick kids out of school so they could send them to us."

There are some programs which have a long-standing relationship with particular teenage problems. But, just as parents become concerned whenever a new teenage crisis receives media attention, some programs seek funding for whichever problem is current, often increasing the perception of the severity of the crisis. A new program which has been set up in Southside as part of a multiple-program agency ("We deal with at-risk teenagers who have multiple deficits and that includes most of the kids in this community") grew out of a program funded by CETA (Comprehensive Employment Training Act, a Carter administration–era program for unemployed youth) to rehabilitate prostitutes aged sixteen to twenty-one. This year it turned its attention to intervening in teenage pregnancies. When we spoke to the director of the program, she said that this was now the major problem for adolescent girls in Southside and that the agency was concerned and wanted to be responsive. When I talked to another program director in the same agency, he laughed and said, "Remember last year there was a *New York Times Magazine* article on teenage pregnancy and CBS did a special too? About that same time agency people began talking about how funds were becoming available for teenage pregnancy programs, and that's really when we became concerned."

The director of one of the smaller rehabilitation programs in Southside said that they had been in drug rehabilitation and juvenile delinquency diversion programs for over two decades but that money was drying up here because these were no longer "in" problems and competition for what little money was available was so tight that the small agencies were being frozen out. "The big agencies grab all of the money, and they'll start a program even before money becomes available because they are tied in with people in the funding sources and help them to decide and define what is a problem for kids and what isn't."

There are some externally funded agencies, however, which are also community-based, frequently with large numbers of paraprofessional community personnel involved. In Southside these agencies are quasi-governmental, often first established by a city, state, or federal agency as an outreach program and eventually becoming semi-independent. The director of a Hispanic multiple-services program described his agency as being responsive to the Hispanic community and an outgrowth of "ethnic politics." He went on to explain that all the major ethnic groups have had their "time" when they have some power in the city. Now, he explained,

Hispanics are becoming increasingly important as a political force and more funding is coming our way. Our biggest problem is with teenagers. The little kids are watched by their parents, but the teenagers are the ones who get into the most trouble and make people think that all Hispanics are criminals. We should start with the little kids, but their families won't send them to us until they are already in trouble.

Our experience with these agencies was that they saw their role as strengthening family relationships rather than replacing or even intervening in them. For the youngsters we interviewed, the co-ethnics who staff such programs were seen as part of the same community as the trainees—more peers or friends than adult caretakers or parent surrogates. Brenda, for example, a fifteen-year-old black girl, told us how she was getting along in the "Black Pride" program at the agency. She talked about how friendly everyone was in the program and how she had been able to "open up" with the black professionals as she sometimes did at home but never could at school except with her friends. She had made a lot of friends here, and they had begun to share some of their social life outside the program as well. The professionals were very friendly, but they also wanted you to learn and to make something of yourself. There seems to be an entire range of accountability standards which the students here must meet in order to continue in the program. These include completing tasks and producing a finished product in their skills areas, learning to discipline themselves by being on time, keeping accurate time schedules and not falling behind in their work, and helping to make as well as follow rules.

Not everyone, however, agreed that there was either a need or a future for such community organizations. One of the precinct policemen said that the community-based agencies were little more than another form of welfare:

> They are the place where blacks and Hispanics get their first political job and then move up as they prove themselves and get better known. I don't know that they do that much for the minority kids. They tell them what their rights are, like helping their parents get welfare, and they fill them up with a lot of racial and ethnic pride which is supposed to motivate them, but they still can't get jobs. They call them diversionary programs and that's what they really are. They divert money into the minority community to keep them quiet and off the streets.

There are also a few community organizations in Southside which are both community-based and community-funded. Actually, it would be more accurate to say that they are ethnically based and funded, and they usually see their principal function as developing ethnic consciousness in their youthful constituencies. There are such programs for every major ethnic group in the area, but the most highly organized are in the Chinese community, where they serve to augment, rather than replace, the school as well as the family. One member of our team, who is himself Chinese-American, spent three years observing and interviewing teenagers and adults there:

In Chinatown teenagers learn the traits, symbols, and behavior of traditional Chinese culture not at home but in the local agencies such as the Pak Hok Kung Fu International Association and the Chi Ku Tuk Chin Association. Over the last six months I have been able to observe and participate in both of these agency-school settings. The Kung Fu Association's school uses the martial arts as the basis for getting Chinese kids there, but they also emphasize learning Chinese culture. During the first two days of Chinese New Year, I went to the school's celebration banquet with Sam (fourteen years old) and William (nineteen years old).

William was very respectful to the *sihans* (teacher-brother) and said to the Grand Master, in Chinese, "I wish you a Happy New Year and that ten thousand things will come out as you wish this year." This is a very polite and adult *gon bui* (toast) in traditional Chinese society. William called his *sihans* "Chin Pui," or "Respected Forward Generation." When I asked him about this he replied, in Chinese, "Even though I am a *chuk sing* (bamboo sprout) I respect my elders."

Later "Uncle Liu," an elder at the Kung Fu Association's school, said, "We have to tell them what to do. In English school the teachers never teach them how to address their elders. They never teach about politeness, and their parents are so busy working and have not learned English, and so these young people need our school to teach them how to respect their elders."

I also spent some time at the Chi Ku Tuk Chin Association (the Filial Piety and Respecting of Elders Association), which is for young people from ten to twenty years of age. The adolescents learn the forms of address and politeness by practicing here in school. The first few times they seemed a little awkward and embarrassed, but they soon learned. For example, they learned to give the Tong ancestor salute, or *kowtau*, and when they learned it properly they were rewarded with a *lai si*, or little red envelope with money in it, and they were soon laughing. During the course of the day they did the *kowtau* again and again and were constantly encouraged: "You are *tai go tsui* (a big boy) now."

There are social agencies in Sheffield, and Newtown as well. But, in contrast to the extracommunity character of most social agencies in our urban inner-city sites, the social agencies in Sheffield and Newtown are intimately related to the family and the school rather than competitive with them. A police officer involved with adolescents in Sheffield comments:

> Of course the problems here are very different than those you see in the city. Just about the most serious problem is kids taking their parents' cars and driving over lawns, or, as in one case last year, when kids stole liquor from their parents' houses. They were finally discovered when they took a very expensive case of champagne from one house to celebrate a soccer victory. I guess everything here is family-centered.

Throughout the conversation he kept coming back to the topic of the influence of families in deciding what social agencies there will be and how they will operate.

> All of the organized recreational and social activity is controlled by families either through membership in country clubs, in churches, in community groups, or through their influence on the schools. Talk about interlocking directorates—the same people sit on every board and some on as many as four or five different ones.

A good deal of the social agency activity in both communities is oriented toward athletic programs or cultural enrichment, offering community-based activities which families cannot provide but which they support and approve. In Sheffield, for example, every church as well as every school maintains an athletic program. There are organized leagues for sports such as soccer and hockey which travel to various parts of the state and are highly competitive. The hockey league has a number of different teams. It begins with an informal program for kids five or six through eight called "Mites," and then moves through a series of more highly organized teams: nine- and ten-year-olds belong to the "Squirts"; eleven- and twelve-year-olds are "Pee Wees"; thirteen- and fourteen-year-olds are "Midgets"; and after that comes the senior team. A father told me that his twelve-year-old son had been playing organized hockey for six years. The father, who coached this team, said that one of the biggest problems was how to motivate the kids. He said that it was very important to have a practice before each game since the kids needed that extra push then. He mentioned that he was not having a good season, that the kids were just not "putting out" the way they could; they just were not playing up to par. In another interview, a former head of the Sheffield Athletic Association said that "the parents in this town are very hyperactive.

That's how they got to where they are and what brings them to this community, and that's the way they want their kids to be."

Why such a heavy emphasis on sports? A teacher who works after school as a coach for one of the local teenage soccer teams explained:

When I first came here I resented the kids, and their parents even more. I felt that the parents in Sheffield were using sports and recreation as a means of getting their kids into some activities and maybe out of their hair. I couldn't schedule practice sometimes because half the team would be off in some other activity their parents set up for them. It didn't take me long to find out that if we didn't win there was a lot of complaining from parents, the mothers almost more than the fathers. I remember one lady quoting Vince Lombardi to me: "Winning isn't everything, it's the only thing."

Church social activities also center heavily on sports but include comprehensive programs ranging from behavior counseling to organized trips in and outside the community. A young priest who directs one of the largest church-centered teen programs talked about a great deal of parental involvement in the program as well as cooperation from the school. As a result, "there is no crap going on, no smoking, no drinking, and very strict rules that the kids know about." His program is, he explained, like a family in that it builds relationships of mutual trust and dependence. The end products, he said as he introduced me to two program members who were high school seniors waiting to hear from Ivy League colleges, are the easiest part of the whole process. "It's the organization and planning and the ideas that go into the program—the leadership, the responsibility, and being able to work together to create unity—that are important. The end product is all enjoyment; it's building a life for these kids that puts a new set of family relationships with other kids on top of the family relationships they already have."

We also observed and interviewed the teenagers who were in the program, as well as their parents. The teenagers run a "youth mass" twice each month which all parents attend, and they also have a council which decides on what programs to have. The priest explained that in the beginning the kids voted on who would be officers, but "as it became bigger and more complicated, I couldn't take a chance on who would be voted in, so that in the second year that I was here I began to choose the officers myself because I couldn't deal with anyone who isn't going to give one hundred percent.'' We also talked about the sports programs in the schools, and he observed that the community tries to make them as competitive as possible to keep the kids active and involved.

One of our field research assistants went to a number of the church-sponsored social events in Sheffield and describes a dance held every Friday night at one of the local churches:

> I went to the teen center one Friday night where there was a dance with a live rock band, and the kids (there were about 160 of them) paid 25 cents to get in. There were two chaperones, a married couple, and a number of mothers and a few fathers who were there to help with the food. The rules were that once you leave the center you can't get back in. Then the next day the priest will ask your parents what time you got home and see to it that they know you left the center at 9:00 P.M. but didn't get home until 10:00 P.M.
>
> During the dance I had a chance to talk to some of the parents, and they told me that the program also held a number of ''self-search'' retreat weekends where the emphasis was on Christian family values: ''The program tries not to substitute for the family but to tie the family into their belief. The purpose is to bring the whole family together.'' One father talked about his role on the community's interfaith council and how they were working to get all of the various sports committees not to schedule any sports programs on Sunday until afternoon.

Social agencies, in the sense that they exist in Southside or even in Sheffield, are not present in rural Green Valley, nor did we find many in other rural areas we studied. As mentioned earlier, the major social agencies in Green Valley which would correspond to Southside's youth programs are located in the county seat; and there is virtually no outreach from there nor do many Green Valley youngsters seek them out. The community itself has organized some recreational activities for youth which are family-related. The chairman of the town recreation committee, who is also a local shopkeeper, told one of our fieldworkers about the program.

> I'm the chairman of the town recreation committee. It's a volunteer position and there really isn't any committee because I'm it. We have basketball in the winter, about one hundred kids and ten teams,

which is held at the high school, but we've had trouble because we couldn't find a parent to coach it. Our Little League baseball team, on the other hand, has been very successful because there is a father who really enjoys coaching. Parents who do coach usually have kids in the programs. These programs are town-supported and open to everyone in town.

He went on to point out that he has a working arrangement with the school in that he takes care of the recreation and athletic programs until the kids are thirteen, and then the school picks them up. The school, he says, usually has trouble with older kids because "once they get a car you can forget about them; they're off and away."

Some of the town businesses support teams among adults as well as kids, but, he explained, it is the "old families" who participate rather than the newer arrivals:

We had some trouble last year when some people broke into the recreation building down at the lake and stole a lot of our equipment. We're pretty sure it was some of the people who are moving into town. Most of those commuters' kids have not participated in the recreation program and they haven't felt what it's like to be close to other people in town. Those are the kids who destroy things for others. We had a budget hearing to get money to replace the equipment, and I knew that there might be some trouble. I tried to convince some of the townspeople to come and support us. In this town, if you can get a bunch of parents to be pissed off about something and get them into the town meeting, then anything they want will be passed. I told them to get together, to bring their kids. Stick a pencil in the kid's butt to make him cry so that everybody will think it's the missing equipment he's crying about. But it's winter now and nobody can think ahead, so very few came and we didn't get the money. Now there are about eleven mothers who are organizing themselves for the recreation program this summer. They do anything they can to get the money: raffles, bake sales, garage sales, anything.

What the town's recreation chairman was telling us was more than just that it's necessary to work through the family to get anything done in Green Valley; he was also indicating that there are no other resources available to youngsters—at least those who, as members of the "old families," are isolated in family environments. One reason the commuters' kids don't get involved in the township's athletic programs is that they have their own through parents' country clubs or elsewhere in the county.

There is, however, one other social context available in Green Valley, particularly for the farm kids. The Grange, the 4-H Club, and Future Farmers of America are very active in the community. The Grange, we were told by the local representative, was started in 1867 by a clerk in the Department of Agriculture to unify farmers. It was a rural organization for farmers until the beginning of the century. As the number of farmers declined, membership in the Grange declined along with it. The organization then became more socially oriented, working with farm communities' families, which meant that you didn't have to be a farmer to belong. The representative explained that the Grange began as "a farm fraternity." There are secret membership rites, secret salutations, and a secret password that changes every year, and meetings are not usually open to the public. This is a "throwback" to the time when farmers were fighting against railroad expansion and didn't want railroad spies coming to their meetings. "Today," she added, "we call ourselves a rural family organization."

School personnel we talked to in Green Valley were very supportive of the Grange, Future Farmers of America, and 4-H programs in the area. They saw them as part of the "old farm work ethic" tradition. The agricultural teacher at the high school (who was also the local leader of the Future Farmers of America) described some of the Grange programs:

> You can join the Junior Grange at age five and then move to the Subordinate Grange at thirteen, because we consider kids to be adults at thirteen even though some of them are not really ready until age fifteen, when they must leave Junior for Subordinate. Kids join the Grange because it's a going organization. I never have to go around and ask anybody if their kids want to join. We have a lot of activities—square dances, bake sales, flea markets, first aid and hunting-safety classes (the high school closes on the first day of hunting season), roller skating, and picnics; we do so many things I can't keep track of them. We also try to give the Juniors some sense of being involved; there are forty-six of them, and thirty-three are officers or leaders of some kind. . . . You don't have to have your parents in the Grange to join, but most of the membership is family membership. I suppose that is why we call ourselves a rural family organization.

The same attitude toward the independence and cohesion of rural family life and support for the Grange's role in it was shared by most people we spoke with in the area:

The town supervisor said, "We're like farmers everywhere. We try to do everything we can by ourselves before going to 'Big Brother' in the county seat for help. Parents have to take charge of their kids' lives. That means you have to have good parents to have good kids."

A teenager called Mark said that being a farm kid, he likes to work, and that it is important to him to be working. "I really don't know why I work; I gotta. Ever since I can remember I was working."

Another teenager said that he and his friend used to drink. "But since my friend became the county representative of the Future Farmers of America, he won't go drinking anymore. He is afraid that if he is seen drinking by somebody who knows who he is, it will be bad for him and the Future Farmers."

A youth named Dick recalled that he used to drive around town in his father's pick-up when he was fifteen but the cops wouldn't bother him because they knew he was on farm or Grange business. He mentioned the curfew and said he doesn't know if anyone has ever gotten caught because he would stay out until 2:00 A.M. sometimes and no one ever bothered him. "The cops do pick up some of the new kids who have bad reputations," he said, "like ones who have been arrested before or who are hanging around smoking dope or drinking. That crowd never changes."

These farm adolescent–oriented programs are not active in another rural community we studied in the South, where most "farm children" are actually migrant workers. In fact, there is little such social support outside the school and the family for these youth. There is a migrant workers' union beginning to organize which maintains some youth programs, but generally they are county and state operated. Here again the absence of an established community structure seems to preclude extrafamilial services, despite the dim view that most local residents take of the efficacy of family socialization for the migrant children.

When we look at these rural communities and the small number of non-kin mentors available for teenagers there, compared with places like Southside or Sheffield, the significance to adolescent development of how a community is organized and what social opportunities it provides becomes apparent. While the family is an important setting for such formative influence, adults in other social contexts also play a critical transitional role for teenagers. The social worlds outside the family—such as the peer group and the school—not only provide new vistas and hence new insights; they also modify the child who was crafted by the family, and in so doing change the family as well. Various communities, and the very different patterns of family alignment and the social and emotional environments which form within them, deal differently with the teenager's need for continuity and congruence in her relationship with adults. These aspects of adolescent development are scripted and cast in family dynamics, but they become far more important when they are acted out in the world outside the family. We found, for example, that feelings about controlling one's fate developed in the family have a great deal to do with how adolescents approach school and career futures. We also learned that it is not possible to understand schools without asking how they are linked to the families that sent students to them and how the schools are linked to the world of work for which they are expected to prepare these students. Viewed in this perspective, the adolescent transition is a process in which the child becoming an adult needs loving but consistent guidance to move from childhood dependency to the interdependence of the adult social world, avoiding along the way, ones hopes, the loneliness which is the price of true independence.

4

From Home to School

If growth from dependent child to productive and procreative adult is the fundamental developmental task of adolescence, its contemporary social setting is in the movement from the world of the school to the world of work. The transformation of child-student to adult-worker is probably the most commonly agreed upon standard by which we judge a successful adolescence, even though the age at which it takes place can and does differ dramatically from community to community as well as among socioeconomic classes. In all societies it is necessary for the young to pass through a period of dependency.[1] During this time physical maturity is attained and skills and knowledge necessary for adulthood are learned, but the length and nature of dependency vary according to the culture, as does the substance of learning. The extension of compulsory education into the late teens and the substantial increase in the number of students in postsecondary education have made the school the primary environment for adolescents. Increasingly, however, the school, and particularly the high school, is being designed and evaluated not just as a place for academic education but as a preparatory institution, a staging area for moving children from their family origins into a variety of very different occupational roles in society.

Schools are a major feature in the lives of adolescents, not only because they spend so much of their waking time there, but because the school is assigned a role at least commensurate with the family in the preparation of adolescents for later life. Not only occupational preparation, but health care, self-discipline and social discipline, and becoming a good citizen are all expected, even demanded, from the educational experience. In fact, we have a tendency to see the school—

and particularly the high school—as the principal remediator for social ills, and the inclusion of new courses in the curriculum as the best chance for prevention as well as cure. When there were first perceived to be widespread problems with drug abuse, drug education courses were introduced; when drinking became a concern, alcohol education was initiated; and sex and AIDS education programs have been controversial but inevitable consequences of their related social crises. In the aftermath of the Watergate political scandals, courses in civics and citizenship were once again emphasized in the secondary school. The introduction and continuation of such courses, however, is much more a matter of community sentiment and sensitivity than of any educational policy at the state, let alone national, level.

Just as communities differ, so do their schools. Despite consistently bad report cards when compared to other countries, American education has made significant strides since World War II. High school completion has more than doubled, and there have been even greater gains in the number and proportion of teenagers who go on to and complete college. These gains, however, are not equally distributed throughout the country or among the various ethnic and socioeconomic groups in the population. High school attendance and completion statistics show that Hispanics have had the lowest rates throughout this period: a result, most educators maintain, of their recent immigration and impoverishment. The effects of socioeconomic deprivation on educational development are demonstrated once again in the research findings which indicate that Hispanic youngsters show just about the same rates of high school enrollment as black or white children when they are matched by social class.[2]

Major gains in the educational lives of black youngsters since the civil rights movement have resulted in a closing of the enrollment gap between black and white adolescents; up until about age seventeen, virtually the same proportion (over 90 percent) of black and white high school–age students are enrolled in school, as compared to Hispanics, whose rate has already dropped below 85 percent by that age.[3] Dropping out of school, however, a sign of present and potential disenfranchisement, still shows the effects of racial and ethnic differences in the adolescent experience. While blacks have only marginally higher dropout rates than whites throughout early and middle adolescence, when students go on to higher education, black enrollment drops well below that for whites, and Hispanics have an even lower rate than blacks. Yet once again poverty and socioeconomic status are most powerful, and regardless of race, poor students are more likely to drop out than their more affluent age-mates.

The schools themselves differ regionally and by type of community. Those states and locales with the highest rates of poverty, unemployment, and minority populations also tend to have the highest dropout rates and the lowest student achievement scores.[4] Similarly, schools in major urban centers, particularly those in inner-city poverty areas, differ from suburban schools in what has come to be called "the culture of the school" as well as in enrollment, dropout, and achievement scores. To some extent this can be attributed to differences in the racial and socioeconomic composition of their student bodies, and in how the schools are run. But the influence of the community on its schools is so strong that it makes the notion of a school culture or school effectiveness independent of the community culture questionable. Certainly the influence of educational authorities in making their schools effective places to learn is important, but families and the school community get the schools they earn.

Communities differ in how they structure and empower this pattern of relationships, and its dynamics can be more important to adolescent development than the individual contribution of the family, school, or peer group. While each can have a facilitating or restricting effect on preparation for adulthood, multiple deficits in these areas can combine and reinforce each other with devastating effects on the life course. To say this in a somewhat more positive way, it is possible for an adolescent from an impoverished background—even one where there is little or no commitment to education by parents—to succeed. It is also possible to overcome early educational deficits or association with peers who derogate school, and numbers of individuals have and will continue to do so. But these are individual efforts, involving exceptional intrinsic motivation on the part of the individual adolescent, a family which values and encourages educational attainment, a teacher or school dedicated to success, or some fortuitous combination of all of these.

Every community can and should model the relationships among these institutions into a network of values and opportunities which produces and sustains an environment for cooperative learning. The messages which each of the institutions send to individual adolescents should be mutually reinforcing rather than disharmonious or even at cross-purposes. It should go without saying that this structure of opportunity should be available to all children and not only to a fortunate few. Such, however, is not always the case. Three of the sites we studied were all in the same Gulf Coast county in the South. All of the public schools there are under the jurisdiction of the same county-wide school system, but it is the local community, not the county government, which shapes the aspirations and opportunities associated with schooling, and in so doing sets the educational environment for life in those schools.

SEMINOLE COUNTY

Seminole County, on the Gulf Coast of the Southeast, describes itself as one of the last frontiers in America. The sprawling million-and-a-quarter-acre political unit oversees a visibly differentiated topography of swamplands, fertile farm country, dozens of resort communities on miles of Gulf beaches, and literally thousands of islands. There are about eighty-five thousand year-round residents in the county, over half of whom have settled there in the last decade, primarily in the resort-retirement communities along the beaches. The patterns of migration have added to the already dramatic differences which geography, population characteristics, resources, and economic opportunity produce in the life styles of these communities and so of their schools.

Smyrna Beach is the political and population center of the county. Situated on a long peninsula of land which reaches out into the Gulf, it has a permanent population of about 50,000 people which triples to 150,000 in the winter tourist season. The permanent population is growing rapidly, and the influx of new settlers brings mostly retirees from the north central and northeastern states, although there is an increasing number of young migrant families seeking the better life of the Sunbelt. As a result, youth-oriented programs and facilities are not as well developed as senior citizen facilities: the local hospital has a large and separately housed geriatrics unit, but there is only one adolescent psychiatrist in the city. Winter visitors here tend to be middle or upper middle class, white, and Protestant, and are looking for family-oriented activities rather than nightlife and entertainment. Smyrna Beach High School has twelve hundred students, 96 percent of whom are white, 2.8 percent Hispanic, 0.9 percent black, and 0.02 percent American Indian.

About a half-hour's drive inland from Smyrna Beach is Ranchville, a farming community located on a hammock which is the only high

land in the swampy internal part of the county. Ranchville was originally an area of Indian encampments which was settled in the mid-
1800s by white hunters, traders, and cattlemen. An Indian school
had been established there at that time, but it attracted only white
students and so it gradually became the local public school. The permanent, year-round population is about ten thousand, most of whom
are cattle ranchers and vegetable farmers, their employees, and the
personnel needed to service human and commercial-agricultural needs.
In addition to these "old white" families, there are Indians who
live on a nearby reservation, some blacks who work on the farms,
and a few Mexicans who tend herds on the cattle ranches.

Every winter, which is harvest time here, thousands of migrant
workers come to Ranchville to pick the fruit and vegetables, almost
doubling the size of the population, and creating massive problems
connected with housing, sanitation, law and order, race relations,
and education. Most of the migrants are Mexicans, with a smaller
number of blacks coming as well, and they live the bitter and impoverished life of migrant workers everywhere. There are virtually no special
services for them and their children, many of whom also work on
the farms or in the packing houses. The tension existing in the town
when the migrants are there is illustrated by the sign which appears
every winter on the local drugstore forbidding more than two teenagers
at a time to be in the store.

The Ranchville High School, like the Smyrna Beach High School,
is grades 9–12 and comes under the jurisdiction of the same county
superintendent of schools. Its student body of about seven hundred
is 46 percent Hispanic, 31 percent white, 21 percent black, and about
2 percent American Indians. The school reports that about 30 percent
of its students migrate every year.

Cypress City, the third community we studied in Seminole County,
has been a fishing village located in a remote coastal mangrove swamp
area since the turn of the century. It also has a small hotel-inn for
housing the sports fishermen and hunters who come here every winter
from all over the country. The fishing and shrimp boats operating
out of the commercial wharf were once all owned or controlled by
the same man, but in the 1950s what was actually a company town
became an incorporated city. The population is almost entirely white,
with a few blacks and Hispanics serving as household or service
workers.

While fishing is the major industry here, Cypress City is also said to be a major center for the smuggling of illegal drugs by boat and by plane from South and Central America. This new industry has left its marks on the culture as well as the economy of the area. Some of the fishing boat owners have discovered that they can make as much money in one trip out to a "mother" drug ship in the Gulf as they can in a season of commercial fishing. While the new industry has produced a number of signs of affluence, it has also meant that federal and state drug enforcement agencies keep the town under almost constant surveillance. This scrutiny includes the middle school, where teachers pointed out to us the sons of drug smugglers—easily identified, they said, by the multiple gold chains they wore around their necks. The teachers also talked about the effects of the new wealth in making it possible for some youngsters to go into Smyrna Beach or even to larger, more distant resort areas for entertainment and excitement. "It is," said one teacher, "making it a lot harder for us to teach them because the community is too small and too close for them now." When I asked him in what ways, he went on to say that they were no longer "under the control of the community" and were becoming more and more like the kinds of teenagers they mingled with in these other communities.

Talking with the county-level school officials in Seminole County revealed how differently they thought about the schools in each of the communities. Smyrna Beach High School, for example, was described as a "fast track" college-bound school, where there is a no-nonsense approach to discipline as well as learning. Parents were said to be "very supportive" of the strong discipline, which includes actually locking up disruptive or recalcitrant students in a study-detention center for hours or days at a time. Ranchville's high school, on the other hand, was seen as a place where the probability of directly entering the world of work following graduation, or, more frequently, dropping out, meant greater concentration on what were euphemistically called "life skills." Not all of the parents in Ranchville agree with this approach, and a number of parents and some teachers argued that it really represents the political power of Smyrna Beach residents in comparison to the disenfranchised migrant workers in Ranchville.

One example they cited was the decision by the county school board to impose a regulation setting a firm minimum for the number of days a student had to attend classes in order to receive credit for a course. The reason for the new rule seemed to be that parents in Smyrna Beach had been complaining about their teenage children cutting class and then not doing well on exams, which in turn meant lowered prospects for getting into a good college. Teachers and administrators in Ranchville pointed out to me, as they had to the county officials, that most of their migrant students would certainly be absent the minimum number of days and more because of the need to work during the winter picking season. It was to no avail, because, as they said with some bitterness, "Ranchville doesn't get treated any different from Smyrna Beach when it comes to the rules, only when it comes to resources." Cypress City doesn't have a high school, and the county officials explained that it is just too small and isolated to support one. Cypress City students go to other county high schools, where, reported the officials, they are easily recognized, keep pretty much to themselves, and make few if any friends outside their own group. "Just like," they added, "the folks in Cypress City have always done."

There is a process of social categorization, or "sorting," that we found in every school we studied. Students and the education they will receive are classified along a number of different dimensions. One dimension is the formal process of putting students into "tracks," such as vocational, commercial, academic, and so on. Another is ability grouping, where students are sorted on the basis of aptitude and achievement. There is a third, less formal process by which students are sorted (by themselves as well as by teachers) into a series of informally recognized distinctions that indicate what is valued and what condemned by the school. To some extent, the basic characteristics which establish the categories for sorting, and determine who will be sorted into or out of particular categories based on their real or assumed qualities, beliefs, and behaviors, are established outside the school and carried over into it.[5]

In rural Ranchville, just as in urban Southside, the dominance of racial, ethnic, and social class affiliation as the major source of social identity in the community is reinforced in the high school. Green Valley is also a rural community, but its high school brings together students from a number of different communities and the town of residence has always been a major criterion in the sorting process, although more prominent differences between "old-time families" and "commuter types" have been muting some of these distinctions. Cypress City is just as isolated as Ranchville or Green Valley, but there is virtually no racial or ethnic differentiation, and all of its students are from local families. What sorting we did see here was largely based on a very broad distinction: those families who had money and those who didn't—a distinction made even stronger by the influx of drug money.

Each community influences the sorting process in its schools to a greater or lesser degree by the beliefs about social differentiation that teachers and administrators, as well as students, bring into the schools from their homes and communities. But even where two communities have similar sorting categories, many of the specific beliefs, values, and concerns which shape these group identities may differ.

Some criteria for sorting are generated by the school itself, as an institution charged with teaching and learning responsibilities in the community. In a community such as Sheffield, where there are few social distinctions to be borrowed from the social organization of the community, school-based differences, real or assumed, form the basis for at least the earlier stages of how the school sorts students and how they sort themselves. Whether the student responds negatively or positively to school activities and rules (Is she "disruptive" or "supportive"?); how well or badly the individual performs academically (Is she a "good student" or a "poor student"?); how much acceptance and influence the student has with peers and teachers (Is she "popular" or "unpopular"?)—these are common distinctions made in schools. Our experience has been that teachers and administrators often develop a correlation between tracking, or streaming, of students and the sorting process. We found, as have others, that many teachers and administrators have a tendency to assume that social class–based cultural characteristics, disruptive behavior in the school, student life style, and low academic skills are usually found together in the individual student.[6] Teachers in every community reported that "the same kids who have trouble learning create most of the trouble in the school." School officials and teachers alike estimated that these students make up anywhere from 10 to 20 percent of the school population (lowest in the suburbs, highest in urban inner cities, and varying between these extremes in rural areas). Such students were variously referred to as "troublemakers," "the difficult kids," or "the hard-core group," but they were identified and labeled in every school we studied.

When we asked why that should be so, school personnel almost always associated the learning as well as the behavior problems with deficits in the students' social, cultural, and particularly family background. A countywide administrator in Seminole County, for example, comparing students in impoverished Ranchville and affluent Smyrna Beach's high schools, insisted that "it's all in what they bring to school with them on the first day they enter the door, and if they don't look forward to learning then, they never do, and just see it as a place to raise hell." The school official went on to say that even in Smyrna Beach there is a small percentage of students who "are failing everything and always in trouble, and when you meet their parents and see how they live you come to understand why." In some places this same association was based on race or ethnic differences, as between Chinese and black or Hispanic students in Southside.

What happens in a child's school life can often be a direct result of how a community sorts its young learners and the reality of the bases they use to justify the process. The reflective, evaluative aspect of the self-concept and its associated sense of self-esteem develop within a social milieu. Sorting establishes social boundaries in schools, isolating some students not only from other students but from access to the school's resources as well. Sorting also describes and to some extent hands out the possible identities which schools present to adolescents. While the sorting process provides some basis for affiliation and selection of friends, sorting categories serve more as an individual's internal self-identifiers than as the basis for the formation of actual groups in the school. In other words, there are not actually social groups of "good students" or "bad students"; most teenagers simply come to know where they fall in that continuum. This in turn produces a perception of shared social identity. To the extent that the school formally (or, more frequently, informally) uses social, racial, and ethnic identification to sort students' access to educational resources, the perception confuses and confounds the consolidation of authentic identity. Ethnographers Signithia Fordham and John U. Ogbu have argued that one reason black students do poorly in school is the ambivalence and dissonance they experience from "the burden of acting white."[7] Many academically able black students, they find, do not put forth the necessary effort because they are caught in the bind between a school system which refuses to acknowledge that black students are capable of academic achievement and a black community which comes to consider academic striving as "acting white."

How one is sorted subjectively in a school can also have more influence than more objective measures in reaching formal decisions about a student's progress and placement. One of the field researchers who spent a year working with teachers and administrators and specifically studying the sorting process in Sheffield reported that she frequently witnessed scenes where teachers "abandoned all of the 'scientific data' that they had available to them, and made decisions on the basis of their feelings or personal opinions." She also found, as we did in most other schools in urban and rural as well as suburban areas, that the importance and frequency of such decision making could not be ignored: "Even teachers and administrators are aware that their sorting decisions fall into some gray area between 'objectivity' and 'subjectivity' and expressed how anxious and uncertain that makes them feel."[8]

In some ways, the effort the teenager expends to control the process of being self-sorted as well as sorted by others may be seen as an effort to manage the development of an identity. One major task is to individuate from the family and to find new milieus within which to achieve mature development. To the extent that a school's sorting system reinforces the identity images inherited in the family, it makes the seeking of new and individuated identity that much more difficult. In fact, it seemed to me that doing so was an almost impossible task for Josie Delgado of Southside. It was extremely difficult for Bruce Megan of Sheffield as well, but for very different reasons.

Following Josie into her high school in Southside reveals how her social identification as a Hispanic segregates her and her life chances just as surely as if she went to a separate and unequal school. If you spend any time in the school, you can't help but notice the correlation between the formal tracking system which assigns students to particular educational experiences and the informal but powerful sorting system which is based on race. Most of the students and families we talked to attributed this to racism, but many of the teachers and most of the administrators there will tell you that this is just the way student motivation and application work out. They place the major burden on the educational deficits of the families the students come from and the disdain for schooling by the peers with whom they associate. They also point out, and they are right, that parents are just as prone to identify students (and sometimes their abilities as well) on the basis of race.

When Josie enters the school building at about 8:35 she goes immediately to the third floor stairwell, which is the gathering place for her friends in the section of the building that is the Hispanic gathering place. She finds herself a niche on the steps (much of the initial surge of traffic is past), where she sits and talks (in both Spanish and English) to her closest friends. Then she goes to her first-period gym class and begins the round of classes for which she is scheduled.

Mr. Katz, a young Jewish teacher wearing a yarmulke, fills the front board with the cryptics of mathematics, earnestly emphasizing the points with the tip of his chalk, but Josie and her friends seem unimpressed. There is a low but constant stream of chatter among the Hispanic students. In this class, as in most others, Josie sits with her fellow Hispanic students, just as most Chinese and black students sit with their ethnic peers. Gradually but inevitably the teacher, faced with the obvious disinterest of the Hispanic students, uses his body position to edge Josie and her friends out of the major stream of conversation about the lesson. Soon he talks facing a small group of Chinese students. Meanwhile, a group of black students sit in the rear of the room quietly; no pretense was ever made by the teacher of talking to them.

Josie's family is little involved in what happens in the school, not only because they feel incompetent to deal with the education of their children in America but because the school is, as one teacher described it, "parent proof." What is a parent-proof school? The teacher explained that when the city had decentralized its elementary and junior high schools under pressure from black civil rights leaders, they had kept the high schools centralized so that "we can get the final shot at overcoming the educational deficits that families give their children." She went on to say that there is virtually no parent involvement in setting the program or standards of the school; that, after all, educational questions require professional judgment, and most parents have neither the requisite background nor the interest for getting involved. Chinese parents sometimes come in to inquire or complain about what is happening to their children, but black and Hispanic parents are "content to leave the driving to us." We found this same perception of the lack of parental involvement in each of the urban inner-city and rural areas we studied, and it stood out in sharp contradistinction to the descriptions of community involvement and even complaints of interference by parent groups we heard about in the suburbs.

There are Hispanic students, like Josie's cousin Victor, who travel back and forth between the different and sometimes conflicting worlds of community and school with ease as well as determination; they will surely succeed. But there are many others—and Josie seems to be one of them—who will not make it in this school, in no small measure because the language, culture, and motives of her learning environments outside the formal boundaries of the school are alien to it. So she goes to her classes, still just barely motivated by dreams of economic mobility, good grades, and social favor, but mostly because her friends are there. One of the pieces of educational folk wisdom quoted by most teachers is that experiencing success leads to positive perceptions by others, which leads to self-esteem, leading to more success that further enhances self-esteem, and so on. Research evidence indicates that students, especially those who for whatever reason are low achievers, need to experience an approximate 80 percent success rate in their graded work in school to feel any progressive sense of motivation.[9] When you talk to Josie about what she considers to be her successes, she always begins by telling you how she gets along well with her family and friends and how warm and comfortable she feels when she is with them. If you ask about school she shrugs her shoulders and makes a face, and you can see in the gesture that she has just about given up on the dream just as surely as she believes that the school has given up on her. These same attitudes and opinions about schooling were expressed by many of the students we met in Southside and other urban inner-city areas, and, not surprisingly, as many as half of them fail to complete high school. It is the effects of poverty and deprivation, however, rather than race or ethnicity, which account for poor performance in school. When we compared similar communities we found, as so many others have, that class-shared values and aspirations for youth as well as the family's educational values were far more important than ethnicity in developing those characteristics which insure success in school and, later, on the job.[10]

There is sorting in Sheffield's high school also, but its dimensions and its relationship to family background are quite different. There are social identities among students that follow the almost universal patterns of conforming "jocks" and nonconformist "freaks," but most of the eight hundred students in the school are social "nobodies," unassigned to any such grouping.[11] The transient nature of the younger and on-the-move families in Sheffield—over 60 percent have lived here five years or less—means that many children spend the major portion of their school lives becoming recognized. Bruce, for example, who lived in three different communities during his elementary school years, jokes about his father always wanting to pay his country club dues on a monthly rather than annual basis because he never knew when his company would assign him elsewhere. Bruce also talks about how much difficulty he had finding his place in the new schools he had to attend.

In Sheffield, adults, school personnel, and the many parents who have direct involvement in school programs also differentiate students, but primarily on the basis of academic ability, prowess in sports, special talents, participation and particularly leadership in student activities, and other performance indicators. All of these characteristics are incorporated in an assessment of the individual student's ability to achieve both in school and in later life. They combine to describe what Sheffield parents and educators alike describe as "educational mobility": going on to the right college to prepare for the right career as a result of individual effort. The social and cultural differentiation which color life in Southside's high school are not present in Sheffield, and parents and educators alike want to keep it that way. One open letter from a school administrator, concerned about the formation of cliques there, proclaimed:

> I am concerned about the growing fragmentation within the student body. A school which once prided itself in the ability of its students to transcend narrow stereotypes is now "choosing up sides" and "staking out turf." . . . Why is this phenomenon occurring? In my opinion it reflects the growing insecurity of Americans, and teenagers in particular. The media is winning as it peddles the concept of group identity. There must be something wrong with not being part of the "Pepsi generation" or not being able to affect the "Jordache look." . . . Sheffield was always different. I fear that the students themselves are creating the constraints of group identity that ultimately will reduce their freedom.

The similarity among families and their aspirations for their children increases rather than mediates the pressures for individual success, for standing out from the crowd. The school responds to this message from parents.

Newtown parents, at least those we met within the racially integrated middle-class community we studied, have the same family characteristics and aspirations for their children that we found in Sheffield and all of the other suburban sites. In fact, the two communities are quite similar except for the presence of a number of black families in Newtown. Newtown also differs from Sheffield in that within the former's larger-community context of the planned city, there are children from lower-income housing areas who attend the same schools as other children there. These differences seem to have made some difference in the ambience, if not the result, when both communities, like many others, abandoned the "open space" concept for their middle schools under pressure from parents for a more traditional structure in which to house the "back to basics" movement.

We were present in Sheffield during this debate, and the issues were clearly linked to the notion that the freedom and lack of control which many parents (and not a few educators as well) associated with the open space school were responsible for declining academic standards and declining S.A.T. scores, with important implications for college and career futures. This all happened in Newtown before we started our research there, but parents who were there at the time talk about racial and social class undertones which surrounded the back to basics movement in the community. As in Sheffield, preparing for college and careers were reasons given in Newtown for abandoning the open space concept, but the problems of low achievement and motivation became popularly focused on three schools in the racially mixed, subsidized housing areas of the community. What really necessitated the restructuring of schools, it was said, was the inability of the youngsters there to handle the lack of structure and the requisite more self-motivation popularly associated with open schools. Because the students in Sheffield were homogeneous, this justification for a return to a more conservative educational philosophy of "back to the basics" was not available to Sheffield or most of the hundreds of other affluent suburban school systems throughout the country which closed up their open schools at about the same time.

If social class differentiation and group identity are not available for the social sorting of students in Sheffield, there are individual differences which are. Schools use a grouping system to develop levels for students and adjust the curriculum accordingly. The programs, which are numbered instead of named, range from an accelerated program for the top level of students, a middle-range program for good students, a low-average program for average students, to a remedial program for any student having difficulties. Since few Sheffield parents want their children in a low-average program, the school accommodates, and, if a parent insists, a student will be placed in a higher-level class, even an accelerated class, on a provisional basis.

Teachers and administrators in Sheffield often described their educational program as "parent related," which any observer soon realizes means "parent driven." School personnel often talked about what they called a "corporate mind-set" on the part of the parents. Sometimes they used this term in describing their response to individual or collective parental pressures. Many fathers are young executives who are used to issuing directives in their companies and getting some immediate response. They direct the same stance to the schools and, reported one principal, think nothing of calling the school and saying they want to get some information or have something done by two o'clock that afternoon. Mothers behave in the same way, not only because they are involved in their husbands' careers, but because they tend to have an educational philosophy of their own, often expressed in terms of what the schools had been like in a previous community in which they lived. Not infrequently, commented one administrator, the critical commentary from a mother will begin with "I used to be a teacher myself and I found. . . ."

There is, however, a second sense of the "corporate mind-set" which influences the education of children and adolescents in Sheffield. The superintendent of schools once remarked to me that the schools there are working with "a terrific product" because of the conducive home environment and the strong parental support. Task orientation among students is high and absenteeism and morale problems are low because the work and activity schedule in school leaves little time for hanging out or getting into any real trouble. Parents, say the teachers, are "invested" in their children's education. One open letter from an administrator during the "back to basics" era asked: "Has any generation planned more carefully for the success of its children than ours?" The letter went on to answer: "We suburban parents have invested generously and programmed carefully for the happiness, education, and cultural enrichment of the next generation."

The more one hears about the pressures to excel which set the standards for Sheffield adolescents, the more one also hears about the stress and anxiety which surround these pressures, particularly as college admissions time approaches. Counselors in the middle and high school programs described stress symptoms, which begin in elementary school, as being the results of placing children in early, continuous competition not only with peers but with themselves as well. As good as parents think the schools are in Sheffield, they are not good enough to satisfy many parents' search for excellence. Prestigious colleges and universities tell parents they are looking for well-rounded individuals who have interpersonal skills and enriching experiences, and so whatever time is left over from academic preparation goes into a round of out-of-school learning experiences. Tutoring and coaching for college entrance exams also compete for time. Many of these activities eventually find their way into the school programs and into the daily lives of the students as well. The following items from our field notes when we were observing in Sheffield schools give an idea of the prevailing attitudes:

The middle school has a ''Brain Bowl,'' a revival of the old ''College Bowl'' TV game show. Kids take trivia tests in homeroom and have to score at least 20 right in order to be in the Brain Bowl.

The principal explained that kids compete against local norms on standardized tests (rather than national, regional, or state norms) in order to be placed in accelerated classes, ''so they compete with kids from this school rather than other schools and that makes the competition keener.''

During the awards ceremony in the middle school the number of awards presented seemed very high. There was an award for each academic subject as well as for each sports activity and a number of sub-awards for various activities during the school year. The principal commented that he wanted to give out as many awards as possible because winning seemed so important to parents in this community.

Mrs. Grey explained to the students at an assembly about the awards that would be given out on the environmental field trip: best and neatest cabins, best behavior in dining halls, and a number of other individual awards for ''personal best effort.''

Kim's mother said she is getting her daughter ready for the next Olympic games, which are three years from now. Kim is eleven years old and has been training with a private coach, before and after school every day and on weekends, since she was seven. Her mother has been pushing the school system to start a girls' gymnastics team in the middle school Kim attends. The mother also said that an organized gymnastics program should begin in the elementary schools: ''In this sport you're already over the hill when you're seventeen years old.''

The principal said that the high school maintains a central calendar for all its own adolescent activities as well as schedules for other major programs, such as the town's athletic programs and those of the churches, to make sure that the activities don't conflict.

The pressures to compete begin to be internalized very early in the academic lives of Sheffield's children. In a third grade class, we overheard the following exchange among three students:

BOY 1: What page are you on?
BOY 2: Page 16.
BOY 1: Top or bottom?
BOY 2: Top.
BOY 1: Well, I'm ahead of you then. I'm on the bottom.
BOY 3: You are not! I know you're on the bottom of page 15, and I'm on page 17!

Kindergarteners and first graders in Sheffield have already learned the difference between play activities and "getting to work." One third grade youngster mentioned that if you are "smart enough and work hard to finish your workbook" before the others, you get to do art work. Most students we talked with believed that their teachers did not want them to share answers with other children; they insisted that "you do your own work." By the late elementary school years students have come to accept the individualized ability grouping. They have also learned the sorting pattern which it develops. "We have red, blue, and purple books. . . . Purple is higher and I used to be in purple but I dropped back." Another student added, "I'm in higher math and my parents feel good about it because I'm not with all the kids that are stupid and stuff."

The early childhood experience also seems to continue and even to be reinforced throughout adolescence. For example, two students were talking about how well they were doing on college admissions tests. When one told the other his math scores she commented, "That's good, John, but I'm still ahead of you."

The themes of educational mobility and the corporate mind-set combine to program the developmental years in Sheffield so that "school" and "work" are synonymous. Schooling is seen as the necessary basic training for social and occupational campaigns in the future. The superintendent of schools recalled, somewhat ruefully, the mother who complained about the elementary school her daughter was attending, explaining that she planned to send her daughter to Princeton someday. In the old days, mused the superintendent, it was only the boys who were pushed like that. He went on to talk about the pressures he is also getting to establish sports activities for girls as well as boys, because being in sports and being active in clubs and activities often make the difference in terms of college admissions. Sheffield parents take school sports programs seriously, insisting that the school should incorporate their character-building benefits as early as possible.

The importance which athletics and its competitive character-building potential has in the school, as well as in the community, is transparent in the school's daily bulletin, read by all the teachers during the first period class:[12]

> Please have the following members of the ninth grade basketball team report to the Medical Office today at 9:00 A.M.

Once on a team, you can be excused from school early:

> The basketball team will be excused at 2:08 today for the game at Oak Ridge.

Such resources are not only open to males:

> Please excuse the girls' basketball team at 2:45 today to attend a basketball game at Cookstown.

Once you've won a letter for sports you can have even more opportunities to cut classes with official sanction:

> All boys who have won two Varsity letters report to the auditorium sixth period today (Monday) for a meeting, reorganization, and election of officers for the Varsity "S" Club.

And, on Friday of the same week:

> Varsity Club executive meeting today in third period in the Student Activity Office.

Participation in sports can have fringe benefits as well. If you're the team captain, you can escort the Homecoming Court in a fall assembly:

> The following people are excused during first period in order that they may prepare for the Homecoming Election Assembly scheduled for 9:08 A.M.

Nor need access to avoiding classes be confined only to team members:

All persons who wish bus transportation, leaving school at 2:45 today, to the basketball game must have signed up and paid $1.00 in the Student Activity Office before noon today.

The point here is not whether sports activities are frivolous or valuable. Rather, it is that in "parent driven" Sheffield, where time on task in academic subjects is a major requirement of the school and of the parents who set its tone, athletics are considered important for developing and honing the competitive edge. Some amount of competition is present in almost all of the activities in the schools, from formal, schoolwide events such as the "Brain Bowl" to informal, classroom games such as one known among students as "Screw Thy Neighbor," in which students try to stump their fellow-competitors with difficult questions. Athletics, like all of these activities, is both generative of and adaptive to the sorting system here.

In Southside, by the way, there are no school-sponsored sports activities because, said school officials, there is a real danger that they would engender conflict and possibly even violence. This caution, it was pointed out, is a reflection of the school's racial and ethnic sorting, which establishes the various ethnic "turfs" within and around the school, reinforcing the residential separation of the various ethnic enclaves in the community. It also suggests that one reason why the school is "parent proof" is because of administrative concern that too close a linkage of school with community might result in moving the community's conflicts inside the school. We heard something similar to this in other urban inner-city communities.

While Sheffield has a large number of teen-oriented but parent-controlled social and athletic programs for older adolescents which are sponsored by the town, the schools, and the churches, we were struck by the absence of such programs in Newtown. We heard two different but related reasons for their absence from teenagers we interviewed there. One was that the town planners had not anticipated that there would be older adolescents remaining in Newtown, since they would all be off at college; when the subsidized housing appeared and not all adolescents went to college, there were no facilities for those who remained. The other reason we heard was that there had actually been teen centers, which, like the interfaith centers, were localized in each "village," but they became too troublesome and disruptive and were closed. Here again there were suggestions that this was at least coincident with, if not attributable to, the emergence of the subsidized housing.

In homogeneous Sheffield, however, where extracurricular community and school activities for young people abound, competition abounds too. Most parents in Sheffield would insist that the competition instills confidence as well as competence. But it can also lead to atomization. The price paid for the competition is reflected in the guarded selection of just a few close friends and the loneliness which individual adolescents spoke of in interviews. One student in the high school, for example, described what he discovered to be the clear rewards of conforming. He also illustrated how students as well as parents and teachers come to accept and in many cases value the importance of competing for good grades despite the frustration and anguish it can bring.

> I came here from a private school and at first I was really disillusioned with the place. I thought it was going to be a lot more open than a private school and so I messed up the first few years. I got into the high school thing really well at first, real rah-rah, went to the pep rallies, did the whole routine, but nobody paid much attention to me. Nobody said, "Hi, friend, welcome to Sheffield." So I got hurt and mad and started to knock the place. In November of my sophomore year me and three "liberated" girls wrote a newpaper article for what was supposed to be the sophomore free press. We were really outrageous. We cut down some of the things the seniors were doing that year. We sort of cut down the school and, in a way, the people in it. Mind you, I was a sophomore, and you know how sophomores are. They aren't scared because they are still new to the school like the freshmen, but they haven't learned how to work the system yet either. So the repercussions were pretty bad. I guess I expected it from the grown-ups, but I wasn't prepared for what it would do for my reputation with the other kids because this was my first year here.
>
> This is a very cliquey high school. Word gets around very fast in a small town and a small school. Some people even called my parents and asked what the hell was wrong with them. So all of this was very bad and I had a bad image for about a year. Mostly it was the jocks who gave me a hard time, but the freaks didn't

exactly like me either even though they might agree with what we had said in the article. Who was this out-of-town jerk who was stirring up the place? Well, I'm a sort of passive guy, and when the kids would just sort of call me names I'd just say well, big deal, you know. I guess it did hurt, though, because my grades went down. Some of it was my fault, but I think maybe some of the teachers sort of had it in for me, too. This all lasted about a year.

In my junior year I started to get my head together and my marks started to go up. This is when kids started to take notice of me. When marks go up, kids psychologically say, "Hey, this kid is smart. If he's smart, he must be a good guy." I think they saw a difference in the way teachers acted toward me and maybe their parents eased off some, too. That's the way high school kids think.

Well, so like last year I got interested in a whole mess of things. My marks kept going up. I was just generally doing a good job. I am not a very sociable type of person. Like, I didn't party very much. But this year I just really started to get into it. So like my junior year was just getting used to the place after kids started accepting me. Don't misunderstand me: most of the jocks and lots of the freaks still don't trust me, but at least they admit that I'm alive. The thing is in high school, your junior year is a big year and everybody is scrambling because that's when the colleges look at you. So you have to pull really good marks. I would just study on the average for about three hours every day, about four hours on Sunday, which is pretty phenomenal for a high school kid, because usually high school kids spend about an hour and then close up the book. I don't mean anything conceited, but I was really busting my rear end. It paid off, I got straight A's. So hopefully I can go to a good college.

Not all of Sheffield's children buy into the structure of competition, but those who do sometimes become confused about the difference between doing well and trying to outdo others. This becomes particularly difficult for those who work for the tangible symbols that indicate that they are better than others only to find that not all of their peers accept athletic symbols as a sign of success or a measure of respect. Athletic prowess, for example, considered an important symbol of success by "jocks" in Sheffield and in other suburban communities, is not as valued by many of the students if it is not combined with academic success. In an interview with an athlete who was a team captain, I heard about some of the frustration he felt despite his considerable popularity as one of the leading jocks:

> I found in the high school (this is my fourth year) how the varsity jacket used to be a status symbol. It used to be a big thing, you know. And you know, the idea that in college, even in high school, the big football player gets all the recognition, all the girls. I'm on the football team and there are a lot of students who look up to me, but there are all kinds of kids who don't want to know me. I wear the varsity jacket a lot more downtown, where adults will wave to me and ask me how I'm doing, than I do in school, where it's no big deal like it used to be.

There is still another price exacted by the emphasis on competition, and that is a feeling on the part of many of the students I interviewed of not being "on track": not working toward some goal. The socioeconomic status of the parents means that work in the sense of paid employment and the consequent notion of unemployment are alien to youth in this community. Many of the kids have "chores" to do, but invariably we were told that homework comes first. Since schoolwork is the real "employment" of most youngsters here, anything which interferes with it, even those rare occasions when the teachers do not assign any homework, produces the same emotional tone as being unemployed. Parents will frequently ask for more homework at earlier grades for their children. The students themselves appear to expect and accept homework as long as they can see it as related to some evaluation and to progress. A number of students said they thought there would be fewer complaints about the amount of homework if they were sure that when it was assigned it would be collected, and when it was collected it would be graded, and when it was graded it would be returned.

The school's conception of discipline, supported by parents who, as with homework, often demand more than the school assigns, is also tied into the competitive drive toward the future. We heard a number of stories about this in the teachers' lounge at the high school:

> Everybody agreed that Mr. Wright was a very popular math teacher, but parents began to say that he was popular because he didn't give a lot of homework and was lax about discipline in his classes. There was one case where a junior didn't do well on his math

S.A.T.'s even after he took them a second time, and his mother came to school and showed the principal all of his math homework, all with A's and even some A-pluses. She demanded to see the grades of other students who had done better on their math S.A.T.'s, but, of course, the principal said he couldn't do that. You know, she contacted every parent she could find whose kids had been in her son's math class and then came in and said, "He gave *everybody* A's and A-pluses; he has no discrimination!"

We had our "battle of the books" just like a lot of other school systems did but ours was different; nobody complained that we should remove books because they were dirty or irreligious; we were told that some of the things that children were being asked to read just were not challenging enough.

I was opposed to all of this parental pressure when I first came to teach in Sheffield because I thought that it was directed against the teachers. It really isn't. If I have to discipline a student, one of the best ways to do it is to call his or her parents and say, "Look, I'm having trouble with little so-and-so; could you help us?" They almost always agree to and ask what they can do. I don't know what happens at home after my call, but there are at least a few days when I see a very chastened and conforming child. I have to admit, I sometimes now just threaten to call home and that seems to work, too.

Parents, too, reported that they expected the schools to give the maximum amount of homework and to impose firm rules in what they considered the best interests of their children:

When Mrs. Clearwater was asked how she felt about ability grouping she said that she was all for it but that she couldn't understand why there were so few ability groupings in math because she knew that her son was capable of doing better work if he was just challenged more. She said that she had spoken to her son's teacher and she had been told that the reason was there just aren't enough different ability level textbooks for them to use, but they are hoping to move in that direction in the next few years. "The problem, of course, is that my son can't wait a few years, so I have arranged for a special tutor in math for him."

The superintendent said that parents complain about what they consider "classroom disruption" but what is sometimes just teenage exuberance. He mentioned one incident in which some students had sneaked into a library room during the spring break and turned all of the books upside-down. He got a number of calls from parents asking if he was going to prosecute, and he replied that it didn't seem to be that serious and how would the caller like it if it turned out to be one of their children. "You might be surprised to know how many of them said that they would still want to see the culprits punished."

And this was sometimes true of the students themselves. Whenever we asked about rules, there seemed to be general agreement that the rules should be tougher, particularly about things like no smoking. Some students spoke especially about the fact that despite the ban on smoking, the bathrooms were often used as smoking areas and this made them smell. One student said that there was a clump of trees outside the school where some seniors went to smoke and that one of the assistant principals would periodically go out and walk around the clump and sniff the air. If it was tobacco smoke he smelled it was O.K., but if it was marijuana he would charge in and try to grab whomever he could. "What's the use of having rules," this student said, "if they are not enforced?"

Student discipline has always been a significant concern for parents nationwide, and year after year parents reply to questions in polls about what is wrong with America's schools by citing discipline as the major problem. During the early stages of our study of adolescents, some of us also began looking at schools in different parts of the country as part of a national study on school crime and violence. That research, which came to be known as the Safe Schools Study, resulted from national, and particularly congressional, concerns with activities taking place in schools ranging from disciplinary problems through disruptions to actual serious crimes.[13] One of the things we discovered was that the ability of the principal and the staff was of considerable importance in setting up an environment where learning as well as social development could proceed in order rather than chaos. In every successful school we examined, we found that "a structure of order which represents the enactment of the governance system was described as 'fair, firm, and most of all consistent.' "[14]

Every school we have studied since that time reaffirms this finding that a sense of social order is necessary for both cognitive and behavioral development for youngsters. Sheffield's approach to it, however, may seem a little too regimented. In the middle school cafeteria we observed that students waited in an orderly line for lunch, picked up their food quietly, and after lunch waited for dismissal until a teacher blew a whistle. When the whistle blew, the students stood behind their chairs waiting to be excused until the teacher had checked the tables to see that chairs were replaced correctly. This disciplining process begins in kindergarten and extends into the academic programs of the middle school, where students march from class to class with virtually no noise. After school they wait outside with just a little more childish exuberance for some mother (usually their own but sometimes another, who is the car-pool driver that day) to pick them up, ask them what they did in school, and take them home to start on homework.

While this may sound like "all work and no play," life in Sheffield is as pleasant for most of the adolescents we interviewed as it is predictable. It is that predictability, in fact, which makes growing up there a smooth if sometimes stressful process. Even the stresses are predictable and to some extent manageable, since they represent what is a common set of values about competition and achievement and consistent pressure from the community to excel. Unlike Southside, where the future orientation of the home and the school are often at odds because they literally—sometimes—can't understand each other, the social environments in Sheffield speak the same language of progress through school and into careers. This congruence and continuity did not, of course, assure security or success for all of the youngsters we observed and interviewed in Sheffield. One type of discontinuity seemed to be particularly troublesome for many teenagers in Sheffield, and in all of the other communities as well.

Across the country we found that school transitions are often traumatic for adolescents, as has already been shown in Bruce's description of his problems adjusting to a new school as well as new peer expectations. The movement from the elementary to the secondary school, which usually takes place in the seventh grade, is particularly difficult for many youngsters.[15] We came to call it "the problem of the seventh grade." It usually signals an abrupt change from the child-centered, self-contained classroom, in which there is one teacher (just as there is one mother at home), to the subject-centered, less intimate secondary school, where the student must move from class to class and teacher to teacher after a short session with the "homeroom" teacher.[16] It also usually means leaving the neighborhood school and the close associations with the home and the family there, and for many young-sters it is the first time they come into sustained contact with culturally different peers. Some youngsters in Green Valley, where virtually all of the students are bused into the secondary school from a variety of communities, said that they were afraid of getting lost, of being lonely and alone in a strange place where no one knew them. As the seventh graders move from class to class they must also fit into a changing and often different group of peers. In the Safe Schools Study the seventh grade turned out to be the place where teachers, parents, and students themselves saw and reported the greatest problems of adjustment and the most disruption.[17] Some researchers and clini-cians believe that changing from one school to another is one of the factors associated with the sense of loss which characterizes some teenage suicides.[18]

The anonymity of large schools makes school transitions particularly difficult for new students.[19] But we found that, paradoxically, South-side's characteristic ethnic diversity seems to ease that problem some-what. Despite the size of the high school there, students seem to experience less stress from such transitions, probably because of their familiarity with diversity. The ethnic sorting pattern also allows them to identify fairly quickly with others similar to themselves. Yet, while the presence of peer figures with whom one can identify may make the transitional process more certain and so less traumatic, it perpetuates the self-concept problems which sorting imposes. Sometimes, how-ever, sorting can provide positive avenues for developing self-esteem, particularly where they are reinforced by families.

Most of the teachers and educators we met gave us examples of how important the family can be in shaping a child's effective learning environment, even in those places where the community at large does not profess high hopes for the education of their children. We found a number of such families among blacks and Hispanics in Southside, but it was among the Chinese—as we heard from teachers, social workers, and others—that this family influence was most visible and effective.

An illuminating example is the story of Amy Chang, a recent immi-grant to the United States from Hong Kong. She lives with her parents, three brothers, and two sisters on the edge of the Chinatown section, which is about twelve blocks from the school. Her parents both work long hours at low-paying factory jobs in Chinatown, and Amy works at the same factory after school and on weekends. The six-story tene-

ment building in which she lives has, like Southside itself, seen changing migrations of immigrants. The building is in the section of
Chinatown which was once settled by Jewish families but which
changed quickly following the fivefold expansion of Chinese in the
area in the late 1960s and early 1970s. All of the families in the
building are from Hong Kong and they maintain a close association
with each other, differentiating themselves from the Taiwanese and
mainland Chinese, whom they often call "Bamboo Heads," establishing a sense of social distance. Hong Kong, they will tell you, is
much more urbanized than the mainland and so they are more cosmopolitan. But they are still poor and struggling, and Amy's parents see
America as a land of promise for their children but not really for
them.

Amy, who has adopted an American name but whose name is
actually Mai Ling, and her brothers and sisters are bilingual, but
their parents are not. Amy says that there is no need for them to
learn English, since everyone they work with and the few relatives
and friends with whom they socialize—on those rare occasions when
there is time for it—also speak only Chinese. Amy had some language
difficulties herself, but she has been doing very well in school, and
after only one year she passed out of the English as a Second Language
sequence into the regular English classes. Teachers commented on
how well she participates in class, her diligence with schoolwork,
and her "positive attitude," and would sometimes contrast her attitude
and behavior with those of most black and Hispanic students.

What makes Amy so special? It's not just Amy, the teachers replied;
it's the Chinese students and even more so the families they come
from that provide "a positive learning environment." The teachers
would make the almost inevitable comment that both the Chinese
students and their families are like the Jewish students and families
who used to be so plentiful in the school—both kinds of families
investing themselves in the education of their children. Then the examples would begin. The Chinese parent who came to see the principal
to complain that there was too much class discussion in his son's
advanced math course: "My son is here to learn from teachers, not
from other students who don't know any more than he does." How
did the principal respond? He was so pleased to have a parent come
in and say he respected what the school and his teachers were trying
to do that he thanked the father for his complaint. Again the comparison
with the Jews in a story by one of the older teachers, who remembered

the Jewish student coming to class one day without his reader because his father had fallen asleep trying to learn to read it late at night after his son had finished it. And then the comparisons go the other way, and the teachers compare the Hispanics and blacks with the Italians, who always believed that you should not educate your children beyond your own level or they would forget the family.

These differences in the educational values which various ethnic groups are said to have for their children may account for some of the perceived differences in their children's educational motivation and achievement. But as powerful as families can be, they need help from other social environments in reinforcing such values. In the case of the Chinese students in Southside, for example, the family is not the only—and in some cases not even the primary—source of educational values for children. I have already described the role of the community based and organized agencies, such as the Pak Hok and Chi Ku Tuk Chin associations in Chinatown, in setting values for youngsters there, particularly where "their parents are so busy working." The emphasis there is not on replacing the family, but on buttressing it.

Explaining why Chinese students in Southside seem to do so well in school begins with some in-school factors but inevitably reaches outside the school into the family and the Chinese community. One important factor is that administrators as well as teachers expect them to do well because, in the school's sorting system, Chinese students as a group are characterized as good students and high achievers. As a result, teachers hold them more accountable for both attitudes and efforts as well as performance and results in class, and they express surprise and even disappointment when some Chinese students do not live up to these expectations. Individual Hispanic or black students who show the same interests and abilities as are expected of the Chinese students are also favored by teachers but are considered to be different from most of their ethnic peers. When we had the opportunity to view Chinese students in classes with other ethnic and racial groups, as in Josie's math class, it was often the case that the teacher both engaged and obviously felt engaged by the Chinese students as a group more than any other.

As mentioned above, however, these in-school factors, important as they may be in the students' educational development, do not tell the whole story. The Chinese community is unique in Southside in its ability to develop a structured system of relationships among the school, the family, and the community which provide a supportive learning environment for its youngsters. Once again, there are individual students from other racial and ethnic groups for whom their families or some social agency provide this same facilitating environment, but in most cases these arrangements lack the collective power to influence the school's programs or to project educational attainment as a basis for self-esteem. Because the sorting system at the school tends to segregate students into classes and programs by race and ethnicity, the social bonding into peer groups which results among students reinforces the school's predictions: Chinese students, who are expected to do better, do so, and others, who are expected to do poorly, also live up to what is expected of them. Observations in other communities provided other evidence to support our proposition that communities and their families must collaborate with the schools not only in setting educational goals for youngsters, but in holding all students accountable for these goals, no matter how they are sorted socially.

When the academic sorting process reflects rather than intervenes in the racial or social class sorting system of the community, the school compounds and perpetuates whatever deficits students bring with them when they enroll. If the social organization of a school and its sorting standards serve as barriers rather than avenues to greater integration than community residential patterns allow, it is small wonder that some students will continue and even expand their neighborhood-based peer groups and establish their identities within them. Our observations in a middle school in another of our sites illustrate the effects on learning of sorting patterns which bring or keep together youngsters who reinforce each other's potential for disruption and indifference to the school's academic program.

RIVERTON

Riverton is a small, predominantly white, suburban city of about thirty-five thousand people. Located in the same Middle Atlantic state as Sheffield, about thirty miles eastward, it is the prosperous seat and commerical center of an adjacent county. While there are some well-to-do sections which have the same verdant and settled feeling as Sheffield, Riverton also has a large central shopping district as well as a number of sprawling shopping malls on its outskirts, high-rise office buildings to accommodate the county government offices, and a number of small factories and the lower-cost housing needed for their employees. Unlike Sheffield, most of the people who live in Riverton work there as well, but over 70 percent of them are renters rather than owners. Riverton also differs from Sheffield in that most of the people who work there don't live there, and the daily influx and exodus of the county government workers during the week and their absence on weekends highlights a feeling of transience. Although Riverton has been described as "more of a lively casserole than a melting pot," there is enough local perception of social class differences to lead a city official to observe, "One major problem is that the costs of community services are not borne equally by the people who use them."

Most of the whites who live in Riverton are from families which have been there for a long time, but it also has a more recently settled Italian community that emerged as a dominant local political force in the post–World War II period, and many of the teachers, school administrators, and other social service professionals are Italian-Americans. In recent decades Riverton has also experienced an influx of blacks, adding to a small but long-established black community, and a smaller influx of Hispanics, but their integration into the community has been quite different. One place where the difference is most observable is in Riverton's schools, which are considered by residents and nearby communities alike as among the best in the area. Not only the excellent academic program, but the strong and effective discipline, have always been a source of particular pride to the old-time residents.

Riverton's middle school, like the four elementary schools which feed it, is a two-story red brick colonial building in a park-like setting near the center of town. Despite its relaxed and comfortable appearance, the school has a strict, almost authoritarian social order, with constant supervision and control of students. The system of ability grouping, which literally sorts kids into different wings of the building for upper-level, on-level, or lower-level classes, also acts to limit peer association in an informal, unofficial, and perhaps even unconscious process of segregation. Teachers told us that there is virtually no trouble with discipline, nor are there any "problem groups" in the school. Visiting the school would seem to confirm this; everything is in place and in order. The hallways are immaculate; there are no graffiti; you could hear a pin drop if anybody dared to drop one. Yet, after we observed and interviewed students in classes and in the community, a somewhat different picture emerged. The casual observer does not see disenfranchised and disruptive cliques of students walking down the hallways of the school, but they are there.

In classroom and individual interviews the students told us about some of them. The Stickup Boys is a clique of about ten seventh and eighth grade black and Hispanic boys, all from the same neighborhood and all part of the same young adolescent network there. They don't actually carry out stickups, but their name is a leftover from the fact that they did at one time engage in thefts from other students. Nor are they violent, although we did hear that they were responsible for a food fight in the cafeteria. They described themselves as just a group of "fellas who got together to chill out whenever we could—nothing special." Except for two members who are in "on level" classes, all of the other members are in "below level" classes.

The Lords are a group of older students characterized as more like a gang than the Stickup Boys, and their membership includes black, Hispanic, and a few non-Hispanic white teenagers, all of whom had met as a result of being sorted into the lower track. They were described as being violent—"The Lords, well they break bones"— but back in their neighborhoods rather than in the school. What makes them different from the Stickup Boys? They had, we were told, already begun to drop out through cutting classes and skipping school. Some had already been in difficulties with the police and were in trouble in the community. There were also some female student cliques mentioned—the Earth Queens and the Foxy Force, for example—and also a number of what were called "crews," a seeming derivative from the break-dancing crews found in Southside and elsewhere. The Breakout Girls, for example, are a crew of about six eighth grade black girls from the same Riverton neighborhood who have developed a reputation for dancing as a group. They also smoke cigarettes together in the girls' bathroom and sometimes get involved in fights.

The invisibility of these disruptive students reflects what teachers and administrators themselves refer to as "dumping" or "warehousing" students who are not making the grade academically into largely custodial classes and then ignoring them unless they make trouble. This begins a cycle of failure and resentment leading to disruptive behavior and withdrawal from in-school activities and eventually the school itself. Peer groups such as the Stickup Boys begin their association in their neighborhoods, and the school's tracking and sorting systems reinforce those early associations. Once in the lower tracks, teenagers come into association with similarly disenfranchised peers and the result is the formation of more disruptive gangs such as the Lords. The formation of crews and cliques and eventually of gangs further concentrates these negative effects. Unless there are more positive bonds available at home or in the neighborhood, or they can be negotiated in the school or through some other community agency, peer groups become increasingly influential in their members' educational development.

When sorting systems sustain the circle of failure and lowered self-esteem in schools, they are doubly problematic, since they not only interfere with cognitive development, but hinder socialization and enculturation and have implications for the individual and for society which reach into adulthood. Piaget's dictum that "human intelligence develops in the individual in social interaction" is equally true of social knowledge and skills development.[20] While I earlier described peer groups as transitory in their existence, the development of disruptive groups like the ones in Riverton is a key example of how they can have lasting effects, because they mediate the influences of educating institutions, creating deficits which can last throughout the life course. Recent research confirms that social categorization can lead to identification with a particular group or grouping, even where there is no particular attraction among those sorted into the category, and can also influence how that group behaves or misbehaves.[21] Teenagers, particularly in the early years when they are becoming increasingly aware of peer-sanctioned as contrasted to family-sanctioned behavior, are fascinated by deviant behavior, especially in the absence of some positive valuation of conventional behavior.[22] The segregation of students, formally by ability group and informally by race, ethnicity, or social class, means that social impact and influence are similarly segregated.

It could be and has been argued that the school is simply responsive to those characteristics which students bring in with them from their families and communities. To accept this argument only maintains the school in a passive role, defaulting on its major responsibility for orienting students to the values of knowledge. It is also important for students to feel that teachers and administrators care about them as persons: showing that they have positive expectations of them and care how well they are doing. Many years ago Freud suggested that mature, self-sustaining love of knowledge can grow from an early and positive identification with teachers.[23] It can just as easily be stunted or exterminated by a real or imagined sense of rejection by them. While nearby Sheffield may be teaching its students to try to outdo others, the message to the negatively sorted group of students in Riverton may well be that no one thinks there is any real chance for them, so why try. When I conducted the classroom interviews in schools in the various communities and indicated to teachers that they could stay or leave, it was almost invariable that in lower-track classes the teacher would choose to leave, while in above-grade-level or gifted classes the teacher would remain, and sometimes became involved in the discussion as well.

The comparisons I have drawn among schools in Southside, Sheffield, and other sites are not really concerned with the merits or demerits of ability grouping or whether orderly schools are better than those with some degree of "creative chaos"—both being points which are still at issue in educational circles.[24] Rather, these comparisons are meant to show how the social sorting process in schools really begins in the community, and particularly in the relationship between the family and the school, before the student ever arrives. These glimpses of school life as we saw and heard them also reveal the self-categorization and self-definition which can result from channeling peer association in tracking. Both Amy's and Josie's experiences in Southside's high school are significantly affected by how they are sorted and how the ethnic category to which they are assigned, and with which they align themselves, is perceived. The possible selves Bruce enjoys in the sorting process which is driven by Sheffield's pressures for achievement are no less constrained by what is expected of him and no more conducive to seeking an "independent" identity. The school's role is too often one of reinforcing the community's sorting categories by formally or informally tracking or academically streaming students along these same dimensions. Families continue to be important in this process even after the school becomes the major institutional locus of adolescent development as well as the "responsible" agency *in loco parentis* for socialization and enculturation.[25]

Without overidealizing the family as the only social institution in town which relates to the school, it is important to consider how profound its effects can be on schooling, not only in terms of direct impact on the quality of the schools children attend, but on how the children make use of their academic opportunities. Just as family influence is still at work when the student is in school, the school's influence can also follow the student back into the home to inform a wide variety of attitudes and behaviors in areas such as health and citizenship as well as education. It is just as important to consider how schools can intervene in the educating environments of families to help prevent or reduce the risks of academic deficits as it is to develop programs to deal with them once they are identified in the school.

The very different educational exposure teenagers experience in Smyrna Beach, Ranchville, and Cypress City, despite the fact that all three communities are under the same county educational jurisdiction, argues against expecting that community differences can be adjusted by some centralized educational authority. Even in a community like Riverton, where many students do achieve academically, the deficits some students bring with them when they enter seem to resist the power or the will of the school to overcome them. Instead, formal and informal sorting processes perpetuate and exacerbate them, leading to continuing deficiencies in later life as a by-product of the cycle of lowered self-esteem, leading to further lowering of performance as well as expectations. The question would seem to be less one of how schools can remediate all of the social as well as cognitive learning problems of the community and more one of where and how the community can intervene in that cycle. One place to begin is in the critical relationship between the school and the family. It is necessary to reconsider the range and power of the social and cultural as well as cognitive characteristics which students bring into the schools. Communities need to frame some new questions about the role of the family, and eventually of other institutional sectors, in working with schools to implement realistic, achievable educational programs which maximize strengths as well as remediate weaknesses in order to allow students some feeling of success. Teenagers then could and should be accountable at home and in other community settings, as well as in school, for learning efforts and results. Some recent work by two educational psychologists points to a way it might be done by beginning with the school-home connection.

Reviewing the great bulk of educational research on student achievement, Herbert Walberg found agreement on three sets of factors which can be optimized to increase affective, behavioral, and cognitive learning.[26] Two familiar sets of factors are (1) *student aptitude,* which includes ability or prior achievement, development, and motivation;

and (2) *instructional factors,* which include the amount of time students engage in learning and the quality of the instructional experience. While these factors are unquestionably of major importance in learning, they are really only partly alterable by educators and so do not offer the optimal vantage points for educational reform. The third set of factors is *environmental:* (1) enduring affection and stimulation from adults in the home; (2) the psychological climate of the classroom social group; (3) the out-of-school peer group and its learning interests, goals, and activities; and (4) the use of out-of-school time, particularly the amount of leisure-time television watching. These environmental factors seem somewhat more susceptible to directed change or alteration, and so "hold the best hope for increasing educational productivity."[27] Also focusing on the home environment, Benjamin Bloom suggests five elements which he and his students have found to be significantly related to the school achievement of children: (1) the work habits of the family, which are characterized by greater or lesser routine and regularity and by higher or lower priority given to schoolwork; (2) academic guidance and support, or the availability and quality of help, support, and home and community conditions to support the child's schoolwork; (3) stimulation in the home, i.e., the opportunity to explore ideas, events, and the larger environment; (4) opportunities in the home to develop correct and effective language use; and (5) the parents' academic aspirations and standards for the child and indications of their interest in the child's school experiences. Bloom advocates parent education through regularly scheduled meetings between school and family as a medium for improving student achievement, indicating that "the payoff here is likely to be very great."[28]

Some of what both Walberg and Bloom suggest, such as school intervention in "the alterable curriculum of the home," which studies have shown to be twice as predictive of academic learning as family socioeconomic status, will take major changes in communities and so more time.[29] Other prescriptions, such as supervised and graded homework, which seems to have a major effect on achievement in schools where it is required, and has three times the power of socioeconomic status in influencing achievement, are easily followed and the benefits can be immediate. Bloom also points out that while we are rightly concerned about the negative influences which peers can have on attitudes toward schooling, academic expectations and behavior, and so achievement, we ought to also consider that this means they can have a positive effect as well. He proposes, therefore, that schools develop student peer support systems in which small groups of two or three students help each other with review activities.

There are some programs already in place which are making a difference. Some are school-based and rely on the ability of the school to overcome the pre-sorting which students bring with them from the community. Among the most promising are the cooperative learning programs beginning to appear in urban classrooms.[30] Cooperative learning teams of four to five students, mixed by race or ethnicity, gender, and achievement level, work together, discuss assignments and problems, and quiz and evaluate each other in what is intended to become a close-knit support group. Rewards are also shared, and each team is evaluated on the basis of how much each member improves. The message here is one of sharing, and of each student's demonstrated achievement increasing the success of the group.

There are a number of variations of cooperative learning programs designed to be used in different subject areas and using different modes of cooperation, but all stem from the same research-based conclusion: Competition in schools is often damaging to interpersonal relations and to the development of internalized achievement goals because of its emphasis on trying to do better than others, and, in addition, students actually learn better when they cooperate.[31] While the demonstrated increases in academic achievement produced in cooperative learning programs for able as well as less able students are sufficient to recommend consideration of such programs, their negotiated peer groups which seek to mix rather than sort students provide other advantages as well. Research and evaluation studies demonstrate that with few exceptions, students in these programs are more likely than those in conventional classes to name students of other races as best or close friends and to have more cross-race interactions outside as well as inside the classroom.[32] There are also well-documented increases in self-esteem and self-confidence among students in cooperative learning programs.[33]

There are other approaches which, particularly in light of the shrinking of the extended family and the deterioration of the idealized model of the nuclear family, see the school as providing the missing sense of community that is essential for the transition to a productive adulthood. James Coleman and Thomas Hoffer, for example, attribute the greater growth of student academic achievement demonstrated by independent and Catholic schools, compared with public schools, to their ability to provide a better sense of community, perhaps because of shared values or religious association.[34] The public schools we saw were locked into the problems which beset their communities. Schools already offer an astounding number of programs aimed at youth problems such as teen pregnancy, drug and alcohol abuse, dropping out, and AIDS. The programs are often supported by federal or other outside funds and staffed with a variety of social service professionals, and yet they seem to be as ambiguous and controversial as are the problems they hope to resolve. In many cases the programs we knew about were uncoordinated, sometimes competitive for attention and time as well as staff and funds, and took narrowly particularistic approaches to what were often holistic, multiple-risk problems among teenagers. And, from what we saw in many classrooms, particularly in urban areas, they sometimes increased rather than mitigated the complexity of family, criminal justice, work program, and health problems—along with the more standard teenage attendance, behavioral, and counseling problems—by intruding on class time.[35]

The differences I have described in the educational lives of teenagers in Southside, Sheffield, and Riverton neither begin nor end in the schools themselves. Some differences are the result of individual differences in students' abilities, varying patterns of parental concern for their children and their education, or even chance encounters with a caring and stimulating teacher or counselor. In large measure, however, they are the result of how coordinated or divided the community's major learning centers—the family, the school, and the peer group—are in proposing a learning environment for teenagers in which each is held accountable to a common set of educational goals. But other social realities become part of this equation as well. While demographic, economic, and social changes have dramatically altered the shape of the family which prepares the students for the school, the same forces have just as dramatically transformed the workplace for which the school is supposed to prepare them. These changes have also affected the interactions among family, school, and peer groups in setting the occupational futures of youth.

5

After School:
Youth In and Out
of the Labor Market

For most of the twentieth century the defining value of education as the major avenue for social and economic advancement through occupational mobility led ever-increasing numbers of young Americans to seek education at all levels. While we expect schools to prepare youngsters for all of the social competencies as well as skills of adulthood, we judge schools' performance most critically by how well we think they are preparing youngsters for the world of work. We expect high schools, for example, to prepare youth for socially and politically literate as well as healthy lives. But the ultimate test of the high school's success is how well it prepares teenage students for employment either directly in the labor market or for the postsecondary schooling which leads to the first rungs of the higher status career ladders. National and local community economic trends as well as social conditions, however, have made the job of preparing adolescents for economic self-sufficiency as adults more difficult as well as more complex.

Concern over the relationship between work and schooling is evident in the ever-increasing emphasis on career development, from the "back to basics" or the "instructionally effective school" movements in elementary and secondary education through career-oriented college and graduate school programs. One reason for the tremendous growth and expansion of the two-year technical and community college in the 1960s and 1970s was the transformation of the occupational structure in which technical, service, and managerial jobs increased while other forms of skilled work decreased. This extension of the period of schooling has also had the effect of further extending adolescence as well as creating the new "youth" age category during its later stages. Sociologist Burton Clark, writing in the 1960s, described this educational expansion as directly related to the loss of employment opportunities and labeled this latent function of the educational system as a "cooling out" function.[1]

The conventional explanation of the movement of youth populations from early employment to extended education which we heard from professionals in every community associates the shift with changes in the level of skills needed for employability and the consequent need for longer periods of education. In this view, the school serves to prepare youngsters for a more productive and rewarding life in a more complex world of work. The argument here is that expanding technology demands greater literacy among employees and so more schooling. There are, however, some rather clear indications that the displacement of children and adolescents from the labor market actually began in the early part of the century and was largely in response to the availability of immigrant labor. Compulsory-education laws, say the proponents of this view, were enacted and enforced as much to supervise or simply "warehouse" displaced adolescents as to fill a need for extended training.[2]

Whichever view is right—and probably both are—the development of minimum wage and age limitations during the 1930s and 1940s, along with the growth of the trade union movement, further restricted youth from competing with adult workers, albeit for the manifest purpose of producing a more literate work force. High rates of teenage and youth unemployment have been a persistent feature of the American economy since that time. But the effects of youth unemployment in other institutional arenas such as crime, welfare, and family life created a new urgency in the late 1950s and beyond. Changes in the economy and the job market also became reflected in the family life of adolescents as well as in their schooling—and, as I heard in many of the interviews with younger as well as older teenagers, in their fantasies and future orientation as well. Poor employment and career prospects, particularly among minority youth, project a bleak future for many, and the quality of adolescent life is affected by these concerns. The adult world we project as the indication of a successful adolescent transition is an adult world of work.

Most of the young adults we met in the various communities made the passage successfully and without serious incident, and both the family and the school shared credit for the smooth journey. Most of those who did not succeed were in communities where the family and the community did not provide positive models or attitudes toward work and its meaning in adult life, and where academic programs in the schools precluded either successful school performance or any hope for career development. Far from sharing in insuring a successful and relatively painless transition, school and community were frequently in conflict over who had failed most along with the youth.

How well schools prepare students for the world of work was evaluated very differently by the parents and other adults in various types of communities, and, not surprisingly, the parents' assessment was based on how well they thought the schools were working for their children. Parents in Sheffield and Newtown were generally quite pleased with the schools—indeed, the quality of the schools was one of the major reasons why they moved there. When they did complain, it was that there should be even more emphasis on math and reading skills in preparation for college entrance examinations and career paths, and more discipline of the spirit as well as the mind toward the same end. Not only parents but most of the teachers and administrators in the schools agreed with this future orientation, as did potential employers. The result was that Sheffield's and Newtown's youth could envision their adult career roles in this well-articulated and frequently reinforced developmental path which began in the first days of schooling and projected a believable as well as promising future. A similar but less elaborated course was available to those children of skilled blue-collar workers in places like Riverton, or the children of the more prosperous farmers in Green Valley, who could see their future in high-paying skilled jobs similar to those of their parents. Here, however, while parents, teachers, and even employers extolled the importance of basic verbal and mathematical skills for advancement, the youth we interviewed did not agree. They would assent to the need to read, write, and do simply arithmetic but usually argued that job skills and vocational training, not the cognitive skills the school valued, was what would be most important as they sought the job and economic security which combined with a happy marriage to define the good life for them.

In Southside, faced with virtually no job security in the present or much occupational promise for the future, parents, students, even most teachers, saw little fit between academic school programs and the minimal basic literacy demands of the dead-end jobs (and alternating periods of low-paying employment and unemployment) many of the students will drop out of school to seek. Debating whether students flounder academically because of poor motivation and modeling in the home or irrelevance of the school program is futile and does little more than add more tension and distrust to the home–school relationship. As in other urban inner-city areas we studied, it is the most economically depressed populations that provide home environments and models for Southside's youngsters. There is little if any access to opportunities for advancement for adults as well as teenagers. Some of the worst schools in the city are also to be found here, as well as the highest rates of both crime and victimization. Although any one of these problems can produce difficulties for teenagers, they can interact to create a catastrophe.

It is not much more helpful to debate—as human capital versus segmented labor market theory economists have in recent decades— whether it is the lack of qualifying characteristics of the teenager or the decline of opportunity in the labor market which explains why so many of these youth will end up periodically or even permanently unemployed.[3] Both work against Southside's teenagers. They participate in school less because the unskilled manual labor toward which they see themselves headed requires less education. Many high school students in Southside and in other urban inner-city areas told us that peers who drop out of school in their community often have a higher income in the same low-level jobs than recent high school graduates as a result of more time and experience on the job. This fact of working life, by the way, was not unknown among dropouts and potential dropouts we interviewed. A number of them pointed this out from personal experience. But teenagers are also active participants in their own lives, and so in their own fates as well. Their life-style characteristics, appearance, even language, which develop out of what they pick up at home or in street learning from peers, are not those that most employers are looking for, except in those low-level jobs were image doesn't count. The separation of home and workplace has not significantly reduced the major role of the family in orienting children and adolescents to the meaning of work in the life course. The extension of the transition process in the service of more educational preparation for more demanding jobs has made the school liable along with the family for preparing youth for the workplace.

Just as it would be wrong to assume that most teenagers, even in places like Southside, will not somehow make it, it would be a mistake to assume that families and schools fail them out of malice or even indifference. Most of the parents of these youth we interviewed did not devalue education; in fact, many clung to some hope that it could save their children from the fate to which their own lack of education had helped condemn them. This was particularly striking among the Chinese, but we found numbers of parents in other ethnic and racial groups who spoke with obvious feeling about the importance of schooling for self-improvement as well as finding and keeping a job. Many, however, argued that the schools in their community were both unwilling to listen to their demands for a better education for their children and to consider these students as candidates for graduation to a better future. One Hispanic parent, for example, complained that teachers didn't want to be in Southside because "they all want better jobs in other parts of the city . . . my daughter had four different teachers in the second grade." We heard many similar stories from parents who saw education—but not that provided by the schools in their community—as the best and perhaps only way their children could latch onto the American Dream.

Most of the teachers and administrators we met in Southside were not antagonistic to the community; in fact, most of them were teachers there because they chose to be there. What they did complain about was that what little parental involvement there was always came as demands and as challenges to their professional judgment, not requests for help or advice. Teachers and administrators also complained about those same behavioral and life-style characteristics which make Southside's youngsters less attractive to employers, but would usually and indulgently add "Kids will be kids, right?" Once again, it is the quality and character of the relationships among the family, the school, and teenagers themselves as members of particular families and peer groups, not just the failure of any one component, which creates and perpetuates the especially difficult conflicts of inner-city adolescence. In Sheffield and Newtown, family and school agree on both the form and the future of the home-to-school-to-workplace transition, and teenagers there compete to see who can negotiate it best.

In Southside there is little such agreement. Most Southside teenagers are not college-bound and will leave high school with or without a diploma searching for jobs which just are not there. Changes in the labor market as well as high rates of unemployment have made steady, high-paying jobs which do not require some advanced training less readily available and more competitive, particularly for the last-hired-and-first-fired minority youth of Southside. Academic programs in most high schools, and again particularly those in places like Southside, simply are not able to provide the training for entry into these career areas. What are left for these youth are lower-paying, unsteady, often part-time jobs in service or retail areas, and even these are not always available. Urban inner-city parents as well as most of the teenagers themselves see this as a failure of the schools to understand or respond to their needs "because the teachers and the bureaucrats have good jobs and and so will their kids someday." Inevitably, and often unjustifiably, the school comes to be perceived as less than irrelevant—as the local representative of an indifferent and uncaring establishment, which, by failing to do its job, keeps local youth from finding theirs. The resultant dissonance and conflict between home and school combine to make certain that the workplace end of the continuum remains barely above the survival level. It also models a pattern of hostility and conflict toward the school for youth and the peer groups they form. Unlike suburban youth, who compete in school to see who can do best in the transition to careers, Southside youth feel cut out of the competition, and continued schooling becomes a conflict, with their choice being whether to complete the course or drop out of the school and contend as best they can in the marketplace for jobs. More than dropping out of school, they are dropping out of the American Dream of a good, steady job and the family life it can support.

In every community we found some variant of the adult judgment that if adolescents are not in school learning, they must be doing something productive ("working") or they will get into trouble. The details of this principle differ considerably as a result of socioeconomic and demographic variables, but it is present in every community we studied. The widespread and deep belief in this principle helps to explain why there is such widespread concern about what has come to be called the "dropout problem" among modern youth. Ever since the mid-1960s the national rate of leaving school prior to high school graduation has been stuck at about 25 percent.[4] Its recent reemergence as a major problem for adolescence is due to its association with other adolescent social issues such as delinquency, teen pregnancy, and particularly youth unemployment. As a result, it is surrounded by the same confusion and competition among institutional sectors as these other problems.

Almost every state and every educational jurisdiction within these states has its own definition of what constitutes dropping out of school. In various school districts throughout the country, the following circumstances may or may not get a student recorded as a dropout: leaving school to marry, to have a baby, to take a job, to enter the armed services; early college placement prior to graduation; leaving one school or one school district for another; participating in special educational, business, or vocational programs outside the school; being expelled or going to jail—and even dying. The problem of defining who are the dropouts is further complicated by the lack of common agreement even among educators and other professionals as to what constitutes dropping out and who drops out under what circumstances.

Our experience with dropouts seemed to mirror the national statistics; we saw many more in places like Southside than we did in suburban areas, but we also found high rates in rural areas, and particularly in depressed areas like Ranchville. However, we found some dropouts in each of the communities.[5] In the mid-1980s we also did a more focused study of dropouts in a medium-sized city near Seminole County, where the school system and the community felt that the problem was a major one among its minority students. In that research, using a technique we had developed earlier to study adolescent drug abuse, we trained a group of high school students to locate and interview their peers who had been identified as "dropouts" in their school records during the previous two years.[6]

There is an extensive literature on dropouts which indicts a number of contributory aspects of the adolescent's life and life-style both in and out of school. Some studies find the problems to be inherent in the youngsters themselves: some physical or intellectual impairment, some problem in the developmental self-image, low self-esteem, a sense of powerlessness, poor motivation, and a sense of isolation, or anomie.[7] Other studies point to societal factors such as poverty, racial discrimination, and the diminishing of both parental and institutional social controls as the result of a permissive attitude toward children.[8] And a third set of factors often cited are the lack of congruence between the school and the world of work, poor school performance, association with delinquent or non-school-oriented peers, and other school-related circumstances.[9]

In our experience dropouts were most likely to be individuals who suffered multiple deficits spanning each and often all of these predisposing or precipitating factors. Many came from families where the parents had not completed high school and had low employment security and job status, creating a home environment lacking both the experience and the means to encourage the seeking of educational or occupational success. We also met other young people in the same community who came from similar backgrounds and did not drop out. What usually distinguished the dropout was that he was also having trouble in his social and emotional life as well as in school. Many were also from multi-risk families with a history of stress, unable to cope with the social, emotional, and economic problems which were part of their daily lives. And many had been in conflict with teachers as well as parents for much of their time in school. There was rarely a specific, spontaneous "decision" to drop out, but rather a clearly identifiable pattern of relationships and behaviors which reflected a lack of any supportive social bonds in the dropout's life—a pattern which we traced back through school records to early elementary school. Many dropouts came from homes from which parents were absent or where they showed little involvement in the educational or social lives of their children. Most of the dropouts denied that there was any "peer pressure" and insisted that they had talked to no one—not parents, not teachers, not friends—about what they intended to do. In fact, most reported that they felt alone and helpless in facing any number of stresses and "had no one to turn to for help."

We so often heard teachers in so many communities comment "We have known since the second grade" that a particular student would eventually drop out that we decided to look at the elementary school records of the recent middle and high school dropouts to see if there were, in fact, some early warnings. The teachers were right, and whether it was because of early labeling or some predisposition, the youngsters who will eventually drop out before graduation from high school show a progressive and cumulative pattern of school failure and behavioral problems which lead to early leaving. First, the individual loses, or in some cases never acquires, any interest in schoolwork; the consequence is lowered grades and the further result is retention in grade. Frustrated and now "left behind" her neighborhood and school peers, the student begins to skip class and soon comes into conflict with the school authorities. Defensive and angry, she rebels and begins to exhibit disruptive behavior against peers as well as in the classroom. Increasingly, teacher comments and even counseling or psychological reports show that the student becomes withdrawn and feels hopeless, powerless, and isolated; or, in the case of early adolescent females, seeks out an intimate affiliation (which often leads to pregnancy) as an escape from the loneliness felt at home and in school.

The reports also indicate that many of the dropouts were referred to special services or programs because of suspected special education needs or behavior problems in the classroom. Even in the early grades there were frequent indications of requests by teachers for a family conference and in many cases a further indication that the conference never took place. The high percentage of special education students in the dropout population—we found 23 percent in our study of the school records—was also one of the issues raised by some dropouts, as well as our student interviewers, when they asked how realistic it was to assume or assert the educability of all of the dropout population, at least in the regular public school programs. Teachers and counselors also frequently maintained that the lowered cognitive achievement and skills of special education students leads to low grades and frequent grade retention, so that their chances of academic success are restricted. There were similar questions raised about disruptive students, who not only refuse to try to learn but keep others from learning. Special intervention programs are essential for these at-risk youngsters, but it is important to be sure that we target the problems for special resources rather than simply identify the youngsters by labeling and pre-sorting them.

From our review of the school records and what we learned from teachers and counselors, difficulty in acquiring basic skills (leading to an escalating need to play catch-up or to giving up), frequent absences or lateness, early retention in grade, and developing disruptive and antisocial behaviors are, individually and in concert, the most imporant early warning signals. If teachers and counselors or parents can recognize potential dropouts, and provide (1) appropriate treatment programs for those who need psychological or social service help, (2) educational and developmental experiences which they cannot get at home, and (3) some measure of academic success and healthy development of self-confidence, this should prove the basis for an effective preventive program for those youngsters who can benefit from such identification and treatment. Early identification, as important as it is, however, will not solve some of the problems of the complex relationships among family, peers, school, and the workplace which contribute to the long-term persistence of the early school-leaving problem.

One of the most frequent reasons we heard to explain why someone

had dropped out—possibly because it is the most socially accepted—
was the need to find a job to help support the family or the individual.
Paradoxically, the ready availability of low-level, service-sector jobs
in many communities provides ample opportunity for short-term success in finding a job. The immediate gratification of a job which
provides some status in the family as well as some income offers an
attractive but future-limiting escape; for a young woman there is the
added possibility of pregnancy as an avenue out of emotional deprivation as well as school. The price, of course, is that even if schooling
does not relate directly to job skills, education is necessary for developing careers. Dropping out of school also means dropping out of much
else in the developmental growth patterns of adolescence. Peer associations change, as do the attitudes toward the dropout and his associates
by parents and siblings, former friends who remain in school, neighbors, and other adults such as potential employers and the police.
The dropout is viewed, and as a result often comes to view himself,
as being in an arrested developmental role, not only because schooling
is so integral in adolescent growth and development, but because
dropping out so often signals that the family, the school, and the
community, as well as the student, have given up. Many teachers
and school administrators we talked to, black as well as white, tended
to see these children as losers, the offspring of what one teacher
called "families left behind when the civil rights movement finally
brought some hope and advancement to black people." The black
wards in the city which we studied had once been the segregated
home of middle-class as well as lower-income black families. The
fortuitous and welcome mobility of the black middle class meant
that their children went to other schools in the city as their parents
moved up and out. The families who remained behind were the poorest,
least educated, and most socially disrupted families. Even those few
middle-class parents who remained in the area had long since removed
their children from neighborhood schools to send them elsewhere.
Not only were there few if any indigenous role models and mentors
available in the community, but the ability and aspiration levels of
those students who remained in the local schools provided a peer
group pool characterized by low ability and aspirations.

Another reason for dropping out often given was that school was
not helping with what was needed to get on in the world; the dropout
wanted to get practical experience elsewhere. Sometimes the dropout
didn't feel capable of doing the schoolwork. In other cases some

change in the family's or in the individual's life made it necessary or desirable to leave even though the student wanted to continue. And in many cases, particularly among males, they said they just did not like school or particular teachers. Discomfort or dissatisfaction in school, however, was most frequently explained as a lack of any perceived relationship between the educational programs the students were receiving and what they had seen as the work experience of their families and neighbors. One question raised by employers, as well as by students who had dropped out to find jobs, was why dropping out of school to go to work is considered an indication of personal failure since that is what school is supposed to prepare you for anyway. Indicating to potential dropouts that income levels are correlated with years of school completed and that dropouts' lifetime earnings are about one-third less than the earnings of those who complete high school is another long-term promise which was difficult for many of the youngsters we spoke with to accept. Both male and female dropouts indicated that they felt very little of what they learned in school was helpful or even applicable in their present jobs. One frequent complaint was that what was learned at school might "help you be a teacher or somebody who works with his head" but didn't help you learn how to work with your hands or with people.[10] Another was that a student who completed high school often would only find the same type of low-paying sales or service-sector job as a classmate who had dropped out in the tenth grade. To make matters worse, the dropout might end up as the graduate's supervisor, since she now would have two years of on-the-job seniority. Parents often had the same evaluation of the school's programs, and cited their own experience as evidence. When we examined the types of jobs which they held, primarily in service and laboring sectors of the local economy, their statements appeared realistic, particularly since the employers also complained to us, sometimes with the young workers present, that what they had learned in school was of little help on the job.

Schools in places like Sheffield and Newtown can project visions of what career futures will be like and show how what students learn in the academic curriculum can prepare them for further education in that direction. It is much more difficult to show how these same curricula can empower those going into the immediate job market to find or keep those jobs. Both male and female dropouts expressed a strong preference for vocational training programs. When we pressed for some idea of why existing occupational and vocational programs and schools were not being utilized by this group, they replied that they were "too far away from where I live" or "gave preference to veterans" or "don't have the programs I want." Very few individuals expressed any regret about leaving school. It may well be that since we were interviewing recent dropouts, the full implications of their having withdrawn from school had not had sufficient time to emerge, but at this point in their lives they found little reason for wanting to return to school. One question, of course, is whether the low achievement levels and deficient social and family backgrounds which led them to drop out of school would not also be deficits on the job whether or not they completed high school. It may even be that social maturation and experience may be necessary for some youth before they are ready to settle into the world of work.

A number of the dropouts we interviewed spoke of missing their friends in school, even while protesting that they really didn't miss school that much. The ability of our student interviewers to locate and interview their former classmates and friends who had left school, when the school authorities themselves could not locate them, speaks to enduring peer relationships which can be put to the service of keeping dropouts in touch with schooling. There is a good deal of recent research evidence, as well as actual classroom experience in cooperative learning programs, that positive peer group relationships in the school and in the classroom can produce group cohesiveness, satisfaction with schooling, goal direction, and positive self-image.[11] These results and experiences could be put to use in both keeping youngsters in school and attracting some of the dropouts to come back. We continue to focus on trying to convince the individual teenage dropout to return to school because we see his decision to leave as a personal choice. The fact that in-school peer group bonds seem to have failed those youths who leave school early should not discourage efforts to enhance such bonds and to use their most positive elements in any preventive or corrective program. Here again the negotiated peer-tutoring and cooperative education programs I described earlier can help to develop functional and enduring linkages among students which can modify and perhaps even overcome the barriers erected by sorting processes in the community and the school. One advantage could be that such bonds might forge friendships which could help keep students in school.

What we learned about dropping out is that it is not just another example of irresponsibility among youth, nor is it a problem which can easily be assigned to failing schools or depressed economies and changing job markets, or even one which invariably results from an unsatisfactory family background. Rather, the multiple causes of dropping out usually fall somewhere in the untenanted space which develops in the family-to-school-to-work transition when these social contexts are not purposively integrated and coordinated. The potential dropout comes to the school lacking the essential preparatory experiences, positive expectations of opportunities, and self-reinforcing motivation which are the important ingredients of school success. As a result, the school and the student find it difficult to develop and maintain the attachment which produces positive social ties and encourages conformity to the school's norms and expectations. These same deficits and disadvantages follow the dropout when she leaves the school for the labor market. Improving the school portion of the transition by targeting resources better, expanding and enriching instructional methods and curricula, and providing other programs to accommodate the greater diversity of students and learning styles found in schools today is a necessary beginning for reform. Just improving schools, however, cannot be expected to resolve the dropout problem—which often has its origins in early childhood or even prenatally—without the interactive investment of the resources of all the socializing environments of the community. There are also those problems in the school-to-work transition which are part of the changes and fluctuations of the labor market and which confound any predictability on the part of educators. The causes and consequences of dropping out are frequently as much if not more attributable to communitywide social forces than to exclusively individual decision-making by the student or the failure of the school. Given the massive and diverse responsibilities we assign the school for preparing students for adult life as well as remediating the problems they acquire along the way, and given the limited human and material resources schools have to meet these challenges, we must look elsewhere in the community for some help. Some of the problems which dropouts share are just not amenable to educational intervention.

Dropping out is not irreversible. Many students do return, sometimes leaving and coming back a number of times. Even among those who stay out for a long period of time, many eventually do complete their education either by returning to school or completing a General Education Diploma: a popular "second chance" route. In fact, while about 25 percent of high school students nationally drop out before graduation, by age twenty-nine, less than 14 percent of the population is without either a high school diploma or a GED certificate.[12] The real problem adults see with dropping out, we were told by a number of dropouts and a few teachers and counselors as well, was that adults believe that kids are supposed to be in school. They underscored this argument by pointing out that in their state the legislature, bowing to pressures from educators, was proposing to ban the GED so that a person who didn't graduate from a high school could not have a high school diploma. According to these students, being in school, not getting an education, was what adults considered important.

Generally, the individuals we interviewed indicated that they had found schoolwork and the behavioral restrictions associated with it to be in opposition to their life-style preferences, and they did not see their decision to drop out as hindering their opportunities or confidence in a future. In fact, most of the dropouts I talked to saw their decision to leave school as a rational and realistic act, for which they were willing to take the consequences. Again, it may well be that in years to come they will feel differently, but for now, at least, they do not seem to feel that they were forced to leave. Some adolescents did, however, leave school (or a particular school) because of external circumstances over which neither the school nor the individual student had any control. While such circumstances as the death of the wage earner in the family, requiring the student to enter the labor market, are clear examples of involuntary dropping out, the much more frequent case of the female student who drops out because of pregnancy is harder to classify as voluntary or involuntary. Yet the results of both the consequent short-term and long-term educational deficits may well be the same regardless of how much apparent choice the student has over the decision.

While the work problems associated with being a dropout have a high cost for the individual, they are equally high for society. The increasing educational requirements for jobs make high school dropouts more likely to be unemployed and so more likely to require and receive public assistance. Both of these factors have serious repercussions in terms of the individual's self-esteem; he suffers emotionally as well as financially. Yet, despite the higher long-term unemployment rates nationwide among dropouts compared to their high school graduate counterparts, we found that unemployment is not the major problem for dropouts, at least in the communities we looked at. What seemed most critical was that dropouts must, and often are willing to, accept low-paying, dead-end jobs and so have far less chance of advancement, let alone a career prospect, than do their graduate counterparts. High school graduates, for example, are three times as likely as dropouts to obtain white-collar jobs.

The acquisition and development of occupational skills is particularly important for potential dropouts because they will move directly into the world of work, where their success is far from assured. Adolescence, perhaps even more than other periods of the life course, is immediately sensitive to changing economic as well as demographic and social forces. There are also important differences between the exposure and entry points in the world of work for minority youths living in poverty and their counterparts in more affluent surroundings, and these differences are important predictors of the holding power of the schools in any given community. Middle-class youths often take seemingly menial jobs to earn money because they know that these are only "bridging" jobs until they enter college or some career-oriented occupation; for lower-class youths, that first job is often the only occupation they will ever find. An additional problem for minority youths—those who stay in school as well as those who drop out—is the absence of the types of employment networks which could help them to find places in the career world and to later move into positions providing vocational and financial opportunity. The absence of such fortuitous community and family network contacts is an even greater problem for dropouts, who never learn what career patterns are and have few, if any, positive role models to follow.

Jobs and career possibilities differ in various parts of the country and in different types of communities. Urban inner-city areas, for example, seldom offer the type of employment which leads to a career ladder and the social and economic mobility that comes with climbing it. As mentioned above, it is important to have family and community contacts not only at the start of the ladder but at the middle and higher rungs, in order to provide mentors and role models and to lend a helping hand up. Females—white as well as black—who have dramatically increased their labor force participation since the 1970s, also suffer from the absence of networks and models. Finally, the quality of schools and the educational attainment they provide is also unequally distributed and perpetuates the labor market disadvantages of children from minority families.

While work clearly becomes a central concern once teenagers leave school—with or without a diploma—it is an important part of their lives before then as well. According to parents we met in the various communities, whatever their own experiences were or had been, there was general agreement among these parents (and among some, but not all, researchers who have studied teenage employment) that holding a part-time and/or summer job while in high school is beneficial for learning attitudes and habits necessary in the working world.[13] Parents and teachers, as well as youth employment specialists, pointed out that working helps to foreshorten the extension of adolescence; it provides an earlier access for youngsters to the adult world they are moving toward; it helps to build character and industry; and it refurbishes the tarnished work ethic in American society.

In all the communities we studied, many early and most middle adolescents and a substantial majority of older adolescents combined part-time employment with schooling. As might be expected, the type of job and the number of hours worked differed by gender as well as age, with girls much more represented in clerical and retail work than boys, who found jobs wherever they could. Girls also tended to work fewer hours and closer to home.

In addition, the present and future meaning of work differed significantly in the lives of adolescents of different socioeconomic classes and residential areas. The disparity begins in looking for and finding a job. As mentioned earlier, a teenager in an affluent suburban area may take a part-time, summer, or weekend job to earn extra money either for present consumption or for an educational future, but it is unrelated to future employment except as an introduction to the world of work.[14] The same job represents something much more immediate to the poor urban inner-city or rural youngster whose occupational future begins with this employment.

While there is widespread unemployment among both youth and adults in Southside, it is a mistake to believe that adolescents there do not work, and work hard:

"Willie D," a black high school junior, tells me about his rock group. "We get there and set up and I do the mixing and Philip does the MC." They play at parties and usually charge $85 for one session for the night. His group is called "Starship." He mentioned other groups among the high school students: "Master Mind," "Starsky and Hutch," "TNT," and "Astro."

Roy works for a fruit company as a truck loader. He talks about the fact that he works from 4:00 P.M. to 2:00 A.M. and how he thinks maybe he should drop out and go to night school.

Tony worked from 8:00 at night until 4:00 A.M. his senior year in high school and attended school during the day. He would go home and sleep until 8:00 A.M. and then come to school. He had a hard time getting to his first class. Now that he is graduated he works at the same place, but from 4:00 A.M. until noon.

Mai Ling works with her mother in a luggage factory. The mother works the machine and Mai Ling cleans up the floors. It's very nice because they can talk to each other.

Angel dropped out of school because the only job he could find was from 8:00 A.M. until 5:00 P.M.; he goes to night school now.

Juan's father is an electrician who works with his grandfather, who is a carpenter. His grandfather also has a small store where Juan works after school.

Linda was excited about a new job as a part-time clerk for the Justice Department and the fact that they gave her a key to the office door. "They gotta trust me because my fingerprints came in without a record."

Sparky comes in with the turntables, $105 apiece. I ask him where he got them and he says he didn't ask me where I got the money to buy one from him.

Toby says he quit his job at McDonald's because the manager insisted that he had to work during the early afternoon and he couldn't get off from school.

The dean tells me about a student who lives in a cold-water flat and delivers newspapers from 5:00 A.M. until he comes to school.

Spenser got his first job when he was twelve years old, loading and unloading a furniture truck after school and weekends. He later worked for a printer: "Fold 'em and cut 'em, it was easy." He was paid off the books.

Most of the jobs these youngsters had, when they could find them, involved long hours, which often included considerable travel time since they were frequently in downtown commercial areas or in more prosperous sections of the city. In most cases the jobs were short-lived—sometimes because they were temporary to begin with, in other cases because the youth found a better one, and, not infrequently, because the inexperienced youth simply did not work out in the job. Yet for many youngsters, once they found a job it became the most important part of their day and it was school which became part-time and secondary. By the time they had reached high school, many had already begun to make this transition from student to worker and many were attending school only occasionally. They still considered themselves, and were considered by their parents, to be "in school," however—sometimes because it was necessary to retain their student status so that their families could qualify for welfare. School also was where they could meet their friends, find boyfriends or girlfriends, and even sometimes find jobs through their friends or teachers. As high school continued, it became clear that many of them would never graduate. But they still dreamed and fantasized about future jobs and a better life as well:

Billie thought that women should earn money. She couldn't understand how the girls in Puerto Rico just get married, have kids, and never work. She thought that if they did get jobs, they could have money and buy houses and cars and have a better life. She would return to Puerto Rico if she and her husband could find jobs there.

Greta wants to join the air force. She would get on-the-job training, it would give her the chance to travel to some places outside of Southside, and she could take her baby with her after basic training.

Geraldo would like to be a policeman after he graduates. He never wanted to be a cop when he was a kid, but he read somewhere how much they make and how they can collect a pension after twenty years of the job. His father and mother have both been working since they were in their early teens and can't stop because the only "pension" they have is welfare.

Peter Ho was telling us at lunch about working in the family restaurant. He started when he was ten years old helping in the kitchen, and by the time he was twelve he was the cashier. His parents don't want him to take over the business because of the long hours and hard work, and he agrees with them. He would like to go to medical school after college and eventually do research in genetics. He is worried because he has heard that medical schools have a quota system for Asians, just like they used to have for the Jews.

The reality for youth in Southside was that they experienced the same difficulties which beset their parents and older siblings in finding any but the most menial and unskilled jobs:

Angel complains that all the jobs in the newspaper say "experience necessary." One job as a dishwasher required two years prior experience: "No others need apply." He decides that when he graduates in June he will go into the navy to learn a trade.

Hawkins asks the principal if he can skip his lunch hour every day so that he can leave one period early to go to work. The answer is a long lecture about the school's responsibility to provide a balanced diet and how the school would be neglecting its duties if it allowed him to skip lunch.

Anthony comes into the office to explain that he did not get the job as a delivery/messenger boy because the other student (from an uptown school) who applied for the same job got it. He thinks that they were sure he would loot the packages he would be delivering.

What was important here, and for most of the youth in Southside and in other urban centers who worked while going to school, was not only the fact that none of these jobs had any relation to any probable future; they also interfered in terms of both time and interest with the educational program of the school. Not only were working and schooling not related; they were, like so much else in Southside, frequently in conflict, and most of these youth were left to make it on their own. In fact, the realities of the changing job market make the promise of the American Dream of occupational and social mobility out of the ghetto through education questionable for those who hope to pursue that vision; in 1986 only 36 percent of male high school graduates found work in high-wage stable occupations, down from 57 percent in 1968.[15] Whatever the dreams and fantasies about future careers, the social reality is that participation in the labor market is not an equal opportunity for all would-be workers, but is conditioned by a number of factors, some of which, like ethnicity, age, and gender, are givens no matter where an individual lives. Other factors, however—such as education and job training; motivation and work habits; and knowledge about, as well as placement contacts within, particular job and career sectors—are a part of adolescent career development that is dramatically different for Southside's youth when they are compared with those who live in Sheffield.

If work is a necessity for Southside's adolescents, it is an option, even a luxury, for Sheffield's teenagers. Jobs here foster peer group relationships as much as, if not more than, individual skills development and often seem to be obtained and experienced by groups rather than individuals. But despite parental support for, and even insistence on, work as beneficial for older teenagers, it seemed to us that it diminished rather than strengthened family understanding and parent–adolescent relationships. Some of this can be attributed to having less time together or even to the greater autonomy from parental supervision a job affords. More significantly, however, the negative effect results from strains caused by demands for time and attention on the part of the family (in association with the school) that conflict with the demands of the workplace. Also, employers expect, or at least hope, that their youthful employees will be mature enough from the beginning to do the specific job they are being paid to do, and do not share the parental view of the job as a learning and character-building experience for future careers. Most parents we interviewed in suburban areas wanted their teenagers to *learn* what it is like to be a responsible worker, to be at work on time every day, and to be dependable. Most of the employers cited precisely the same "kid stuff" characteristics of teenage workers parents were hoping the job would remediate—being late or not showing up for work, lack of dependability and the propensity to quit—in explaining why they prefer older workers.

In Sheffield we often heard teenage workers complain that their parents had no idea of what they did at work or what it was like. "It's not," Bruce once told us, "that my father doesn't work hard, he does, but he is doing what he wants to do and can't understand that my part-time job is just a job and not a career." Bruce's friend Scott added that his father gave him frequent pep talks about how he had to "make a name for himself" in the garden and building supply store where he works on weekends and summers, making sure that he got identified as a good worker so that he could get good references for the future. The owner of the business knew that he was just working until he went off to college—in fact, called him "college boy" sometimes—and all he was interested in was that Scott come to work on time and do the work he was supposed to do. "My father," explained Scott, "sees my job like it would be where he works and everybody is pushing to get ahead; but really, it's only me, three other guys who work part-time, the owner, and his son, so where is there to go even if I wanted to?" Another area of conflict about the job with his father was over what he felt was his father's intrusion into his workspace: "He thinks he knows more about the job than my boss does and is always telling me how I should work and how I should tell the boss some ideas about improving business, as if I cared or he would listen to me."

There is further conflict when what parents expect their children to acquire from this first exposure to work outside the family is clearly different from the expectations and experience of the adolescents themselves. Seeking peer group acceptance and respect sometimes leads to peer-oriented forms of personal style or conduct which are antagonistic to employers. Unauthorized group food binges, collective absenteeism to go to the beach, and other forms of disapproved peer social activity are not uncommon in Sheffield. Social interaction with peers in collective opposition to adult supervision in the workplace is certainly not one of the lessons parents—let alone employers—expect teenagers to learn. But work binds Sheffield teenagers to their peers and serves to separate them from their families. It is one of the few social environments which is not under the control of the community-centered, family-dominated program for adolescent development, because it usually takes place outside the purview and control of the family and the school.

Working while in school—either because one has or one wants to—almost always restricts youths to the local labor market, and this can make a difference in both the type of job and work availability for youngsters. Most Smyrna Beach teenagers, like those in Sheffield, are college-bound and their jobs have little or nothing to do with their eventual careers; yet most of the older teenagers we observed and interviewed had part-time and summer jobs, which were readily available in this resort community. This was also true in Newtown, where the shopping mall and a number of other fast-food and small commercial enterprises in the community provided adolescents with access to low-pay, low-level jobs. It was less so in Sheffield, since such work sites were not present in this residential community or in the ring of similar communities surrounding it. But even in Sheffield, most adolescents worked during the summer, sometimes traveling a considerable distance to their jobs. In the suburbs, the first "work" experience outside the family often begins in the early teens, with girls baby-sitting and boys doing odd jobs for neighbors and then moving outside the home and the neighborhood to where most of the jobs are. But sometimes there just aren't any jobs where the people who want and need them are.

In rural Green Valley there was a virtual absence of any local job market and poor employment prospects for what jobs were available. The situation was made even more difficult by the fact that subsidized job-training programs were located in the county seat, which was culturally as well as geographically many miles away. The local economy was built on family dairy farms and orchards, and the business and service infrastructure to support these activities had always been the local way of life. If an individual couldn't work on the family farm (and only a small percentage of the youth here could, even if they wanted to), it was usually necessary to leave the area to find a job or start a career. Youth employment agencies in the county seat were concerned about the absence of any job futures for most Green Valley adolescents and had tried to establish job-training programs to help. One program initiative, set up by a federal youth employment agency and the local high school, was to pay three senior students to work with the school custodian as part of a work-study program. The result, said one school administrator, was that they had to pay the custodian more to supervise the student workers, primarily to make sure they didn't injure themselves or cause damage, and he had less time to spend on his own work. "Seemed damn foolish to pay the custodian three times more money to do one-third less work." The agency personnel argued that the school simply did not understand that the real purpose of the program was to provide work experience and to help encourage a work ethic. The student workers themselves said their real concern was getting paid; how many school custodian jobs were there in Green Valley that they could hope to get when they graduated, anyway?

The county-level authorities also set up a special job-training program for adolescents who were eligible for federal program funds. But it was installed in a campus-style educational center which had been built with federal and state funds at the other end of the county, and the students were bused there, an hour and a half each way. From the outset, the students felt alienated in what was a strange new place to them—mixed in with other students from elsewhere in the county and equally unknown "city" people. The people who ran the program were from the county seat, and they had just as much difficulty understanding the rural customs and values which the Green Valley students brought with them. "The first questions," said one of the program administrators, "were 'When do we get paid?' and 'When do we eat?', just like any farm day-laborer would ask the farmer." He went on to add that the real problem was that the youngsters were not really "in tune" with what they were supposed to be doing there, and because they were in "alien territory" among people they didn't know and trust, by the end of the first week the program was down to five students. "Even these kids didn't want to be small-engine mechanics; they stayed for the pay."

Why, I asked, had the program chosen the repair of small engines for lawn mowers, chain saws, and similar equipment as the occupational goal of the program? "Because we thought that kids in Green Valley would jump at the chance to learn how to work on any kind of engine. You've driven around this area, haven't you, and seen the junk cars, sometimes five or six of them, parked in the driveways and in the front yard?" When I responded that I had, and wondered why anyone would clutter up the landscape with cars that clearly had seen better days, he explained how transportation in Green Valley is absolutely necessary to get anywhere and do anything, not just visiting or finding something to do, but getting to work, buying food, and doing all the other things that are necessary to life. The rural poor need cars for transportation like everybody else, and since the cars they can afford are always breaking down or even dying on them, they need other cars around for spare parts or maybe even for actual use if their present car breaks down. They can't afford to have cars repaired, either, so they do all of the work themselves. They are "wheelies" or "car freaks," fascinated by engines, and will spend hours, even days, trying to get a car to run. Since most of the newer people who have moved into the area aren't interested or able, somebody has to repair their lawn mowers and other small-equipment engines. Green Valley youngsters, however, don't see that as any kind of job for them, and they could not become serious about this training program, which was just as different from their experience as it was distant from their community. Why not train them to be automobile rather than lawn mower mechanics, then? "Are you kidding? There isn't much we can teach them that they haven't already learned from their fathers or older brothers or just by trial and error, and besides, there are six or seven skilled and experienced guys waiting for every auto mechanic job that becomes available here."

There were other problems which contributed to the local opposition to, or disenchantment with, federal or state employment programs everywhere, and we heard them elsewhere. Here in Green Valley the opposition was phrased in terms of what was happening to the work ethic. The real problem, one of the administrators told us, was very basic: "In any occupation you have to learn your trade before you start getting money, but in these programs you are paid right away and whether you learn or not." He had tried to convince the students that their real "pay" would be in the future, from what they learned and in their career development. "You learn the skills," he would tell them, "so that someday you can go out and make some money." "In the real world," he said to me, "the reward comes later on, but in these programs you get immediate gratification and so you end up with kids who can't delay rewards and learn to want their satisfaction now." He went on to explain that while there were problems with the program, the real problems were in the home and school life of these kids, who "aren't ready for us when they come here."

The difficulties in this employment-training program are broadly similar to problems we saw elsewhere, but in rural Green Valley they are illustrative of the sense of separation between the community as a place to live and grow and the work world which resides outside that community. This employment-training program is part of a "package" which Green Valley buys from the county's educational center and includes in the school system's budget. Vocational programs were added to the original countywide special education mandate of the center, which provides Green Valley with services for learning-disabled students including a part-time psychologist, a reading specialist, and several special education teachers. The net effect is that much of the work and career related schooling for Green Valley youngsters takes place outside the community—removed from the direct control of the community's schools and families. Interested parents may ride the school bus from Green Valley to the educational center and see the programs in action on the one or two days a year when it is allowed, but in our experience, most of those few who did were the parents of special education students. Other than these "show and tell" sessions, there is no local community involvement in program design, evaluation, or accountability.

This centralization was intended to produce the benefits of specialization in professional service and teaching and to provide economies of scale, both of which it has done. What it has also accomplished, however, is to disperse the social environments available to the adolescents in this community even more. The director of the center, however, attributes the failure of his programs to attract and retain Green Valley youngsters to their early family life.

It's the family that is the crux of the problem for us here, because if the parents can't get their kids to think about their future, there's not much that we can do. [He went on to explain that those kids who come from farm backgrounds think of work as part of their home life and they know how to work, but don't see it as leading to any future.] On the other hand, if a kid grows up in a family where the parents work for some corporation that employs twenty-five thousand people, they don't learn much about working. Dad has a good job and there is enough money to support the family. If there's not, Mom's out there with a second job and kids just don't learn about work. You ask these kids, "Where does your father work? What does he do?" All they know is the name of the company he works for; they have no idea of what he does. They have no concept of work. Now, the farm kids, as I said, know what work is but they have no idea of what they want to do when they grow up. Yet you ask them if they intend to go to college and about 80 percent of them raise their hands. But the kids we get here are not college-bound because the school doesn't send those kids to us. So why do they say that? I think the reason is the same as why anything having to do with cars is so popular with the boys, and cosmetology is the only thing that the girls seem interested in. They can't wait to get out of Green Valley.

In virtually every interview, the youngsters complained that there was "nothing to do in Green Valley." Whenever we discussed career plans they either diverted to some other topic or talked about careers as journeys out of Green Valley and into some nearby small city or outside the area:

Marcy is a sixteen-year-old daughter of a recently retired army noncom who has lived in many parts of the United States as well as in Germany. Her father is an alcoholic, who grew up in a small town near Green Valley and joined the army to get away. Her mother is from another nearby small town. She has a younger sister who runs away from home frequently, usually to stay with friends she met in school but sometimes to the cities in other parts of the county.

Marcy wants to be "an institutional parent" in a residential home for child abuse victims. When I asked her what an institutional parent is, she gave a lengthy description, including where training programs are available (a county community college and the state university) and where she intends to work ("as far away from here as I can get").

Ryan's father is a truck mechanic who has been divorced from his mother for the past eight years. His mother is now divorcing his stepfather. Ryan says that he loves to come to school because it is a chance to meet kids from other parts of the county. When he has to return home (his bus leaves at 2:30 P.M. and he gets home at about 3:15 P.M.) he helps his mother with the housework and then goes out to play. He thinks that he would like to be a state policeman when he grows up (he is now fourteen years old) and looks forward to moving from barracks to barracks in various parts of the state.

Linda is a seventeen-year-old senior who plans on a singing career. She has always sung in the school chorus and took lessons from a voice teacher in the county seat. She has gone as far as she can, she says, and has to get away to a larger city where she can get proper voice training. Another problem is that her vocal talents are not prized in this "culturally backward" area.

Bobby is a seventeen-year-old son of a local dairy farmer. He has three brothers, all of whom are older, one of whom lives in a house on his father's farm. Bobby has a car and drives with his girlfriend and another couple to a small city across the river "several times a week." They just visit shopping malls, sometimes go to the movies, but mostly "get away from Green Valley." He doesn't know what is going to happen to his father's farm and does not want to become a farmer because taxes are now so high that a farmer can't make a decent living. He plans to leave Green Valley as soon as he graduates from high school but has no definite career plans as yet.

These youngsters are representative of the children of the older, rural families in Green Valley, while the children of the commuter families are very much like those of suburban areas such as Newtown or Sheffield. Like Southside's youth, the rural poor teenagers in Green Valley need to work to help their families, but the distances they must travel to find jobs are much greater and jobs are even less available here than in the metropolis. Yet most of the poor youngsters manage to find them as soon as they are able to get a car and go to where the jobs are. Most of those we talked to were eager to start looking for jobs, not only to help their families and for their own consumer needs, but, as previously discussed, because it got them out of Green Valley. But while such young people seek work and have the same hopes for the future as teenagers everywhere, educational futures here are just as bleak as they are in Southside. When we followed up on some of the youngsters just described, we found that few were able to do what they had hoped, at least in the first few years after leaving the high school. Neither Marcy nor Linda have managed to start out on their career plans. Linda married soon after graduation, has a family, and sings in the church choir; Marcy is also married but has left Green Valley for a Sunbelt city, where she and her husband both hope to find jobs. Like his father, Ryan has become a truck mechanic, but he works and lives in the county seat. Of the four, only Bobby has gone to college, and he went from there to veterinary school and plans to practice in Green Valley "someday." Getting an education often means leaving their local community to attend the centralized school in Green Valley; getting a job means leaving Green Valley.

While there is a local high school for the adolescents in Ranchville, the community we studied in the South, the absence of any job future there also means that withdrawal from the community is the only realistic ending for adolescent development. The problems are even more severe for the adolescent members of the migrant labor families who move in and out of Ranchville. They carry with them both the burdens of poverty that are obvious in Southside and the isolation resulting from absence of a total community of institutions that characterizes Green Valley. One result is that since both the school and the community in Ranchville take a strict and unbending attitude toward young people's behavior, the family, probably the only stable institution in their lives, also is the only arena in which tensions can be acted out. We found that frequent family disputes imposed severe strains on family cohesion. In many cases it seemed that only the need to have as many family members as possible working in the fields sustained the family as a unit. The meaning of work in this situation was that everyone was expected to work but no one saw any relationship between that work and any notion of social or occupational advancement. Just as in Southside, working and schooling were unrelated and in conflict in terms of time demands; and for the migrant adolescents of Ranchville working is even more critical to economic survival, since they are usually hired as part of a family and follow their families from job to job until they start their own families. Most of the migrant worker families in Ranchville have little chance for survival and no safety net without the seasonal employment of all family members, including children, since they are ineligible for public assistance and disability benefits, nor can they look forward to any pension or even Social Security benefits. Even the local schools (but not the county school system) recognize this and take a less stringent view of migrant children's absences during picking season.

While they have no greater social status among the year-round residents whether they work or not, and certainly no connections which can help them find better jobs, Ranchville's migrant teenagers have a surprising amount of respect for work. There are, of course, as few intangible rewards in their work in the fields as there are financial ones, but they manage to find some solace and even some joy in being with friends and relatives and "earning my keep and helping my family." Yet even the fantasies the teenagers described to me were impoverished, and they seemed to find it difficult to imagine that anything or anybody could change their certain future of hard work and little to show for it. Even their daydreams about what might happen if their life did change—if, let's say, they hit the *bolita* numbers game or won the lottery—were circumscribed by the immediacy of their present-day hard times. Most of the migrant adolescents reported that they would use the money to help their families rather than to seek escape from poverty themselves; they would pay off all of the family debts, or get needed medical attention for some family member, or they would buy a house "in one place" for their family and settle down. Then, and only then, they would buy themselves a car.

Why do teenagers work? We asked both adolescents and their parents and heard somewhat different answers from each in different types of communities. Suburban parents told us that working was "good for" their children; that it allowed them to see what it was like to take responsibility and to "deal with the public"; that it gave them some understanding of the business world; and, almost incidentally, that they could earn some spending money or put some away for college. Adolescents said that they worked because it gave them a chance to be with their friends; because work gave them money which they could use to buy some of the things they wanted; and because it was something that their parents expected. But, while suburban parents often stressed the "learning experience" and developmental aspects of work, they seemed to view teenage employment in much the same way as they talked about tennis or music lessons: an experience which would be valuable in their children's real careers in the future.

Adolescents, particularly those who had been working for some time, were not buying any of this. Any rewards or job satisfaction they described resulted from the non–work related interactions with friends and peers in the workplace or the consumer power they enjoyed from the money they earned. While there were some exceptions, most saw the work they did for what it was: a short-term job which was generally menial, frequently exploitative, and having little relationship to what they and their families saw as their career futures. In fact, despite their parents' social and business connections, many suburban adolescents found out about and obtained jobs through friends who worked at the same place.

In the suburban areas there was no similarity between the work fathers or mothers do and that of their teenage working children. Job loss is an unpleasant and anxious experience for both Sheffield's parents and their children but does not have the same dreaded urgency as it does in Southside. Sheffield parents and children alike see unemployment as a temporary state and have little feeling for what the subculture of unemployment can be like: ''I can't understand why the government makes such an issue out of teenage unemployment. I can't find a kid to mow my lawn or rake leaves.'' Southside's adults and their children have a different experience and so a different feeling about unemployment; for them it is an ever-constant threat that can be as immediate as this week's paycheck. In the urban inner-city sites, both parents and children had unskilled jobs which, while they might be in different sectors of the economy, were locked into the same low-pay, no-advancement, unskilled, and unsteady labor market. The work characteristics of both adolescents and their parents in the migrant families in Ranchville were even more similar, since they had essentially the same jobs and were even sometimes paid as a family.

Like their parents, teenagers in Southside work because they must, but it would be a mistake to believe that there is any community support for not working whenever there are jobs available. Their parents encourage them to find work, but they have virtually no ability to help them find jobs and are often out on the job market concurrently with their children. Most are effectively barred from the high-salaried occupations by their lack of education, and even from the security of well-paid industrial work and craft union protection. They are the classic example of the marginal unskilled labor force whose members are most subject to the vagaries of economic and labor market fluctuations. Teenagers who are out of school and not working, particularly males, are an unwelcome burden on the family and a potential source of trouble in the community. Yet work is not highly valued, either, and few parents tell their children about the dignity of labor. As Josie's mother would tell her, work is what people like them must do in order to survive, and no sensible person questions it or even hopes to avoid it. Work for Southside youngsters, when it is available, binds them to their families but often interferes with or even precludes education and career development.

To sum up, both the more affluent and the poorer adolescents can visualize their futures in their parents' present life style. Because the poorer teenage workers already share their parents' difficult fate, they develop a more empathetic mutual relationship based on a shared understanding of work's realities. Josie, for example, once told us:

> My mother worked every day since she was twelve years old and she's going to die working. When I was little she would tell me and my sisters how hard it is to work and how nobody thanks you for it. She used to say out loud sometimes, "Am I the only one who put Jesus on the Cross?" I used to wonder why she was complaining so much. Some of the ladies she works for give her clothes, sometimes they give her food to take home, and most of them give her Christmas presents. When I started working in the record store I thought it was great: I could listen to music, meet people, I got discounts on records. Now I don't feel the same. I try to study there sometimes and the manager says, "This ain't no school, clean up the stockroom." Having somebody else look down on you and tell you what to do all the time is not the way I want to spend my life. I look at my mother sometimes and say to myself, "How did you stand it all these years?"

We were able to observe and interview adolescents working in fast-food restaurants in a number of our sites, and the comparisons provide some insights into how even the same jobs can have very different impacts on teenagers in different communities. In the more affluent communities such as Smyrna Beach, Sheffield, and Newtown, these teenage workplaces were essentially organized according to peer groups, and the important relationships were among the adolescent workers themselves. The social interaction among these employees seemed little different from what took place in school, and, as anyone who has tried to get a hamburger prepared "your way" can attest, the work itself is often seen as a distraction. Relationships with supervisors tend to be seen by their young employees in the same way—more related to controlling appearance and social interaction than teaching anything about the work. One seventeen-year-old employee in a fast-food restaurant in Newtown, for example, complained:

> He [the manager] doesn't really care much about us. If we don't work out he can find five other kids who want the job. He took me off the counter because my zits [facial pimples] were oozing and bleeding, and he says, "Look, kid, nobody can eat hamburgers after they see your face." O. K., but what does he do then? He puts me to work on the french-fry cooker, and you know what grease does to zits, don't you? My father says that the employer "owns" the job and he has a right to decide what kind of people work there, but I don't think it gives him the right to criticize how I look. I would quit but my friends all work there, and no matter how hard he tries to keep us from being together, we manage to arrange our hours to be there at the same time.

We heard quite a different story from the employers. Those we talked to were candid in saying that appearance, particularly where "meeting the public" was required, was an important factor in the hiring decision. But once hired, appearance was not the major reason why teenagers were fired. Most frequently, they reported, it was because the teenager was unreliable, came late or missed work without prior warning, would ask for an excessive amount of time off, or wasn't satisfied with work conditions. These findings seem to agree with the reported differences in job satisfaction between youths and their employers; youths are more likely than others to leave jobs because of dissatisfaction, while employers tend to view youths as unproductive and unreliable workers.[16] Among those we observed working or interviewed, job retention was very low. While these teenagers most frequently left jobs because of dissatisfaction or taking other jobs, in well over one-third of the cases we knew of, they left involuntarily, either because of reductions in the work force or business closings or because they were fired.

There were also a few fast-food restaurants in or near Southside and Wharton Hill (an inner-city area near Southside, to be described shortly), and a number in and around Riverton, where most of the employees were black and Hispanic. There was still a good deal of teenage banter and interaction among the employees, but it was more constrained by supervisory control than was true in the suburban areas.

When we interviewed these teenage employees, the importance of the job as a job was obvious. Few of them saw this job as a temporary work experience on the way to a better future; rather, it was a way to earn money that they and their families needed now. It wasn't that they didn't have aspirations and a desire to get ahead; it was that this job had its own immediate return. While few saw it as a learning experience, the relationship between their current employment and their occupational future seemed less tenuous than in the suburbs.

By the mid-1980s we began to see a number of senior citizens, whose relationship to the job market is just as restricted as that of teenagers, working in fast-food restaurants in some suburban settings as well as in cities. In the suburban sites there was little interaction between them and their teenage co-workers beyond what was necessary to the work. I do not mean to suggest that there was any obvious antagonism; they were simply two distinct social networks. They also were not from the same socioeconomic class, since the senior citizens were working to supplement meager retirement incomes. In the urban sites there seemed to be much more interaction among the adult and teenage employees, more exchange and sharing of both social and work-related information. We conjectured that this was more than a shared sense of the importance of this job to survival in the present; it also resulted from the similarity between the senior citizens' past and the adolescents' probable futures.

The emphasis on schooling as preparation for work has come to mean that unemployment among youth is directly linked to the failure of the high school in the social perception. As a result, high rates of adolescent and youth unemployment have more than an economic impact, they become a major sociopolitical and even moral question for the community and for its educational system as well as the basis for a national controversy. When we interviewed youth employment professionals and policymakers, we found that economists, educators, and politicians disagree as to the reasons for both the high rate of teenage unemployment and the disproportionate number of blacks and Hispanics who are jobless. They are in even greater disagreement as to the solutions to such problems. Some see them as inevitable: a function of the labor market, which increasingly will have fewer and fewer jobs available, with youths, women, and minorities having the least chance to be hired. In this view, both a reduction in discrimination—off the job as well as on it—and some fundamental changes in the labor market structure will be necessary for any change. Another viewpoint, more optimistic, sees youth unemployment as resulting from a lack of both schooling and work experience which improved education and job training can remedy. Fundamental to this argument are the relationships among education, employability, and unemployment.

Behind this major social policy problem variously defined as unemployment or unemployability, however, is the still-debated basic question: Does youthful unemployment stem from the behavior of youths themselves and their lack of skills and productivity, or from institutionalized features of the labor market? Understanding how and why youth employment programs developed at a national level seem to flounder in the local community requires first understanding the conflicting federal and local policies and the individual and interactive contributions of the family, the school, and the workplace to the problem. The dilemma was further compounded when the effects of youth unemployment in other arenas such as crime, welfare, and family life created a new urgency to "solve the problem" in the late 1950s and beyond. While unemployment became a national issue, its most dramatic and traumatic effects were in the urban inner city.

WHARTON HILL

Just across the river from Southside, in another major urban center, is Wharton Hill, an inner-city area of decaying houses with only the most rudimentary commercial and service activities, where migrant blacks and Hispanics have largely displaced earlier Italian and Portuguese and even more recent Cuban residents. The city in which Wharton Hill is located is said to be dying, and few of the old-time residents will be around to mourn its death. Once a city of almost one-half million, 80 percent white, it has shrunk to less than one-third of a million, 65 percent of whom are black. Twenty years ago the city had 9,000 businesses and 200,000 jobs; now it has less than half that number of businesses and fewer than 120,000 jobs. Although the city ranks almost fiftieth among the nation's cities in size, it is in the top five in the incidence of murder, and Wharton Hill has the highest rate of homicide of any section of the city. Poverty is evident everywhere in the approximately two square miles that is Wharton Hill, and when the sun goes down, the drug dealers (including some crack dealers in their early teens) and adolescent gangs come out and make life there perilous. No one in his right mind, it is said, including those in the helping professions, would wander in except the police, and even they consider an assignment there "combat duty."

There are families who live there; most are hardworking and many are single-parent, female-head-of-household ones. In some neighborhoods over half the families are on welfare, some for the third or fourth generation as the working poor become the permanent poor. Despite their underclass status, they raise their children with the same hopes we heard in Sheffield but with even more despair than we saw in Southside. Unlike Southside, ethnic succession has been almost complete in Wharton Hill, and the local high school, recently named for a Black Muslim activist, is almost totally black and, to a lesser extent, Hispanic. Most of the teachers and virtually all of the school administrators are also black. The school, however, is just about the only vestige of a once well articulated community of social institutions and services in Wharton Hill. When the Italians and the Portuguese fled from Wharton Hill as the blacks and Hispanics moved in, the local businesses went with them. One of the few white teachers left in Wharton Hill's high school explained what he had witnessed in his twenty-two years of teaching in the area:

> When the Italians left and moved to the suburbs, they left like the Russians left Manchuria; they took everything that could move with them. What they left behind was only the houses, and they were run-down because they were so old. But even when the government replaced some of the houses with housing projects, there just wasn't any community, only a place to live but no feeling of belonging with people you understood and knew what you could expect from. Everybody in the projects are strangers to each other; nobody else trusts them, so why should they trust themselves?
>
> It wasn't only the businesses and the social clubs and agencies that had been built up over the years; it was what everybody called "the system": families that knew each other even if they didn't always get along, the police, the schools, churches; everybody knew what to expect and where to go if there was trouble. They took the system with them too when they moved, and the police and the schools and the churches have never adjusted to the new people who were never part of that "family" system. You know, it sounds funny, but the only people in Wharton Hill who have any of that left are the Gypsies. They are better organized in their own

community than the Italians were. They arrange their own marriages and the family controls their kids for the rest of their lives. They don't need job programs or welfare agencies. They take care of their own.

What the Italians and the Portuguese took with them, of course, was the interactive and interdependent network of relationships among the social institutions of Wharton Hill. It was this community based and locally developed pattern of kinship-like relationships—and the adolescent charter it enacted and empowered—which provided a structure for adolescent development. What came to replace it were massive but insufficient programs—externally funded, organized, and directed—which tried to provide a new "safety net" as a substitute for the old institutional matrix. Only the family and the school were left to the local community, and they soon became the scapegoats for the failure of the federal and state programs. A job developer in a federally funded employment program insisted, for example:

Their families just don't instill the work ethic. Making some money to buy a box [portable radio] or for partying has real meaning for them, but not holding down a job. Look, this isn't some conservative or racist speech. I respect these kids for what some of them are trying to do, but they aren't job-ready; they need to see work in the context of a career, to think about their long-range plans, and then we can worry about a job for them.

The director of a similar employment program asked:

How do you convince a kid that working is better than not working if it isn't something he has learned at home or in school? He has to see it at home from the time he's a toddler; he has to see his father go to work every day, come home and talk about getting a raise, getting a promotion, a sense of accomplishment. . .

And a counselor in the same employment program added:

This is a very difficult population to work with. Most employers don't want to hire them and the jobs we do find for them they don't want. There are a lot of unskilled jobs open in small towns outside Wharton Hill, maintenance work mostly, but they don't want to travel that far and they say they don't want to do maintenance work; "I want a job in an office like you have!"

While legitimate jobs of any real promise are not available, some questionable ones are, adding to social disorganization, often providing more attractive alternatives to what low-level jobs are available, and confounding realistic estimates of unemployment. In Wharton Hill, just as in Southside and elsewhere, there is a burgeoning underground economy among youths (as among adults) for obtaining money illegally or "off the books." Edward Banfield, among others, has argued that the lure of the underground economy causes inner-city youths to refuse low-wage jobs: "Illicit enterprises, too, tend to have the effect of setting an informal minimum wage for unskilled labor which has no relation to the market value and which other employers cannot afford to pay."[17] Most of the youngsters we talked to did not earn much more than the legal minimum wage when they worked in illicit enterprises, but some did, and all managed to avoid taxes. The extreme cases were youths who reported that they could earn $250 to $700 per day selling drugs or stolen goods. Others described a variety of jobs which they could hold in small industries and commercial enterprises where they were paid in cash and consequently not subject to withholding taxes, Social Security payments, or other payroll deductions. We were frequently told by some of these adolescent entrepreneurs that entering training to get a nine-to-five job for three or four dollars an hour did not seem worth it. Some segments of this "other" economy, such as the unlicensed, or "gypsy," cabs found in both Southside and Wharton Hill, are openly accepted, considered by many government officials to be aberrations of the culture of poverty which are hardly worth serious social, let alone legal, concern.[18]

Throughout our fieldwork in Wharton Hill and Southside, we heard from both youth services professionals and politicians alike that one common focus of most adolescent social problems was in "the cycle of poverty and unemployment." Accepting the compelling statistical picture of youth unemployment as a major problem, and the evidence that the problem is most critical among minorities, what appeared central to us was that youth unemployment was almost always said to be connected to a number of other social handicaps (and so a number of institutional sectors) within the adolescent population. Unemployed youths are frequently school dropouts or low achievers who have no skills for entering the labor market, and many come from broken or otherwise inadequate families. Where do you start and where do you concentrate resources in dealing with what everyone agrees is a major problem for society as well as for teenagers?

One of the basic requirements for a sense of community is that we must weave our own social networks if they are to be more than safety nets. When a community has to look mainly to outside sources for support, it loses a sense of independence and, what I think is even more damaging, any sense of interdependence. This absence of a feeling of "ownership" on the part of the recipient community is matched by a feeling of proprietary control on the part of those professionals and policymakers who plan and implement the programs. The interagency network is often imposed on the community, and, in the absence of some established indigenous institutional network, has little chance of being accepted. The values which drive such programs are those of the professionals who run them, and over time these values, rather than the needs which the programs were designed to remediate, become the motive force for the programs. In effect, the sense of community and interdependence develops among the planners and managers rather than among those they seek to help. As is true in any community, when resources become scarce, value conflicts and partisan self-interest can, and usually do, develop.

In Wharton Hill, as I pointed out earlier, the traditional network of community-based social agencies and programs was replaced by an externally funded one when blacks and Hispanics replaced the Italians and Portuguese there. There were increasing complaints, even riots, protesting that these areas had been, as one resident said, "raped, pillaged, and then abandoned" by the local political system. The older, established city agencies which were a part of that political system were unable or unwilling to respond to the needs of the new residents and saw the federally funded programs as an incursive political ploy on the part of "outsiders," whose only interest was in gaining more votes and reducing the probability of more riots while ignoring the rest of the city. Police we talked with, for example, were openly resentful of the job possibilities Wharton Hill youngsters seemed to have, which had been unavailable to them in their youth. One officer said that it was a waste of time—that they would never be able to put the training to use. His partner laughed and said not to be too certain of that. Then he told a story about a young Wharton Hill job trainee who had been placed as an intern in the computer room of a brokerage house. Once he had learned to use the equipment and knew the various mailing lists, he obtained the names of a number of wealthy widowed clients to whom he then wrote asking for financial help for his education.

When we traced the various programs and policies up the administrative ladder, probing federal agency personnel in Washington as well as in their local offices in Southside and Wharton Hill for answers, the reality of inter-institutional jurisdictional conflict soon became apparent. Teachers and school administrators cited the absence of family guidance and hence motivation as the major problem, while employment service professionals quickly pointed to the failure of the schools to provide adequate basic education and skills for job readiness. Employers usually cited the absence of both skills and family motivation, frequently adding that there were problems with child labor laws and mentioning their own unwillingness to undertake the extensive training or retraining which would be necessary.

This sounded like more than simply passing the buck. It seemed to represent a particularistic focus on institutional prerogatives by employers as well as advocates for the family or the school, and that the different sectors developed different expectations in their youthful clients. Inevitably, these conflicting views produced similar conflicts in adolescents in first understanding and then internalizing a set of standards for occupational choice and success and contributed to the very high dropout rates in such programs. Many of the young people we interviewed expressed frustration at what they considered having to "start over again" with learning basic academic skills which they had already had in school and were openly resentful when they were told that their years in school were for naught as far as the employment program was concerned. Youths also frequently complained that they were sermonized on the importance of becoming self-reliant in order to become self-sufficient: "They tell you it's up to you, but they don't realize that when you're down you need some help to get up." The enduring effects of family socialization add another institutional sector to this conflict. Some youths said that the stipends they received from one program or another were insufficient to allow them to help support their parents and younger siblings and that they had to supplement the stipends any way they could or leave the program. Parents sometimes contributed to this problem by opposing or ridiculing "going back to school to learn how to find a job." The need which program specialists felt to deal with faulty socializing in the home—to teach acceptance of authority or even to stress the importance of being on time—led to a sense of cultural difference and even some resistance to what were considered someone else's values. Anthropologist Lee Rainwater characterized the American ethos of socialization as a strategy of "the good life" in the working class, a strategy of "career success" in the middle class, and a "strategy of survival" in the lower class.[19] And Melvin Kohn found that in raising their children, parents tend to stress the values that reflect their work conditions, in effect reinforcing the class structure.[20]

The emphasis of employment programs has increasingly been on the school because of employers' demands for basic skills training and a diploma as a condition of employment. In the mid-1970s we heard many complaints from employment service job developers in Southside. The employment professional would say, "What kind of job can I find for a kid with a third grade reading level, and if I do find one, it won't be what he expects anyway." Then the job counselor might confess, "Frankly, we have to 'cream' and take into the program only kids who can read at an eighth grade level, even though you and I know they can find their own jobs anyway, but there just isn't much you can do with job placement for illiterates." From employers we heard, "If she couldn't learn to read in school, what assurance do I have that she is going to learn to do the work here?" and then the assertion "Education is not my responsibility."

Almost a decade later we heard many of the same complaints and saw a number of the same problems in Wharton Hill, but by then the degree of disillusionment among professionals was noticeably higher. A black high school teacher, for example, told us that the school board's decision to "mandate that no child should graduate from the twelfth grade until he could read at an eighth grade level [had] made a mockery of educational standards; they picked the eighth grade standard because that is what they think is necessary for employability." A police officer who works with schools and juveniles was certain that "the schools fail kids by passing them, giving them A's and B's even though they can't read, and so how do you expect them to get, let alone keep, a job?" He also illustrated the problems of modeling and family structure:

The new high-rise projects they have built actually add to the problems. There are too many of the wrong people and too many kids stacked up on top of each other. Any positive role models get lost, get hidden. They see the men who don't go to work and the women who collect welfare. They see hundreds of them in the same building. They also see the pushers doing well and people who work not having any money.

One change that did occur in the time between when we looked at youth employment programs in Southside and in Wharton Hill was an increase in awareness that unemployment is the result of a number of related problems rather than any single one. When programs for such at-risk youngsters are put into operation, the multiproblem approach gets as much emphasis, if not as much enthusiasm, in the Wharton Hill of the 1980s as it did in Southside in the 1970s. In both cases the emphasis of most agencies we observed is on developing "job readiness skills," responsibility, a new self-image as a productive individual, initiative, and future-oriented skills. One continuing problem, which we encountered first in Southside but which became obvious in Wharton Hill, is the discrepancy between federal "externally developed" program guidelines and accountability—in a precise cost accounting system with actual job placement and retention as the major standards—and the motivations and goal expectations of local agency professionals. Most professionals in the new programs measure their real success by attitudinal and behavioral change in their clients; and they see "numbers," or the measurement of success by the number of jobs obtained and held, as bureaucratic inhumanity. In fact, a number of agency personnel said that attempting to quantify success was counterproductive. The outcome in most cases we followed was development of a list of job-entry skills which satisfied the funding agency but set relatively low standards for accountability.

One persistent problem which we found in both communities, and which seemed not to have changed much in the decade in between, was the trainees' lack of knowledge about the job market and how their skills translate into earning power and work status. Many of the youths we talked to either expressed no specific job preference or listed occupations such as supervisor, professional baseball player, disc jockey, or social worker—and, with increasing frequency, jobs in high-tech areas, particularly in computing. The point is not so much that these levels of aspiration are unrealistic or frivolous or that they are not to be encouraged. Rather, it is that the discrepancy between what the agency saw as realistic for youths in terms of entry-level jobs and the expectations of the youths themselves were ultimately defeating for both programs and participants.

Many parents as well as professional educators we spoke with still cling to that part of our American reliance on education as the great remediator which insists that more skills training, more effective schools, and other improvements in educational preparation will counteract the multiple deficits found among so many unemployed teenagers. When we looked at the behavior and heard the expressions of inner feelings of minority adolescents, a somewhat different picture took shape. A frequent theme in both descriptive and fantasy material in these interviews was a preference for "on the job training" in "the real world," in contrast to school, which is "what you do as a kid." In effect, these adolescents' fantasies or thoughts about work reflected little relationship to a past (schooling, family experience), little future for which to plan (employment programs as career development, a career "ladder"), but a strong sense of wanting immediate job fulfillment in the present. A sixteen-year-old female student in a commercial high school program described her fantasies about working:

> I like to imagine myself finding a job as a secretary to some executive while I'm out on a job placement. He—or it might even be a she—will say to me, "I like the way you work and I'm going to take you on right away." I say, "I won't graduate for two more years," and he says, "That's alright. You will learn everything you need to know here." That's great. I can "earn while I learn and learn while I earn."

One result of both the lack of specificity or realism of the youngsters' occupational choices and the few "real time" jobs which became available was that in a number of programs, this dissonance between program and client expectation led to an implicit understanding that the stipends paid to youths became an end in themselves and a major motivator for youngsters to remain in the program. A number of the projects we observed made special arrangements to pay participants every week or at least every two weeks, because they had come to realize that the stipend served as the chief motivator in program retention rates. This, in turn, led to additional cynicism on the part of staff, who complained that participants "live off the stipends they get for attending class and never bother with really trying to get a job."

Most of the youths we followed who did get jobs were employed in subsidized public sector jobs. While obtaining these jobs was classified as a "positive termination," or program success, there was considerable cynicism on the part of both staff and the youths themselves about the authenticity of the outcome. The professionals said that such jobs were "make work," which would never survive the program subsidies. As one remarked, "Everybody knows that the real job world is in the private sector, but we can't place our kids there because employers don't need or want them even with tax incentives.'' The youths themselves were no less disenchanted. One youth, who was scheduled to go out on a job interview, said:

> There is something unreal going on here. We spend weeks in class role playing on how to be interviewed on a job, even with television programs showing us how to do it, but all the guys who went out on interviews say this is a waste of time. One of the things we spend a lot of time on is how to introduce yourself to the employer, tell him something about yourself, what you do in school, why you want this job. But when you get to the interview, the employer just tells you what time to show up the next day to start work because the job developer had set the whole thing up already anyway.

The ideology behind most of the employment programs has been based upon two questionable assumptions, no matter which political party has been in power. One is that traditional work attitudes such as ambition, achievement motivation, task orientation, persistence, and goal seeking are inherent in work itself if not in potential workers themselves. The other is that the opportunity structures and appropriate training provided by job programs will result in motivation and success. But these old Protestant work ethic assumptions do not underlie what Swedish educator Torsten Husén, for example, sees as a new work ethic based on "personal fulfillment, security, and the chance to devote time to rewarding leisure activities," emerging among all classes of youths.[21]

The conflict continues not only over two opposing institutional views on the origins and persistence of youth unemployment, but over who or what destroyed access to the dream and where to go to fix it. Recent legislation concerning youth unemployment has been not only a policy response to its high levels, but an indirect attempt to deal with increasing high school dropout rates and declining academic achievement among high school students. However, any reconnection of schools with the realities of the economy and the changing job market must include more than the school and the workplace, since families introduce and peer groups help to redefine the places teenagers see for themselves in the adult world of work.

An awareness of this is already present among practitioners in a wide variety of the youth-related agencies we observed, where we found successful as well as less than successful programs for strengthening the relationship between work and schooling. For example, we found that those which are successful stress a linkage that produces a unified view of how education relates to later as well as present work skills and career development. The primary factor seems to be sufficient planning to assure that the work component of the school-with-work collaboration addresses some area of productive enterprise which is valued by both adolescents and the community, and provides some sense of challenge to both.

This does not necessarily mean that productivity is measurable only by pragmatic standards. Certainly programs which are directly linked with business and industry can be important and practical means for a comprehensive career education model that both prepares for and structures the transition to the world of work. But providing skilled employees for business and industry is neither the sole function of the school nor the primary benefit of the successful adolescent transition to a productive, secure adulthood. A second factor which we found in many successful programs grows directly out of the view of work as more than just man's and woman's lot in life. It can and should be viewed as a means of transforming the environment and producing the culture. This can begin in the school. A number of schools where we did research had established programs in which students worked on a variety of community improvement projects.

A third factor of successful programs linking school with work is their focus on providing firsthand knowledge to youths of what the current occupational options are in the area. One of the major criticisms of traditional vocational education programs is that they prepare students for jobs which may well be obsolete in the long-range, if not short-range, future. One of the most promising approaches here is a resurgence of the apprenticeship. Apprenticeships currently seem to be concentrated in the industrial sector, particularly in the building trades, where over 60 percent of the registered apprentices are located. But apprenticeship programs tend to be industry-based, while cooperative vocational education is school-based.[22] The two can work together. Schools can channel well-prepared and interested students into apprenticeships of various kinds in any area of the economy, while still providing the instructional portion of the program.

Finally, successful programs which link the world of work to schooling provide a realistic structure of expectations which tempers possibilities with realities, and which youths can see and evaluate while being permitted sufficient flexibility to allow for differing emphases on schooling and work preparation for different and changing work roles, at different times. One of the lessons of past attempts to integrate work and schooling is that while providing a sense of direction is essential to setting up programs which are task and goal oriented, such programs can become rigid and miss the opportunity or need to change with changing times. It may well be that the problem resides not with our youth, but in what has happened to the American Dream itself. We have seen that family structure, socialization, and enculturation in both family and school, as well as educational achievement and the sorting process associated with it, are the common building blocks for adult careers in both the legitimate and underground economies. What we have sometimes failed to see is how all of these influences combine to produce social bonds for teenagers which can either predispose them to, or preclude them from involvement in, disruptive and delinquent behavior.

6

Pathways to Crime

Throughout the United States there is a growing concern about adolescent involvement in an ill-defined range of behaviors from "youthful mischief" to "crime." Some of our worries about adolescents seem remarkably similar from place to place and from generation to generation and are extensions of the concerns we have about even the most "normal" of adolescents: Will they grow and develop into proper adults and have a happy and productive life? What can I do as a parent to help them along in this? There are also more formidable fears about characteristics and behaviors which we consider abnormal or deviant. Deviant in this sense can just mean different, but it can also cover a host of social and emotional problems which grow with teenagers' newly strengthened aggressive and sexual drives. But changing social values can alter the line between what we consider normal and what we label as deviant.[1]

In seeking causes for deviant and criminal behavior, experts and public opinion have blamed failures of the family, the school, and the community. Peer groups, and particularly deviant peers or groups, are equally suspect in our attributions of blame. We are increasingly using the courts and the legislative system in addition to, and sometimes instead of, the family and the school to establish conformity and control, to correct these perceived failures on the part of a community's social institutions, and to instill a proper commitment to a healthy as well as moral life. One reason for the legislative takeover is the continuing controversy over whether we are being too lenient or too harsh in our treatment of adolescent "status offenders" as well as those who commit serious crimes. A status offender—the teenage drinker, the truant or dropout, the incorrigible, the runaway—is found guilty of an act for which she would not be charged if an adult. There are also distinctly criminal acts, some of considerable violence, committed by adolescents which lead us to fear them as well as fear for them. Often seemingly senseless juvenile crimes are attributed to such youthful social ills as drug abuse or teenage gangs.[2] The result of such thinking, rational as well as irrational, is the imposition of society's authority and control not only over what is considered "deviant" in adolescents' behavior, but over the socializing role of their families and other community institutions as well.

Not only the crime rate but the type of crime committed varies across age groups and the adolescent years as well. Embezzlement, forgery, and the various other "white collar crimes" require adult status and opportunities. There is also a developmental pattern in criminal or delinquent behavior within adolescence, so that property crimes are much more a part of early adolescence than are violent crimes, which increase in the middle and later teen years. In fact, older adolescents (fifteen to seventeen), along with young adults (eighteen to twenty-four), are disproportionately responsible for acts of criminal violence.[3] To some extent this may be the result of the neutralization by incarceration or even death of older offenders, but it also represents the steady escalation of juvenile crime in the aftermath of World War II.[4] But here again I am certain that it is fundamentally the result of the failure of many families and their communities to develop and empower a firm, fair, and consistent charter of behavioral and social expectations for adolescents. The failure of community-based social institutions to interact productively in helping youngsters develop is clear in the fact that adolescents who become offenders are more likely to have trouble at home and in school, to abuse drugs and alcohol, and to come from a minority and poverty background.[5] Those who have been abused as children not only are more likely to become involved in crime, but their crimes also tend to involve more aggressive, even violent behavior.[6]

Whether aggression is the expression of an innate drive, produced by frustration, or socially learned through modeling, it is visibly a feature of adolescent life, particularly among males.[7] The mortality rate among young men in America is almost three times that of their female age-mates. This is in large measure a result of the major role which violence and other aggressive factors play in such deaths. Accidents, particularly in automobiles, account for a major portion of these deaths, but homicide and suicide rates are also high, accounting for twice as many deaths as cancer, which is the leading cause of death as a result of illness among young people. There is, however, the same variability in dying as there is in life for adolescents. Suicide rates are three times higher for males than for females and twice as high among whites as among blacks. White male adolescents are the most likely to commit suicide; black females, the least. Homicide rates, which seem to have stabilized to about the same level as suicides (approximately 12 per 100,000 persons), also present dramatic differences by race and gender. Black males have homicide rates which are six times higher than for whites, and black female rates are four times higher than they are for white women.[8]

But by no means are all of the problems of teenage delinquency the result of impulsive behavior. Sometimes teenagers get into trouble just because of their status—no longer children but not yet adults—by violating moral or social norms through behavior that is not criminal and does not involve a victim in the usual sense. "Incorrigibility" and "moral depravity" are the most controversial status offenses because they are so vaguely defined, allowing a good deal of latitude for parental and police discretion in both the reporting and disposition processes. Juvenile justice critics particularly point to the enormous potential for abuses created by the lack of procedural safeguards for individual rights characteristic of the juvenile courts. In 1967 the U.S. Supreme Court ruled that it was unconstitutional for state laws to provide differential sentencing for the same crime by virtue of age, and that juvenile courts were subject to the same due process requirements as all other courts. Operationally, however, adolescents and children are still subject to different laws and different treatment under the law than adults. Examples—such as movements to impose curfews and to increase the minimum legal ages for drinking, driving, and other behaviors considered adult prerogatives—are commonplace. But at the same time the age at which children can be prosecuted as adults for more serious felony crimes has been adjusted downward in a number of jurisdictions.

There are also considerable differences among communities in terms of the types and the intensity of teenage misbehavior which is judged serious enough to warrant intervention and social control. Such acts can be individual or group and can range from disciplinary problems at home through substance abuse and other health-related abuses, to violence, homicide, or suicide. These social distinctions and community attitudes also affect who is and who isn't apprehended, whether or not they are arrested if apprehended, and what happens to them if they are arrested. Young people throughout the country, for example, are the age group most likely to commit a crime, to be the victim of a crime, and to be arrested. There are, however, significant differences in victimization, offense, and arrest rates by gender and race; and such rates are also a function of residence and are highest in urban inner-city areas and lower in suburban and rural areas. Street crime in the urban centers of America has a major effect on the quality of life for adolescents and presents a unique dimension of concern and anxiety in their social and emotional development.

Wide variations in defining adolescent status, and consequently in identifying and dealing with those behaviors which are considered status offenses, were apparent among and within all of our field sites. In looking at the observational and interview data, what was most striking was that the age-graded definition of delinquency has as its immediate behavioral and social consequences the establishment of wide discretionary powers on the part of the agents of the criminal justice system. The discretionary process begins with the police officer who first encounters an incident. Police officers, probation and court professionals, and parents, as well as adolescents, all spoke of the considerable variability among police officers in their response to adolescents and what might be considered delinquent behavior. At this level, the discretion reflects the individual officer's values, the norms of the police subunit within which she is working, the characteristics of the community in which the activity takes place. A particularly important factor mentioned is the officer's estimate of what will or will not be done by the courts in relation to specific individuals. In Southside, for example, police admit that they will not arrest an adolescent for possessing or even for smoking a small amount of marijuana unless there is some more serious crime involved, because the youthful offender will be back on the streets even before the arresting officer has completed the paperwork involved in filing the charge.

While we found some evidence of deviance and delinquency in every community, we saw the same variations by residence that have been reported nationally. Violence was most common in the conflict-ridden urban inner-city areas and virtually unheard of in the suburban areas. In some rural places like Green Valley, what little violence we heard of was domestic—between husband and wife, father and child, or siblings—and, the police said, was better left to the family to resolve. In Ranchville violence was episodic. The deputies there associated it with payday-night rowdiness, and, so long as the migrant workers kept it among themselves, seldom intervened. There were thefts in every community, and the variations among communities were predictable according to their social organization. Mugging and armed robbery made the streets of Southside, and particularly Wharton Hill, unsafe for residents as well as passers-through, and fear of being attacked for even small sums of money was one of the costs of living or visiting there. In all of the rural areas automobile theft was the most frequently reported juvenile crime, although vandalism and even some burglary by juveniles were also frequently reported. Thefts in Sheffield and Newtown were always said to be by youths from less affluent neighboring towns, although the police did mention that theft of liquor from parents or neighbors was becoming common.

After an adolescent enters the criminal justice system as a result of being apprehended for some violation of the law, there are different routes through it in different communities. For example, both the Southside and the Sheffield criminal justice systems make use of "diversionary" programs to deal with youth as an alternative to incarceration, but there are significant differences between the two. At the ideological level the most frequently cited reasons for such diversionary programs in Southside are overcrowding of court calendars and correctional facilities as well as resistance to placing youth in situations where criminal careers can be established. In Sheffield, on the other hand, the reasoning is much more related to the importance of other settings for social learning. The criminal justice system there explicitly views the school, the family, the church, and other social agencies as being the first step in dealing with wayward adolescents. The system also sees close linkages among these institutions as the basis for good moral and legal learning. A wide variety of sports, recreational, and counseling programs are available to which youngsters can be referred.

In Southside a teenage offender enters the criminal justice system by being brought to the attention of the police officer, after which several things can happen. The youth can be released to the care of his parents or guardians; he can be returned to a specific agency or authority such as the probation department or a residential service program; he may be referred to special counseling or treatment services by the police; or the case may go to the court for prosecution. Cases referred to court are handled either by the family court or by the criminal court, usually depending upon the age of the youth. There is now considerable controversy over whether the seriousness of the offense rather than the age of the perpetrator should determine the decision. Under recent juvenile offender laws, cases involving serious felonies by youth under sixteen are handled as adult cases by the criminal court, which may, however, refer them back to the family court. Changes in the education and social services laws and the Family Court Act have raised from sixteen to eighteen the age at which someone who drops out of school without written authorization can be adjudicated a ''person in need of supervision'' (PINS). The result has been that an estimated tens of thousands of new cases are flooding the courts, and many PINS adolescents, say juvenile experts, are ''falling between the cracks,'' lost in the welter of forms issued by various agencies and the courts. What is important in this context is the use of criminal justice agencies to enforce generalized standards of adolescent behavior because of the perceived inability of the school system to deal with its dropouts.

In Sheffield an adolescent may also become involved in the criminal justice system through apprehension by the police, but once again the suburban safety net of social institutions comes to the rescue. The teenager is dealt with as a communitywide responsibility rather than a deviant individual to be remanded to the criminal justice system. There are a number of factors which could explain this. One is the fact that in Sheffield the police are an integral part of the community, while in Southside they usually live elsewhere and are to some extent alienated from the community. Another factor may be the sheer difference in size and diversity of population in the two sites.

What seems most striking, however, is the coming together of social institutions in Sheffield when a youngster gets into difficulty. The township has its own citizen-based Juvenile Conference Committee (JCC), which according to its original charge is ''mandated to deal with the vast middle ground of juvenile behavior, neither harmful enough to require adjudication, nor innocuous enough to be overlooked by the community.'' This committee can make a number of recommendations concerning disposition of a case, most of which result in referral to one or more community agencies or projects. Even this community-based approach, however, is only one aspect of a larger, multi-institutional community perspective on dealing with delinquency. Project Community Pride, for example, is a police-operated program, covering Sheffield and two neighboring communities, in which youth and their parents receive family counseling as well as work assignments, church referrals, or school counseling. Sheffield teenagers are seldom actually sent to court; most of the disposition of cases occurs before any court appearance. What takes place in the courts, however, is similar to what takes place at the JCC and police levels; youth, as the juvenile judge put it, "are reassigned to the community."

There are two levels of meaning here. First, the offender is literally returned to the community, since the juvenile court is actually in the county seat and the local police term for referral to the court is "sent out of town." But more important, the notion is that the youth is being "reassigned" to community agencies for resocialization. The detective in charge of juvenile programs in Sheffield commented on the "informal community network" which surrounds the youngster who gets into trouble. "There is no question that the kids who get into mischief or even serious trouble in Sheffield are headed for criminal careers," he said. "Sending them to court or institutionalizing them would be a step in that direction, since they would lose the close community support once they left." State correctional institutions, he went on to explain, are crowded with the worst kids from city slums and depressed rural areas, and "our kids just can't survive in those institutions because they aren't tough enough compared with the others."

The support provided by the interaction of the social agencies is demonstrated in a number of ways. The superintendent of schools, for example, often referred to a number of church-based youth programs as places where the school activities were buttressed with good social experiences. The police we interviewed also mentioned these same social agencies (the detective who is responsible for juvenile justice works closely with them) as places where "kids who get into trouble can get a firm hand while being in contact with a lot of good kids at the same time." The most extreme form of criminal justice sanction, according to educational and criminal justice professionals we interviewed in Sheffield, is to remove a youth's driving privileges. This can be done in the community by the police, by the Juvenile Conference Committee, or by the judge. This is an example of the communitywide coherence of institutions, since the removal of the license is an informal (and possibly illegal) sanction applied for any infraction whether or not it is related to driving. An adolescent who is apprehended for possession of a small amount of marijuana (but probably not other drugs such as cocaine or crack), is chronically truant, or is incorrigible at home can have his driving privileges removed and this action will be supported by the school, the family, and the adult community in general.

Rural Green Valley's isolation from the social service programs centralized in the county seat and lack of public transportation access also affect its juvenile justice experience. This physical isolation seems to produce a perceptual isolation as well. We were told repeatedly by juvenile justice program officials in the county seat that they really didn't know much about Green Valley or its youngsters. Once again they cited the remoteness of the region and the people to any outside influence. As the conversations continued, however, it became apparent that there was also a feeling that Green Valley teenagers are adequately "controlled" by their families and communities and that with the exception of vandalism and minor theft, the juvenile crime problem there could not be expected to match the problems faced in the county seat as a result of its multiracial population.

The county probation officer not only agreed with this assessment but extended it. Green Valley, she said, handles juvenile justice problems—both status offenses and delinquent behavior—in the way they should be handled: the formal juvenile justice system is "the court of last resort" for teenagers there. Only when all local resources fail is there any consideration given to turning to the youth authorities. The folklore of America, she added, sees this as the tendency of the small rural community to "hide its dirty laundry from outsiders" and to take care of its own. This is not true, she said—at least in what little experience she has had with Green Valley. Certainly the town is not interested in publicizing any problems, but the fact is there just aren't any major ones. Given the small size of the community and its relatively stable population, just about any problem can be handled locally. After giving some examples of the chaotic criminal justice problems in the county seat, she added again that Green Valley's informal social controls were really the only way to handle juvenile problems.

Community leaders in Green Valley still tend to agree with this assessment of the success of their informal approach. This is usually followed by a disclaimer that, of course, Green Valley doesn't have the magnitude of the problems in the county seat, not to mention places like Southside. But somewhere in that statement there is usually a direct or indirect reference to the importance of the family and the school and the stability which they provide as the real agents of social control. The community's chief of police, who, like the only other police officer, is part-time, cited vandalism as the major juvenile problem in the community. He went on to say that kids steal cars once in a while for a joyride but don't keep them for very long, because in Green Valley everybody knows everybody else's car. The conversation took place in the town's luncheonette and the owner added, "I never have trouble here because I know every kid, his father and mother, and who his teacher is, too."

The state police, who also have local jurisdiction (as they do in all rural areas), also think vandalism is the major problem but add that drug problems are growing with the influx of non-farm families (i.e., outsiders). While both the local and state police agree that marijuana is the only drug that is currently a problem, the state police hint at the beginning importation of harder drugs, again as a result of more "streetwise" youth moving into the community from outside. The local police explain that they know every family in town, and that any problems with youth are immediately brought to the attention of the offender's family, which "usually takes care of it." Once again, however, when we spoke with the state police, they mentioned growing problems with youth who have recently moved into the community.

As in Sheffield, there is a close working relationship in Green Valley between the local police and the school. Unlike the Southside police, who place most of the blame for juvenile misconduct on the family and the school, the police here see themselves as agents of those two institutions. The police chief, who grew up and went to school in Green Valley, spoke with pride of the good work being done by the counselors in the school and how the discipline there contributes to both learning and good citizenship. In large measure, he said, this also results from the town's conservative, agricultural work ethic. Later, however, he commented on how the new families are bringing change. These more affluent families, he said, provide automobiles for their children more frequently and earlier than the older traditional families. Kids in cars, he said, are out of the sight and control of the community and learn to drink and get into trouble. A curfew which requires youth to be off the streets by 11:00 P.M. was instituted a number of years ago to combat vandalism. There is also an ordinance banning the drinking of liquor or beer on public streets. Neither really works very well. Local youths go to other communities to drink, and they aren't afraid of violating the curfew because if they are apprehended by the police after the curfew hour they are simply sent home with a warning. In the old days, we were told, family and community pressure would have been a sufficient sanction, but it isn't anymore.

How typical are these communities of others? While we found many similarities among the communities we studied, no two were exactly alike and so there is not any possible typology by size, demography, pattern of residence, or any other dimension that we could find. But there are similarities, and they do seem to be associated with how the various institutional sectors relate to each other. In looking at the differences among communities in terms of how they dealt with deviant and delinquent behavior, for example, one critical factor was whether the criminal justice system saw itself and was seen by the community as an ally or as an oppressor. One of the communities we looked at was a small, rural suburb in the Southwest, very much like Sheffield and Green Valley in its family structure and schools and in how its juvenile justice program relates to both these institutions in handling local youngsters.

ARGOTOWN

Argotown is located in the Rocky Mountains along an interstate highway about fifty miles from a major city. It was once the center of a thriving gold-mining area, and there are still a number of active metals-mining sites, all operated by the same multinational corporation. There is still some gold in these hills and some nostalgia about finding new and more efficient ways of getting it out and returning to a former affluence and splendor. The old Argo mill, which was the gold-processing center for the area, is still open as a tourist attraction, and it is the tourists—along with the more economically viable if less romantic copper and molybdenum mines—who provide jobs for many of the twenty thousand inhabitants of the area.

The township is also the administrative center of the county school district and the location of its single secondary school. The school district, which covers a 450-square-mile area, includes a number of economically and socially diverse communities. Closer to the metropolitan center is Spruceville, a suburban community with large and spacious houses, estates, and ranches. To the west of Argotown is the county seat of Frenchtown, another old mining town of about a thousand people, which, with two hundred of its original nineteenth-century buildings still intact, is now a year-round tourist center. Frenchtown was once a thriving community of five thousand with an opera house, a hospital, and two newspapers, but the Sherman Silver Purchase Act of 1893, which produced a sharp decline in the price of silver, made it a virtual ghost town until tourism rescued it from continued decline. The effect that fluctuations in the price of metals can have on the local economy is still a concern, evident when declines in the demand for copper or molybdenum produce layoffs, which bring back memories of what can happen in a one-industry company town.

Paradoxically, despite its attraction as a tourist mecca, there are few recreational and entertainment facilities available to local adolescents outside their homes and the school. Once they can drive and have access to an automobile, they go into the big city, particularly when there are major rock or country and western concerts there. The local police and parents, part of a protective social web which surrounds the community's teenagers, don't like that because it leads to drug use and other big-city problems, which are not, they maintain, a part of local life. In what we came to learn were a number of accommodations reached by the parents, the police, and the adolescents to "keep the kids at home," the community informally accepts but does not officially sanction "hill-toppers": spontaneous beer parties in one of a number of mutually acceptable gathering spots in the mountains outside of town.

We were told by a number of adolescents (and it was confirmed by police and parents) that a hill-topper occurs when some group of teenagers or even some individual spontaneously decides to hold one—either as the result of some event, like a victory by the high school football team, or because it is "just time." The word goes out over the adolescent grapevine that a hill-topper is being held at one of the spots that night, and everyone who can get transportation will head for it. Someone or some group—whoever has money—buys the beer at the local convenience store and the partying begins. At some point one of the town's police cars will probably drive up, stop for a moment on the periphery of the party area, and, if everything seems to be in order, drive away.

The informal agreement among the teenagers, parents, and the police includes the responsibility to clean up the site (the partygoers call it "policing") and insure that campfires are out. Parents hear about the arrangements for a hill-topper almost as soon as their teenage children do. Usually they will not interfere unless there is one of the periodic rumors that someone has brought drugs back from the big city, or unless they are disciplining their child for some infraction of a family-based rule. I rode in one of the police cars checking out a hill-topper, and the police officer, who had attended hill-toppers himself as a high school student a few years before, explained that "kids have to raise a little hell every once in a while, and this way they can do it here without being watched and judged by the whole town, instead of getting into things they can't handle in the city or in the back seat of a car."

The homogeneity of the adolescent population of Argotown is reminiscent of Sheffield. There are, however, some important differences as well as similarities. Sheffield's affluence and class homogeneity are not found in Argotown, where there are distinctive if unobtrusive social class differences between the small Hispanic (primarily Mexican-American) and American Indian communities and most residents. But these communities are well-integrated into an institutional system which provides guidance for adolescent development through a locally based, staffed, and funded youth services program. Juveniles who get into difficulty in any of the institutional sectors—the family, the school, the criminal justice system—can be referred by any of the program's agencies. Remediation services, including job training and placement, family and personal counseling, educational programming, and community service, are community-based. They are restricted to local adolescents, and the itinerant "dirt bag hippies" and "ski bums" who come to the town in the appropriate season are not referred to such services but go directly and formally into the criminal justice system. This resistance to outsiders is apparent in the signs reading "Native" which some long-time residents attach to the license plates of their cars. More recent residents sometimes affix "Nearly Native" signs to their plates.

Contrast this community based and supported approach to teenage deviance with what happens in the urban inner-city area of Wharton Hill. Here the criminal justice system is considered and considers itself to be imposed on rather than a part of the community, virtually an occupying force. There are two models of community organization immediately obvious as one moves from the "older" pattern of local institutions that has disappeared from Wharton Hill but is still found in the more affluent Italian and Portuguese wards of the city to the newer, emerging institutions in the black and Hispanic communities, such as Wharton Hill. The older ethnic groups had developed a model of local community organization supported by kinship and kinship-like relationships. Young people did get into trouble and were some-times sent off to correctional institutions, but the first attempts at correction were local, involving the family, the school, and the church. One of the few white teachers left in Wharton Hill's high school explained what he had witnessed in his twenty-two years of teaching in the area:

> The Italians took care of their own, and when a kid got into trouble his father would beat the hell out of him. If that didn't work, then the priest would talk to him and he might beat the hell out of him too. If the kid had trouble in school, they would tell his parents and maybe even get in touch with the church so that they could "talk" him into joining the CYO [Catholic Youth Organization]. It wasn't just that the kids were afraid, although a lot of them were; it was that they knew what was expected of them and what would happen if they got too far out of line. The Portuguese were the same, although their kids seemed to be in less trouble. But when the Italians moved out it all changed. There wasn't anybody left in the community to send the kids to, nobody who really gave a damn. The parents were afraid of their own children, and the schools couldn't control them even if they went to school. The police? They didn't give a damn either as long as they robbed and mugged their own people here in Wharton Hill. They didn't start to worry until the muggers moved outside of Wharton Hill and started hitting on people downtown.

We heard this same explanation for "the two Wharton Hills" from many of the police, prosecutors, public defenders, probation officers, and judges, whether it was framed as "The Italians had their own family system when they were here" or "Nobody would dream of starting trouble because the community wouldn't stand for it." What replaced this community-based system after the racial riots of the late 1960s and early 1970s (always cited as the demarcation point) was a new social support system which was externally funded and, say local residents like this black probation officer, externally directed:

> We were in trouble even before the Reagan administration cut off funds for just about everything. This was not only true in the

correctional programs; it happened in education also. We always heard that if you moved poverty people into modern housing they would soon turn it into slums, but we always thought that was racist bullshit. The real reason it didn't take long was because a community wasn't there to support them. There were no support systems established in the black and Hispanic communities. They were used to white policemen and judges and they always had gone to white agencies for help. After the riots a lot of new programs started, but they were started by people who didn't have any established ties for credibility in the community. They had to try to work out links with the existing structure in the city and to build new structures in the black and Hispanic communities. I just don't know if it would ever have worked, but the budget cuts cut off the outside money and everything started to dry up. Look at the new Wharton Hill and you see abandoned hopes as well as buildings. Now kids who get into trouble think they are lucky to be sent away. Any talk about juvenile diversion is a joke; there are no jobs or social programs to send them to, or local agencies to work with anymore.

The people of Wharton Hill have not, however, given up in the face of poverty, crime, and despair, and there are a number of new community-based initiatives beginning there. One of these initiatives addresses a common complaint against the criminal justice system which we heard here (as well as in Southside): the police ignore crime and violence in the ghetto as long as it doesn't spill outside to more affluent sections. Following a police strike which left Wharton Hill even less protected than usual, a local group of volunteers not only began to patrol the streets themselves but used their cars as ambulances to take the ill to the hospital and the elderly to the services they required. This community-based program continues to develop and expand and is beginning to make a difference. While it is too soon to report any changes in crime statistics to indicate if the volunteers are being any more successful than the police have been in reducing crime, there is a discernible difference in what you hear on the street. People talk about having taken the streets back for themselves, and about feeling safer knowing that neighbors are out there to help. Other community groups are also beginning to work with adolescents and youth, family planning and health care. The difference between the Wharton Hill of the recent past and the new community which is struggling to emerge is expressed this way by residents: "We want our kids to grow up with pride in their community." They go on to say that the first steps have to take place within Wharton Hill and begin with learning to depend on each other rather than waiting for help from others. "We need help to make this into a viable community," said one of the leaders of the street patrol program, "but we have to learn how to help each other before we can even decide what help we have to ask for outside."

Still a different pattern of organization linking criminal justice with the other social institutions is visible in Riverton, which is quite near Wharton Hill. Riverton has also experienced an influx of blacks and Hispanics in recent decades, but their integration into the community has been quite different from the Wharton Hill experience, because of an existing black middle-class community in Riverton which could extend its established social support system to the newcomers. For Hispanics, however, such a supportive base was absent, and, as a result, it seemed to be Hispanic youth who were most frequently in trouble with the law, just as they were most frequently in trouble in the schools and in the labor market. A court officer who had lived and worked in Riverton for twenty-seven years told us:

> There isn't too much trouble with kids here because the county wouldn't stand for it and so they have seen to it that there is good police service here as well as good housing. There have been a lot of blacks and Puerto Ricans moving in over the last ten years, and with all the high priced high-rises here you might expect that there would be a lot more trouble with drugs and break-ins, but it's pretty quiet. Most of the trouble is with the Puerto Rican kids because their families don't have real roots here. When they get into trouble there isn't anyplace they can go except to the juvenile authorities—no church, no civic groups, not even any relatives or family.

All communities display different degrees of concern about deviant juvenile behavior, but all fear teens' potential for delinquency. While poverty and isolation can be influential in delinquency, affluence and planned social contacts are not always safeguards against it. The importance of having an established social order which links institutions to each other was equally obvious in Newtown, the planned community where there had been a well-meaning but ill-advised attempt to design and implement an artificial social system and sense of community.

As part of that plan it was expected that Newtown would be home to different social classes as well as different races. In effect, the plan called for an integrated "city" in which the social support base would be income-blind as well as color-blind. While present-day Newtown does not reflect the social disintegration of the slum, it has begun to experience some of the problems of imperfect social integration. So long as most black residents were solidly middle-class there was little difficulty, but when the planned-for subsidized lower-income housing appeared, it brought with it some unanticipated perceptual problems. A study of the politics of race in Newtown, done in the early 1970s, found "a chain of implication" that "associates crime with subsidized housing, and subsidized housing with blackness."[9] While the study found few open allusions to race as a factor in crime in Newtown, it reported that "cover" terms, such as "problems of racial mixture" among teenagers or the presence of "low-income people," were frequently mentioned.

Ten years later we still sometimes heard the same associations whenever there was talk about trouble, and even some direct references to low-income black teenagers who brought with them "a lack of familiarity" with, or a "resistance" to, the community's social control system. But even more frequently, however, blame was placed on "outsiders"—black teenagers from two nearby metropolitan areas or white youngsters from the surrounding rural county areas—who were not subject to the social control system and came into town "looking for trouble." This view was described in an interview with a young white youth who had moved out of his parents' home in one of the villages into an apartment in a nearby low-income section:

A few years back we had the famous lakeside battle over turf areas which all the parents will tell you was a drug fracas but which was really a racial incident. There are no real facilities for older adolescents here because it was assumed that they would all be off to college. So older teenagers hang around the lake [in the center of Newtown near the mall] to party, and territory gets known to belong to certain groups largely on a racial basis. Nobody said it had to be that way; it was just that white kids gathered in some places and black kids in another, and everything was O.K. until somebody decided that somebody else's section was better. One night the different groups got involved in a fight over turf, and when it got out of hand the Toonervilles [county sheriff's deputies] came in to break it up. There was a lot of talk among grown-ups that it was "undesirables" from outside the community who came in and started it because "our blacks" were integrated into the community.

The persistence with which such racial and ethnic stereotyping influences our attribution of deviance among adolescents is one of the unfortunate prices we still pay for diversity.[10] This same "insiders" versus "outsiders" distinction in treating as well as defining deviance and delinquency can develop, however, even in the absence of race and ethnicity as a basis for justifying current social biases. In the winter resort city of Smyrna Beach, burglaries and thefts were always said to be the work of "tourists," "beach bums," or "winter people," while Argotown always blamed "hippies," "ski bums," or "city kids" who were passing through. Green Valley's old families blamed the new commuter-type teenagers for introducing drugs into the town, while the commuter families in both Sheffield and Newtown were concerned about their teenagers going into nearby cities to obtain drugs. In Smyrna Beach the sheriff's deputies said that there actually was very little crime brought into town by outsiders and that many of the senior citizens who come to live here choose this area because it has not been as hospitable to lower-class migrants who had created major crime problems in other resort communities in the state.[11] In Argotown, on the other hand, the local police confirmed that itinerants —attracted to the town because of its proximity to a major East-West interstate highway—did create a good deal of trouble and were the most frequently arrested young people in the area.

Concerns over rejection of the conventional local values and susceptibility to influences from outside the community also extend to worries about adolescent health, which center on the subsequent life effects of drug, tobacco, and alcohol abuse and teenage pregnancy. There are also the more recent fears of AIDS among sexually active and intravenous drug–using adolescents, who may not have symptoms for years after the infection. Drug use and abuse, however, and how it could bring crime and violence into the community, was by far the major concern we heard in communities, reflecting the sad truth that society is frequently more concerned about adolescent disturbances than it is about disturbed adolescents.

Alternating periods of concern with drug or alcohol abuse ignore the evidence that substance abuse is a generic rather than substance-specific problem; people who currently drink are six times more likely to use drugs than are nondrinkers.[12] While drug use declined among adolescents in general in the late 1980s, the incidence of cigarette smoking remained constant.[13] Despite the decline in the overall use of drugs, including cocaine, the use of crack, a form of cocaine, became a problem of considerable concern in urban areas because of its addictive patterns and relationship to violence and crime. Patterns of alcohol and drug use differ according to residence in one region of the country or another, residence in urban or suburban settings, and socioeconomic status, and these same differences appear among teenagers.[14]

When asked why they used drugs, teenagers in the suburbs most often offered curiosity about drugs and the peer pressure of "everybody does it" as explanations. Many also maintained that they had observed fathers having a cocktail or two when they returned from work, or mothers using legal drugs for stress relief; these teenagers saw the "soft drugs" they used as simply another form of the stress-relief syndrome. Answers to these same questions about drug use put to urban inner-city teenagers were quite different from the peer pressure and curiosity factors we heard about in suburban areas. Youths here spoke of poverty, unemployment, and alienation; many minority youths described their drug problems as the result of police indifference to, or even collusion in, the drug trade in ghettos. Some even spoke of a calculated plot on the part of a racist establishment to keep black youngsters down by letting drugs spread in urban inner-city areas.[15] The severity of the type of drug used by youths in the urban inner city—heroin and later cocaine and crack—was a further indication of how different the drug problem is there than in less socially disorganized communities. Although the use of these "hard" drugs depends to some extent on their availability in urban areas, it is also a result of the pattern of relationships among the major social institutions in a community and their interactive involvement with adolescent development. Police in the suburbs reported that parents and educators would come to them for help whenever there was any indication of drug use and would "go berserk" if they heard of any possibility of hard drugs, while many parents and some educators we talked to in Southside and Wharton Hill would agree with the teenagers' allegations of police indifference or worse.[16]

Whether in the suburbs or the inner city, popular opinion, supported by some research, holds that peer pressure and a drug culture associated with peer groups is what is most instrumental in teenage drug use.[17] Other research, however, presenting a different view of how peer groups influence drug use among adolescents, indicates that it is often acquaintances—not friends—who first introduce individual adolescents to drugs.[18] Still other research has shown that drug users are not close to their parents, and even that conflicts with parents are directly associated with drug use.[19] Another study found that parental relations were associated with adolescent drug use but peer influences—as measured by scales of social adequacy, social isolation, and independence—were not. Still other studies suggest that the drug user may be "the adolescent who is the loner in this culture, the adolescent without family and friends."[20]

In Seminole County we were able to observe the effects of three very different forms of community organization and three very different patterns of community response to juvenile deviance, all within the criminal justice jurisdiction of one political-administrative unit. There is little or no difference among the three communities in terms of the availability of juvenile justice services. The sheriff's office maintains a countywide Youth Relations Deputy Program in which younger sheriff's deputies are assigned full-time duty in schools. The deputy makes classroom presentations on the work of the police, carries out individual and small group discussions of problems related to drug dependency or delinquency "before it becomes a serious legal problem," and, as a resource person, refers adolescents to appropriate community agencies as necessary or requested. The deputy is, however, "first and always a law enforcement officer," and at the principal's request will investigate criminal violations committed by students attending his particular school. A Youth Relations Deputy, who is uniformed and armed, is assigned to each middle and high school in the county.

When we talked with this deputy, as well as with other police officers, about juvenile problems in schools in Seminole County, there was no mention of gangs or other disruptive groups or any real problems with delinquency or crime. The major problem, they said, was drugs and drug-related theft, perhaps due to the easy availability of drugs in that region. Parents, youth-related professionals, and even adolescents themselves echoed the major, countywide concern about drugs. The police, however, saw very different ways of dealing with the drug problem in each of the communities, and their characterizations of social integration and control mechanisms in each place were confirmed by subsequent interviews with social agency personnel, teachers, and teenagers themselves. When we looked at our data on drug use, we once again found that the availability of opportunities for conventional bonding—being close to the family, making a good relationship with the school—provided the best barrier against deviant bonding and delinquent learning structures.

Smyrna Beach police, and most of the adolescents and adults we interviewed there, saw teenage drug users as either alienated from the local controls of community social institutions or, less frequently, as "outsiders": recent arrivals in town who were as yet unintegrated into the community. My own sense at the time was that in this family-oriented resort-retirement community, fear of drug-related adolescent deviance from the strong family values and the fears of the retirees about the potential for drug-related crime were reflected in the community attitudes. The key to solving the drug problem, everyone agreed, was to strengthen the role of the family by educating parents about the immediate and long-term hazards of drug abuse. In fact, one of the major national parent-centered teenage drug abuse prevention programs began and is still headquartered in Smyrna Beach. However, an alternative view was voiced by a psychiatrist who specialized in adolescent problems and the psychologist who worked with her. They maintained that the dependence on tourism and the consequent need to maintain an orderly community had led to a strong sense of "wanting to keep the lid on" local kids. The "complete power" which the family and political structure of the community exerted over youngsters to insure this provided a restrictive and, in their opinion, oppressive environment for adolescent development. The Smyrna Beach teenagers I interviewed did comment that "cutting up and dragging [driving through] or even hanging out downtown is a no-no," but there was no discernible sense of oppression or resentment on their part. Rather, they seemed to have accepted this as the way things were. They did their cutting up, dragging, and hanging out in beach areas just outside of the downtown area, and their parents and the police accepted this compromise. Some youths from nearby communities such as Cypress City or Ranchville mentioned that they were hassled and roused by the police in Smyrna Beach if they appeared in the downtown areas, or could not present an acceptable reason for being anywhere else in town.

In the migrant worker community of Ranchville we were told that there was little difficulty with adolescents as far as the criminal justice system was concerned. To some extent this was the result of the "tight lid" the growers kept on the community, but, said local residents, the migrants' children were quickly integrated into the family work team and spent much of their time working on the farms. There were some problems with drugs, but these were beginning to come under control because the police authorities and the school system were cracking down. When I asked about working on drug prevention with families, as was already happening in Smyrna Beach, I was told that families were powerless to do anything because it was peer groups which were at fault. When the Smyrna Beach–based drug prevention program did try to start a program in Ranchville, the organization was unable, I was told, to find enough parent support to make it worthwhile. The principal of the Ranchville high school, whose wife was an administrator in the Smyrna Beach high school, explained that "the parents who could relate to the program were not those who had kids who were using drugs, and the kids who were using them had parents who couldn't relate to the Smyrna Beach people who ran the program."

In Cypress City, where juvenile delinquency was almost unheard of a decade before our visits, there were beginning to be some problems with drug use by adolescents. Police officers and teachers told us that cocaine use was becoming "frequent" among the newly affluent children of drug smugglers. This assertion was combined with descriptions of a decline in family values attributed by the authorities to the sudden wealth of families who were ill-prepared for it. What had happened, they said, was that a community which had a strong sense of "moral order and decency" now found itself involved in the drug trade and "all of the old respect for family and community" was gone. While our research did not have the historical base to evaluate these assertions, we did find differences in the orientations toward drug use expressed in the interviews with adolescents here and those in Ranchville—both isolated, working-class communities. When drug use came up during the Ranchville interviews, the most frequent affective tone was one of peer-accepted deviance from adult values, not unlike talking about drinking or premarital sex. In Cypress City, however, the affective tone was one in which external authority rather than parental or even community sanctions were seen as the organizer of the law, rule, or convention being disobeyed. One eighteen-year-old male student from Cypress City, for example, said:

They [federal Drug Enforcement Administration agents] just come into town whenever they want and impound people's boats and airplanes because they say they are being used for drugs. Then you never see the boat or plane again unless the narcs themselves use it or put it up for auction. That's not right. We don't grow drugs here and we don't have anything to do with the fact that people all over the country use them. We never have any trouble here, so why don't they work on the people who use the drugs and stop hassling us.

Whether or not peer group influence is what leads to teenage drug abuse, drugs were an important activity and medium of social exchange among deviant groups. In every community there were groups identified by teenagers as "heads," "burnouts," "druggies," and similar terms, who were known to be heavy drug users. One important characteristic of these groups was that they provided a social setting in which teenager members could escape adult supervision. Quite frequently members became involved in other forms of deviance and delinquency as well. These peer groups, however, were usually loosely structured, temporary groupings which often changed membership over time. There were also other groups of peers in each community who, in isolation from adult supervision and guidance, formed more structured deviant groups.

Urban-slum fighting gangs, with their distinctive "colors" and intimidating names, as we saw in *West Side Story* and numerous films since then, are what first come to mind when we think of such adolescent and youth groups. The popular image is a vivid one, especially associated with the dominance of the peer group over parental and other social influences in the lives of lower-class youth. Fighting gangs still exist in urban areas, and their violence is a frightening reminder of the impulsive aggression as well as hostility and anger we associate with adolescence. There are also less aggressive but still deviant adolescent cliques, or what have come to be called "disruptive local groups," which collectively engage in antisocial or even illegal acts such as shoplifting, vandalism, drinking, or drug use. We found both of these forms of deviant youth groups in the various communities we looked at, as well as a number of self-styled "crews": gang-like peer groups in middle or high schools which seem more prone to mischief and rebellion than to any serious disruptive behavior.

While accurate information on the size and scope of juvenile gang activity in the United States is difficult to come by, the National Institute of Juvenile Justice and Delinquency estimates that there are approximately 120,000 law-violating youth groups with about 1.5 million members in the 2,100 American cities and towns with populations of 10,000 or over. This number represents about one-fifth of the male adolescents in these communities. Such disruptive groups, however, are not all gangs in the classic sense. Although they regularly associate with each other and become involved in illegal actions, they do not necessarily have the permanence, tight structure, and identifiable leadership one finds in a gang. There are about 2,200 organized gangs with approximately 96,000 members located in approximately 300 American towns and cities. Popular opinion has always thought of such gangs as the products of the inner-city areas of a major metropolis, but about half of them, and about one-third of all gang members, are found in cities with populations of half a million or less.[21] Ninety-six percent of documented gang members are under age twenty-five, and 70 percent are between sixteen and twenty years of age.[22]

Differentiating among the various types of deviant groups seems simple at first. For example, the Foxy Force, the break-dancing crew we found in the Riverton middle school, and the Ghost Shadows, a violent street gang we looked at in Southside's Chinatown, are clearly different in terms of what their members come together to do. There are also a few gangs or groups (such as the Guardian Angels, who patrol high-crime areas as surrogate police) who have chosen socially constructive forms of behavior. Even the fighting gangs sometimes perform socially constructive services, such as when they drove drug pushers out of their neighborhoods in Southside in the late 1960s and early 1970s. Whatever deviant groups do, they bring young people together in a peer group with its own social structure, which frequently binds them more closely than any other affiliation. What is it about such groups that bonds their members together, and why do they become involved in delinquent and sometimes openly criminal behavior?

We found that gangs and other disruptive groups emerged where adult caretaking environments such as the family or the school did not provide a clear and accessible structure of social order and expectations. What seemed to bond the members of these various deviant groups was some shared sense of an unmet need for affiliation, a search for what Erik Erikson called "fidelity": "something or somebody to be true to."[23] Virtually all of the adolescents who belonged to street gangs as well as disruptive peer groups continued to live at home, and even the fighting gangs lived at home most of the time. Yet, in our observations of family life and in interviews we found that many of the members of disruptive groups and almost all of the street-gang members came from broken or severely disturbed and deprived homes. While these social conditions can be disruptive in themselves, the interviews with youth-gang members in Southside and Wharton Hill, supported by the few opportunities we had to observe their family life, indicated that neither of these factors alone or even in concert was the key determinant of what leads some young males to find their primary social bonds in gang membership. Many if not most of the adolescents in both Southside and Wharton Hill suffer these same potential deficits, but only a small number join and an even smaller number remain in youth gangs. And, while young women do associate with gangs, they usually do so as auxiliaries of male gangs, and so, in our experience, the gang phenomenon is peculiarly a male phenomenon, to some extent explainable by male bonding for self-esteem, prestige, and mutual protection. But, again, these pressures and needs are present for all male youth in most urban inner-city areas.

What we found to be different was that gang members experienced and expressed a stronger need than other urban inner-city youths to distance themselves from inept or uncaring home environments which lacked even the most rudimentary family structure to support some form of a competent parent–child relationship. Many were from single-parent families where the mother had been unable or unwilling to establish adequate behavioral controls over her male children. In many other cases there was a stepfather present against whom the teenage gang member rebelled, not infrequently because of feeling that his mother was being abused or degraded. Youths of this type became alienated from their families and had fled or sometimes been chased out to the streets at an early age and banded together there. Most were still in school, although with frequent and often long periods of truancy. They felt little or no affiliation there—perhaps as much the result of the stress caused by family disturbances as of anything the school did or did not supply. They soon came to be considered rebellious, unruly, even dangerous troublemakers in the school as well as in the community. Welcome and "understood" only among others like them, they sought out the structure and the often severe strictures of organized deviant peer groups, where fidelity is to the group or gang rather than to family or school. If conventional roles in the home and the school do not provide a means of achieving an identity which fosters some minimum sense of self-worth, peer groups do—and usually with more excitement and immediate gratification. Once in the deviant peer group, the teenager learns and shares whatever forms of delinquency and criminal behavior he and his fellow members know. Younger gang members, for example, usually learn the techniques of robbery from older members and, in turn, pass them on to the next group coming up.[24]

In more affluent communities we found that quite frequently the home and the school exerted too much pressure to compete and too high a level of expectations for achievement for those youngsters who became involved in deviant and delinquent groups. These youngsters spoke of never being able to satisfy their parents or their teachers; of being judged and judging themselves as failures at an early age; of a diminished sense of self-esteem. The behaviors and attitudes they shared with other youngsters who felt negatively evaluated by parents, teachers, and more conventional peers as well were often hostile toward both the family and the school. Vandalism in the community, particularly against the school, and thefts from parents and neighbors expressed their sense of being "losers" in these social environments. Kenneth Polk found that even among middle and lower class adolescents who were not members of gangs, deviant behavior was highest among "peer-oriented" boys, those most involved in such activities as "hanging out" or "cruising" streets or shopping malls with friends, as contrasted to "parent-oriented" boys, whose activities were centered in family and home activities such as chores and doing homework.[25] The most important factor, however, was neither peer orientation nor parental orientation. Rather, school involvement seemed so critical that Polk described two opposing subcultures: one school-oriented and the other involved in "youthful hedonism and intergroup loyalty." We also found that members of gangs and disruptive peer groups had little interest in school as a learning environment, regarding it mainly as a gathering place. In our research, however, while antagonism to schooling could help account for the formation of school-based disruptive groups such as the Stickup Boys and others, we found that in many communities it was insufficient to explain the more elaborated and compelling subculture of the youth gang world. The territorial imperative of staking out and maintaining control over one's turf in a disorganized and conflict-laden community, and the violence this generated, were the forces which organized and sustained the street gangs we followed in the urban inner cities.

Why are some deviant groups more violent and more criminal than others? We did not find named fighting gangs which are involved in criminal behavior anywhere but in the urban inner-city areas of Southside and Wharton Hill. Here the disorganized, impoverished social environments do not individually or collectively hold the promise of any resources to control criminal behavior, nor are they strong enough to reverse the progressive attenuation of conventional social bonds which results. Not only youth gangs, but the organized adult criminal gangs they often grow into, flourish in the absence of a coordinated set of controls that could link the social environments of the urban inner city. Both types of gangs feed off their own communities before moving outside in search of victims.[26]

As mentioned earlier, there are fighting gangs in both Southside and Wharton Hill, and even a few instances where gangs with the same name appear in both. While there are a few gangs in Southside that are, like Southside itself, multiethnic, almost all are ethnically homogeneous and encamped in a specific piece of turf. What is clear in looking at the relationship between race or ethnicity and juvenile gangs, moreover, is the historical fact that every major ethnic group which has been ghettoized in America's major cities—the Irish, the Jews, the Italians, the blacks, the Hispanics, and more recently, the Asians—has produced youth as well as adult criminal gangs at one time or another.[27] Ethnic and racial demarcation of territory provides the bonding bases for both types of groups, sometimes even reflecting divisions and distinctions within the ethnic group itself.

In Southside's Chinatown, for example, membership in the several street gangs we followed was defined in terms of ethnic origin in China, and dominance among the gangs was established through a process of shifting loyalty or fidelity.[28] The first major gang, the Continentals, seems to have been formed in the early 1960s by American-born Chinese as a counter to black, Italian, and Hispanic gangs which surrounded the Chinese colony. Soon, however, the defensive function turned to extortion of the local merchants by selling them protection, first from outside forces but later from the Continentals themselves. Probably because of internal dissension, or perhaps even because the original members matured out, the Continentals dissolved in the mid-1960s. The lure of the gang remained, and some members formed a new gang, the Chung Yee Tong, and another offshoot, the White Eagles. At about this time, when immigration from Hong Kong soared, a new gang, the Quen Ying, began to form, and the establishment of the *dai pong*, or mini-empire of each gang, began as well. The Chung Yee Tong gave way to a derivative group called the Flying Dragons, and the three gangs—the White Eagles, the Quen Ying, and the Flying Dragons—controlled all of the streets of Chinatown, which they divided among themselves. This relative peace was short-lived, however, and soon some of the members of the Quen Ying formed a new gang called the Leung Shan Tong, taking over some territory of the White Eagles, which was breaking up as dissidents formed a new group, the Black Eagles.

By 1970, when the Leung Shan Tong was replaced by the Ernieboys, there were four rival gangs: the White Eagles, the Black Eagles, the Flying Dragons, and the newly formed Ernieboys. Over the next few years the Flying Dragons emerged as the most powerful of the four gangs, but a new group, the Ghost Shadows, appeared and grew to a membership of over two hundred immigrant youths from Hong Kong. From about 1977 on, the history of the gangs of Chinatown is one of continuing strife, which often erupted into shootings and other violence in what had always been considered a self-policing community. Some of the disruption came with internal strife among the Ghost Shadows; some, when still more new groups—such as the Chuen Ying (The Unforgettable Heroes) and the Chung Yee, an off-shoot of the Flying Dragons—were established. The earlier migrations from China had been primarily by peasants from the mainland, who settled together, and, perhaps even more than the other ethnic groups surrounding them in Southside, kept their village culture intact. Their children, however, had to leave that cultural enclave to attend school with the children of other ethnic groups. The ethnic sorting in the schools kept the Chinese children together as a social group, but in the school they lacked the familiarity of Chinatown. Like the children of every ethnic group that settled in Southside, they banded together for protection, first against the gangs from other ethnic groups and then to prey on their own neighborhoods. As the migration from China shifted from the mainland to Hong Kong and Taiwanese mi-grants, new gangs developed among these more urbanized youth, who vied for power with the established gangs, disparaging them as ''bamboo heads.'' The extortion continued and spread to protecting illegal gambling houses in Chinatown and even some Chinese-controlled massage parlors uptown.[29]

Youth gangs continue to thrive in Chinatown because they have become tied into the underground economy, where many "off the books" jobs in stores, factories, and restaurants, as well as in the Tongs and in gambling houses, offer easier dollars than seem possible from the labors of school and work. This is the other side of teenage life in Chinatown, which exists despite the current stereotype of the studious and industrious Asian-American youngster and of the strong community support which was so important in shaping Amy's world. Most Chinese gang members we met had experienced the same inept or uncaring home environments we found to be characteristic of other gang members in Southside and Wharton Hill. Many had also dropped out of school.

What we concluded from years of observation of disruptive peer groups in general and street, or fighting, gangs in particular is that they grow up in the cracks which appear in the social structure of communities under stress when their institutional systems are incongruent, unavailable, or even alien for the youngsters who live there. What the juvenile gang, and to some extent the adult criminal gang as well, provides for its membership is the certainty of a structure of social control which for some reason is missing in their contacts with the more conventional social structure of their communities. Youths seek out the support of street gangs because they did not have the "good enough" socialization from family and community institutions which would facilitate their seeking more conventional bonds and relationships. Resentful, often feeling cheated, having only each other to depend on, and blocked from access to careers in legitimate society by their lack of schooling, they act out their resentment in violence against that society and each other. Many of the delinquent youth I interviewed on the streets and in detention centers expressed anger and hostility, but usually against some generalized "society" rather than any specific part of their community such as family, school, or even the criminal justice system. One eighteen-year-old Puerto Rican teenager, for example, said at a youth board hearing on youthful violence against senior citizens:

> I was raised on the streets. My life has been one of many difficulties, problems, frustrations, and violence, for at the age of eight I was already into street life. . . . . I left school at the age of ten, because

I was sentenced to three years in a correctional facility. . . . I was the Supreme President of the Savage Samurais [a street gang], which can be a goal many youngsters dream of. . . . Young Puerto Ricans and blacks are people who are faced with so many problems at a very early stage in life. In order for us to partake in this so-called American Dream, then society will have to take a much closer look at us and try to understand us instead of putting us away, abandoning us, or psychologically destroying us. . . . The young people of today are very misguided and so very frustrated with life. But how can all the blame be put on us, or our parents, for not bringing us up right? I say the blame falls upon you—yes, you, the American society. It is time we all reach some understanding and start helping each other, instead of turning our backs.

There is, however, little that "society" can do without the will and effort of the local community and its social institutions, which is where deviance and delinquency begin. This particular youth was part of a juvenile diversion program which operated in Southside and was now finishing school under the guidance of the program. In the absence of any models to guide such youths back into the legitimate world, they emulate the only role models they see. One young adult, already launched on a career in organized crime, told me, "If the people I saw driving Lincolns and Cadillacs in my neighborhood had been doctors or lawyers, that's probably what I would have wanted to be, but they weren't; they were drug dealers and pimps who were making it." The failure to find a way back becomes even more certain when youths are sent to correctional institutions in the hope that they will be reformed, rehabilitated, and resocialized before being returned to the same community with the same not-good-enough environments. What usually happens is that most of them are soon in trouble again.

A small number of teenagers—less than one percent of older adolescents and even fewer of the early and middle adolescent population—are placed in institutions, usually as a result of their behavioral, social, physical, or emotional problems. A very small proportion are in mental hospitals or institutional settings for the mentally handicapped. By far the largest number of confined young people is in juvenile detention or correctional institutions as a result of a variety of criminal or juvenile justice offenses. Once again, blacks and Hispanics are disproportionately represented among the institutionalized, and there are also many more males than females and higher rates in urban than suburban or rural areas. The absence of the traditional socializing influence of communities, combined with the effects of the impoverished cultural environment and association with peers who share an orientation to deviance, clearly makes the institutional setting a particularly troubled environment for the adolescent transition.

We followed some of the adolescents we were observing through the courts and into correctional institutions and spent a number of years in the major juvenile detention center to which Southside's young people are sent when they get into trouble with the law. Despite the isolation and anomie of jail life, or perhaps because of it, social bonding and personal identity are even more important here than they were on the outside.[30] Life within the walls is, in many ways, a continuation of what goes on outside them for many of the young men here, but with some important modifications. One is that they come here as individuals without even the minimal association and protection they had from families. However inadequate or even destructive family relationships may have been on the outside, most inmates we spoke with felt alone and vulnerable without some family contact. Kinship, particularly among Hispanic inmates, is a link which more than any other serves to bond and protect. When Roberto and José Perez came to register for classes with one of our graduate students who was working in the inmate school, Roberto insisted that he be assigned to the same class as his younger brother because he was responsible for taking care of him. Similarly, Juan Ortiz, a newly arrived inmate, risked the wrath of one of the corrections officers on duty by rushing through the hallways looking for his cousin, who was already an inmate. He needed to find his cousin because he was the only one he could trust to keep his valuable leather jacket safe for him.

On arrival the inmate is stripped of all of the sources of support which structured his social world. The inmate population must, therefore, create its own social order based on a value system which consists primarily of the shared values which got them into confinement in the first place, as well as those values which allow the individual to deal with the debasement and degradation of correctional routine. Faced with this necessity, two related patterns of social relationship develop. One is the "court": small groups of peers, developed by the inmates themselves, based primarily on ethnicity and sometimes on prior association on the outside.[31] A court, which is similar to the neighborhood street-gang on the outside and is just as hierarchically structured, takes precedence over the imposed patterns of interaction among cell mates or work groups. A second pattern is the selection of a close associate or two with whom the inmate maintains what would be in the outside world of adolescence a "best friend" relationship. These relationships, variously called "my main man," "my man," "the man who watches my back," or, among Hispanic inmates, *mi compadre,* are essentially defensive alliances. The harsh realities of institutional violence make it essential that the inmate should have someone on whom he can depend for assistance when necessary and who will, in effect, protect his blind spots. The relationship allows for empathy and expressive exchange between two individuals who have no other social supports available to them. When we interviewed inmates, we found that they formed peer groups and friendships as much to combat the loss of identity and control which came from being alone in the face of the compelling and frequently terrifying danger, as out of fear of injury or death.

Gangs which operate outside also sometimes move inside. Two or more members of the same gang doing time together re-bond when they are inside. The members of the gangs which are most well developed and powerful outside bring the reputation and the influence of that membership with them when they are incarcerated. One of the most powerful networks of gangs we encountered in our fieldwork was the Posses, derivative from Jamaican gangs and heavily involved in drug traffic. The groups we saw had a paramilitary organizational structure, with a "general" in charge and "captains" controlling smaller groups of "soldiers." Members of the Posses have replaced the traditional pimpmobile with the Jeep, and sport pit bulls as part of an ostentatious life style as well as for protection. In a number of major cities throughout the country, they are reaping and displaying a profit from their drug trade which makes them the unconventional role models for inmates inside as well as teenagers outside the detention center. The Posse as a means of personal protection and social control moves inside from the streets among the almost exclusively black and Hispanic inmates. Inside, the Posse serves many of the affiliative functions it did on the outside; by banding together inmates enjoy the benefits of mutual support and protection. And since inside as well as out the best defense is a good offense, the gang members bully the inmates and control most of their activities.

How do you get into the Posse? There is really only one way, and that is to prove yourself, or, in the language of the inmates, "to take no shorts.'' As soon as a new inmate arrives he is tested by the Posse, either through a direct physical challenge by one of the "soldiers," or fighters for the Posse, or, more often, by having some of his belongings stolen—his sneakers, if possible, particularly if they are the high-status Puma or Adidas brands. If he puts up a good fight, he may be asked to join, or he may be tested several more times before a decision is made. If he avoids the testing or backs down, he is marked as a victim for the rest of the time he is there. There are, however, some other possible ways to gain protection from other inmates. Someone from the same neighborhood, or a "homeboy" in another symbolic relationship brought in from the outside, could help, but this is infrequent, since sharing strength and power can diminish one's own safety from predation or direct attack. This makes the lot of the few white inmates particularly difficult unless they are a "Mighty Whitey," a "live one"—with personal power because of demonstrated strength or aggressiveness. Other white inmates are at such peril that the staff often try to find some means of segregating them. Relationships with the correctional staff, however, do not offer protection, and one maxim learned by each new inmate is "Snitches get stitches," so few try to survive by informing to the staff.

The isolation and insulation from the world of social institutions outside the detention center promotes the development of alternate informal networks among the inmates, which has the further effect of reinforcing antisocial and illegitimate value systems. Although we found this same pattern in some of the communities we studied, it was most obvious in the isolation of the detention center. To some extent this could be attributed to the concentration of individuals with socially deviant values among the inmates, but it also resulted from a lack of a clear alternative structure of socially sanctioned and prolegal values among the prisoners themselves. Prestige and position among the inmates was based on the presentation of a pro-criminal and opportunistic public image which conformed to the deviant values of toughness, looking for trouble, and surrender to whatever fate brings—values we found in street gang culture in Southside and Wharton Hill.

While the educators who operate a school for the inmates we studied publicly oppose these values, they have few meaningful and available alternatives to offer. As one inmate remarked, "What can this school do for me? Even if I could learn something, my prison record will make sure I can't get a job anyway." Another inmate, who was sitting nearby, added, "Some of the teachers try but most of them agree with the CO's [the corrections officers, or guards] that we got no place to go after we get out but to come back here." Even more important than the school's inability to engage the inmate-students is the fact that the corrections officers, most of whom come from similar social and cultural backgrounds as the inmates, openly give support to these values, not only by showing favoritism toward those inmates who most clearly represent them, but by adopting those same values in their own behavior. A guard will, for example, show the same toughness and "street smarts" as inmates in dealing with rebelliousness or deviance contrary to the formal rule structure of the institution.

It is the inmate culture, reinforced by the tacit agreement of the corrections officer not to interfere as long as there is no obvious trouble, that runs the day-to-day life of the detention center. In fact, several corrections officers asserted that this is the only way they can operate the institution given their small numbers and the potential for violence among the inmates. Status and power are determined by strength even more than by wealth. If you don't have it and can't get it by becoming a member of the Posse, you have to buy it from someone who has it. There are a number of ways of doing this. You can become a "Maytag" or "Hoover" and do a stronger inmate's laundry or cleaning in return for his protection. Or you can "pay your rent" and buy protection from a stronger inmate with commissary items, particularly with soap, which is major currency for exchange. You can also use other items such as cookies, deodorant, cigarettes, clothes, or, if you can get them, drugs. Again, the relationships from outside are parodied here and the dependent inmate becomes known as the "son" of his more powerful protector. You can also pay for protection by "turning out," or engaging in homosexual activities. There are also "crabs" or "lobsters," inmates who are dirty or unkempt; strangely, this offers a form of protection also, because they tend to be avoided.

We found a similar process of establishing a small but intimate peer group—usually but not always one person—in the two psychiatric wards we studied. Like imprisonment, confinement in a psychiatric setting cuts off or reduces association with the outside community. There was, however, an interesting difference between the two psychiatric programs. One of the wards was in a famous teaching hospital and its program served youths from all over the world. In the other hospital patients came from the local neighborhoods. In the more cosmopolitan program the patients often talked about "my best friend" among the patient population, but the intimate primary relationship was even more frequently established with a staff member and it was frequently not the patient's therapist. In the other hospital the patients did form close relationships with fellow patients, and particularly with one very maternal social worker, but more frequently, strong ties to family and neighborhood precluded any consistent pattern of forming primary social bonds with another patient or even with staff members. In both hospitals, however, the availability of a caring and supportive professional staff (absent in the detention center) provided the transitional role models necessary to restructuring lives. One nineteen-year-old male in the adolescent ward of the teaching hospital with problems of depersonalization told me:

I've learned a lot from Dr. Levin. She doesn't give me all the bullshit I always got from other people here, which wasn't very different from what I got outside. I understand what some of my problems are now, but what's more important is that she has helped me to see that there is a way to learn how to get along in life.

Similarly, a fourteen-year-old black male teenager, sent to the other hospital because of school problems and adjustment problems in a single-parent family, said:

Mirta [a social worker] got me a ticket to see a *Dream Girls* matinee about two years ago and fixed it so that I could go backstage and meet some of the cast. They asked me if I wanted to come back the next day and I said "yes." Ever since then I can go in anytime I want and they give me acting and dancing lessons. I even go to the Stage Door Church with them sometimes. I applied to Music and Art [a performing arts high school] and it looks like I'll get in, and now I know what my life is going to be.

In these and other interviews there were frequent and sometimes extensive mentions of having developed a relationship with some staff member or, less frequently, with another patient who was a constant source of help and support. The image which was internalized was of a guide or exemplar of what was necessary to operate in this new and strange social context, devoid of the outside sources of support. Not only did the new "friend" help in understanding this new world;

frequently it was anticipated that he would help to bridge the transition to the future world as well. Perhaps the complete dependency which the total institutional environment of these wards imposes on the individual adolescent is what makes the relationship so intense a socializing experience. But we saw similar, if less dramatic, examples of this relationship outside a confining institution: with parents, teachers, social agency personnel, an older sibling or neighbor, a religious functionary, a martial arts teacher or master, a coach, or sometimes even a more experienced or valued peer. The relative absence of such transitional figures in the detention center is explained, if not justified, by the difference in the value-orientations of the prison and the hospital—correcting individuals who have committed crimes against society as contrasted to healing those who are ill. In the psychiatric ward, adults who have established facilitating relationships with the patients can serve as powerful role models, becoming internalized as part of the newly developing identity of the adolescent patient. In the juvenile detention facility, on the other hand, the absence of any contextually valued adult role models leads to reliance on the formation of strong partnerships with peers for protection against danger and anomie. When inmates leave the detention facility, these partnerships either dissolve, leaving individuals with an even greater sense of instability and isolation in the outside world, or they continue to link former inmates together, usually to their and the community's detriment.

What we saw inside the detention center as well as in the community is further evidence of how important it is to forge community consensus and linkages among the family, the peer group, the school, and the law to develop social constraints over conduct and pro-social values and behavior in children and adolescents. Of all the problems we associate with adolescents, antisocial and delinquent behavior are the most perplexing as well as the most troubling. Adults feel righteous anger and dismay but also some responsibility and not a little guilt about the failure of social controls over their children. Asserting that something must be done, we lash out at permissive parents or failing schools, or place the blame on the rejection of our moral values by teenagers and their peer associations. Teenagers seem just as confused as adults about the locus of responsibility and remediation for delinquency. A national survey found that throughout the country, high school students see juvenile delinquents as kids who get into trouble as well as troubled kids; as coming from rich as well as poor families but essentially as coming from families which do not care for them; as being the victims of peer pressure; as having special needs and psychological maladjustments, but also as not being very different from other kids except (particularly among urban adolescents) that they happened to get caught. In general, delinquents were feared by rural students, held in contempt by suburban students, and often seen as "normal" by urban students. Their prescriptions for preventing or controlling delinquency were better and closer family relationships with more discipline and trust. They mentioned just growing up and seeking professional help as the best ways to end delinquent careers.[32]

Nor are scholars who study delinquency or the practitioners who must deal with it any more in agreement as to what causes it and how we can prevent or cure it. One longstanding approach, for example, has been the view that juvenile delinquency is a subculture of deviant communities in society and that youths are molded by and responsive to its values and mores. If the neighborhood is organized against crime, then youths can utilize available legitimate means to achieve important life goals; if it is organized for crime, with pressures and opportunities to engage in illegal activities, then youths either cannot utilize legitimate means or they must be effectively socialized to seek them out.[33] Another body of theory emphasizes social controls, and sees delinquency resulting when inadequate or ineffective socialization leaves the individual free to become involved in delinquent behavior.[34] Unlike cultural deviance theory, which proposes that youths do become effectively socialized, but, unfortunately, to deviant rather than conformist values and norms, control theorists see improper socialization leading to nonconformity to *any* set of values or norms. Cultural deviance approaches place the onus on the deviant or criminal culture to which a young person becomes socialized, while control theory sees deviant behavior as emergent from the individual and would argue that we would all be deviant if we could get away with it.[35] Social learning approaches maintain that it is the consequences rather than the prior causes of behavior which determine what young people will learn. They therefore emphasize rewarding conforming behavior and not rewarding or negatively reinforcing deviant behavior. In this approach, delinquents are the product of a faulty or incomplete socialization which results from poor or absent parenting, school failure and attendant prospects of occupational failure, relationships with delinquent peers, and the problem of an often uncaring and unresponsive governmental and legal system.[36]

The problem is that while each of these competing ideologies tells us something of value, no single one can explain fully why youngsters become delinquent, let alone why some do and others do not. Most recent approaches to explaining delinquency now tend to combine a number of theoretical approaches.[37] But regardless of the mix, the fundamental emphasis on socialization in remediation and treatment programs is based on an ideology which relates youthful crime and deviance quite directly to the family, the school, and the peer group. Still at issue, however (as it is elsewhere in adolescent-oriented theory and practice), is the relative importance of each social institution in the development of delinquent and eventually criminal patterns of behavior. Citing some single cause such as disorganized neighborhoods, broken homes, inadequate schooling, unemployment, or associating with deviant peers obscures the interactive effects of teenagers' experiences with different institutions within a community. As a result, we often also ignore the importance of how these relationships can encourage or discourage attachment, belief in, and commitment to conventional, as contrasted to delinquent, values and behavior.

We saw a number of very different types of programs to prevent or combat juvenile delinquency and crime in different communities, and some worked but most did not. Where they failed it was usually not because of the lack of good will and intentions on the part of the adults, but rather because the teenagers themselves were not interested or involved. Most frequently teenage clients in such programs complained of not seeing any possible change in their lives as a result of what the program was hoping to do for them. "Look, there is no way they are ever going to get me a job by teaching me to read," said one Wharton Hill teenager who was attending a program designed to make dropouts literate and hence employable. "There are lots of guys in my block who can read and they don't have jobs, either." Or, in what was really another version of the same perspective, the teenagers would talk about how overcoming one problem such as lack of a job wouldn't really help very much with other deficits such as a police record, a drug habit, or having to take care of a baby.

When programs did work they were oriented toward an interactive social development approach looking to multiple causes, rather than focusing on some single factor thought to be causal in and of itself, and the program used a variety of interrelated means of resocializing the adolescent. Some of the techniques were developmental, such as psychological and life-skills counseling and encouraging new peer networks among program participants as well as between participants and more conventional institutional settings. Other techniques, such as providing job training and education, were empowering, so that participants could function more successfully in those environments and feel some sense of competence. But others were more controlling, reducing the teenager's interaction with deviant peers and adults, setting firm and consistent standards for performance in the program, and demanding accountability rather than simply dispensing treatment and support without an evaluation of their individual and collective effectiveness. And some techniques were clearly based on negative reinforcement, lowering the opportunities for young people to get involved in deviance and, at the same time, increasing the costs to individual adolescents and their caretakers when they did. But while some of the programs we saw were working, their high costs compared to their generally low rates of success are a powerful argument for communities to deal more directly with preventing youthful alienation from and rejection of conventions, rules, and laws, since that alienation is often a precursor to deviance and delinquency.

The various social settings in culturally homogeneous communities like Sheffield present a generally consistent moral code which can usually be applied in any social environment. This concordance among the social environments also means that while the social norms of the home and the school and those of the peer group are not always the same, they are seldom in conflict. Children very early on are able to differentiate social rules by the setting that presents them and to tolerate some degree of inconsistency among the settings.[38] When we observed and interviewed children in elementary schools, for example, we found that while there was uniformity in the moral messages of the home and the school, the pupils understood that you could do things at home that were not appropriate in school. Teachers' injunctions in the earliest grades, such as "You have to learn to do your own work" or "We don't do that in school," underlined the necessity to learn new ways of relating as well as behaving. Parents told their children the same thing, and over the next twelve years of schooling, the moral and ethical principles learned in school were usually reinforced in the family because of the basic agreement between the codes (as well as how they should be inculcated) of the two social settings derived from similar social and cultural values. Although the peer group made minor modifications to update the norms, basic principles remained the same and those few teenagers who rebelled were identified as "freaks" by their peers as well as by adults. This was also true in the other suburban communities and, again to a lesser extent, Green Valley as well. But in the urban inner-city sites, diversity and disorganization among the value-setting institutions produced competing social and cultural norms and, sometimes, conflicting moral codes.

Americans tend to think of urban inner-city areas as unconventional and as our new lawless frontiers, but in both Southside and Wharton Hill there were as many different and often conflicting conventions and codes of formal and informal rules as there were settings in which teenagers learned them. Earlier we saw that there were characteristic differences between the rules and conventions of the home and the school and that teenage peer groups, particularly street gangs, had even more stringent rules than most adult social groups. The presence and power of social agencies, which intervene with a different set of conventions and rules in the lives of inner-city youths, add another dimension of diversity. The adolescents my associates and I observed and interviewed in urban areas have a much more complex task of finding a cohesive set of rules or principles to integrate into identity and to serve as moral guides. Unlike their suburban counterparts, they do not hear the same moral messages from each social setting; in many cases, what they hear is in conflict. Additionally, many of these youngsters do not have a solid and stable connection to any social group larger than the family or the peer group. As a result, there is no larger social entity to which they can appeal to evaluate moral and ethical questions.

In every community, social and moral development take place within the *interactions* among value-setting institutions—the family, the peer group, the school, and the criminal justice system—rather than within any one of them exclusively. Inconsistent or antagonistic relationships among these settings make it difficult or impossible for youths to develop a bond of commitment to a coherent set of values which can be internalized as moral guides. Inadequate or inept socialization in the family begins the pattern of antisocial behaviors and failure to achieve social and academic skills. The antisocial behavior and the lack of skills can lead to rejection by more conventional peers or their families and to the type of sorting and placement in the school which further reinforces the deficits. The pattern of association then continues, and the child enters adolescence with poor or inadequate preparation for bonding with conventional peers and community values. Communities tend to respond to what they see as the immediate needs of individual institutional areas—improving education, finding or creating new jobs, strengthening families, separating good kids from bad—but adolescents themselves are much more likely to experience problems holistically, as a sense of success or failure, of something learned or better forgotten, or as a matter of bad luck or poor fate control. Ultimately, what is most important is how well the public worlds of the adolescent's peer group, family, the law, and morality become integrated and available for internalization in the individual's personal and private worlds.

7

Tell Me Who I Am

Ginny Johnson was seventeen years old when I interviewed her in Newtown. She was one of those teenagers who took rather easily to talking about herself, filling each of the five, hour-long interviews with nonstop self-description. When Ginny arrived for the first interview she came straight into the room and announced, "I'm just your average person, not too different from anybody else you'll meet here." Over the course of the interviews she described how and why she had become "satisfied to be just me."

All of her early life had been filled with trying to become what somebody else told her she could be if only she worked hard and set high standards and goals for herself. It is difficult to believe that her childhood was as "driven" as she described, but that is how she remembers it. Her parents "bombarded" her to "try harder" every time she brought them what she hoped would make them proud of her. In kindergarten the teachers talked a lot about learning to accept each other's differences and to become part of a sharing group with one's classmates. They encouraged the children to bring little gifts to school every day to share with each other. Every morning Ginny and her mother would talk about what she would take to school to share that day. It soon became a game of deciding what would be the gift that would outshine everyone else's contribution. Ginny remembers running all the way home after school and breathlessly telling her mother that she had shared the best thing anyone had brought to school that day. Her mother was pleased, and they began to talk about what she might take to school the next day that would be even better. "For a long time I swallowed it; I wanted to be prettier or smarter or better liked than I was, always making sure that I was doing my best." Her biggest fear was that she would fail. Fail at what? Anything or everything. "What I used to dread was that I hadn't tried hard enough or that I had set my goals too low and that even if I succeeded it wouldn't be enough; I was never satisfied with myself."

All through elementary school the pressure to excel accelerated. It was, Ginny told me, as if there were some rule that good enough was not good enough, and that if you took time out to contemplate what you had accomplished it would all go away because you had let the person behind you overtake you. Teachers joined her parents in the exhortations to achieve. Just reading a book for relaxation, for example, was not enough; it was supposed to add to your knowledge and help you to become a better reader. And, of course, there were books you could read and those you couldn't because they didn't add anything to the pursuit of excellence: "You get the same thing in the movies and on television and even in the books you read. Everybody ends up a success even though they may go through all kinds of disappointments to get there; the message is that if you stick to it and work at it, you will win in the end. What makes the story is the struggle, and you are supposed to learn that part of success and reaching your goals is working hard and suffering. That is supposed to make the victory sweeter."

When Ginny was fourteen, something happened which she remembers as the most important turning point in her life. She had always been considered to have a talent for artwork, and, at the suggestion of one of her teachers, her parents had arranged for her to take Saturday art lessons at a museum school in a nearby city. At first she was a little reluctant to go because it might interfere with her schoolwork ("Or was it because I was afraid I was not good enough?"), but her father drove her to the city for the first session and she enjoyed it and decided to stay. She liked the art class, but even more she liked Ruth Healey, the painter who taught the class. Ruth told her soon after she began that it was obvious she had talent but she was trying to do things without feeling them first. Technique and skill were important, but to understand what you were doing meant that you had to concentrate on what *you* felt and not what somebody else said you should feel.

"I thought about that all the way home in the car that day and realized that something had been missing for me and now I had found it," she recalls. "I finally figured out that always trying to do better than you did yesterday has to be self-defeating at some point. What I learned was that you only do your best once in a lifetime and that what you should be striving for is to get your average performance, what you do every day, to be quality work. Then you can feel that you have been a success every day, not just once. Just be average every day and not always try to outdo other people and even yourself. Now I enjoy what I do because I know that the results will be my own best average work and nobody can ask more than that from me. Since I learned that, I can't tell you how much better I feel about myself.''

While Ginny still feels that Ruth was the major source for her new sense of purpose and identity, she credits the other students in the art class for helping her to "see things in a different way than I had before.'' Over the course of that year she spent more and more time at the museum and was pleasantly surprised to find that her parents did not object—probably, she surmises, because she still managed to keep her schoolwork up. She became "best friends'' with another teenager from Newtown who was also in the art class, and when they entered high school they became part of the Sensitive Seven, a clique of artists and writers in the school. When I last spoke with Ginny she was still planning to be a pre-med at an Ivy League college, where she had already been accepted, and eventually to become an epidemiologist.

What Ginny was telling me (although I am not sure she would agree with my interpretation) was not really that Ruth Healey had changed her self-concept and given her a new identity, or even that she had found her identity in art, but rather that she had modified, and to her new way of thinking, improved, her beliefs about herself as a person and her place in the world. Despite her insistence that Ruth had "made a new person out of me,'' it was obvious that what the art teacher had done was to give her a new perspective in which to cast the same values she had learned at home and in school. Her parents and Ruth agreed (although, as far as I know, they never actually met) that hard work and achievement were important and that they would pay off in the long run. There were some differences, such as the notion of perfecting "your average performance,'' between the role Ginny played as a daughter and as an art student—and even between her student roles in school and in the art class—but there was a harmony among the roles in their agreement on the salience of commitment to the role of productive student. Even her school chums in the Sensitive Seven agreed with this view of the world, and, although their dress and life style were visibly different from that of the more conformist "jocks" and "preppies" in the school, all planned to go off to college just as their parents had insisted they should since childhood.

In describing adolescents' search for a productive yet satisfying place in a complex and changing society, Erik Erikson, and most others who have followed after him, proclaimed a need for individual integrity as essential to an orderly and coherent development to adulthood.[1] Unless the adolescent achieves personal mastery over who and what he will be, he will be unable to pursue autonomy, to individuate from earlier identifications. He will suffer confusion or diffusion of identity. How does the adolescent achieve the all-important sense of an integrated identity? Erikson believed that a large portion of the early stages of such development are fostered within the family.[2] First, of course, the child must successfully negotiate each of the previous stages of the life cycle, learning trust in infancy, then successively incorporating autonomy, initiative, and industry into the developing ego. What must be resolved in adolescence are the major questions and conflicts about who one is and where one fits into social contexts outside the family. One must learn to relate intimately with others without fear of the loss of personal identity. While all of this seems to be very task-oriented, Erikson also described adolescence as a psychosocial moratorium, a time of social play, an "as if" period in which one can experiment with a number of different roles without an immediate need for real commitment.[3] If the adolescent identity crisis is successfully resolved, a new and coherent self-structure bridging childhood and adulthood is created with a sense of personal and social well-being; if the adolescent fails in this task, the probable result is continuing intrapsychic and interpersonal crisis, no sense of wholeness and continuity.

What we found in the ten years in which we studied teenagers is in general agreement with Erikson's view of the achievement of identity during adolescence. Finding out who you are and what you will be was a major concern for most of the young people we saw and heard in each of the ten communities. Determination of identity was indeed a crisis, and failure to resolve it did lead to any number of personal and social traumas, even tragedies, as teenagers became increasingly dissociated from personal and social reality. But we also found impressive evidence that it is possible to intervene in the lives of adolescents who have experienced inadequate, even adverse life chances in childhood to help such youngsters achieve healthy, productive identities and promising futures. Like Ginny, many teenagers told me about having met some adult, read some book or seen some film, come in contact with some new ideology or life style, "taken up" running or health foods, entered a program, found religion, or discovered any number of other environments or contacts which "completely changed my life." In virtually all cases they described what they felt was a transformation of self as a result of these new vistas or departures. What they were and hoped to be now was, they explained, completely different from what they were or wanted to be before. In many cases these changes did not go very deep into their character structure, and some were clearly cosmetic; it was easy to recognize the "old me" under the "new me." This is not meant to trivialize these shifting perspectives, because they were very real and meaningful to the young people who experienced them. I merely want to separate these from the more fundamental cases of adolescent identity change, where a basic structure for identity laid out in childhood was completely—sometimes dramatically—altered in adolescence. One illustrative example from Southside is Josie's cousin, Victor.

When Victor was a kid nobody in the Dominican community in Southside where he lived in the same block as Josie thought he would amount to much. His father had never actually married his mother, and, after a stormy eight-year period in which he frequently beat her, he left her with Victor and his two younger sisters to take care of as best she could. "In a neighborhood of poor people, we were the poorest," Victor remembers. "My mother was twenty-seven years old and two months pregnant when my father left, and she was sick all the time and couldn't work." The family had been on and off welfare even while the father was living there (again, on and off) but still couldn't make ends meet. Victor says, with what seems to be a mixture of shame and defiance, "There wasn't any such thing as a budget; we lived from day to day. My mother would send me to my Aunt Dominga [Josie's mother] at six or seven in the morning to ask her for a dollar so that we could buy rice." He would give his mother the money and then leave the tenement and wander the streets. What was he looking for? "Trouble, I guess, and I usually managed to find it.'' He "seldom" went to school after the fourth grade, and he remembers coming home one afternoon to find the truant officer waiting for him: "I just turned around and walked out, with her yelling after me to come back and my mother crying and saying I was going to be just like my father.''

From the time he was old enough to go out on the street, he had been hanging out with older boys and getting involved in a daily round of "trouble." Every morning on the days that they went to school they would walk or run down the street to the Italian open-air markets and steal fruit or vegetables, cans of tuna fish, anything they could lay their hands on. Some of it they ate; most of it they just took home or even threw away. Other days they would go to the open-air markets in Chinatown or to the outdoor clothing stalls in the Jewish section and steal "whatever was loose." When Victor was eleven years old, he got caught. A Chinese merchant grabbed him and held him, kicking and screaming, until a cop who happened to be there on the street took him in and he was booked and let go. He never told his mother about it, and he waited for the authorities to come after him, but nothing happened. Whether the police had simply pretended to book him in order to frighten him or if it all got lost in the paperwork shuffle he still doesn't know, but nothing ever came of it.

Nothing about his life changed as a result of getting caught, and he continued in the same petty thefts, moving up to indoor markets and snatching purses and gold chains. The money allowed him and his gang to buy drugs and beer, and by the time he was thirteen he was smoking three or four marijuana joints a day and drinking maybe two or three cans of beer at night. What about school? "I went pretty much because it was something to do and I was considered a 'smart Spic' by teachers, who used to tell me I had a gift that I was wasting." Victor knew that the work in school did come fairly easily to him although he never studied, never did any of the assigned homework, nor does he remember that any teacher was willing to take the time to try to get through to him or turn him around.

Victor got caught by the cops again when he was fourteen, and this time he did not get away with it. He had been snatching purses uptown in the area of the high-priced department stores, and when he grabbed at the purse of what looked like an easy mark it turned out to be a female decoy cop dressed as a middle-aged woman. Victor let go of the purse, kicked the decoy in the knee, and started to run, but the two male officers who were backing her up soon caught him, wrestled him to the ground, and handcuffed him. As he was being put in the squad car to go to the precinct house for booking, the decoy cop gave him a savage kick in the crotch, and, through the pain and the humiliation, Victor could hear the two back-ups laugh and some of the onlookers cheer.

He was booked and brought to trial, but once again something intervened to keep him from incarceration. The way Victor tells it, his court-appointed public defender, who was a young female Hispanic lawyer, "took a liking" to him because he was smart. "At first she really let me have it, telling me I was a real scum-bag who made her ashamed of being Hispanic, and I told her I didn't ask for or need any help from her or any other social worker. She really got mad then and said that she could understand how a lot of Spanish kids got into trouble, but someone smart like me should be using what he had to make other people look up to us rather than feeling for their wallets when one of us walked by." The lawyer didn't just lecture him, though; she also managed to get him probation and to put him into a juvenile diversion program which specialized in working with "high risk, high potential" Hispanic teenagers.

This is the encounter which Victor insists reorganized his internal as well as external world and got him to "see things as they could be instead of what they had always been." We heard of such turning points from Ginny and other teenagers also, which may not have been as critical as they thought, but in Victor's case his own analysis just may be true. The diversion program saw its mission as more than diverting him from a life of crime; it was also necessary to help him develop a new sense of himself as someone "who could," someone who had a promising future despite a disabling past and disoriented present. The program arranged tutoring and homework help to keep him in school. As he began to respond in class, he found that some of his teachers were interested in him, but even if they weren't, he could and did do the work. The caseworker assigned by the diversion program also worked with his family, helping his mother to get medical attention and eventually getting her enrolled in a job-training program. But it wasn't, points out Victor, all one way, all having someone do something for him. The program also found him a part-time job working in a lawyer's office as a runner, helping to put some of the responsibility for his new identity on him as well. In his senior year Victor won a scholarship to a Catholic college, where he plans, not surprisingly, to take pre-law. While his story ends much like Ginny's in his going off to college, it began a lot differently, and nobody who knew him as a kid would have written this ending to his adolescence.

How to account for this dramatic reversal in Victor's sense of identity and future orientation? It may well be that the intervention of the Hispanic public defender, someone who obviously cared what happened to him, started him off in a new direction. A more cynical view might be that the prospect of going to jail, or even the ''good swift kick,'' were enough to convince him that he had better mend his ways. There is, however, little question, as Josie will attest, that he was ''a completely different person'' from the time of his second arrest than he had been for the previous fourteen years. Whatever led him to seek a new identity as a college-bound student with a career in his future and to abandon his identity as a troubleseeking street kid on a dead-end course happened after, not before, he was arrested. There is nothing I can find in his previous life which would have insured that he had, in Erikson's terms, successfully worked through earlier periods of resolving industry versus inferiority or even trust versus mistrust as he was growing up. According to Victor there had been no models of industry to emulate, nor anyone he could or did trust before he came to the attention of the diversion program staff. In Victor's case, and in others that I saw, years of previous neglect and not-good-enough environments were overcome when a new and good-enough social environment was made available. Sadly, I also saw other cases where even the most facilitative of new environments could not erase the impoverishments of childhood. There were many more cases where interventions did work, not usually as dramatically as with Victor, but sufficiently to improve life chances. What may have been different for Victor is that he was obviously intelligent. But the question remains: Was his adult identity, in some fundamental sense, the fulfillment or expansion of a preexisting identity, preserved by his intelligence from the ravages of the deprivation and disorganization of his childhood? Would that identity have emerged without the intervention he experienced?

This question is, to some extent, entangled in a continuing debate: Does one discover or actualize an internal ''true self'' or, instead, create or construct an identity from externally available alternative identities or identity elements?[4] From what we saw and heard, I would propose that identity formation in adolescence is a developmental process which involves *both* discovery and creation. It is the individual who "finds" an integrated and internalized identity in the adolescent transformation. But that identity is also produced by an interactive process of social development: it is constructed from a repertoire of possible identities offered and valued by the various institutional environments of the community. Just as biological endowment places limits on the adolescent identity, so the available roles presented to adolescents by the environment limit the possible identities they can construct.[5]

The discovery of possible future selves as goals for identity development begins in what significant adults and the community's public belief system about adolescence display as possible and preferred future roles, along with methods of achieving them.[6] For Ginny, these social environments were in harmony throughout childhood; hence adolescence required a recognition or, at most, a discovery of their equilibrium. She saw and heard similar people, even some of the same people, in each setting: a teacher, say, might be a neighbor, and another neighbor might be the coach of her after-school swimming team. The adults she came into contact with in each setting also expressed support for the values and expectations of the other settings of Ginny's life and encouraged her to participate in them. This consistency defined the community within which Ginny was learning about the roles available to her and all teenagers there. Ginny happened to come from an intact "traditional" family, but some of her friends did not. Yet the intact and functionally integrated community of institutions was there for these youngsters as well, and they could pick up the same messages, see the same role models, and learn the same role ideals from these institutions that she did. As we have seen, however, Ginny was not a passive recipient of her community's presentation of preferred roles and life styles. She could and did make other interpretations and choices. But the fact that there was basic agreement among the adults and youths of Newtown on the possible roles teenagers could assume meant that its adolescents could be more concerned with learning those roles than with having to find new ones in different settings.

In Sheffield, too, and similar communities, a congruent pattern of possible identities was modeled in each and all of the social environments as a way of evaluating and interpreting the present self. The image of the husband-as-good-provider was not in competition with the role of productive corporate citizen that was also projected. Similarly, the role of caring and competent mother fitted with the role of wife who helps further her husband's career, and both these feminine images complemented the ideal male role as well. Emerging feminist protests about the bias inherent in these role descriptions had not modified their value content very much over the period of time that we were observing and interviewing. Most parents—mothers as well as fathers—explained that certainly women should prepare for careers, since that adds to their personal development and will make them better mothers. Many of the teenage girls I interviewed in both Sheffield and Newtown spoke about future careers, and, as elsewhere, if there was some indication of conflict, it was over how best to combine family and career, not over which took precedence. What was expected to be internalized by youngsters was a sense of mastery over present and future life events through diligent effort and competitive drive. While career growth was projected as largely under one's own control, its benefits were to be shared and made socially productive in a combination of work and family life. The school, the church, neighbors, and most peers as well subscribed to these models of present and future roles and the values they represent. For better or worse, adolescents were gently but firmly led by parents and other adults through the process they had to negotiate to become similar adults.

Victor's chaotic as well as socially and economically deprived childhood did not provide this stable stage on which to develop a sense of continuity and support. Neither did it provide easy access to a variety of socially sanctioned and consistently evaluated roles. His family life (what there was of it) was not conducive to even the minimal requirements of the role of student. He seldom went to school, and when he did the teachers could do little with him to instill any sense of the importance of learning and the study habits from which it proceeds. From what we know of his childhood associates, they learned the same negative lessons at home and in school, and they banded together as "street kids," further diminishing their roles as family members and as students. While there was homogeneity and even some stability in Victor's peer group, he seldom if ever saw the same people involved in more than one of the various adult institutions with which he was required to interact. In fact, he comments on the fact that the high turnover among teachers in Southside's schools, combined with his own record of being absent for long periods, meant he would often have as many as six different teachers during the same school year. "I never," he says, "got the final test at the end of the term from the same teacher who gave out the books at the beginning of the term." He also had four different probation officers in the two years he was on probation. Cultural differences among the institutions in his community added to the conflicts in defining roles. His neighbors were other Dominican immigrants, and, while there is no evidence that they devalued education or the role of teenage student, there were no role models available to demonstrate that it could lead to later success. Victor's peer group joined him in the conviction that it would not. Even when his teachers pointed out to him that he was bright and could do well in school and so insure a better future, he did not hear the positive message or see its possibility at that time because no other institutional sector of his life validated it.

The deficits in and conflicts among the social settings in Victor's life were not of his making; they were there for most of the youngsters in Southside and in Wharton Hill as well. Family and school seldom worked together in presenting a clear picture of how education could be related to future lives much different from those of older siblings, parents, and neighbors. These adults were the believable figures to whom most of Southside's teenagers could relate as role models. The criminal justice system and employers saw Victor and others like him as inevitably headed for these same future lives. Peer groups set their own agendas, which were present-oriented rather than future-oriented. What became internalized here was a sense of powerlessness, frustration, and resentment in the absence of a coherent and stabilizing pathway through adolescence. Youths like Victor were left to chart their own course, or, much worse, to pick a route from among the often confusing signals put out by the family, the peer group, the school, and the workplace. Defeatism, acting-out behavior, and a resistance to any authority structure were some of the consequences we observed. A surprising number of teenagers "make it" even in such a non-facilitating environment, but usually as the result of unusual nurturing in one of the adult institutions—a strong and supportive family system, a caring school, some social agency which intervenes in their lives, or even one caring and supportive person in one of those settings—or because of the individual's own personal emotional strength or resilience.

The important point in Victor's story, however, is that all was not lost. It was possible for him, with some help, to overcome the early deficits. What the caretaking adults he came into contact with were able to do was to develop for (and with) him a good-enough environment within which to develop a coherent sense of identity; this identity not only linked him to that environment and introduced him to some new worlds, it also coordinated and stabilized the previously chaotic relationships of the antagonistic social worlds in which he grew up. The diversion program got him a part-time job in a law office, introducing him into a world of work and a vision of a possible future to which his family could not and his previous schooling would not have provided him access. This vision moved him to take school seriously, and the program provided a tutor and homework help to allow him to make up for what he had previously lost. The program stabilized his family life (as much as any outsider could) by helping his mother to obtain health care and to enter a job-training program. Most importantly, the program kept him out of jail. That, of course, is what a diversion program is supposed to do; but diverting Victor back into the same not-good-enough environment would only have meant postponing his inevitable imprisonment. No one of these interventions in and of itself would have been sufficient to overcome a lifetime of conflict and deprivation. Keeping him out of jail without ameliorating the impropitious environments in which he lived would have continued him at risk. *Only* finding him a job, or *only* helping him to get back into school would not have done much to provide an alternative developmental environment to his chaotic home life, or shown him a vision of a future worth striving for and possible to attain. Looking back on his childhood truancy, Victor recalls that his mother was always saying he should go to school but then telling him he had to stay home to care for her when she was ill. Multiple sources of risk require a multidimensional approach, but the interventions should be as integrated as we hope the newly emerging identity will be. What the caring professionals at the diversion program did was to make Victor's everyday life more predictable and to project roles in each of his social environments out of which he could assemble and consolidate an identity. They also gave him an opportunity for a moratorium, a place to be until he could tolerate the divergence between his past and the future he could now see for himself.

It could be argued that the real difference between Ginny and Victor is socioeconomic and that life in the ghetto is always more uncertain and disruptive for individual development. While the social disorganization which characterizes the inner city does present a more complex challenge to adolescents who seek identities there, most of the young-sters we met managed to achieve an identity status with which they, their peers, and the adults with whom they came in contact were satisfied. Some of these youngsters displayed what Fritz Redl called "ego resilience," the ability to withstand pathogenic pressures or to recover from them spontaneously "under conditions which seemed unsupportable to health."[7] Others, like Victor, found some means of avoiding or resolving personal as well as social conflicts through the help of a particularly strong and caring family, the intervention of some adult caretaker or program, or, with quite different end results, in a gang or other peer group. Many, however, simply adjusted to the disorganization among their institutional environments by develop-ing a decentralized set of situational identities, or what Edward Samp-son has described as "a pantheon of selves within a single body."[8]

Communities influence the development of identity in adolescence by sorting. This means that adolescent identity achievement can be as complex as the social structure of the community within which it emerges. In Southside and Wharton Hill, and in Ranchville as well, the multiethnic and social class groupings create "natural" bases for sorting which come to dominate the identity process. The family "gives" the child an ethnic and class (as well as gender) identification, but each of the community's other socializing institutions may sort individual adolescents by using these same personal characteristics in somewhat different ways. The staff of the high school in Southside, for example, sorts youths by ethnicity, pointing out that the blacks, male and female, are potentially violent; the Hispanics are prone to forming close-knit, kinship-like networks; and the Chinese are the most studious. The local police precinct, however, has a different view, and police officers there will describe the Hispanics as the most potentially violent ("real crazies"), the blacks as having a stronger sense of group coherence ("watching out for each other"), and the Chinese youth gangs as the most serious threat to the social order of the community. Southside's teenagers are well aware of these character-izations and how different they can be from one setting to another. A black youth in Southside who was a freshman in an Ivy League college when I interviewed him told me, "Teachers like smart niggers and cops hate them, so I had to behave one way in school and another way on the street." He went on to say that his parents encouraged him to study but that he had to deny being smart to his street peers and would lie to them when he went to the public library at night and on weekends: "I would say I had a 'squeeze' uptown and I was going to spend time with her or that I was going out to do some heavy hustling, which made it O.K." There are fewer such social identity differences, and so less strain among roles, in homogeneous and socially integrated communities (Sheffield, Newton, Argotown) than in multiethnic and discordant communities (Southside, Wharton Hill).

It is not essential that each community make a modal identity available to all youngsters in order for them to achieve an integrated identity, but some modeling and cultural support for the variety of identities which can be negotiated is necessary. In building a "master identity" for adulthood, teenagers draw on the various situation- and context-specific roles we observed in social interactions in the various community settings and heard about in fantasies. Growing up anywhere involves experimenting with a number of roles at the same time as well as consecutively. Every parent who has ever wondered at how the passive, even sullen, teenager he or she must deal with at home is transformed into the active, participating companion in the peer group has observed this phenomenon. The role identities of adolescents can be as myriad as the salient social contexts in which they must operate: A teenager may have one identity at home, another with peers, a third at school with teachers, and a number of others depending on what social contexts are available and important to him and to adult caretakers. A religious teenager or one whose family has strong religious beliefs may have an identity in the church group which is not available to or valued by other adolescents in her community. Even in the same institutional setting—such as the school—a teenager may have a variety of role identities which emerge vis-à-vis teachers or with particular teachers, students who are or are not included in his sorting group, coaches, and administrators. At home, relatives or older siblings or even each of the parents may present quite different perspectives on future as well as present ways of being. The task of identity building is facilitated or made more difficult by how the adult institutions work individually and together to make multiple but consistent roles possible and available.

Communities such as Southside do not offer complementary or even always compatible roles. Sometimes, as in Victor's story, the adolescent himself must coordinate the very different roles, and the attitudes and behaviors associated with them, presented or permitted in the home, in the school, and in the peer group. Victor, and many other youngsters like him that we met, was expected to show loyalty to his family by contributing as soon and as much as he could to their protection and support, particularly in the absence of his father. His neighbors as well as his family expected that he would aggressively seek a job, any job, not prepare for a career by going to school. In school he was expected to adopt the passive role of student, to follow the rules and conventions of the school, and to work toward graduation into a future which was at best little different from the life he already knew. His neighborhood peers valued aggressiveness and "street smarts," and encouraged and even demanded loyalty to their rules in defiance of both home and school. In such communities as Southside the adolescent often must choose among incompatible roles. Other communities manage to make the role identities available in all or most institutional settings similar enough to enable the youth to consolidate his identity, rather than developing separate identities for each sphere of his life. In these communities the teenager is encouraged to seek out a full set of role identities even when a full portfolio of roles is not available locally. In Argotown, for example, adults encourage and guide such outward-bound ventures outside the family, elsewhere than in the school, even outside the community to find sources for developing competence. I heard how one eighteen-year-old has embarked on such an "identity project" of reaching out and finding support wherever she could, with the full support of her teachers as well as her parents.[9]

I was introduced to Jill by the teacher who had been asked by the principal in her high school to help me arrange for some interviews with students. We were walking down the main street in the small downtown area of Argotown, where the teacher was giving me a tour to illustrate an earlier comment of hers that there were no recreational activities available for teenagers anywhere except at the school. Jill drove by in her 1960s Ford Thunderbird, blew her horn and waved, and then pulled over to tell the teacher that she had been able to get "the absolute last ticket" to a Rolling Stones concert which was being held in the nearby metropolis where her father worked. The teacher, who was also the faculty sponsor for the school's drama group, teased her mildly about how she was able to accommodate her sometimes expressed hope to become a concert pianist and her enjoyment of the cavorting of rock musicians. Jill took it with the same good humor with which it was given, saying that she got different and yet similar satisfactions from each.

As the teacher and I continued down the street, I commented that the Thunderbird, which was almost twenty years old, seemed to be in first-class condition. The teacher said that Jill maintained the car herself and that she had bought it the year before and restored it. Jill went to a class in auto mechanics the high school gave in the evening and now was her own "grease monkey" on the car. Nobody seemed any more surprised at this than they were at her interest in art and fashion or in the drama club. The teacher explained, "We encourage a lot of interests in the kids and try to get them to work them out for themselves because there is so little for them to do here unless they go into the city."

During the interviews, when I asked Jill about fantasies they spilled out in a jumble of images and relationships which seemed to link her current concerns with future goals. She imagined winning a scholarship to an Eastern university with a well-known school of music. In talking about it, she said that her music teacher in the nearby city had told her that she had taken her about as far as she could and there was no place in the area where she could get the training she needed. Then Jill spoke of how she worried that her father might "not be too keen" about allowing her to go to the "big bad city" where the university was located and what she could possibly do if he balked when she talked to her parents about it. In an earlier interview she had described how she and her parents had a "family powwow" whenever a decision of this sort had to be made. Sometimes her parents resisted what she wanted to do ("You should have heard my mother when I told her about the car!") but virtually never without some explanation that she could accept. The meetings usually resulted in one of three decisions: (1) most frequently, everyone would agree and develop a plan for carrying out the decision; (2) sometimes the decision would be that she needed more information, and her parents would suggest that she talk to a teacher or counselor or even write away for the information; (3) there were occasions when they would say that they didn't think it was a good idea, and that would be that—"at least for now."

She also talked about what she would do with her car if she did go, since it would never survive life in the city. While there was some obvious anxiety in her presentation, it seemed much more related to having to make choices than to any fear that everything would not come together for her someday. She finished recounting her fantasies by observing that, since she was only a junior, she had time to work it all out. With a smile she said, "Like Scarlett O'Hara really meant to say, I'm sure I'll worry about that tomorrow."

A critical part of the self-concept is developed in relations with friends and peers during adolescence. In suburban areas, friendship patterns tended to be established first in neighborhood play groups, and then to move farther and farther away from direct parental control as the teenager moved out into the school and peer group relationships. As we saw earlier, the sorting pattern of the school also acts to influence both chance and choice in governing a teenager's identification with some individuals rather than others. Yet, while most of the teenagers we observed in suburban areas sought to conform to the social and behavioral standards of the peer groups to which they belonged, it was always possible to modify or even change one's role: for example, to emulate some admired teacher or to "be like" some new friend. Ginny and Jill are case examples of suburban teenagers who tried a number of different roles at different times without any apparent major friction with parents, friends, or teachers.

In urban inner-city areas, on the other hand, friendship patterns, like residential and high school sorting patterns, were frequently based on ethnicity. To the extent that ethnic identity was the major determinant of mutual acceptance into peer groups, this permitted less experience with different life styles. Victor, for example, once said that he worried what life would be like for him at the college he would soon be attending: "I don't look like them, I can't dress like them, I don't even talk like them; so I'm going to be 'that black Spanish kid' when I get there." He went on to say that he didn't think they would give him any trouble; rather, they would be "super-careful to be nice because I'm different from them." Similarly, Amy once told us that whenever she started in a new class the teachers would assume that she was going to be "Super Student" because they could see that she was Chinese. What we expect of teenagers often depends on who and what we think they are. A teenager's racial identification did not have any intrinsic effect on self-regard but was important in self-esteem to the extent that it was featured in the community's, or more frequently in some component social institution's, identity-ideal for adolescents.[10] Youngsters come to be pre-sorted in the various institutional settings; a youth who is labeled and treated as a delinquent or as a poor student learns to think of himself that way. As we saw in looking at schools, such labeling can become a self-fulfilling prophecy reinforcing both the identity concept and the social perception of the teenager. Self-esteem and a sense of self-consistency can also suffer, since the teenager's feeling of worth and purpose is also gained or lost in situational and institutional contexts.[11] We often heard "I feel better about myself" in reference to entering some specific social world of the community, or, just as frequently, "I hate to go there; they make me feel crummy about myself."

Some teenagers solved this problem by investing heavily in one specific environment—and so in one particular sense of self—as a student in the school or as a member of the family or as a peer in a friendship group. Others diversified their identities as a basis for seeking self-esteem, using school, family, church, peer group, or other arenas in which to perform. We saw both approaches work, but in each case, how the individual teenager envisioned herself vis-à-vis the community's identity-ideal was the most important measure of self-esteem. Ginny and Jill, for example, "chose" to diversify the settings in which they looked for self-esteem. Ginny was seeking complementary identities as an artist and as a student, both of which were valued by her friends as well as by her parents and school. Jill was having a little more difficulty both because she found fewer complementary roles and because her local community could not provide the learning environment for some of the identity elements she wanted to achieve and so could not immediately indicate the positive evaluation of their accomplishment. In Victor's case the congruence of his social worlds was, in effect, an artificial one, created by the social agency which invested in him because of his intelligence. His transitional role identity as student seemed to be the only one which could survive in the fragile balance which rested between his past deficits and his future hopes.

Comparing the fantasy and reality life of adolescents in the various communities provided some additional evidence that both their internal and external relationships are, in fact, patterned by the systematic relationships among the institutional contexts of their communities and that these patterns are manifest in their everyday lives. Different norms and roles emerged from different institutional domains, and the way the community organized and valued those domains established and sanctioned the available models for the definition of the self and the consolidation of identity. Still, adolescents had to go beyond the reality of the moment and create (or imagine) a personal theory about the future within which to weave fantasies and construct identities.

Attempts at self-insight, a concern with inner or personal truth, and reality testing were the means by which they sought to adjust their inner worlds with the outer worlds of their communities.

While the problems of coping with inconsistencies and the need to consolidate an identity out of the roles presented by the environment were particular problems in the inner city, I heard about variations of both the problems and the means of coping with them in the fantasy life which teenagers use everywhere to begin the work of consolidation. A large part of deciding who and what one will be is the result of both one's past and one's perceived and believed-in future. Both are related to, but separable from, who or what one is in the present. Positive and negative images from the past, memories of warm or rejecting relationships with parents and peers, successes or failures in schools—all these are always with us to shape our self-concept.[12] Fantasy serves many of the same functions in adolescence that it does in childhood and in adulthood: seeking conflict resolution; helping to overcome fears; fulfilling wishes; anticipating aspirations. In fantasy adolescents try out a number of possible scripts, but these scripts, and the possible roles teens may or may not rehearse to play in them, are, as we have seen, limited by the worlds they know about or believe are available to them. Adolescence has always been considered a special time for fantasy and the play of the creative imagination. With the pubertal refocusing of libidinal energies outside the family to the peer group, much of the content as well as the motivation of adolescent fantasy is said to be sexual, although some recent research indicates that a very small proportion of a person's fantasy life is overtly sexual.[13] I heard many fantasies described in the interviews I conducted, and overheard many more during observations; not many of them were manifestly sexual in either content or apparent motivation. This does not contest the importance or the prevalence of sexual fantasies in adolescence, but, rather, seems to be the result of how the interviews were conducted. I always asked about fantasies and daydreams as part of the third of the five interviews and probed only those fantasies which the teenager reported, rather than asking about or suggesting particular fantasy subjects. Given the sensitivity which most young people (and many older ones as well) feel about revealing sexual fantasies, it would be reasonable to assume that repression and reticence screened out many overtly sexual fantasies.

What I did hear, however, was clear evidence that while we often think of fantasy as an introspective device in which the adolescent "withdraws" into himself, its uses in trying to understand or control external reality are particularly important in adolescence. By fantasizing about situations which are puzzling, frightening, or simply unknown or unknowable, we can manipulate them and even dream up alternative strategies or possible conclusions. Fantasy allows us to foreshorten the future, to compress time so that we do not have to wait until tomorrow to see how the story ends. It also gives us access to the past so that we can use previous experience and insights to guide us in current situations. We may not be able to predetermine or will the outcome, but we can conceive of the possibilities and imagine the achievement of goals. Most of the fantasies I heard were not illusions; they indicated a growing awareness of, rather than an attempt to escape, reality. Similarly, the use of fantasy can strengthen a clear sense of what is inside and what is not. [14]

Far from blurring the distinctions between imagination and reality, the fantasy life of the adolescents I interviewed served to make reality more "real." For example, a teenager would say, "I would like my parents to let me stay out later but I can imagine why they worry about what might happen to me." Another contrast between what was desired or hoped for and reality might be, "I really want to get into Columbia. I can spend a lot of time daydreaming about what it would be like to live in the city, all the museums and the shows, but I gotta get my grades up to have any chance." Or even, as I heard from one Wharton Hill teenager, "When the teacher talks about 'being a good citizen' I look outside and wonder if a good citizen could make it here." What was real and not real, like what was "me" and "not me," acquired meaning in the way they contrasted with each other. Fantasies are indispensable in the development and integration of identity, and they provide a vivid portrayal of the conflicts and compromises involved. But there were some clear differences, as well as common characteristics, among the fantasies I heard in the different communities.

In all communities fantasies showed a characteristic change over the course of adolescence. In early adolescence they were often organized around concern over growing independence and separation from the family, combined with some apprehension about the world outside. They spoke to the loss of the certainty of the world of childhood guaranteed by parents, and the uncertainty of the new world beyond. One twelve-year-old girl in Smyrna Beach said, for example: "I hate to recite in class, and when the teacher is going around the room calling on people I get nervous because you can tell when she is getting close to calling on you. Sometimes I wish that my mother was there.'' Another example comes from a thirteen-year-old Riverton boy (the only child of a single mother), describing a father-son field trip he went on with a church youth group to a soccer match:

> I felt good because I could tell the other kids what was happening
> because my mom had explained the difference between football
> and soccer to me. Father [the priest who accompanied the group]
> said I knew more than anybody else, and I thought about telling
> Mom that when I went home. The other kids teased me about it
> and asked how I got to know so much, and when I told them
> they teased me more about being a mamma's boy and how did
> she know so much about soccer, anyway. Father said not to pay
> any attention to them and to come over and sit next to him, but I
> wished that I had my dad there like the other kids.

What was evident in these and similar fantasies was not a real or imagined concern over actual loss of the parent, but, as in infancy, a strong fear of losing the parent's love.[15] This fear combines with the unfamiliarity of new places and people, leading the newly emerging adolescent to have difficulty distinguishing between the real-world role of a new person or place and her need for or use of it.[16] Teachers, and the other parent-surrogate adult caretakers with whom the early adolescent now comes into contact, were described by this age group as if they were particularly there to meet the needs of the child. Comments such as ''The teacher picks on me'' or ''Mr. Diaz [a social agency youth worker] says that I am special'' were not only frequent, but such adults were seldom mentioned without some reference to how they related to the life of the adolescent reporter.

In a transitional state between two worlds—that of the familial and familiar relationships worked through in childhood and that of the new relationships the child seeks but dreads to work out in the wider community—the child tries both to take some of that old world with him and to look for familiar figures or relationships in the new one. So, as Freud observed, ''past, present, and future are threaded, as it were, on the string of the wish that runs through them all.''[17] The physical and social onset of adolescence is like the early life of the infant, which Winnicott once described as one of absolute dependence but equally absolute, if unwanted, independence.[18] Driven to leave the nest and yet still uncertain of the ability to fly, the adolescent

uses fantasy to establish a reasonably secure transitional world somewhere between the one he is leaving and the one which waits ahead.
Peers, for example, were sometimes incorporated into the fantasies I
heard, but were much less frequently mentioned than were adults,
while siblings, like parents, seemed to remain important fantasy figures
from the childhood world to add familiarity to the new life of the
child-become-adolescent. This fantasy life, as well as the physical
and cognitive changes that signal the beginning of the journey, may
account for the peaking of creativity as well as the anxiety which
have been observed to take place at the beginning of adolescence.[19]

Fantasies were also used by older adolescents to smooth over or
ease the discomfort of discontinuities and transitions in their lives.
Teenagers who moved from one community to another often spoke
of thoughts about returning to the lost earlier environment with the
same nostalgic reconstruction that often characterizes the early adolescent's looking back on the lost gratifications of childhood. Not all
such memories were positive, however, and in some cases the wish
was to return to undo some real or imagined wrong, again in a way
which seems reminiscent of the early adolescent's looking back with
hopes to repair the unrealized gratifications and the losses of an earlier
period. The loss of a friend or the death of a parent also produced
fantasies which dealt with separation and reunion, and, not infrequently, there was an underlying theme of desertion sometimes containing a wish for revenge. But such themes which seemed to linger in
the past were not characteristic of most of the fantasies I heard from
teenagers in the middle and later periods of adolescence. In middle
adolescence they were more oriented toward the present, usually centering on problems with family and friends or at school, and by the
late teens fantasy became a stage on which plots and plans for the
future were worked out and rehearsed.

Most of the fantasies of the midteen youngsters I interviewed were
focused on defending against fears of feeling rejected or looking foolish.
Rejection themes referred to parents and other significant adults
throughout the midteen years but shifted perceptibly to peers as the
teenagers matured. A rejection theme in the early midteen years could
deal with the same loss of object love which we saw in early adolescence, often containing an almost magical return to a real or imagined
feeling of parental love by projecting the same relationship onto a
teacher or some other adult. For example: "Yesterday Mr. Hamilton
[a soccer coach in Sheffield] told me that he was proud of what I

had done this year on the team, and I guess I felt good because I knew he liked me. Last year he was always on me for not doing anything right, just like my mom and dad were, but this year he has been really proud of me.''

More frequently, however, and more characteristically as the teens progressed, there was evidence that concerns about relationships were moving outside the family into what David Elkind has termed an ''imaginary audience.''[20] A fantasy reported by a fifteen-year-old boy considered a ''cowboy,'' or country-and-western music fan, by his classmates in Argotown illustrates the underlying fear of looking foolish or being ridiculed and also tells us something about one source of content for adolescent fantasies: ''I saw this old movie on TV last week called *Blood and Sand,* and it was about this kid who wants to grow up to be a bullfighter and how he sneaks out every night and goes into the fields and fights these bulls with his jacket. Wow! It was great; he could do what he wanted to do and not have to worry about other people laughing at him or telling him that what he wanted to do was stupid.''

During the midteens a number of differences between boys and girls begin to emerge in their inner lives. In the earlier teen years both boys and girls focus much of their attention on their school life. But it was the girls in each community who exhibited more liking for and excitement about school and schoolwork, more pride of accomplishment in grades and positive comments from teachers, more interest in being popular with classmates and teachers, and fewer school-oriented escapist fantasies. From about fourteen years of age, however, it was the suburban boys who showed the greatest satisfaction with their schooling and urban minority girls who exhibited the least. From the interviews with these girls, what seems to have happened is that the feminine conflict of family versus career had already begun to demand some resolution in terms of a future orientation to one or the other, or required some balancing to avoid decentralizing identity. This suggests another possible dimension of teenage pregnancy, as an acceptance of which way the future is likely to go and an early decision to escape role confusion. Similarly, some dropouts may be walking away from the role of student because they are unable to see any link between the education they are being given and their imagined future role as a worker.[21]

By the later teens, the character of the fantasies had changed again, and now there were more differences between those reported by young men and young women, as well as between urban inner-city minority youths and suburban youths. In all of the sites older teenagers described fantasies which projected concerns into future problems or promise. While I did not find universal feelings of a general malaise in the present or a sense of impending doom, there were some future states which caused concern for all teenagers regardless of where they lived. Illnesses, health problems, and injuries were mentioned as worrisome by about half of the teens of all ages I interviewed in each of the communities, but in only a few cases did they appear as the major concerns. Where they did, they usually came up in association with some personal experience on the part of the teenager, a member of the family, or some peer. There were also some variations between younger and older teens and by gender and place of residence. Girls expressed more concern than boys, particularly in early adolescence. Early adolescents, both boys and girls, seemed to be most concerned with current fears of getting ill, often presenting obvious wishes to find again the loving and longed-for mother who cared for them in childhood: "Sometimes I think about what it would be like if I got real sick and had to stay in bed for a long time. . . . My mom always used to make French toast for me when I got sick and couldn't go to school."

By the middle teens (and on into the late teens) the concerns had moved to future states of illness or injury which could "affect my whole life." This is particularly important, since many health problems of adult life—such as high blood pressure and cholesterol levels and tobacco, alcohol, and drug use—are the result of choices and behaviors established in adolescence. The significance of the environment in generating such fears is obvious in the much greater concern voiced by both male and female urban inner-city adolescents over the possibility of being injured as the result of violence or accidents. Less obvious is why "some crippling disease" seemed to be of greatest concern in suburban areas. One possible cause may be the suburban preoccupation with the competitive drive for success, which is dependent on good health; a major disease could take the competitor out of the running. Or it may be that suburban teens have less cause to worry about the violence and poverty that loom large in the lives of their inner-city age-mates, so disease emerges as the main worry by default.

Over the ten years from the mid-1970s to the mid-1980s during which most of the interviews were carried out, there was a perceptible change in illnesses and health conditions which seemed to cause greatest concern. Early in the research pregnancy, or "getting into trouble," and weight problems were most frequently mentioned by girls; ecological destruction and toxic pollution were mentioned by males and females both. From the mid-1980s on, AIDS had already begun to enter the public awareness and to be of some concern among teenagers. These changes in the specific health concerns we heard about over the period of the research are evidence of an awareness of health promotion programs on the part of teenagers. School programs were most frequently mentioned as the source of the information. These expressed concerns give further support to the importance expressed by health educators for early interventions, not only to improve adolescent health, but, as a result, to improve health throughout the rest of the life course. While it might seem that teenagers, like adults, have a proclivity for avoiding or postponing behavioral change which leads to health improvement, there are some important advantages they have over adults. First and foremost, they still have the time to make changes which can have lifelong effects. This means that there is an opportunity to prevent adult diseases before they become tenured in the life style. A number of effective health promotion programs for preventing initial smoking, for weight control, and for reducing the risks of alcohol abuse in the teen years have been reported.[22]

Important as health was to the teenagers we studied, it was not their main concern. By far the most common characteristic of the fantasies I heard voiced by older teens concerned what they would be doing in the future "after high school." The themes were similar in all of the communities, but there were major differences in both the content and the ambiance of the fantasies presented by the minority youngsters of Southside, Wharton Hill, and Riverton from those of their majority contemporaries in Sheffield, Smyrna Beach, Newtown, and to some extent, Argotown. All spoke of what they wanted to be and why, but the certainty and character of that future, and to an even greater extent, the availability of the means to get from here to there, differed between white and minority youths, and to a lesser extent, between boys and girls. The impoverished and disenfranchised youngsters of the urban inner city faced the future with less optimism and confidence that their efforts would pay off; it always seemed necessary for some change or intervention to occur in the present or future to assure success:

When we sat in on the "Preparation for the World of Work" sessions in the youth employment program in Southside, all the kids laughed and yelled "a hook" or "a rabbi" (colloquial terms for a well-placed sponsor in the civil service system) when the instructor asked what was the most important ingredient in finding and keeping a good civil service job.

During the interview with Angel in the detention center, he talked about how he kept hoping for "one big score" when he was snatching purses and mugging people on the subway. He was sure that if he had gotten enough money he could have found the time to check into a program to get him off drugs, so he could find a job, but he could never get far enough ahead in life to get himself together.

Mary, who is fifteen and pregnant, told me that she "dreams" [fantasizes] about getting married to somebody who will take care of her and her baby so that she can finish school: "Don't laugh; it could happen just that way if the right guy comes along. It happens on TV all the time."

Suburban teenagers, on the other hand, saw both their current and future education as empowering them to compete directly for the careers they wanted, and their anxieties were over their own ability to follow through on the promises of privilege:

Art plans to take business administration courses in college and probably to get an M.B.A. later. He wonders whether he should go straight to graduate school or maybe work for a while to get some experience. The counselor in school told him that experience would both help him to get into a good business school and give him a "head start" on the other students.

Gilly has been talking with her friend Terry about when it is best to have children. She certainly doesn't plan to have any until after college but doesn't know when she should get married. Her mother is always telling her that "there is plenty of time," but she wants to be a young mother so that she can go back to school or work and not just sit around waiting for her husband to come home.

Jeffrey thinks that he will become a minister. He worries sometimes if he has the kind of personality that will allow him to be successful. He has been working with the youth minister at his church and it seems that there is a lot he has to feel as well as do to become a minister. He is not too concerned with doing the learning work that is necessary, but he isn't sure he has enough of a "calling" to be a good pastor.

It was powerlessness and the lack of access to opportunity, rather than simply poverty, which seemed to dampen the future orientation of urban minority youths, and personal empowerment which stoked it for suburban teenagers. For a suburban youth, the course of events in the future was under his control and a personal responsibility; for an urban minority youth, the future was controlled by external forces that he could not influence.[23] Suburban youths talked about planning, personal responsibility for success or failure, and their future as the result of "my own efforts" much more frequently than their urban minority counterparts. In both groups males were more positive about this type of future orientation than females, yet suburban females were generally more positive than urban minority males. Even success in the future as the result of chance was perceived to be out of the reach of minority youth. Although winning the lottery or hitting the numbers was more frequently mentioned by urban minority youngsters as something they daydreamed about happening *now* to insure a future, being "lucky" in future life was more frequently mentioned in the fantasies of suburban youths.

I did not hear enough about the fantasy life of teenagers in the rural or isolated communities of Green Valley, Ranchville, and Cypress City to extend the comparisons to include them. There was a greater reticence to talk about fantasies in these communities—particularly in Ranchville and Cypress City—which was part of a more general sensitivity to my being an outsider in a closed community. Among the few fantasies that were revealed to me (and even these were told reluctantly as if I might make them public or even take them away with me), flight, escape, and withdrawal were usually the organizing themes. When there was some mention of projected roles and imagined futures, they were usually identified with some other place. The lack of a complete set of social settings in the local community from which to draw a full cast of possible future roles seemed almost to compel teenagers to look elsewhere for some role elements to incorporate into hoped-for identities.

In all of the communities, in observed behavior as well as in reproductions of that behavior and the supporting beliefs contained in fantasies, the adolescent identities I saw and heard about were anchored in and mirrored the social organization of the community in which they occurred. There are, however, forces from outside the community which operate to blur the differences among adolescents no matter where or how they live, providing role models as well as fantasy images to model identity. Television, films, records, and videocassettes reach out across the barriers of region and race, social class and community, to instruct as well as to influence. They serve to reveal the secrets once restricted to adult status. As a result both children and adolescents increasingly know more than they ever did (and some say more than they should) about once taboo subjects such as sex, violence, or crime. Television and other media also instruct young people—sometimes to the benefit of society and the local community but at other times to their detriment—making instantly available the forms and methods of personally and socially disruptive or even destructive behavior.

Parents and other adults who guide the lives of adolescents also learn and are influenced by the media. Notions of what is normal or age-appropriate behavior, as well as new knowledge and trends in child health and other aspects of development, are instantly shared throughout the nation. Parents and communities also learn about acute social problems such as teenage suicide and drunken driving, and they anticipate and sometimes manage to find the symptoms of such problems among their own teenagers. But no matter how homogenizing these extracommunity forces are, they are always filtered and hence modified by the local community, the family, the peer group, and the individual, thereby insuring the continuing development of heterogeneity among adolescents.

Adult antagonisms toward teenage music, so prominent in the concerns about youth rebellion of the 1960s, waxed and waned over the course of the 1970s (in varying degrees depending on the particular community and even the particular family).[24] When it became obvious in the mid-1970s that the youth rebellion which was feared in the 1960s and early 1970s was no longer even an imagined threat, attention turned elsewhere for some explanation of why teenagers refused to conform completely to our visions of what they should be; to grow up like we did, or even better. But, possibly because of changes in the genre, or perhaps because of the growing popularity and availability of video versions of rock group performances on TV and videocassettes, the fears and concerns returned. Now the concerns were about the destructiveness of personal rather than social rebellion.

In the 1980s it was sufficient to simply indicate that the four adolescents who committed a joint suicide in Bergenfield, New Jersey, were "devotees of heavy-metal music" to suggest its dire influence in their death pact. We also found, in several of the suburban and rural communities we studied, a number of parents and even a few professionals who insisted that the record industry uses "backwashing" to implant sexual or even Satanic content in rock music recordings. They maintained that the sexual or evil messages are recorded backward on records so that they can be perceived unconsciously by adolescent listeners, with consequent effects on morality and behavior. At a Rock-and-Roll Seminar which was held in a suburban church center but had also been presented in some of the local schools, for example, one speaker played tapes of mostly 1960s-era rock groups and insisted that Charles Manson had been driven to murder by listening to the Beatles' "White Album" played backward. He went on to associate a number of current youth problems such as suicide, teen pregnancy, and drug abuse with resurgent interest in rock-and-roll. Although rock-and-roll music was widely appreciated among our teenagers, tastes in music showed the same diversity we found among teenagers themselves. There were differences among the various communities in the type of music to which teenagers listened, and these differences were in turn related to their affiliations and identity in the community. In Argotown and in all three of the communities we studied in the southeast, country-and-western music was popular among teenagers, as it was among their parents. Similarly, some youths in Southside and Wharton Hill had preferences for ethnic music, such as reggae or Latino music, which they shared with their parents as well as ethnic peers.

It was also inevitable that during the "youthquake" of the late sixties and early seventies, commentators would link television to youthful rebellion. Many argued that television provides "a premature sophistication," which extends not only to violence but to "intimations of sex" and to "cynicism about the operation of the adult world."[25] Television encourages youth to take a blasé attitude toward the virtuosity in sports, drama, dance, and all of the other performing arts which they view constantly. But, inevitably, they become frustrated when they attempt to imitate such "easy" virtuosity. This, combined with the inability of the media to portray positive values or anything good in society except in synthetic stereotypes, leads to an overexposure to evil.[26] Television also reinforces what anthropologist Geoffrey Gorer had earlier described as the "Dionysian element" in rock-and-roll music: a sense of freedom from rational social and individual control which underwrote the adolescent rebellion.[27] James Coleman, writing for the President's Science Advisory Committee in 1974, reported that "the proliferation of media channels that cater to youth" was a major factor in the disruption of juvenile and adult norms, and thus in the solidification of the youth culture.[28] The counterculture, in Coleman's view, arose when adults lost control of the media—when, in response to market possibilities, films designed to appeal to youth, radio stations which played their music, and underground newspapers addressed to youth-oriented issues nationalized the peer group. This permitted deviant norms to spread more easily beyond the locality of origin. As a result, teenage culture could and did come to be considered a nationwide phenomenon which intervened between the adolescent and the local adult community.

While fears of the media sparking a unified national rebellion among teenagers have dissipated, there is still a legacy of concern about the influence of television on teenagers. One major concern, centering on the debasing of the popular culture to which young people are exposed, is frequently expressed as catering to adolescent tastes for "violence, crime, and filth."[29] We found such concerns to be most common in suburban areas, particularly among the more conservative parents, who also had similar complaints about some of the literature available through the schools. In both cases the criticism was that such information sources and the problems they dealt with were produced and developed elsewhere and only inspired imitation among local teenagers. When, for example, condom ads began to appear in an effort to curb the spread of AIDS, a number of suburban parents complained that the disease and its transmission were not a local problem and that the ads only served to stimulate sexual experimentation among adolescents in their communities. There were some similar, but usually less vocal, adult protests in rural areas about the effects of television on teenage tastes and behavior, probably because of the perceived distance between what was being presented on the screen and the realities of local life. In the urban areas the drama on the streets was much more vivid than anything portrayed on television and we heard few criticisms there.

At other times, television was described as pulling youngsters away from other pursuits such as reading. In all of its many forms, however, the central concern was with the relationship between schooling and television and what effects television would have on the learning experience of adolescents. The problem, teachers told us, is not just that adolescents can't read; they don't feel related to the system of symbols upon which reading is based. Additionally, teachers often cited a distorted sense of reality, passivity, a minimal attention span, and even declining S.A.T. scores and motivation as important side-effects.[30] One important question here, of course, is, Just how much do adolescents watch television and what seems to make a difference in both the amount and the focus of their viewing?

We found, as have others, that in every community viewing began in early childhood—before exposure to schooling—and increased through the elementary school years, beginning to show a decrease in early adolescence (at about the time when the youngster started junior high school) and continuing to decrease through the high school years. Adolescents, however, still managed to watch a substantial amount of television despite this decrease; our estimate was between fifteen and thirty hours each week, depending on the type of community. In the suburban communities the overall number of hours per week of television viewing among adolescents was lower than elsewhere, and there was also more parental control of what could be watched. When we asked suburban teenagers and parents why, the answers were almost always related to the conflict with schoolwork, or less frequently, to concerns about such issues as violence, drug and alcohol abuse, and sex. Parents also attempted to control when teenagers watched. They often set up regulations concerning homework completion prior to watching during the school week and allowed more viewing on weekends—frequently, we heard, "to try to keep them at home."

There was more viewing of television by teenagers in the urban inner-city areas than in the suburban areas, and much less parental control of what was viewed. There was also less control over when television could be watched than in suburban areas, but particularly among black and Chinese families, there were often strict regulations as to when elementary as well as secondary school students could watch. The highest levels of television viewing were in the isolated rural communities, particularly in Ranchville, where television was the only "local" recreation possible. There were also differences in familial patterns of viewing. In the suburban communities older teenagers tended to watch alone or with friends, whereas younger ones watched with parents. This was also true in the urban inner-city sites, but while we often heard complaints about being forced to watch "special events" or family shows together, even older urban youth seemed to accept or even enjoy watching with the family.[31] These differences were also reflected in the reasons older teenagers gave for not watching as much as they used to: in the suburban areas TV competed with school; in the urban inner city it conflicted with time spent outside the home with peers; and in rural areas it conflicted with the need to escape from the closeness of family and community.

The types of shows, if not particular shows watched, remained fairly constant throughout the period of the research. In all the communities situation comedies were always popular, and to a lesser extent, so were feature films and dramatic shows involving the police—a menu of preferences not very different from that of adults and possibly representing what was available at the times when youngsters could watch. While situation comedies, which usually dealt with the foibles of family life, were popular at all ages with males as well as females in each community, we did notice some differences, over the span of the study, by age, gender, and type of community. Late-afternoon soap operas seemed to increase in popularity in the late 1970s among teens of all ages and both sexes, possibly reflecting the changes in patterns of family structure which left many unattended in the late afternoon. Not surprisingly, boys seemed to prefer action-oriented shows more than girls, while girls seemed more interested in romantic themes than boys. Horror or mystery shows were more popular in suburban areas, and adventure series which featured automobile chases were particularly popular in rural areas.

What effect did television have on the fantasy life of adolescents in the various communities? There are two clearly contradictory perspectives on the relationship between fantasy and external, overt behavior. One proposes a direct link between the two so that what is learned in the outside world is internalized in fantasy and becomes part of the inner world of thoughts, attitudes, and imagined behavior. The other sees fantasy as originating internally as the result of wishes or needs that cannot be fulfilled in the real world being redirected toward fulfillment in fantasy.[32] We found some evidence to support both points of view. There was considerable use of symbols and ideational material drawn from television in many of the fantasies I heard, but the basic themes or plots emerged from real problems or issues in the personal lives of the teenagers themselves. A fantasy story about vampires recounted by a thirteen-year-old, for example, could be traced to a horror story he had seen on television a year before the interview, but he also made associations to concerns about the bodily changes he was undergoing. The fantasy was one which he experienced over and over, until, as with children and fairy tales, he began to develop a sense of mastery over both the imagery in the film and his concerns about his own transformations.[33] Similarly, a sixteen-year-old girl's daydreams about being a hostess on a luxury liner drew its cast of characters from a television series she watched, but the problems she described in finding friends in her small community came from real-life experiences. Daydreams served to allow youngsters to bring problems they were struggling with in the public worlds of their community into the private world of fantasy where they could try to work them out for themselves. Television, and other make-believe media, supplied the imagery for the stories, which were free of the meanings and consequences of real-world symbols, figures, and locales. There were, however, differences among the various communities in the nature and use of the imagery borrowed from television.

Although adventure series were popular with boys of all ages in every community, the themes transposed from the screen to the fantasy world differed between the urban inner-city sites and the suburbs. In Southside and Wharton Hill it was the physical conflict involved which was most frequently featured in describing daydreams. In the suburban areas, however, where the same action-filled programs were just as popular, it was the rivalry between opposing forces or contending characters which was focused on in fantasy. Films about *ninja* and the martial arts and films about war, for example, were popular in both types of community, but what was internalized and reappeared in fantasy differed. In the urban inner city I frequently heard, often with considerable body language as well as the sounds of combat, about the clashes and the violence. The suburban youth focused more on the contending forces involved—how one group or individual outdid or outsmarted the other. One Sheffield teenager said that he liked to watch adventure films which had some element of anxiety and suspense, some pursuit "so that you can see how plans work out if you decide what has to be done and stick to it."

There were less sharply counterposed differences between girls in the urban and suburban sites. The one clear difference was in the intensity and immediacy of identification with the imaginary characters. Girls in the urban inner-city area, in describing daydreams which had characters or situations drawn from television, usually related what they were reporting to their own present life situation. Talking about a teenage or even adult television character having problems with her family or husband, the girl would empathize with the feelings involved and might even make a direct association with some problem in her own life. It did not seem to matter if there were obvious differences in social class, race, or ethnicity between the character portrayed and the viewer; the identification was with the situation and its applicability to the girl's perception of her own life situation. Suburban girls, in describing a similar incident or situation in a television portrayal, would depersonalize their reactions and talk about the emotions or the life principles involved, sometimes even citing examples of situations in someone else's life. The frequency and immediacy of such problems in the urban teenager's life made it easier for her to identify with the situation, which was less real—and perhaps more feared—for suburban girls.

These differences among the various communities indicate the inability of television and other media to single-handedly shape adolescent identity formation in the face of contrary pressures from the social environment. The family and the peer group impose a number of controls on identity formation which intervene between the national media and the local culture. While television and other media do influence the fantasy lives of teenagers by providing material for use in imagination, almost all of the teenagers I interviewed were able to make clear distinctions between what is real and what is not, and reality always seemed to be closer to home.[34] Perhaps there are more direct influences by television on beliefs and behavior in childhood, but by adolescence young people have been socialized to the medium. They are able to split its fantasies from their own daydreams and to maintain "the importance of the true self relative to anything false."[35]

Listening to the accounts of their inner lives by teenagers in the various communities, we found again that the critical question in understanding identity development is not the relative role of the individual versus society, but rather how the community is organized to provide a stable structure for the life course and the role projected for adolescence within it. Adolescence is an important but not unique period in this process; neither self-concept nor identity, after all, begin or end in the teen years. What makes adolescence so important in identity development is that this is the time we tell youths they must get serious about deciding who they are and what they are going to be. Adults, however, must be just as serious about giving teenagers the latitude to choose their own identities. Using our own memories of adolescence to decide what today's teenagers should be like can be just as arbitrary as most of our memories of "the good old days" tend to be. A society which prides itself on individualism cannot insist on treating adolescents as if they are all the same, an age-graded class of individuals who can be collectively identified as "the Me generation" or "a generation on the skids."

Peers, too, are an important influence on how the adolescent negotiates between fantasy and reality in formulating his identity and his future. Part of what adolescents share, in what adults sometimes interpret as slavishly conformist behavior in their peer groups, is a sense of wonder and mutual discovery, what Erikson called the "rituals, creeds and programs" which provide structure to the condition of being between social states.[36] In the communities we studied, intimate peer groups mediated teenage music, films, and other cultural as well as social influences through the shared fantasies of their individual members.[37] Such collective fantasy was much more frequently shared by teenagers with peers than with adults. Teenagers, particularly in the suburban and rural communities, often go in cult-like groups—virtually never alone—to see horror films in theaters, drive-ins, or less frequently, on television or videotapes at home. Anyone who has observed them as they scream and turn away in real or feigned horror, reach out to grasp at each other, and then comment on how "stupid" or "camp" the films are can see the films' real function in providing a collective source of fantasy, away from adult scrutiny, that contains many of the behaviors and dangers their parents warn them about.

In primitive societies was the pubertal rite of passage, a time of social learning as well as initiation which institutionalized and consequently clarified the transition to adult status. Such rituals were for groups of age-mates and involved adult instruction and indoctrination. As British anthropologist Victor Turner has demonstrated, the unreal world of the initiation ritual was used to introduce the neophytes to the rationality of the real cultural world.[38] One way of viewing such a process is to see it as a means of moving individuals from the egocentricity of childhood to the social reality of adulthood, with the mediating adults as guides. If the adolescent world is somewhere between these two worlds, then these adult transitional guides and the "transitional sphere" which they inhabit can be the adolescent equivalent of Winnicott's "facilitating environment" in childhood. Arnold Van Gennep long ago reminded us of what is still true in the adolescent transition: pubertal rites of passage involve imbedded social clues, symbolic behaviors, and prototypes of social rules.[39] He also recognized that they separate us from previous identities, help us make the transition to new ones, and help us incorporate the new identities into a new social role or status. It is in this creative time and space between childhood and adulthood that significant adults can be most influential. It is also one of the areas of enculturation and socialization which is often ignored as a means of easing the self into "not-me" learning of the consequences of the roles of others, which is a necessary part of consolidating an identity as part of adult society.

Adolescents do generate their own norms and identities, but this process does not and cannot develop in isolation from the institutional context of the community in which the adolescent lives and learns. Teenage norms and the identities they help shape may be in harmony or in conflict with the "ideal" values of the community or of particular institutional segments, but they are never independent of them. Ethnic and social class values as well as community characteristics do play a role, but none of these is determinant of the character and form of adolescent psychosocial development. Rather, we have found, such development is the complex product of all these factors within a particular community—each interacting with all the others. Innate individual differences or biological predispositions are also a factor, but it is how the community chooses to interpret and act on them that makes them more or less deterministic in defining the self.[40] Daniel Yankelovich has identified the two "truths" we all know about the self: "One is that the self is private, and alone and wholly encased in one's body. The other is that one is a real self only to the extent that caring and reaching beyond the self continue."[41] The teenagers in every community we studied were reaching out into their social environments to find a personal narrative which would give meaning to their present and future lives. Communities can and should care about and reach out for the self-development of their young as well. Coordinated social interventions by a caring community into the life course of adolescents can lead to the joint construction of a shared and mutually acceptable life story which links the past to a believable future.

8

The Search for Structure and the Caring Community

We started this look at adolescent life in ten different American communities from the rather pessimistic viewpoint that it is the problems surrounding the adolescent transformation which generate such widespread interest in it. Looking at the interaction of the institutional environments of the community, which organize but can also disorganize the transition, should have set a number of critical issues for adolescent development in some perspective. One is the continuing controversy over the immutability or even the necessity of a period of development between childhood and adult status. Inevitably, questions here revert to the problems inherent in defining and describing a period in the life of an individual which starts with the observable biological fact of puberty but is only considered ended when a variety of social perceptions indicate that the individual is now prepared to function as an adult. Adolescence is composed of a sometimes bewildering complex of physiological, emotional, and social processes which are not synchronized according to chronological sequencing or biological development. Neither are they coordinated by any socially agreed upon agency or institution.

Adolescence is a demanding period for youngsters, and the demands come from many directions: from their own physical and cognitive development, from family and peers, and from the environmental settings of the community. This is fertile ground for conflict, and a variety of conflicts do in fact exist, not all of which are the result of the unevenness of social and biological maturation. Nor is it just a question of innate or imagined inner turmoil and intrapsychic conflict.

Differences between the two dominant social worlds of the adolescent, the family and the peer group, are always a source of potential conflict. Even as the teenager becomes increasingly dependent on peers for social approval and companionship, the family remains a source of continuing influence. There continues to be considerable congruity between the values expressed by parents and their teenage offspring. But new and tentative relationships to a variety of institutional worlds, the roles they project, and their changing demands and resources for social competence lead the teenager to question his identity. The dilemma of adolescence is not simply how to develop a self-concept; it is a question of where to look for the personal guidelines which will allow a teenager to satisfactorily relate the sense of self with the social structure he must negotiate. This task is one faced in childhood and adulthood as well, but we have made it the special mission for adolescence.

Most problems commonly associated with the teenage years are not really unique to adolescents, since the crises and conflicts they face are societal ones and affect all of us. For adolescents, however, these problems are particularly troublesome, since they have neither the protective dependency of childhood nor the independent competence of adulthood to help them deal with personal crises. They are, in a word, individually and collectively *alone* amidst a maze of institutional contexts which alternately compete for primacy in authority and protest their inability to deal with the task alone. As early as the 1830s Alexis de Tocqueville described Americans as a nation "locked in the solitude of their own hearts." More recently another French observer, the psychoanalyst A. Haim, writing about adolescent suicide, described the similarities in the dynamics of mourning and the emotional tone of adolescence in the same language of estrangement. For the developing teenager is required to give up the gratifications, the goals, even the familiar objects, which organized her childhood world.[1] The anguish and the uncertainty which comes with loneliness is particularly acute when people do not feel connected to some intimate collective, such as a family or a caring community, which they can fall back on for support. For adolescents, required to give up the family and still unfamiliar with the community, it is the transient peer group which often provides the only possibility for what Edmond Burke called "the little platoon": the intimate and supportive social group we all seem to need in order to feel secure. The progressive decline of the family, the church, and the school—

institutions traditionally charged with the intimate socialization of the young—was supposed to be in the service of creating a supportive network of social institutions working together to create a common, community-based locus for socialization. At the heart of the eventual failure of this new structure to materialize is the loss of the sense of the caring community. One result has been the fragmentation of the adolescent experience, as the various social environments function as independent, sometimes isolated, and at times competitive or even conflicting settings for teenagers. It is this community-level dissonance, and the disaffection which develops because of it, rather than any nationwide rebelliousness toward adult society, that exacerbates the conflicts of the adolescent identity crisis into the ''adolescent problems'' we hear so much about.

Deciding who and what one will be is a function of both one's past and one's perceived and believed-in future. Both are related to, but separable from, who or what one is in the present. Positive and negative images from the past, memories of warm or rejecting relationships with parents and peers, successes or failures in school, are always with us to shape our self-concept. What we believe we can be or will be in the future is no less affected by what others tell us or show us is possible. The adolescent helps to shape the effective environment within which his transformation will take place, but in turn seeks help and guidance from others. In every community, urban inner-city as well as suburban or rural, we found that not only age-mates but a variety of continuing relationships with family members, relatives and neighbors, institutional settings, and the significant adults who are part of them serve as exemplars and guides for individual or groups of adolescents. Congeniality among their values and clarity and consistency in their guidance are essential to the adolescent, who is engaged in a *search for structure,* a set of believable and attainable expectations and standards from the community to guide the movement from child to adult status. If the values expressed by different community sectors are at odds, if their directions are unclear or inconsistent, the teenager cannot be expected to accept their good will or trust their judgment.

Teenagers learn and express these standards and expectations not so much as sanctioned rules as a loose collection of shared understandings which operate to limit the variability of permissible behavior. If, for example, we asked a teenager why she did or did not become involved in some activity, seek some goal, avoid some risk, or behave in one way rather than another in any situation in which there was a possible "choice," the reason was seldom attributed to any specific rule or even particular authority system such as family or peers. Rather, what we heard was a much more generalized explanation, usually phrased as "I don't know why, it seemed to be the right thing to do" or "That's the way it is here in Argotown." Both parents and teachers were equally nonspecific in describing the reasons for what they expected from their teenage children and students. Parents, in explaining what time they expected a teenager to be in at night, would usually cite the general perception among neighbors or community residents that youngsters of a particular age should be in "at about" some specific time, and we seldom found any great discrepancies among families. Teenagers might protest that the curfews were too early but would usually cite the same general time limits as parents. The teenagers could also describe how much leeway would be granted and what extenuating circumstances would or would not be acceptable, again in impressive agreement with parents and with each other. Asking teachers about homework assignments or school administrators about discipline almost always brought the same type of reference to "what this community expects."

We came to call this unwritten, "sensed" set of expectations and standards the community's "youth charter."[2] While it is nowhere set down or codified, both youngsters and adults usually know the limits set by the charter for various areas of behavior. Much of the daily life of the teenager proceeds from the conventions which emerge from its shared understandings, rather than from any explicit set of rules or laws. Like so much else in life, the charter begins in the family, where the growing child learns from the comments and choices of parents and older siblings to value or devalue individual and group traits, as well as to evaluate the "shoulds" and "should nots" of individual and social behavior. For most youngsters the family continues to be more influential than any other social setting. From the early adolescent years peers become increasingly important in spontaneous decision-making, but their judgments are considered along with, rather than as replacements for, parental influences.[3] As the school and other social worlds of the community become increasingly important in the teenager's life, the community establishes a comprehensive frame of reference which both integrates and transcends the influence of any particular institutional sector. The youth charter establishes a quasi-independent and relatively stable system of conventions and normative behavior. In doing so it sets the parameters of behavior and provides role identities and ego ideals rather than expressing specific and definitive rules. Consequently, it is intended to defend against conflicts between teenagers and important adult caretakers and to reduce internal conflict between the fulfillment of personal desires and social requirements. However, our interviews and observations revealed that it is too often the individual adolescent and not the community, the society, or even the culture that must ultimately produce the integration required for social and cultural competence.

It is through the youth charter that teenagers can become active, constructive participants in getting to know themselves, their social worlds, and who they are and can become within them.[4] Within the various community institutions and environments, adolescents can observe the interacting effects of their actions and the actions of others, and thus evaluate and modify their own behavior in response to the judgments of others. A youngster can, for example, decide to view himself, or to behave, "like" a particular person or group depending on the judgments attached to that model by peers, significant adults, or both. The charter provides the source for feedback about who one is and how one is doing as the individual develops a set of self-evaluations as a son or a daughter, a student, and a friend.

Teenagers, who are generally preoccupied with learning about themselves, compare their own traits and behavior against those of others even more than adults do, and in so doing find themselves in their interactions with other people.[5] Anthropologist Clifford Geertz locates our determination of what we mean to say somewhere between thinking it and hearing it: "the art of understanding is inseparable from the art of presentation."[6] So it is with the teenager as she projects the possible roles which will order her developing identity and hears and sees how they work or do not work for her. It is in this interaction in the day-to-day life of the community that teenagers attempt to develop a coherent and integrated life story out of their previous developmental history, their present experiences, and the possible future selves they can envision. The family's encouragement or discouragement, the school's sorting system, the peer group's message as to what is "in" or "out," operate individually and in concert to set standards and to hold the adolescent accountable. This accountability, however, like the standards and expectations which formulate it, is local and not global. The teenagers I interviewed did not see or evaluate themselves in comparison to those throughout the country; they compared themselves with their neighbors and friends and sought their approval and acceptance.

If adolescence is a process of psychological and social separation and individuation from the family, then the uncertainty and emotional instability which are imposed by the new realities and unanticipated relationships must be just as anxiety-producing as they were in infancy. In fact, given the development of the imagination and the extension of experience, they may be more frightening, particularly since there is more uncharted space for negotiation between the teenager and the wider social world of adolescence than there was between infant and family. The attachment to a previous security worked out in the family required creative and imaginative development of a transitional world beyond immediate persons and things. It required that the established sense of belonging must be incorporated or merged into a new one rather than simply surrendered. In talking about the enculturation of the infant, Winnicott located cultural experience in the potential space between the individual and his environment; "an intermediate area of experiencing, to which inner reality and external life both contribute."[7] He proposed two important aspects which the mother must develop in the relationship in order to encourage and integrate the capacity for concern and through it the ability to care, first for her and eventually for others. One is that she must learn to tolerate the infant's unknowing frustration and aggressive seeking for satisfaction. The "good enough mother" (later including the father and, eventually, the family) creates a "holding environment," an embracing and supportive presence and availability, giving the infant time to learn to trust that she will be there ("survive") for him. The other crucial factor is that the child must also be given the "opportunity to contribute," the chance and indeed the necessity to work on and help accomplish the development of that facilitating environment himself.[8] But transitions are not restricted to childhood; they occur throughout the life course and adolescence owes its very existence to its transitory function in society.

Just as the transitional world of the infant requires a degree of object constancy, or stability, in the environment in order to fix reality, so does that of the teenager—and probably more so. Adolescence is notoriously a period of changing certainty as well as uncertainty, as new objects, new experiences, and new ideas compete for incorporation into an emerging and expanding self. The teenager defensively projects his own uncertainty into the outer world and then brings a perceived or construed reality back inside in fantasy.[9] Margaret Mahler set the recipe for successful individuation in childhood as a measure of constancy among the objects in the external world and a measure of self-constancy in the child, and that formula takes on a new urgency in the adolescent individuation.[10] In order to maintain some sense of stability for the adolescent during her individuation from the largely parentally sanctioned reality of childhood, she needs the supportive presence of adults as transitional objects who can represent, model, and introduce her to the new adult worlds she must enter. This requires an especially caring involvement of adults, because adolescents, unlike children, can choose among particular people and places in the external world as sources for competence and self-esteem.[11]

As I have illustrated in describing each of the social environments of adolescence, adult caretakers can help conduct teenagers through this transitional phase by offering them the security of an expectable and "good enough" environment.[12] Predictability is important to teenagers because it provides the sense of stability and self-assurance attendant upon the familiar, but youth charters must also be responsive to change. Some communities adjust to social change rather naturally, almost spontaneously; their youth charters also adapt their symbols and injunctions to changing demographic, cultural, and economic conditions. The social institutions in such communities work through these changes together, either through some formal mechanism such as a communitywide planning group or through longstanding informal relationships such as those we saw established in Sheffield and Argotown. Other communities do not respond to change in a coordinated way. Their component social institutions march to different drummers, and the discord makes for confusion among the expectations and standards presented to teenagers.

Every community communicates its youth charter through a series of distinctive yet sometimes overlapping channels of interaction. It organizes a socialization system through which the individual learns the cognitive, emotional, behavioral, and social skills which define adulthood in that community. This structure also includes the interactions through which adults are socialized to accept the values of the specific community, as well as its definition of youth's role in the variety of institutional contexts. These definitions may differ not only from community to community but from institution to institution in the same community. Thus, as we saw in looking at work and school, youth "work" is seen as schooling in suburban Sheffield and Newtown and in Argotown, while in Southside, Wharton Hill, and the migrant labor center of Ranchville (and to a lesser extent in rural Green Valley), work is defined for adolescents as what takes place outside school hours. These differences among communities, which are representative of the many others described throughout the preceding chapters, attest to the fact that what society sees as adolescent conformity or deviance depends upon how particular behavior is defined in the particular environment in which it takes place.[13]

Youths also learn who is empowered and who is not to make and enforce rules and decisions, and what sanctions can or will be applied. Communities and institutions within them differ; in some only the adults make decisions, while in others it is a more shared process. When a community sees itself as having a significant youth problem or rebellion, it is within this authority-power structure that it often seeks to bring about remediation by applying sanctions, such as curfews, which can be counterproductive to the developmental goals of growing independence which are part of the socialization system.[14]

Over time, the charter which expresses the pattern of relationships among the institutions becomes more and more a personal possession of the maturing adolescent and serves to organize the emerging self of adulthood. This takes place as the objects and places of their external environments and their feelings and beliefs associated with them are "internalized" and become part of the teenagers' own inner world.[15] What the charter does or can do is to serve as the community's "mind," for thinking about, imagining, and planning the adolescent transformation by imposing some cultural form on otherwise incomprehensible material and providing a structure within which various roles and relationships can be experienced and evaluated by a congruent set of standards.[16] The charter should provide a stable but broad enough base to give room to explore relationships at increasing distances from the self-perception worked out in childhood; at the same time, it should still provide role models and standards for mastery. Our society has traditionally looked to the self to provide unity and integration to the individual. The requirement of such autonomy is confounding enough for adults, let alone the teenager in transition from a childhood which frowned on too much autonomy. As I listened to teenagers talk about their relationships within the various communities, it was clear that autonomy is not the same as integrity, and that as the analyst W. R. D. Fairbairn suggested, a very strong ego has the capacity to be split and, at the same time, integrated.[17] Teenagers have more opportunity to explore identities and think longer about decisions with less need to commit early if the community youth charter is capable of providing a basis for integration. As adolescents internalize the standards and values exemplified in the charter of their community, they develop judgment criteria themselves based on how the charter defines the limits of acceptable and unacceptable behavior. What should develop over time is a new and shared sense of reality.

While a community's standards and expectations are often unwritten and unspoken, explicit articulation can be an invaluable contribution to a "good enough" nurturing and the facilitating environment within which adolescents can contribute to their own development. A community's youth charter can and should provide the firm, fair, and consistent expectations and achievable standards to allow adults and teenage citizens to develop and sustain a caring community. The charter is, in effect, both the declaration of independence and the constitution for this new transitional state, which should provide an unhurried migration from childhood to adulthood as an integral part of the life journey.

PROGRAMS THAT WORK

In the early years of our study, concerns with the traumas and the tragedies of teenage social problems led to a widespread sense of urgency in getting programs started up to deal with each adolescent "crisis" as it was discovered and diagnosed. The fragmentation of this categorical approach is now becoming clear to youth professionals as well as researchers, who have learned, as we did, that problems develop as multiple risks in youngsters' lives without regard to the bureaucratic dominion of the particular problem which initially causes concern.[18] Attempts to treat that presenting problem often reveal other deficits associated with or underlying it. Today, an appreciation of the importance of providing comprehensive rather than circumscribed remediation and social support is emerging in a wide variety of locally developed youth-related programs. Although such successful programs are as diverse as the communities which have developed them, they do share certain characteristics that seem to be important in their success.

One of the most important aspects of successful programs is an emphasis on support systems which link adults and adolescents in a wide variety of formal and informal social networks. Being part of a group or network of individuals can provide a number of benefits, but what appears most important is that the networks include both adults and youths working together on productive tasks and problem-solving activities.[19] Mentoring programs, which have become wide-spread throughout the country, are one type of linkage program. These developmental alliances, which range from continuous and very intense encounters to fairly superficial arrangements, take different forms. Some programs relate youngsters to adults in a one-to-one relationship. Others extend their reach to groups of youngsters. The "I Have a Dream" Foundation, for example, resulted from a 1981 visit by indus-trialist Eugene Lang to his old Harlem school; rather impulsively, he offered to pay the college costs for an entire sixth grade class. Lang soon discovered that while the money might help make the dream possible, the students needed the encouragement and support which only a comprehensive and supportive mentoring program could offer, and one came about through East Harlem's Youth Action Pro-gram. The program has now expanded to many other cities and includes individual mentoring programs as well.

Most mentoring programs—like Inroads, in Chicago, which pairs a minority youngster with a person from the business or corporate sector throughout high school and college—are based on a caring one-to-one relationship in which the adult serves as general adviser to his protégé. Some programs, however, are much more oriented to dealing with particular needs of teenagers. The Learning Web in Ithaca, New York, for example, matches young people who wish to learn a particular skill with adults willing and able to teach it.[20] Tutoring programs, such as Columbia University's Project Double Discovery, in which college students act as mentor-tutors for disadvantaged neigh-borhood youngsters, are another way of forging links between adults and teenagers. Most tutoring programs link a single adult tutor with a younger learner, and it is often the mentoring and caring aspects as much as the teaching and learning relationship which are most important for both tutor and learner. Columbia's "double discovery" has been that learning advantages accrue to the tutor and to the community as well as to the youthful learner. Mentoring-teaching relationships are also an important aspect of many of the more success-ful new programs which prepare youths for the world of work. Some, such as the Boston Compact, provide business executive mentors who play continuing roles in the job lives of students as well as being instructor-tutors in schools. Apprenticeship programs—in which there is currently a resurgence of interest—are another approach to learning work skills and attitudes. These programs also rely on the mentoring relationship. In a program in New York City, youth work with skilled artisans who are restoring the cathedral church of St. John the Divine.[21] The Rent-a-Kid Program in St. Paul, Minnesota, matches teenagers who want to work with jobs in the community which need to be done.[22]

There is still not complete understanding of how mentoring works, or even complete agreement on its relative benefits, but from what we saw, it can be a major source of help for teenagers. Those programs where it was successful did more than simply provide an adult caretaker or role model; they provided the mentor with the resources—learning and skills development materials, trips to museums and theaters, opportunities for the protégé to meet new people and other teenagers—to guide the protégé toward the new worlds she was hoping to enter rather than simply helping the youngster to adjust to her present environment.[23] What mentoring programs have demonstrated is the importance of finding new adult roles for working with teenagers which grow out of the cooperation of shared involvement rather than perpetuating the often competitive or conflictual attitudes characterizing some of the present youth–adult relationships. In many ways the mentoring concept is a formalization of what have always been the informal mediating relationships which develop in communities between youngsters and some adult with whom they share interests and mutual respect and caring.

Mediator roles themselves can be formal (e.g., parents, teachers, police, employers), but many informal roles also emerge in the pattern of relationships established in the community. While even the poorest communities have untapped resources for mentoring, there are many communities where youngsters' social networks do not include potential mentors. Programs such as Big Brothers and Big Sisters have long tried to supply mentors for those youngsters whose life experiences do not provide a pool of adults to serve such roles. Mentoring or mediating roles need not, of course, be hierarchical, and in our experience those which were based on a more collegial relationship worked best. The mediating role of social agency personnel with their teenage clients seems to be particularly important in communities such as Southside and Wharton Hill, and to an even greater extent in Ranchville, where formal role models are not available or not congruent with young people's adult-identity ideals. Informal mediating relationships may also be based on ethnicity in urban communities that have a majority of black, Hispanic, or other minority youngsters and only a small number of formal adult models from those same groupings. We found, for example, that many of our graduate student field researchers unconsciously came to serve that function for some of the youngsters they worked with as part of their research with groups of teenagers. Daniel Levinson, among others, has proposed the conscious development of a pattern of model-mentors for youngsters: someone young enough to identify with, yet old enough to have the experience to be a believable model.[24]

Another important characteristic of successful programs is that they link teenagers together. As indicated in earlier chapters, the social networks of teenagers are fairly limited and the sorting process tends to insure that they will not meet many age-mates different from themselves. Expanding youth networks allows youngsters to experience and share the diverse talents and experiences of others and to develop relationships which broaden their community consciousness beyond their own immediate neighborhoods. Such expansion can also provide a sense of belonging to the insecure, and enable teens to help peers who are confused or uncertain. Programs such as Positive Educational Experiences in Relationships (PEER), sponsored by the Youth Research Center in Minneapolis, were developed to provide a structured set of experiences to help youths learn their personal strengths and potential while also developing group skills and better understanding of individual differences. Groups of six to twelve teenagers work with an adult leader to learn communication skills and improve interpersonal relations through greater acceptance and understanding of the self in connection with others.[25] Other programs, such as New York City's School Mediators' Alternative Resolution Teams (SMART), use students trained in mediation and counseling techniques to settle disputes in schools.

It is important that adults be included in these new social networks, just as they are naturally a part of teenagers' lives. The relationships in these negotiated intergenerational social networks should demonstrate that adolescence is part of a continuous developmental process and allow for development of adult skills and attitudes while still holding youthful members accountable for participation and performance. This means that such networks should work on real problems and tasks as they occur in the community, rather than on "make work" projects or projects that deal solely with adolescent problems.

The programs should also allow leadership to develop among the youthful members, and while not choosing who will or will not lead, help to develop a process which assures that everyone has an opportunity to share in governance and to evaluate the results of their work. Most successful peer-based programs accomplish these goals of continuity, relevance, and shared responsibility by developing a strong sense of commitment and service to the local community. Interestingly, most of these programs are found in major cities, where alienation of youth from the community has always been considered a major problem. One of the oldest of such programs was the New York City Volunteer Corps, in which youths provide necessary services and assistance to the elderly, the homeless, the indigent, and others— over half a million hours of service every year. The East Harlem Youth Action Program in the same city has youths escorting and protecting senior citizens in housing projects. Since 1984 a Boston program, Youth as Resources, has worked with a high-risk student population who clean up their own neighborhoods and plant flowers as well as tutor peers. In Tampa, Florida, the police department has established Teens on Patrol, a program in which older teenagers assist police in providing protection and maintaining the peace in public parks, swimming pools, and retirement centers; and in Madison, Wisconsin, high school students on the Positive Youth Action Team are teaching elementary school students about the problems of, and methods of dealing with, drug and alcohol abuse, sexual abuse, and suicide.[26]

The possibilities of peer-based community programs are as limitless as the energy, enthusiasm, and talents of the young people and adults who direct and participate in the programs. There is some evidence that creating opportunities for young people to serve their communities both reduces alienation and develops a sense of self-worth.[27] It also provides direct experience with the possibilities as well as the problems of community life and identifies possible solutions. In one program we developed at the Horace Mann–Lincoln Institute, Teachers College, Columbia University, teenagers took pictures of dilapidated and unsafe buildings in their neighborhood and decided to send them to the borough president, asking him to meet with them and discuss what could be done. He did, and as a result nine of the twelve buildings they had photographed were restored.

As suggested above, creating opportunities for young people to work together to serve their communities and establishing new linkages between teenagers and adults also provides a network of social support for youngsters who might otherwise be alone and vulnerable. A solid and stable connection to some larger social entity, whether family, peer group, neighborhood, or community, can help develop competence and promote self-esteem, and may even result in improved resistance to disease.[28] But creating support networks for individual youngsters is not an easy or inexpensive task, nor is there complete agreement that providing a youngster with this protective web is always in his best interests.[29] If it is designed and imposed by adults, it can lead to resentment from the very youngsters those adults are hoping to help; they may feel that it is intrusive, even demeaning, to be targeted for such help. Such programs work best when they are mutually desired and designed, but here again, it can be an arduous and sometimes thankless task, particularly when the adults and the teenagers come from different social or cultural backgrounds and may not agree on what is necessary and desirable for development. Formally developed social support systems or groups can also take power and prestige away from caretaker institutions, such as the family or the school, which society should be moving to empower. But when parents and children, teachers and students, genuinely work together, both benefit and learn from the interaction. Finally, and most significantly, changing or modifying the behavior of the individual child or adolescent or even small groups of them is valuable and important, but does not have the lasting transformational effect on the community that changing its component institutions and modifying their relationships to each other can.

What can have this lasting transformational effect are youth programs which create new linkages or modify existing ones among the family, the school, the workplace, and the criminal justice system. Such programs are proliferating, both because of the growing recognition of their interdependent roles in teenagers' lives and because of the multiple problems which each and all of our institutions face. The progressive decline of the influence of family and schools, the escalation in unemployment and delinquency among youth, have led many communities to reassert the importance of the community as a holistic context for the development of youth.[30] We saw and heard about a number of programs which are hoping to make better linkages among some of the community's institutions. One of the major new program thrusts is to make the school-to-work transition more predictable and productive for society as well as the individual young worker-to-be.[31]

Many of these programs are school-based, or like the Career Intern Program developed by the Opportunities Industrialization Center in Philadelphia, establish alternative education programs which combine a supportive atmosphere with intensive academic and job counseling and attempt to make the school experience relate to realistic life goals. Other programs link the schools directly with the world of work in a partnership model.[32] Adopt-a-school programs—in which industrial and business concerns work directly with schools, providing expertise and job opportunities—and initiatives such as the Partnership Program, in which private employers in various communities worked with schools in twenty-one sites to redesign curricula, have shown some success. After five business executives spent a year studying school programs, a partnership with the Kodak Company was formed and led to the establishment of the Rochester Brainpower Program, which placed a company-paid job counselor in every high school of that New York State community. What is most promising in this group-to-group mentoring approach is its potential for providing career networks to those youngsters for whom family and community resources and contacts to further careers are not available.

Most dropout programs continue to concentrate their efforts on pre-employment training in the school-to-work transition, and a number of new approaches to such training have developed into successful programs. The Job Readiness Program is an experimental mini-school jointly sponsored by Chicago United, a nonprofit business organization, and the Chicago Public Schools, in which ninth grade students considered at risk of dropping out receive training in basic skills and then are gradually enrolled in a vocationally oriented school-within-a-school. In rural Massachusetts the Cooperative Federation for Educational Experiences (Project COFFEE) has established an alternative school, with connections to small business and the Digital Equipment Corporation, which trains students in computer maintenance, horticulture, buildings and grounds maintenance, and other skills by having the students run small businesses. Rich's Academy is an alternative high school, operated by the Atlanta Public Schools and the nonprofit education agency Exodus, Inc., which holds classes on an unused floor of a major department store. Students draw on the store's resources and are paired with employee-mentors to learn about various vocations; they also receive counseling from Atlanta social service professionals. In San Antonio, Texas, the Valued Youth Partnership Program prepares teens to tutor other teens, involves parents in the training process as well as teachers, and has had a 6 percent dropout rate compared to the 37 percent among similar students in the city.

A wide variety of "second chance" programs pick up and hope to salvage students after they drop out. In Chicago the Alternative Schools Network of thirty-five alternative schools and youth centers has developed a computerized, self-paced basic skills program which helps dropouts work toward the GED, or high school diploma. Privately operated but state-supported Educational Clinics located in seven counties in Washington State help dropouts toward the same goals. Washington also has a pioneering Secondary Credit Exchange Program in which migrant worker youths in their middle and late teens are given a chance to finish school programs they began in other states. Two other states, California and Colorado, have now established similar programs. While all of these programs differ somewhat in their approach, their directors all attribute their successes to the commitment and caring of their staffs, and the students all credit the programs' supportive environments.[33]

Successful linking programs are also being developed by the criminal justice system in an attempt to prevent and control juvenile delinquency and youth crime.[34] Some are based on a community youth development model which attempts to involve young people, particularly those who do not show a strong commitment to the school, with new links to education and to other legitimate activities and groups. There are variants of this approach in programs such as the Community Arbitration Project in Anne Arundel County, Maryland, in which juvenile offenders, their victims, and the offender's parents are brought together in an informal session in the courtroom with an attorney designated as the Juvenile Intake Officer who arbitrates the case. If the offender admits the offense and consents to arbitration, she is assigned (or "sentenced") to a specific number of hours of community work or restitution, counseling, or an educational program. A number of other programs which come out of this same model place emphasis on reconnecting youthful offenders with their families or communities. First Massachusetts and subsequently other states have closed large, overcrowded juvenile training centers and have diverted most juvenile offenders into a network of privately operated and community-based service programs, with more serious offenders going to small, secure settings. While there is still some controversy over the long-term benefits of this approach among young offenders, some of the recent evidence indicates that recidivism rates are lower among youths in intensive community-based programs than among those who are re-leased from training schools.[35] Similarly, the Guilford County Wom-en's Residential Day Center in Greensboro, North Carolina, provides alternative programs to incarceration for young women who have children or are pregnant. The Dorchester Youth Collaborative in Massa-chusetts, working through a broad coalition of youth, the elderly, schools, police, and business people, has established teams of teenagers paid to work with the elderly for their protection and also to prevent vandalism and arson. In return, the requirements for remaining in the program are "staying in school, off drugs, and out of trouble with the police." Philadelphia's Crisis Intervention Network sends out trained youth teams (which include former gang members) to patrol their neighborhoods, intervene in conflicts, and work with police, parents, and youth. These teams have been instrumental in reducing gang-related murders from forty to two per year.[36] In California the State Task Force on Youth Gang Violence has pressed for new programs which focus on strengthening caring family and community programs to deter youngsters from participating in gangs.

Not surprisingly, it is in education that linkage programs are receiving the most attention and promising the most important results for social as well as cognitive development. The school–community relationship has often been a controversial issue in American education. While the focus during the civil-rights movement was on greater community access to the schools, the current emphasis is on moving the programs and influences of the school out into the community as well as moving some community-based programs into the school.[39] The school–busi-ness partnerships and the adopt-a-school, tutoring, and mentoring pro-grams described above are examples of this latter movement, but some of the most promising programs are attempts to move the school to reach out into the community.[40] One of the most frequent (and as indicated earlier, most promising) initiatives involves joining the home and the school in a cooperative teaching and learning team. Remember-ing the differences between Sheffield and Southside in home–school understanding, cooperation, and support, it is understandable that most such programs focus on poor and minority children. Chicago's Parent Plus Project, for example, enrolls parents and pupils in a cooperative learning session one hour each week in the home, and in San Diego, California, the Partnership Program has established parent-student-teacher teams to set learning objectives and means of achieving and evaluating them. It also trains parents as tutors. In New Orleans parents are provided with home-study materials, prepare as tutors, attend in-service workshops related to the skills their children are learning in school, and receive frequent computerized feedback on how their children are progressing. Other programs prepare parents to be reading partners with their children, train parents as tutors or coordinator-aides in the school, or develop new home-instruction or home-counseling arrangements.[41] Each of these programs has proven successful not only in retaining children in school and improving their achievement levels, but also in serving to join the family with the school in a learning consortium.

A number of school-based and school-related programs have been developed which reflect a concern with linkage among students and between students and other community institutions. One type of program focuses on the improvement of governance by involving students in school policymaking, particularly in such areas as drug abuse, and insuring that a wide range of students, not just "leaders," are involved. One such program was developed at New York City's South Bronx Samuel Gompers Vocational-Technical High School, where 95 percent of the fifteen hundred students are from low-income families. A new principal, who instituted cooperation with the local police precinct, set up a jobs program with industry, and established drug education programs for parents as well as teachers and students, turned the school—once considered a drug "war zone"—around, leading to a 22 percent increase in the number of students reading at or above grade level. Similar programs, which add law-related education or prevocational education and career exploration to school curricula on an experiential basis as early as the middle or junior high school years, are being tried elsewhere. A somewhat different approach places more emphasis on social control aspects. Programs like Los Angeles's Say YES (Youth Enterprise System) or San Francisco's Centro de Cambio look to prevention and remediation by using cooperative gang members or former members to intervene in school crises, and by training teachers and administrators in crisis intervention techniques, information gathering, and rumor control.[37] The Centro de La Comunidad Unida Delinquency Prevention and Youth Outreach Program in Milwaukee provides individual and family counseling, gang mediation, and educational and occupational programs which have proven successful with high-risk youth, particularly in job placement.[38] Meanwhile, in Jacksonville, Florida, a program called Accountability in Citizenship Training (ACT) has been working successfully to reduce disruptive behavior in the schools by setting up a "caring team" of parents, students, and teachers to help students accept responsibility for and modify their behavior. An important aspect of this program is that it does provide for student accountability to a set of expectations and standards by having each student commit to one agreed-upon behavior change at a time, specified in a behavioral prescription or contract.

There are also programs which work directly with families, such as the Albuquerque, New Mexico, New Futures School for parenting and pregnant teenagers, or the Leslie, Michigan, public school–sponsored Family Learning Center, which provide day care and education to help teens with children continue toward a diploma. Other programs attempt to empower families even more directly by involving them in programs to learn about conflict resolution, drug abuse, sexuality, and other areas where parents can help youngsters. Some communities are also involving parents more directly in law-enforcement programs. One program which has proven so successful in Tacoma, Washington, that it is now being adopted in Chicago and New York City's Bronx section is Homebuilders, which assigns teams of social workers, counselors, and psychologists to work closely with schools and juvenile justice agencies in helping distressed families overcome crises and develop long-term coping strategies.[42] Still other new initiatives intervene in early childhood education in an effort to instill the values and skills that will prevent students from dropping out later.

Some dropout programs in places like Roanoke, Virginia, or New York City depend heavily on connecting with community resources and work through community groups who know local families and neighborhoods, as well as the students who are likely to drop out. Attempts to negotiate peer group formation to enhance social network development are also beginning to appear. Twelve Together is a peer group program sponsored by the Metropolitan Detroit Youth Foundation which uses structured peer groups of potential dropouts, caring adults, and students who seem destined to remain in school to work together to encourage the dropout-prone to stay in school. The possibilities here seem almost limitless, from "turning" youth gangs into groups which protect communities outside their own turf to having suburban and urban youngsters work together on self-help and community development programs which are based on the very different skills and insights they can bring to each other.

Although we saw a number of programs and heard about many others that are making a difference, it is not really possible to determine what works for every community. Some things, however, seem to be necessary for programs to work anywhere. Not only must the programs link adults and teenagers, but both need to learn each other's appropriate role in the relationship. Adults need to make public their desire to help, but they must include a firm explanation of what they expect from youngsters and how both will know when it has been achieved. Young people have to learn to ask for help when they need it, but they also have to accept the fact that not all adults can offer every kind of help. Thus they must seek out the kinds of adult mentoring and guidance they want and need. Adults have to be available and willing to help, but young people must also agree to commitment and involvement in programs rather than giving up. Finally, modeling by adults seems to be the best way to develop such commitment and to foster caring relationships both between adults and teenagers and among adolescents themselves.

Ironically, most of the successful linkage programs we saw were operated in isolation from others, even in the same community. Many had no financial or other relationship to the community, but tended to be supported by foundation or government grants. Whatever good they did do—and in some cases it was considerable—was for small numbers of youngsters and often left other problems and deficits unattended. Adding more programs is not going to make that much more difference. The adolescent experience is not a collection of isolated experiences; rather it is an organization of experiences and exposures in the various social worlds of the community. Programs for adolescents should grow out of a community youth charter which promulgates the expectations and standards which can meet the developmental needs of the adolescents in the specific community. A well-integrated and consciously developed pattern of relationships can provide a stabilizing transformational structure that produces equally integrated identities as workers and citizens and parents; no single institution has the resources to develop all of these roles alone.

Just a few short years ago it was not uncommon to hear about the "death of adolescence" in the face of media, parental, and popular cultural influences in compressing the years of childhood by early exposure to adult life styles. It is perhaps typical of the confusion our society generates in thinking about adolescence that during this same time there were grumblings about the problems youths were facing and creating as a result of their prolonged adolescence. The portrait which appeared in the media (and in the minds of many adults) of a deeply troubled, rebellious generation of young Americans is not the picture we saw emerge over the decade of our research. By the second half of the 1980s, adolescent pregnancy was down to 51 per 1,000 teenage girls from the 68.3 per 1,000 in 1970 and 89 per 1,000 in 1960. The increased acceptability of single motherhood reflected in this change may be a positive development to the extent that it allows pregnant teens to avoid marriages that have little chance of success. However, the children of poor, young single mothers are among the neediest members of American society.[43] Therefore, there is certainly cause for concern in the increased proportion of teen mothers who are "going it alone." Educational attainment, particularly among blacks, has increased steadily and the dropout rate has declined as well. The importance of giving young people time to overcome crises is underlined by the fact that 86 percent of all adults aged twenty-five to twenty-nine have earned a high school diploma, twice the percentage of 1940, and 22 percent are college graduates, four times the 1940 rate. There have also been significant decreases among youths in drug use and some leveling off or decrease in crime, homicide, and suicide rates as well as alcohol abuse.[44]

What is needed now to capitalize on these trends, and on the success of the individual programs, is comprehensive community planning.[45] In Minneapolis, for example, Project City's Children is an attempt to bring together planning groups of teachers, youth workers, human services providers, police, businesspersons, judges, researchers, and others to create a vision of the type of environment necessary for children and adults in future years and to develop a comprehensive plan for moving in that direction. Such a planning process is necessary as a first step, but some means of involving youngsters in planning the future in which they will live is just as necessary. A well thought out, mutually designed, and publicly proclaimed community (again, not national) youth charter can provide a basis for reducing the unnecessary uncertainty which affects adults as much as adolescents. It can also make explicit what the community expects of youth and why, as well as what youth can expect from the community.

When I first undertook this ten-year research project, the development of such a youth charter was a dream. We even included a caution in our early proposals and reports citing Freud's *Civilization and Its Discontents,* in which he asks, "What would be the use of the most acute analysis of social neurosis since no one possesses the power to compel the community to adopt the therapy?''[46] Now, over a decade later, at least one community is doing precisely that. Sparked by both research and a number of program initiatives, the city of Seattle, Washington, has adopted and made explicit a Policy Plan for Children and Youth, which was developed to: (1) gain better understanding of the status of children and youth in Seattle and current efforts to address their needs; (2) promote community agreement on goals and priorities to establish a clearer understanding and consensus on the roles to be played by various jurisdictions and organizations in the service system for children and youth. This policy framework, which looks to youth as a resource, makes the community's youth charter, or what it identifies as a community youth agenda, clear and available to all. The agenda proposes to: (1) help parents better fulfill their responsibilities to their children; (2) improve the health and well-being of children and youth and protect them from harm; (3) prepare young people for a successful transition to adulthood; (4) help young people better understand cultural differences and value the ethnic diversity of the community; (5) project a vision to all young people of high expectations and hope for their futures and a sense of the responsibilities they bear; (6) involve children and youth as active participants in the community. The Policy Plan, which goes on to describe the responsibilities as well as the rights of all the constituent social institutions including those of children, has now become the ''official'' policy of the city. It is overseen by a committee of officials and citizens, including two young people elected by their peers.

It is the next step that Seattle is taking which can convert what is essentially a planning process into a youth charter. Groups of thirty teenagers meet frequently to convert the plan item by item into a series of expectations and standards. They have conducted youth-to-youth surveys to determine how best to disseminate and make these available to all youngsters in the city.[47] It is, of course, somewhat soon to say ''Well, there it is'' and to assume that this or any other such formalization of a community's adolescent charter can be made to work as a new or expanded chance for a smoother, more productive transition to adulthood. It does, however, offer the hope that communities are accepting their local responsibility to treat adolescence as a period in which the child becoming adult requires a stable, consistent environment in which to grow and develop. It also is a good example of how a community can, given the will, develop and proclaim a structure through which to move from dependence to interdependence, from the egocentrism of early adolescence to the social competence of the young adult. Encouraging young people to participate in defining the community's youth charter also facilitates their movement from accepting the definitions of who they should be, as offered by a variety of others, to gaining a sense of control over their own individual identities. If they are helped and encouraged to explore and experiment, this liberating potential for self-development and self-management can and should provide for a healthy diversity in developing adult personalities.

The teenagers I met and interviewed expressed a considerable confidence that they could make choices and decisions about present and future life styles given the time and adult guidance they know they need. It was the adults we observed and interviewed who seemed to be in a hurry for teenagers to "settle down" into being grown-up, often ignoring or forgetting that identity achievement proceeds as much from the guidance and encouragement provided by the community as from the teenagers' own resources and motivation. As we heard over and over from these young people no matter where or how they lived, what they want out of life—to find a good job which they enjoy and to have a happy family life—is precisely what we all want for our children as well as ourselves.[48] With a firm but sensitive set of expectations and standards, and with our acceptance of the fact that there is still time, adolescent crises can become less urgent and can even provide an opportunity for learning and progress toward these mutually valued goals.

Our focus should be on how we can integrate adolescence into the life course as a time in which teenagers seek personhood rather than independence, and we should provide an explicit guidance structure they can work within, rather than benign neglect or outraged moralizing. The transitional role of adults and adult-mediated institutions should be one of patient tutoring. The youth charter can be an ideal place to map out a joint effort which transcends narrowly conceived generational perspectives, since it is more accessible for discussion and negotiation than is teenage fantasy but has less immediate and critical consequences than the expedient reality we so often insist teenagers must face. Articulating a youth charter can provide a community with an intergenerational forum for expressing diverse views and a medium for making them public. Youth charters, and the structure of expectations and standards experienced through adolescent life in the community, interact with individual personalities in a variety of social worlds to produce behaviors and motivations, attitudes and transitional role models, for the movement to adult status. It is in the coordinated harmony of these social worlds that adolescence can and usually does become a period of joy and challenge as well as a nostalgic journey from what must be left behind in the migration to the new adult world.

Notes

CHAPTER 1

Growing Up in America

1. *Newsweek,* "The Copycat Suicides," March 23, 1987, p. 28.
2. Ibid., p. 29.
3. *Time,* "The New Whiz Kids," August 31, 1987, p. 46.
4. Ibid., p. 45.
5. Our fieldwork was based on traditional ethnographic field methods in an approach which we had developed and used in a number of earlier studies in which events became a focus for observation and interviewing. (See F. A. J. Ianni, *A Family Business: Kinship and Social Control in Organized Crime,* New York, Russell Sage, 1972; E. Reuss-Ianni, *Street Cops vs. Management Cops: The Two Cultures of Policing,* New Brunswick, N.J., Transaction Press, 1983.) The fieldworker, who had a long-term participant-observer relationship with the social setting being studied, recorded the individual and social action of a particular event: sometimes as dramatic as a food fight in the cafeteria or as routine as a teacher calling the role in class. Following the observation, the participants in the event were interviewed and the accounts were analyzed along with the observer's perceptions of what took place and why. Field notes by each of the fieldworkers were recorded and transcribed and made available to other team members. In addition, each field researcher prepared memos on any interesting event or observation and summary analytic memos for distribution. We also gathered archival data on each community, using standard sources such as demographic data sets, previous or ongoing research on the particular community, and a review of available materials on its cultural history. In addition, we interviewed local youth profession-

als about the available programs for teenagers as well as local and federal-level policymakers responsible for programs for adolescents.

Since the research was based on a qualitative methodology, we began our analyses of the data from each of the sources from the outset of the research. We conducted first-level analyses of the data from each community and then did comparative analyses across communities. In both stages of the process, our aim was to identify those major themes—latent or manifest principles underlying the conventions that shape attitudes and behavior within a social system by providing cultural meaning—which we believed characterized the adolescent transition. (For the theoretical basis of this approach to analyzing field data see R. Benedict, *Patterns of Culture,* Boston, Houghton Mifflin, 1934, and M. Oppler, "Themes as Dynamic Forces in Culture," *American Journal of Sociology,* vol. 53, 1945, pp. 198–206. For a full explication of a similar approach see J. P. Spradley, *The Ethnographic Interview,* New York, Holt, Rinehart and Winston, 1979.)

6. The opening topic area for the first interview was always a personal and family history, as well as self-image material; for the second it was social relationships, friendships, and social networks in which the adolescent was involved. The third session concerned future orientations, relations to objects and people, positive and negative attachments to authority, power and powerlessness, and concepts of and feelings about responsibility. In the fourth session we turned to significant adults and how the adolescent related to them, attitudes toward self and others, ideas about work and productivity, and, if they had not come up in earlier sessions, dreams and fantasies; the fifth and final session was open-ended, with the adolescent choosing either to talk about earlier topics or introduce new ones. We also compiled a number of life histories of some of the adolescent interviewees to tap specific features of community, personality, and educational experiences before as well as during adolescence.

The interviews were carried out over a period of six years from 1979 to 1985. The youngest interviewee was eleven years old and the oldest twenty; the median age was fifteen. In addition to the 311 interviewees who completed all 5 interviews, an additional 41 began but did not complete the interview series. I conducted at least 10 interviews in each of the communities; there were 163 in urban areas, 119 in suburban areas, and 29 in rural areas. Eleven of the urban interviews were with teenage patients in two adolescent psychiatry wards (one inpatient and one outpatient) and two were with recently released inmates of a juvenile detention center in the same city.

7. Our approach was based on the focus group interviewing technique which has been so successful in market research. The basic procedure in this

form of interviewing is to encourage a group to discuss feelings, attitudes, and perceptions about a particular topic, or focus. Like group therapy, focused interviewing is based on the premise that individuals who share a problem, concern, or interest will be more willing to talk about it as part of a group of others sharing the same problem, concern, or interest. The use of focus group interviews developed in the 1950s as a reaction to the large-sample polling techniques which were the basis for most market research at that time, and which provided lots of numbers but little of the meaning or "why" behind the numbers. (See R. K. Merton. M. Fiske, and P. L. Kendall, *The Focused Interview,* Glencoe, Ill., Free Press, 1956.)

8. The late Swiss psychologist Jean Piaget, for example, placed the emergence of formal operational thought—the ability to think abstractly and reason logically—at about the same age as puberty because this developmental stage was characterized by significant social as well as physical change. (See J. Piaget and B. Inhelder, *The Psychology of the Child,* New York, Basic Books, 1969.)

9. Some, Arnold Gesell and J. M. Tanner, for example, have been primarily interested in developmental processes and maturation, identifying overall trends or "norms" of behavior against which the progress of the individual's maturation could be compared. Hall's biogenetic influence is best reflected in the work of Gesell. Like Hall, Gesell perceived adolescence as a distinct and observable stage in a hereditary process of physical and mental growth and intrinsic maturation—one which was abruptly triggered by hormonal production and terminated in the early twenties. Unlike Hall, however, Gesell did not see adolescence as a period of inevitable storm and stress but rather as one in which genetic differences or irregularities produced differential rates of development of abilities and attitudes which made some youngsters more or less ready to take on the adolescent task of finding oneself. While it was genetic forces which produced, guided, and controlled the maturational sequences of growth and development, these were only observable as behavioral manifestations which were indicative of normative variations or individual differences in the population. Some individual differences could result from environmental factors, which Gesell called "acculturation," as well as from genetic factors, but since maturation was a prerequisite of learning, the environment always played a secondary role.

It was from these observed behaviors that overall trends or "norms" of behavior could be aggregated and against which the progress of the individual's maturation could be compared. This belief that it was possible to establish a normative sequence allowed Gesell to describe what the typical, or normal, adolescent should be able (or unable) to do at each age level as a result of maturation or readiness. For many, Gesell seemed to confirm the epigenetic view of adolescence and to add a new insistence on the primacy of innate biological maturation and the universality of the trends and sequences of development. For many others, Gesell's research was flawed by his use of a sample of youngsters who were not only drawn from the same geographical area, but tended to have high-average to superior ability. Gesell, however, insisted that the developmental patterns he was witnessing were universal and could be applied to all populations. More importantly, Gesell and his followers initiated a growing realization that adolescence is not a single stage, but rather a number of developmental steps, and that there are individual differences in readiness as well as in performance.

Others have focused on the cognitive changes leading to and characterizing adolescence. Here the most influential and best known work is that of the late Swiss psychologist Jean Piaget, who proposed that the child must progress via a finite set of stages of cognitive, or intellectual, development to become an "adult" rational thinker. The end result of this progression and a major goal of adolescent development should be a cognitive style which Piaget called "formal operations," described in note 8 above. The adolescent who has mastered formal operations can deal with concepts such as beliefs and propositions and do so with a logic based on abstract form rather than particularized content. (See J. Piaget, *The Moral Judgment of the Child,* New York, Free Press, 1965; idem and B. Inhelder, op. cit., 1969, note 8 above.)

10. E. H. Erikson, *Childhood and Society,* New York, Norton, 1950. Sigmund Freud placed little emphasis on adolescence as a stage, but he did recognize it as such, and later psychoanalytic writers have seen adolescence as a critical and necessary life period ushered in by puberty and marked with internal emotional upheaval. Anna Freud gave puberty a major role as the crucial factor affecting character formation. (See A. Freud, *The Ego and the Mechanisms of Defense,* New York, International Universities Press, 1948.) Conflict, both internal and external, results from an upsurge in instinctual urges upsetting the precarious psychic balance developed in childhood. These internal forces and the nascent sexuality which they develop drive the adolescent to seek new love objects in the world outside of the family. Peter Blos expanded these themes and described the adolescent years as a "second individuation" resulting from the "revival and renewed resolution or transformation of the oedipus conflict." (See P. Blos, *On Adolescence: A Psychoanalytic Interpretation,* New York, Free Press, 1962; idem, *The Adolescent Passage: Developmental Issues,* New York, International Universities Press, 1979.) Just as Hall's conception of adolescence as a "second birth" focused on the biogenetic emphasis in his work, Blos's characterization

of adolescence as a "second individuation" was an indication of a movement away from biogenetic determinism. The idea of an individuation process, or a movement begun in infancy and usually completed by the third year of life in which the child sees himself as an individual apart from others and particularly as a self distinct from the mother, was first developed by Margaret Mahler from her studies of children. (See M. S. Mahler, F. Pine, and A. Bergman, *The Psychological Birth of the Human Infant: Symbiosis and Individuation,* New York, Basic Books, 1975.) This process develops as a result of the infant's acquisition of new skills and social experiences which make it possible to distinguish between internal and external reality. An important aspect of this new-found ability to differentiate is the ability to conceptualize and internalize models or representations of others and to attempt to be like them. For Mahler, the principal internalized object in the first individuation is the mother. For Blos, the second individuation results in disengagement from the idealized representation of the family and a search for new objects in the social environment from which to model a new sexual and social identity. Blos confirmed the view of the importance of the sociocultural world, commenting that after decades of clinical research on adolescence he had concluded that "adolescent closure occurs at a biologically and culturally determined time, be this in a normal or abnormal manner."

11. At about the same time that the evolutionary paradigm of Social Darwinism had directly influenced the development of Hall's theory of adolescence, a new, revolutionary paradigm began to emerge in reaction to the biogenetic dominance of scientific thought about human nature and society. Franz Boas, the undisputed *doyen* of the formative years of cultural anthropology in America, launched a critique of evolutionary anthropology which led him and his students to a cultural determinism that became as dogmatic as the biological determinism which had irritated it into reaction. In his book *The Mind of Primitive Man,* which appeared in 1911, he attacked not only the hereditarian emphasis of social evolutionary thought but the eugenics movement and the doctrines of racial purity which developed with it. It was two of Boas's students—Ruth Benedict and Margaret Mead—who applied cultural determinism and the exogenetic nature of culture to a challenge of the universality and biological certainty of adolescence.

Ruth Benedict, drawing on the evidence from these field studies, described the effects of culture and its social institutions in the development either of continuous patterns of growth or of discontinuities between childhood and adult roles in society. (See R. Benedict, "Continuities and Discontinuities in Cultural Conditioning," in C. Kluckhohn and

H. A. Miller [eds.], *Nature, Society, and Culture,* New York, Knopf, 1948.) She suggested that it is the culture of societies and not the genetic structure of individuals which perpetuates and transmits those behavioral and emotional traits we associate with the adolescent transition. While most primitive societies are characterized by a continuous and gradual transition from child to adult, Western industrial society has produced a series of role discontinuities which confound the adolescent transformation. Children are required to be submissive, asexual, and generally free from productive responsibility, while their parents, as adults, are expected to be dominant, sexual, and responsible. Modern society has produced a cultural pattern and role for a new life period called "adolescence" which makes those transitions uneven and uncertain. Benedict's work, and that of her student and colleague Margaret Mead, sparked a debate which has continued in one form or another as a fundamental controversy over how we think about adolescence. Mead's books *Coming of Age in Samoa* and *Growing Up in New Guinea* popularized to millions of American readers the contention that anatomy is not destiny and that there are cultures which do not exhibit inevitable storm and stress in a movement from childhood to adulthood. (See M. Mead, "Adolescence in Primitive and Modern Society," in G. E. Swanson et al., *Readings in Social Psychology,* rev. ed., New York, Henry Holt, 1952.) While neither Benedict nor Mead denied adolescence as a biological process, they saw its contemporary character and content as culture-molded. This newer, sociogenetic approach redirected attention from the adolescent to society, and eventually to some aspect, problem, or change in society.

12. N. Ackerman, *The Psychodynamics of Family Life,* New York, Basic Books, 1958.

13. P. Goodman, *Growing Up Absurd: Problems of Youth in the Organized System,* New York, Random House, 1960; K. Kenniston, *The Uncommitted: Alienated Youth in America,* New York, Dell, 1965.

14. J. Bernard, "Teen-Age Culture: An Overview," in H. Silverstein (ed.), *The Sociology of Youth: Evolution and Revolution,* New York, Macmillan, 1973.

15. E. Z. Friedenberg, *Coming of Age in America: Growth and Acquiescence,* New York, Vintage Books, 1963.

16. T. Parsons, "Youth in the Context of American Society," in E. H. Erikson (ed.), *The Challenge of Youth,* New York, Doubleday, 1965; idem, "Social Structure and the Development of Personality: Freud's Contribution to the Integration of Psychology and Sociology," *Psychiatry,* vol. 21, 1958, pp. 321–340.

17. D. Riesman, *The Lonely Crowd: A Study of the Changing American Character*, New Haven, Yale University Press, 1950.

18. J. S. Coleman, *The Adolescent Society,* Glencoe, Ill., Free Press, 1960.

19. See D. P. Ausubel, *Theory and Problems of Adolescent Development,* New York, Grune and Stratton, 1954; J. Bernard, "Teen-age Culture: An Overview," in H. Silverstein (ed.), *The Sociology of Youth: Evolution and Revolution,* New York, Macmillan, 1973, pp. 62–82; J. S. Coleman, *Adolescents and the Schools,* New York, Basic Books, 1965; M. Mead, "Adolescence in Primitive and Modern Society," in G. E. Swanson et al. (eds.), *Readings in Social Psychology,* New York, Henry Holt, 1952; J. H. Plumb, "Children, the Victims of Time," in *The Light of History,* London, Penguin Press, 1972, chap. 2; E. Shils, "Mass Society and Its Culture," *Daedalus,* Fall 1960, pp. 280–301.

20. J. S. Coleman, *Youth: Transition to Adulthood,* Chicago, University of Chicago Press, 1974.

21. E. H. Erikson, *Identity: Youth and Crisis,* New York, Norton, 1968.

22. J. S. Coleman, op. cit., 1974, note 20 above.

23. See G. H. Elder, "Adolescence in the Life Cycle: An Introduction," in S. E. Dragastin and G. H. Elder (eds.), *Adolescence in the Life Cycle: Psychological Change and Social Context,* New York, Wiley, 1975; J. Adelson, "Adolescence in Historical Perspective," in J. Adelson (ed.), *Handbook of Adolescent Psychology,* New York, Wiley, 1980; and, for a comprehensive summary of theories of adolescence, R. E. Muss, *Theories of Adolescence,* 4th ed., New York, Random House, 1982.

24. P. Blos, op. cit., 1979, note 10 above.

25. L. Steinberg, "Impact of Puberty on Family Relations: Effects of Pubertal Status and Pubertal Timing," *Developmental Psychology,* vol. 23, 1987, pp. 451–460.

26. See J. Brooks-Gunn and A. C. Petersen (eds.), *Girls at Puberty: Biological and Psychosocial Perspectives,* New York, Plenum Press, 1983; J. Brooks-Gunn et al., "Time of Maturation and Psychosocial Functioning in Adolescence," parts 1 and 2, in special issue, *Journal of Youth and Adolescence,* vol. 14, nos. 3 and 4, 1985; N. G. Caine, "Behavior During Puberty and Adolescence," in G. Mitchell and J. Erwin (eds.), *Comparative Primate Biology* (vol. 2, part A: *Behavior, Conservation and Ecology*), New York, Alan R. Liss, 1986.

27. J. R. Wetzel, *American Youth: A Statistical Snapshot,* Washington, D.C., Youth and America's Future: The William T. Grant Foundation Commission on Work, Family and Citizenship, June 1987, pp. 2–3.

28. A. C. Petersen, "Pubertal Development as a Cause of Disturbance: Myths, Realities, and Unanswered Questions," *Genetic, Social, and General Psychology Monographs,* vol. 3, 1982, pp. 205–232; D. Offer, *The Psychological World of the Teen-ager: A Study of Normal Adolescent Boys,* New York, Basic Books, 1969; idem with E. Ostrov and K. Howard, *The Adolescent: A Psychological Self-Portrait,* New York, Basic Books, 1981. Petersen and her colleagues concentrated on the early adolescent years and found that over half of the males and females had little if any significant trouble, another 30 percent had only intermittent problems, and only 15 percent seemed to experience major problems or turmoil.

29. S. Freud, *The Interpretation of Dreams,* in J. Strachey (ed. and trans.), *The Standard Edition of the Complete Psychological Works of Sigmund Freud,* vol. 7, London, Hogarth Press, 1953, p. 497.

CHAPTER 2
Peer Worlds and Adolescent Development

1. E. Durkheim, *Le Suicide,* Paris, Alcan, 1897, rev. ed., 1930.

2. P. Ariès, *The World of Children,* London, Paul Hamlyn, 1966.

3. V. C. Seltzer, *Adolescent Social Development: Dynamic Functional Interaction,* Lexington, Mass., Ballinger Press, 1982.

4. Cf. F. A. J. Ianni, "New Institutional Models for the Preparation of Educators," in W. Foshay (ed.), *The Professional as Educator,* New York, Teachers College Press, 1970.

5. J. Brooks-Gunn and A. C. Petersen (eds.), *Girls at Puberty: Biological and Psychosocial Perspectives,* New York, Plenum Press, 1983.

6. A. C. Petersen et al., "Heterosexual Behavior and Sexuality Among Normal Young Adolescents," in M. D. Levine and E. McAnarney (eds.), *Early Adolescent Transitions,* Lexington, Mass., D. C. Heath, 1988.

7. M. McCarthy, *How I Grew,* San Diego, Harcourt Brace Jovanovich, 1987.

8. D. Offer, *The Psychological World of the Teenager: A Study of Normal Adolescent Boys,* New York, Basic Books, 1969; M. Rosenberg, *Society and the Adolescent Self-Image,* Princeton, N.J., Princeton University Press, 1965.

9. See D. R. Clasen and B. B. Brown, "The Multidimensionality of Peer Pressure in Adolescence," *Journal of Youth and Adolescence,* vol. 2, 1985, pp. 121–133; J. K. Ide et al., "Peer Group Influence on Educational Outcomes: A Quantitative Synthesis," *Journal of Educational Psychology,* vol. 73, 1981, pp. 472–484.

10. V. C. Seltzer, op. cit., 1982, note 3 above.

11. J. R. Wetzel, *American Youth: A Statistical Snapshot*, Washington, D.C., Youth and America's Future: The William T. Grant Foundation Commission on Work, Family and Citizenship, June 1987, pp. 27 and 29.

12. Ibid., p. 29.

13. See H. Hendin, "Suicide: A Review of New Directions in Research," *Hospital and Community Psychiatry*, vol. 37, 1986, pp. 148–154; P. C. Hollinger and D. Offer, "Prediction of Adolescent Suicide: A Population Model," *American Journal of Psychiatry*, vol. 39, 1982, pp. 302–307.

14. See H. Hendin, *Suicide in America*, New York, Norton, 1982; E. Robins, *The Final Months: A Study of the Lives of 134 Persons Who Committed Suicide*, New York, Oxford University Press, 1981.

15. T. Dorpar, J. Jackson, and H. Ripley, "Broken Homes and Attempted and Completed Suicide," *Archives of General Psychiatry*, vol. 12, 1965, pp. 213–216; J. Jacobs and J. Teicher, "Broken Homes and Social Isolation in Attempted Suicides of Adolescents," *International Journal of Social Psychiatry*, vol. 13, 1967, pp. 139–149.

16. S. Greer, "The Relationship Between Parental Loss and Attempted Suicide: A Control Study," *British Journal of Psychiatry*, vol. 110, 1964, pp. 698–704; J. C. Sabbath, "The Suicidal Adolescent: The Expendable Child," *Journal of the American Academy of Child Psychiatry*, vol. 8, 1969, pp. 272–289.

17. H. Hendin, "Growing Up Dead: Student Suicide," *American Journal of Psychotherapy*, vol. 27, 1975, pp. 327–338.

18. D. C. Garell, "Motivating the Adolescent: Special Needs and Approaches," in R. Carlson and B. Newman (eds.), *Issues and Trends in Health*, St. Louis, Mosby, 1987, pp. 266–275; S. M. Radius et al., "Adolescent Perspectives on Health and Illness," *Adolescence*, vol. 15, 1980, pp. 375–384.

19. A. C. Petersen and E. Craighead, "Emotional and Personality Development in Normal Adolescents and Young Adults," in G. Klerman (ed.), *Preventive Aspects of Suicide and Affective Disorders Among Adolescents and Young Adults*, New York, Guilford Press, 1987.

20. See H. Kohut, *The Analysis of the Self*, New York, International Universities Press, 1971.

21. D. Elkind, *Miseducation: Preschoolers at Risk*, New York, Knopf, 1988.

22. For a comprehensive summary of the recent research on "invulnerable children" see E. J. Anthony and B. J. Cohler, *The Invulnerable Child*, New York, Guilford Press, 1987.

CHAPTER 3
"Home is Where We Start From"

1. D. W. Winnicott, *Home is Where We Start From: Essays by a Psychoanalyst,* compiled and edited by C. Winnicott, R. Shepherd, and M. Davis, New York, Norton, 1986.

2. D. A. Blyth, J. P. Hill, and K. S. Thiel, "Early Adolescents' Significant Others: Grade and Gender Differences in Perceived Relationships with Familial and Non-Familial Adults and Young People," *Journal of Youth and Adolescence,* vol. 2, 1982, pp. 425–450.

3. P. M. Blau and O. D. Duncan, *The American Occupational Structure,* New York, Wiley, 1967; A. J. Reiss, Jr., *Occupations and Social Status,* New York, Free Press of Glencoe, 1961.

4. J. S. Coleman, T. Hoffer, and S. Kilgore, *High School Achievement: Public, Catholic, and Private Schools Compared,* New York, Basic Books, 1982.

5. See R. A. Richardson et al., "Young Adolescents' Perceptions of the Family Environment," *Journal of Early Adolescence,* vol. 4, 1984, pp. 131–153.

6. R. Montemeyor, "Parents and Adolescents in Conflict: All Families Some of the Time and Some Families Most of the Time," *Journal of Early Adolescence,* vol. 3, 1981, pp. 83–103.

7. E. M. Hetherington and E. R. Anderson, "The Effects of Divorce and Remarriage on Early Adolescents and Their Families," in M. D. Levine and E. McAnarney (eds.), *Early Adolescent Transitions,* Lexington, Mass., D. C. Heath, 1988.

8. A. Russell and G. Russell, "Mother, Father, and Child Beliefs About Child Development," *Journal of Psychology,* vol. 110, 1982, pp. 297–306.

9. R. A. Richardson, loc. cit., note 5 above.

10. J. G. Smetana, "Adolescents' and Parents' Conceptions of Parental Authority," *Child Development,* vol. 59, 1988, pp. 321–336.

11. M. D. Janus, *Adolescent Runaways: Causes and Consequences,* Lexington, Mass., Lexington Books, 1987.

12. G. R. Adams, "Runaway Youth Projects: Comments on Care Programs for Runaways and Throwaways," *Journal of Adolescence,* vol. 3, 1980, pp. 321–334; idem and G. Monro, "Portrait of the North American Runaway: A Critical Review," *Journal of Youth and Adolescence,* vol. 8, 1979, pp. 359–373.

13. R. Johnson and M. M. Carter, "Flight of the Young: Why Children

Run Away From Their Homes," *Adolescence,* vol. 15, 1980, pp. 483–489; A. R. Roberts, *Runaways and Non-Runaways in an American Suburb,* New York, John Jay Press, 1981.

14. D. Verleur, R. E. Hughes, and M. D. de Rios, "Enhancement of Self-Esteem Among Female Adolescent Incest Victims: A Controlled Comparison," *Adolescence,* vol. 21, 1986, pp. 843–854.

15. E. Spillane-Greco, "Characteristics of a Helpful Relationship: A Study of Empathetic Understanding and Positive Regard Between Runaways and Their Parents," *Adolescence,* vol. 19, 1984, pp. 63–75.

16. T. Brennan, D. Huizinga, and D. S. Elliot, *The Social Psychology of Runaways,* Boston, D. C. Heath, 1978; Bernard Lefkowitz, *Tough Change,* New York, Free Press, 1987.

17. D. Verleur et al., loc. cit., 1986, note 14 above.

18. A. L. Otten, "If You See Families Staging a Comeback, It's Probably a Mirage," *Wall Street Journal,* September 25, 1986, p. 22.

19. L. Steinberg, "Impact of Puberty on Family Relations; Effects of Pubertal Status and Pubertal Timing," *Developmental Psychology,* vol. 23, 1987, pp. 451–460.

20. *New York Times,* March 20, 1988, p. E–6.

21. R. Dworkin and A. N. Poindexter, "Pregnant Low-Income Teenagers," *Youth and Society,* vol. 2, March 1980, pp. 295–309.

22. Bureau of the Census, Department of Commerce, *Fertility of American Women: June 1985,* Washington, D.C., U.S. Government Printing Office, 1986, pp. 13–14.

23. Thomas J. Silber, the pediatrician who has been influential in adolescent research, points out that the sociology of adolescent pregnancy differs in various cultures. In countries such as Bangladesh, India, Pakistan, and Tanzania, over 70 percent of females between the ages of fifteen and twenty are already married. The special health problems associated with teen pregnancy and childbearing there are not really very different from those we find here. Infant and maternal mortality rates are greater for teenagers than for adults everywhere, whether or not they are married. In addition, adolescent pregnancy and maternity everywhere are not only associated with educational deficits and reduced occupational chances for the mother, but there is evidence of child abuse, developmental lags, and behavior problems for the child regardless of the marital status of the mother. T. J. Silber, "Abortion in Adolescence: The Ethical Dimension," *Adolescence,* vol. 15, 1980, pp. 183–193.

24. C. G. Ortiz and E. V. Nuttall, "Adolescent Pregnancy: Effects of Family Support, Education, and Religion on the Decision to Carry or Terminate

Among Puerto Rican Teenagers," *Adolescence,* vol. 22, 1987, pp. 897—917.

25. M. L. Sullivan, "Teen Fathers in the Inner City: An Exploratory Ethnographic Study," unpublished report to the Urban Poverty Program of the Ford Foundation, April 1985.

26. National Center for Health Statistics, Department of Health and Human Services, *Advance Natality Statistics, 1984,* vol. 35, supp. 4, July 1986, pp. 31–32.

27. Ibid.

28. *New York Times,* March 20, 1988, p. E–6.

29. T. Silber, loc. cit., 1980, note 22 above.

30. D. Youngs, cited in L. A. Westhoff, "Kids with Kids," *New York Times Magazine,* February 22, 1976, p. 15.

31. V. Abernethy, "Illegitimate Conception Among Teenagers," *American Journal of Public Health,* vol. 64, pp. 662–665.

32. J. S. Coleman, *Youth: Transition to Adulthood,* Chicago, University of Chicago Press, 1974.

33. V. C. Seltzer, *Adolescent Social Development: Dynamic Functional Interaction,* Lexington, Mass., Ballinger Press, 1982.

34. See J. Youniss, *Parents and Peers in Social Development: A Sullivan-Piaget Perspective,* Chicago, University of Chicago Press, 1980.

35. See D. W. Winnicott, "Transitional Objects and Transitional Phenomena: A Study of the First Not-Me Possession," *International Journal of Psychoanalysis,* vol. 34, 1951, pp. 89–97. Reprinted in idem, *Collected Papers: Through Paediatrics to Psycho-Analysis,* New York, Basic Books, 1958, pp. 229–242; P. W. Pruyser, *The Play of the Imagination: Towards a Psychoanalysis of Culture,* New York, International Universities Press, 1983.

36. C. Lasch, *Haven in a Heartless World,* New York, Basic Books, 1979.

37. Ibid.

CHAPTER 4
From Home to School

1. S. Kimball, *Culture and the Educative Process,* New York, Teachers College Press, 1974.

2. J. R. Wetzel, *American Youth: A Statistical Snapshot,* Washington, D.C., Youth and America's Future: The William T. Grant Foundation Commission on Work, Family and Citizenship, June 1987, p. 15.

3. Ibid., p. 17.

4. "The Secretary's Wall Chart," Washington, D.C., United States Department of Education, 1987.

5. See C. Calhoun and F. A. J. Ianni, "Notes on the Social Organization of High Schools," in idem (eds.), *The Anthropological Study of Education,* The Hague, Mouton, 1976, pp. 217–226; H. Varenne, *American School Language: Culturally Patterned Conflicts in a Suburban High School,* New York, Irvington Publishers, 1983.

6. R. L. Crain, R. E. Mahard, and R. E. Narot, *Making Desegregation Work: How Schools Create Social Climates,* Lexington, Mass., Ballinger Press, 1982.

7. S. Fordham and J. U. Ogbu, "Black Students' School Success: Coping with the Burden of 'Acting White,' " *The Urban Review,* vol. 18, 1986, pp. 176–206.

8. S. V. Goldman, "Sorting Out Sorting: An Ethnographic Account of How Stratification is Managed in a Middle School," unpublished dissertation, Teachers College, Columbia University, 1982, p. 227.

9. See C. W. Fisher and D. L. Berliner, *Perspectives on Instructional Time,* New York, Longmans, 1985.

10. See, for example, A. B. Hollingshead, *Elmtown's Youth and Elmtown Revisited,* New York, Wiley, 1975, especially pp. 384–386; S. F. Hamilton, *The Interaction of Family, Community, and Work in the Socialization of Youth,* Washington, D.C., Youth and America's Future: The William T. Grant Foundation Commission on Work, Family and Citizenship, March 1988; H. M. Levin, *Educational Reform for Disadvantaged Students: An Emerging Crisis,* West Haven, Conn., National Education Association, 1986; M. D. Levine, *The Differences That Differences Make: Adolescent Diversity and Its Deregulation,* Washington, D.C., Youth and America's Future: The William T. Grant Foundation Commission on Work, Family and Citizenship, April 1988; L. Schorr, "Environmental Deterrents: Poverty, Affluence, Violence, and Television," in M. D. Levine et al. (eds.), *Developmental-Behavioral Pediatrics,* Philadelphia, W. B. Saunders, 1983.

11. My colleague Hervé Varenne, the anthropologist who led our first team to study Sheffield's high school, has written extensively and with insight about the social and symbolic functions of sorting. See, in addition to the source cited in note 5 above, his "Jocks and Freaks: The Symbolic Structure of the Expression of Social Interaction Among American Senior High School Students," in G. Spindler (ed.), *Doing the Ethnography of Schooling: Educational Anthropology in Action,* New York, Holt, Rinehart, and Winston, 1982, pp. 211–235.

12. This is part of a composite daily bulletin developed by Rodney Riffel and presented at the Annual Meeting of the American Anthropological

Association in New Orleans as part of a paper entitled "How to Skip School and Get Away With It," 1974.

13. The National Institute of Education, *Violent Schools–Safe Schools: The Safe School Study Report to Congress,* Washington, D.C., U.S. Government Printing Office, 1980.

14. F. A. J. Ianni, "A Positive Note on Discipline," *Educational Leadership,* March 1980, pp. 57–59.

15. See D. Blyth, R. G. Simmons, and S. Carlton-Ford, "The Adjustment of Early Adolescents to School Transitions," *Journal of Early Adolescence,* vol. 6, 1986, pp. 105–120; and L. Fenzel and D. Blyth, "Individual Adjustment to School Transitions: An Exploration of the Role of Supportive Peer Relations," *Journal of Early Adolescence,* vol. 6, 1986, pp. 315–331.

16. F. A. J. Ianni and E. Reuss-Ianni, "The Social Organization of the High School: School-Specific Aspects of School Crime," in E. Wenk and N. Harlow (eds.), *School Crime and Disruption,* Davis, Cal., Responsible Action, 1978, pp. 21–36, and see also 127–137; A. Petersen, "The Early Adolescence Study: An Overview," *Journal of Early Adolescence,* vol. 4, 1984, pp. 103–106.

17. F. A. J. Ianni, loc. cit., 1980, note 14 above.

18. W. H. Snow et al., "Preparing Students for Junior High School," *Journal of Early Adolescence,* vol. 6, 1986, pp. 127–137.

19. C. Calhoun and F. A. J. Ianni, loc. cit., 1976, note 5 above.

20. J. Piaget, *Biology and Knowledge,* Chicago, University of Chicago Press, 1971.

21. J. C. Turner, *Rediscovering the Social Group: A Self-Categorization Theory,* chap. 3, Oxford, Basil Blackwell, 1987.

22. D. R. Omark, F. F. Strayer, and D. G. Freedman (eds.), *Dominance Relations: An Ethological View of Human Conflict and Social Interaction,* New York, Garland, 1980.

23. S. Freud, "Some Reflections on Schoolboy Psychology" (1914), in J. Strachey (ed. and trans.), *The Standard Edition of the Complete Psychological Works of Sigmund Freud,* vol. 13, London, Hogarth, 1953, pp. 241–245.

24. W. Brookover et al., *School Social Systems and Student Achievement: Schools Can Make a Difference,* New York, Praeger, 1979; D. H. Hargreaves, S. K. Hester, and F. J. Mellor, *Deviance in Classrooms,* London, Routledge and Kegan Paul, 1975.

25. J. L. Epstein, "Toward a Theory of Family-School Connections: Teacher Practices and Parent Involvement," in K. Hurrelman, F. X. Kaufmann, and F. Losel (eds.), *Social Intervention: Potential and Constraints,* Ber-

lin, Walter de Gruyer, 1987, pp. 122–131. See also, in the same volume, M. Cochran, "Empowering Families: An Alternative to the Deficit Model," pp. 105–121. Educational theorists have long insisted that the cognitive traits that students bring to school are at least as important as good materials and effective teaching strategies in designing educational programs. (See, for example, B. Bloom, *Human Characteristics and School Learning*, New York, McGraw-Hill, 1976; J. Carroll, "A Model of School Learning," *Teachers College Record*, vol. 64, 1963, pp. 723–733; R. W. Tyler, *Basic Principles of Curriculum and Instruction*, Chicago, University of Chicago Press, 1960.) Much of the back to basics movement and the instructionally effective schools movement that followed it as part of the school reform demands of recent decades reflected this concern with student abilities as indicated by test scores and other measures. (K. L. Alexander and A. M. Pallas, "Curriculum Reform and School Performance: An Evaluation of the New Basics," *American Journal of Education*, vol. 92, 1984, pp. 391–420; The College Board, *Excellence in Our Schools: Making It Happen, Conference Proceedings of a National Forum on Educational Reform*, New York, The College Entrance Examination Board, 1985.) I also believe that school reform is important but, based on our field studies, I am even more certain that it is only a subset of the reforms needed in how communities coordinate and empower the various educating institutions of the community, and that schools must be just as concerned with the social and cultural traits and needs their students present. (F. A. J. Ianni, "The Effective Community and Educational Reform: Implications for Instructional Design," in H. Sirois (ed.), *Instructional Design*, Albany, N.Y., New York State Association for Supervision and Curriculum Development, 1988.)

26. H. J. Walberg, "Improving the Productivity of America's Schools," *Educational Leadership*, May 1984, pp. 19–27.

27. Ibid., p. 21.

28. B. S. Bloom, "The Search for Methods of Group Instruction as Effective as One-to-One Tutoring," *Educational Leadership*, May 1984, pp. 4–17.

29. H. J. Walberg, loc. cit., 1984, p. 25, note 25 above.

30. D. Johnson et al., "Effects of Cooperative, Competitive, and Individualistic Goal Structures on Achievement: A Meta-Analysis," *Psychological Bulletin*, vol. 89, 1981, pp. 47–62; E. Aronson et al., *The Jigsaw Classroom*, Beverly Hills, Russell Sage, 1978.

31. R. Slavin, "Cooperative Learning: Applying Contact Theory in Desegregated Schools," *Journal of Social Issues*, vol. 41, 1985, pp. 45–62; C. Ascher, "Cooperative Learning in the Urban Classroom," *Digest*,

New York, ERIC Clearinghouse on Urban Education, Teachers College, Columbia University, no. 30, August 1986.

32. R. Weigel, P. Wiser, and S. Cook, "Impact of Cooperative Learning Experiences on Cross-Ethnic Relations and Attitudes," *Journal of Social Issues,* vol. 3, 1975, pp. 219–245D.

33. R. Slavin and E. Oickle, "Effects of Cooperative Learning Teams on Student Achievement and Race Relations: Treatment of Race Interactions," *Sociology of Education,* vol. 54, 1981, pp. 174–180.

34. J. S. Coleman and T. Hoffer, *Public and Private High Schools: The Impact of Communities,* New York, Basic Books, 1987.

35. E. Farrar and R. L. Hampel, "Social Services in American High School," *Educational Leadership,* December 1987, pp. 297–303.

CHAPTER 5
After School: Youth In and Out of the Labor Market

1. B. Clark, "The Cooling-Out Function in Higher Education," *American Journal of Sociology,* vol. 65, no. 6, 1960, pp. 569–577.

2. P. Osterman, *Getting Started: The Youth Labor Market,* Cambridge, Mass., MIT Press, 1980.

3. E. Ginsberg, *The Optimistic Tradition and American Youth,* New York, Columbia University Press, 1962.

4. D. O'Neill, *Education in the United States: 1940–1983,* Washington, D.C., U.S. Government Printing Office, 1985.

5. We found that in our urban inner-city areas, well over half of all students would drop out of school at some time or other. In some cases the students would return one or more times before finally dropping out. We did not follow dropouts for any period of time, so we cannot give a very meaningful estimate of how many did eventually receive a diploma. The rural areas also had a high rate of dropping out, particularly in Ranchville, where my estimate would be that the true dropout rate— that is, the number of students who would never finish school—was even higher than in the urban inner-city sites: probably as high as 60 to 70 percent of the migrant labor youth. The schools and parents in the suburban communities we studied estimated that the dropout rate there is under 5 percent and that about 95 percent of the graduates go on to college.

6. See F. A. J. Ianni and B. D. McNeill, "A Self-Study Approach to Youthful Drug Abuse," *Youth and Society,* vol. 12, 1971, pp. 173–193.

7. See L. Barber, *Dropouts, Transfers, Withdrawn and Removed Students,* Bloomington, Ind., Phi Delta Kappa, Center for Evaluation, Development

and Research, 1984; M. T. Orr, *Keeping Students in School,* San Francisco, Jossey-Bass, 1987.

8. J. Cardenas and J. First, "Children at Risk," *Educational Leadership,* September 1985, pp. 4–8; A. Hahn, J. Danzberger, with B. Lefkowitz, *Dropouts in America: Enough Is Known for Action,* Washington, D.C., Institute for Educational Leadership, 1987; R. W. Rumberger, "Dropping Out of High School: The Influence of Race, Sex, and Family Background," *American Educational Research Journal,* vol. 20, 1983, pp. 199–220.

9. J. P. Comer, "Black Family Stress and School Achievement," in D. S. Strickland and E. J. Cooper (eds.), *Educating Black Children: America's Challenge,* Washington, D.C., Bureau of Educational Research, Howard University, 1987, pp. 77–84; L. Steinberg, P. L. Blinde, and K. S. Chan, "Dropping Out Among Language Minority Youth," *Review of Educational Research,* vol. 54, 1984, pp. 113–132.

10. In a provocative article in the *New York Times Education Section,* November 9, 1986, p. 23, Harvard psychologist Howard Gardner makes this same point: "We subject everyone to an education where, if you succeed, you will be best suited to be a college professor."

11. See D. Johnson et al., "Effects of Cooperative, Competitive, and Individualistic Goal Structures on Achievement: A Meta-Analysis," *Psychological Bulletin,* vol. 89, 1981, pp. 47–62; C. Ascher, "Cooperative Learning in the Urban Classroom," *Digest,* New York, ERIC Clearinghouse on Urban Education, no. 30, August 1986.

12. *The Forgotten Half: Non-College Youth in America,* Washington, D.C., Youth and America's Future: The William T. Grant Foundation Commission on Work, Family and Citizenship, January 1988, p. 34.

13. While most researchers have proposed a positive relationship between teenage work and good attitudes and skills in the later world of work, not all agree. See J. G. Bachman, "Premature Affluence: Do High School Students Earn Too Much?", *Economic Outlook U.S.A.,* vol. 10, 1983, pp. 64–67; R. D'Amico, "Does Working in High School Impair Academic Progress?", *Sociology of Education,* vol. 57, 1984, pp. 157–164; E. Greenberger and L. D. Steinberg, *When Teenagers Work: The Psychological and Social Costs of Adolescent Employment,* New York, Basic Books, 1986.

14. P. Osterman, op. cit., 1980, note 2 above.

15. Youth and America's Future, op. cit., January 1988, p. 3, note 12 above.

16. G. L. Mangum, *Youth Transition from Adolescence to the World of Work,* Washington, D.C., Youth and America's Future, The William

T. Grant Foundation Commission on Work, Family and Citizenship, 1988.

17. E. Banfield, *The Unheavenly City,* Boston, Little, Brown, 1968.

18. F. A. J. Ianni, "Generation Gap for Organized Crime: The Godfather Is Going Out of Business," *Psychology Today,* vol. 9, December 1975.

19. L. Rainwater et al., *Workingman's Wife: Her Personality, World and Life Style,* New York, Oceana Publications, 1959.

20. M. Kohn, "Job Complexity and Adult Personality," in M. Smelser and E. H. Erikson (eds.), *Themes of Work and Love in Adulthood,* Cambridge, Mass., Harvard University Press, 1980.

21. T. Husén, "Problems of Securing Equal Access to Higher Education," *Higher Education,* vol. 5, 1976, pp. 407–422.

22. See S. F. Hamilton, *The Interaction of Family, Community, and Work in the Socialization of Youth,* Washington, D.C., Youth and America's Future: The William T. Grant Foundation Commission on Work, Family and Citizenship, March 1988.

CHAPTER 6
Pathways to Crime

1. For an excellent analysis of how we interpret and respond to juvenile crime, see J. Gilbert, *A Cycle of Outrage: America's Reaction to the Juvenile Delinquent in the 1950s,* New York, Oxford University Press, 1986.

2. N. Weiner and M. Wolfgang, "The Extent and Character of Violent Crime in America, 1969–1982," in L. Curtis (ed.), *American Violence and Public Policy,* New Haven, Yale University Press, 1985.

3. Bureau of Justice Statistics, Department of Justice, *Report to the Nation on Crime and Justice,* NCJ–87068, Washington, D.C., U.S. Government Printing Office, 1983, pp. 31–32.

4. See D. Moberg, "Old Age and Crime," *Journal of Criminal Law, Criminology and Police Science,* vol. 43, March–April 1984, pp. 764–776; T. Sellin, "Recidivism and Maturation," *National Probation and Parole Association Journal,* vol. 4, July 1958, pp. 241–50.

5. J. R. Wetzel, *American Youth: A Statistical Snapshot,* Washington, D.C., Youth and America's Future: The William T. Grant Foundation Commission on Work, Family and Citizenship, June 1987, p. 32.

6. See J. W. Duncan and G. W. M. Duncan, "Murder in the Family: A Study of Homicidal Adolescents," *American Journal of Psychiatry,* vol. 127, 1971, pp. 926–934.

7. See C. R. Keith, *The Aggressive Adolescent: Clinical Perspectives,* New York, Free Press, 1984.

8. National Center for Health Statistics, Department of Health and Human Services, *Advance Report of Final Mortality Statistics, 1984,* vol. 35, no. 6, supp. 2 (PHS), 86–1120, p. 15.

9. L. C. Burkhart, *Old Values in a New Town,* New York, Praeger, 1981.

10. See G. Fishman, A. Rattner, and G. Weiman, "The Effect of Ethnicity on Crime Attribution," *Criminology,* vol. 25, August 1987, pp. 507–524; C. Spohn, J. Gruhl, and S. Welch, "The Impact of Ethnicity and Gender of Defendants on the Decision to Reject or Dismiss Felony Charges," *Criminology,* vol. 25, February 1987, pp. 175–192.

11. See R. L. Akers et al., "Fear of Crime Victimization Among the Elderly in Different Types of Communities," *Criminology,* vol. 25, August 1987, pp. 487–506.

12. See D. Elliot, D. Huizinga, and S. Ageton, *Explaining Delinquency and Drug Use,* Beverly Hills, Sage Publications, 1985, for a good compendium of the suspected causes of drug use as well as delinquency.

13. L. D. Johnston, P. O'Malley, and J. Bachman, reported in *National Trends in Drug Use and Related Factors Among American High School Students and Young Adults, 1975–1986,* Washington, D.C., U.S. Government Printing Office, 1987; also reported in "Details of Annual Drug Survey," press release by The University of Michigan's Institute for Social Research, January 13, 1988.

14. University of Michigan, op. cit., 1988, note 11 above.

15. See F. A. J. Ianni, "Attitudes Towards the Relationship Among Stress Relief, Advertising and Youthful Drug Abuse in Two Recent Field Studies," in The National Commission on Marijuana and Drug Abuse, *Drug Use in America,* Washington, D.C., U.S. Government Printing Office, 1974.

16. Ibid.

17. W. F. Matchett, "Who Uses Drugs? A Study in a Suburban Public High School," *Journal of School Health,* vol. 41, 1971, pp. 90–93; A. P. MacDonald, R. Walls, and R. LeBlanc, "College Female Drug Users," *Adolescence,* vol. 8, 1973, pp. 61–80.

18. R. H. Blum, *Students and Drugs,* San Francisco, Jossey-Bass, 1974; N. Tec, *Grass is Green in Suburbia,* Roslyn Heights, N.Y., Libra, 1974.

19. D. V. Babst and R. Brill, "Drug Abuse Patterns Among Students in an Upstate New York Area," *Journal of Drug Issues,* vol. 3, 1973, pp. 48–60; W. L. Tolone and D. Dermott, "Some Correlates of Drug Use Among High School Youth in a Midwestern Rural Community," *International Journal of the Addictions,* vol. 10, 1975, pp. 761–777.

20. G. G. Tuder, D. M. Petersen, and K. W. Clifson, "An Examination

of the Relationship Between Peer and Parental Influences and Adolescent Drug Use," *Adolescence,* vol. 15, 1980; pp. 796–797.

21. W. Miller, "Youth Gangs: A Look At Numbers," *Children Today,* March–April 1982, pp. 10–11.

22. Ibid.

23. E. H. Erikson, "Youth: Fidelity and Diversity," in idem, *Youth: Change and Challenge,* New York, Basic Books, 1963, p. 35.

24. M. L. Sullivan, "Getting Over: Economy, Culture, and Youth Crime in Three Urban Neighborhoods," unpublished dissertation, Columbia University, 1985; idem, *Getting Paid: Economy, Culture, and Youth Crime in the Inner City,* Cornell University Press, forthcoming, 1989; F. A. J. Ianni, "The Italo-American Teen-ager," *The Annals,* vol. 338, November 1961, pp. 70–78.

25. K. Polk, "A Reassessment of Middle-Class Delinquency," in H. D. Thornburg (ed.), *Contemporary Adolescence: Readings,* 2nd ed., Monterey, Brooks/Cole, 1975.

26. F. A. J. Ianni, "New Mafia: Black, Hispanic and Italian Styles," *Society,* vol. 3, March–April 1974. See also G. D. Suttles, *The Social Construction of Communities,* Chicago, University of Chicago Press, 1972.

27. F. A. J. Ianni, "Mafia and the Web of Kinship," *The Public Interest,* no. 22, Winter 1971; reprinted in L. Rainwater (ed.), *Family and Society,* Chicago, Aldine-Atherton, 1975.

28. The data on gangs in Chinatown were gathered by Simon Chow as part of a study supported by the U.S. Department of Justice, Law Enforcement Assistance Administration (grant no. 80–IJ–CX–0069), in which we were co-investigators.

29. See B. Rice, "The New Gangs in Chinatown," *Psychology Today,* May 1977, pp. 60–69.

30. Our association with the detention center actually predates our formal research there. I, along with some of the members of the research team, had been involved in developing educational and social programs for the center from 1966 to 1970. Much of the material presented here was gathered by Claudia Ulbright for her dissertation "The Inmate Culture of Male Adolescents Who Attend School Within a Detention Center," Teachers College, Columbia University, 1986.

31. F. A. J. Ianni, *Black Mafia: Ethnic Succession in Organized Crime,* New York, Simon and Schuster, 1974.

32. D. Hedin, H. Wolfe, and J. Arneson, *Minnesota Youth Poll: Youth's Views on Reputations and Delinquency,* St. Paul, Minn., Center for Youth Development, 1980.

33. See E. H. Sutherland and D. R. Cressey, *Principles of Criminology,*

New York, Lippincott, 1970; R. A. Cloward and L. E. Ohlin, *Delinquency and Opportunity: A Theory of Delinquent Gangs,* Glencoe, Ill., Free Press, 1960; C. Shaw and H. McKay, *Juvenile Delinquency in Urban Areas,* Chicago, University of Chicago Press, 1942.

34. T. Hirschi, *Causes of Delinquency,* Berkeley, University of California Press, 1969.

35. For an analysis of the various theoretical approaches, see D. Elliot, "The Assumption that Theories Can Be Combined with Increased Explanatory Power: Theoretical Integrations," in R. Meier (ed.), *Theoretical Methods in Criminology,* Beverly Hills, Sage Publications, 1985.

36. See R. Akers, *Deviant Behavior: A Social Learning Perspective,* Belmont, Cal., Wadsworth, 1977.

37. See J. D. Hawkins and J. Weiss, *The Social Development Model: An Integrated Approach to Delinquency Prevention,* Seattle, Wash., University of Washington, Center for Law and Justice, 1980; J. Weiss et al., *Jurisdiction and the Elusive Status Offender: A Comparison of Involvement in Delinquent Behavior and Status Offenses,* National Institute for Juvenile Justice and Delinquency Prevention, Washington, D.C., 1980.

38. See J. C. Gibbs and S. V. Schnell, "Moral Development 'Versus' Socialization," *American Psychologist,* vol. 40, 1985, pp. 1071–1080; B. M. Gfellner, "Ego Development and Moral Development in Relation to Age and Grade Level During Adolescence," *Journal of Youth and Adolescence,* vol. 15, 1986, pp. 147–163.

CHAPTER 7

Tell Me Who I Am

1. E. H. Erikson, *Identity and the Life Cycle,* New York, International Universities Press, 1959; C. Gordon and K. J. Gergen, *The Self in Social Interaction,* New York, Wiley, 1968; A. G. Greenwald, "The Totalitarian Ego: Fabrication and Revision of Personal History," *American Psychologist,* vol. 35, 1980, pp. 603–618; D. N. Robinson, "Cerebral Plurality and the Unity of Self," *American Psychologist,* vol. 37, 1982, pp. 904–910.

2. In his early work (*Identity: Youth and Crisis,* New York, Norton, 1968) Erikson placed particular emphasis on the influence of family experiences on identity status, but later (*Life History and the Historical Moment,* New York, Norton, 1975) he emphasized the effects of historical events such as war or depression on the identity of those adolescents who were affected by them.

3. Ibid., 1968.

4. The elements of this debate are elegantly laid out in a series of articles,

commentaries, and rejoinders in the *Journal of Early Adolescence:* A. S. Waterman, "Identity Formation: Discovery or Creation?", vol. 4, 1984, pp. 329–341; idem, "Identity Formation, Metaphors, and Values," vol. 6, 1986, pp. 119–121; M. D. Berzonsky, "Discovery Versus Constructionist Interpretations of Identity Formation: Consideration of Additional Implications," vol. 6, 1986, pp. 111–117; idem, "Identity Formation, Metaphors, and Values: A Rejoinder to Waterman," vol. 6, 1986, pp. 123–126.

5. Berzonsky makes a similar point in his rejoiner to Waterman cited above, p. 123.

6. See A. Freud, "Adolescence," in *Psychoanalytic Study of the Child,* vol. 13, New York, International Universities Press, 1958; P. Blos, *On Adolescence,* New York, Free Press, 1962.

7. F. Redl, "Adolescents—Just How Do They React?", in G. Coplen and S. Debovci (eds.), *Adolescence: Psychosocial Perspectives,* New York, Basic Books, 1969, p. 98.

8. E. S. Sampson, "The Decentralization of Identity: Toward a Revised Concept of Personal and Social Disorder," *American Psychologist,* vol. 40, 1985, pp. 1203–1211.

9. R. Harré, "Identity Projects," in G. Breakwell (ed.), *Threatened Identities,* Oxford, Blackwell, 1983.

10. G. Devereux, "Fantasy and Symbol as Dimensions of Reality," in R. H. Hook (ed.), *Fantasy and Symbol: Studies in Anthropological Interpretation,* New York, Academic Press, 1979. See also J. A. Burland, "Illusion, Reality, and Fantasy," in R. F. Lax, S. Bach, and J. A. Burland (eds.), *Self and Object Constancy,* New York, Guilford Press, 1987, p. 397.

11. See M. Rosenberg, *Conceiving the Self,* New York, Basic Books, 1979.

12. H. Hartmann, "Contributions to the Metapsychology of Schizophrenia," *Essays on Ego Psychology,* New York, International Universities Press, 1953; J. Piaget, *The Construction of Reality in the Child,* New York, Basic Books, 1937; idem, *The Origins of Intelligence in Children,* New York, International Universities Press, 1936.

13. See J. L. Singer, *The Inner World of Daydreaming,* New York, Harper and Row, 1975; E. Klinger, "Modes of Normal Conscious Flow," in K. S. Pope and J. S. Singer (eds.), *The Stream of Consciousness: Scientific Investigations into the Flow of Human Experience,* New York, Plenum Press, 1978.

14. See J. B. Rotter, "Generalized Expectancies for Internal Versus External Control of Reinforcement," *Psychological Monographs,* vol. 1, no. 609.

15. E. Kris, "Notes on the Development of Some Current Problems of

Psychoanalytic Child Psychology," *The Psychoanalytic Study of the Child,* vol. 5, New York, International Universities Press, 1950, pp. 24–46.

16. J. B. McDevitt and M. S. Mahler, "Object Constancy, Individuality, and Internalization," in R. F. Lax, S. Bach, and J. A. Burland, op. cit., 1987, pp. 11–28, see note 10 above.

17. S. Freud, "The Relation of the Poet to Daydreaming," first published in *Neue Revue,* vol. 1, 1908. This quote is from Philip Rieff, *Delusion and Dream and Other Essays,* Boston, Beacon, 1956, p. 127.

18. D. W. Winnicott, *Pediatrics and Psychiatry,* New York, Basic Books, 1948, p. 163.

19. G. Smith and I. Carlsson, "Creativity in Middle and Late School Years," *International Journal of Behavioral Development,* vol. 8, 1985, pp. 329–343.

20. D. Elkind, "Egocentrism in Adolescence," *Child Development,* vol. 38, 1967, pp. 1025–1034.

21. See S. Berryman, "Breaking Out of the Circle: Rethinking Our Assumptions About Education and the Economy," occasional paper no. 2, National Center on Education and Employment, Teachers College, Columbia University, New York, July 1987.

22. See J. C. Gordon, "Crisis in Adolescence: Special Needs and Approaches," in R. Carlson and B. Newman, *Issues and Trends in Health,* St. Louis, C. V. Mosby, 1987, pp. 276–283.

23. See E. W. McClain, "An Eriksonian Cross-Cultural Study of Adolescent Development," *Adolescence,* vol. 10, 1975, pp. 527–541.

24. Cf. P. M. Hirsch, "Sociological Approaches to the Pop Music Phenomenon," in F. G. Kline and P. Clarke (eds.), *Mass Communication and Youth: Some Current Perspectives,* Beverly Hills, Sage Publications, 1971; J. Rockwell, "Is Rock the Music of Violence?", *New York Times,* December 27, Section 12, 1979, p. 11.

25. E. Shils, "Mass Society and Its Culture," *Daedalus,* Fall 1960, pp. 280–301.

26. J. Bernard, "Teen-Age Culture: An Overview," in H. Silverstein (ed.), *The Sociology of Youth: Evolution and Revolution,* New York, Macmillan, 1973, pp. 195–208.

27. G. Gorer, *The American People: A Study in National Character,* New York, Norton, 1948.

28. J. S. Coleman, *Youth: Transition to Adulthood,* Chicago, University of Chicago Press, 1974.

29. F. Hechinger and G. Hechinger, *Teen-Age Tyranny,* New York, Random House, 1962, p. 125.

30. N. Postman, *Teaching as a Conserving Activity*, New York, Delacorte Press, 1979. Postman, however, is saying more, and is specifically indicting television for destroying conventional socialization and developing an unnatural precosity which must eventually obliterate adolescence, if not childhood.

31. J. W. Bryce, "Families and Television: An Ethnographic Approach," Ed.D. dissertation, Teachers College, Columbia University, May 1980. At the conclusion of her ethnographic study of the various ways in which families live with television, Jennifer Bryce comments on television's role as a mediator—setting a schedule for the temporal organization of family interaction as well as the uses of attention and the physical environment of the home, and even setting the agenda for family interaction and influence in the ways in which family members talk to one another—and so as a determinant of social learning in families. She goes on to point out, however, that while television has the capability of influencing the individual and the family, "the family has far greater power to influence the child's use of the medium" (p. 352).

32. M. Spiro, "Culture and Personality: The Natural History of a False Dichotomy," *Psychiatry*, vol. 14, 1951, p. 20.

33. I heard two similar fantasies about vampires from early adolescents beginning to undergo pubertal changes. A similar fantasy was reported to me by Tamar Z. Kahane, an intern in clinical psychology, during a supervisory seminar at St. Luke's Hospital, New York City. In the context of addressing the issues of separation-individuation, an early adolescent female patient described the image of a person who was half vampire and half a real person. The patient explained that before the person could become a complete vampire, he/she needed to kill. For a fascinating description of the fantasies of children (and some adults as well), see D. Bloch, *"So the Witch Won't Eat Me": Fantasy and the Child's Fear of Infanticide*, New York, Burnett Books in Association with Andre Deutsch, 1979. See also B. Bettelheim, *The Uses of Enchantment: The Meaning and Importance of Fairy Tales*, New York, Knopf, 1976.

34. D. W. Winnicott, "Adolescent Immaturity," in *Home is Where We Start From*, compiled and edited by C. Winnicott, R. Shepherd, and M. Davis, New York, Norton, 1986, p. 154.

35. Idem in ibid., "The Concept of the False Self," p. 66.

36. E. H. Erikson, "The Problem of Ego Identity," *Journal of the American Psychoanalytic Association*, vol. 4, 1956, pp. 56–121.

37. P. W. Pruyser, *The Play of the Imagination: Toward a Psychoanalysis of Culture*, New York, International Universities Press, 1983.

38. V. W. Turner, *The Ritual Process: Structure and Anti-Structure*, Chicago,

Aldine, 1969. See also M. Apprey, "Liminality as Metaphor in Adolescent Psychotherapy and Psychoanalysis," *The Journal of Psychoanalytic Anthropology,* vol. 6, Winter 1983, pp. 3–16.

39. A. Van Gennep, *The Rites of Passage,* translated by M. B. Vizedom and G. L. Caffee, London, Routledge and Kegan Paul, 1960.

40. M. Rosenberg, op. cit., 1979, note 11 above.

41. D. Yankelovich, *New Rules: Search for Self-Fulfillment in a World Turned Upside Down,* New York, Random House, 1981, p. 240.

CHAPTER 8
The Search for Structure and the Caring Community

1. A. Haim, *Les Suicides d'Adolescents,* Paris, Payot, 1969.

2. F. A. J. Ianni, *Home, School, and Community in Adolescent Education,* New York, ERIC Clearinghouse on Urban Education, Teachers College, Columbia University, 1983.

3. Cf. P. Benson, D. Williams, and A. Johnson, *The Quicksilver Years: The Hopes and Fears of Early Adolescence,* San Francisco, Harper and Row, 1987.

4. Most theories of the self are based on some form of reciprocity between the self-concept of the individual and the social structure. We found that adolescents constantly rediscover and recognize themselves in interaction with the social structure of institutions, and ultimately, as sociologist Ralph Turner says, "social roles constitute the organizing framework for the self-conception." See R. H. Turner, "The Self-Conception in Social Interaction," in C. Gordon and K. Gergen (eds.), *The Self in Social Interaction,* New York, Wiley, 1968, p. 24. Similarly, in expanding his concept of the "selfobject," the undifferentiated relational self of infancy, Heinz Kohut describes a "transmuting internalization" of the psychological environment which crystalizes a "nuclear self." In each case elements of the social structure are selectively imported by the individual as the organizer of a view of herself which allows her to live with herself as well as with others. See H. Kohut, *The Analysis of the Self,* New York, International Universities Press, 1971, p. 18.

5. See I. Markova, "Knowledge of the Self Through Interaction," in K. Yardley and T. Honess (eds.), *Self and Identity: Psychosocial Perspectives,* New York, Wiley, 1987, pp. 65–80.

6. C. Geertz, *The Interpretation of Cultures: Selected Essays,* New York, Basic Books, 1973.

7. D. W. Winnicott, "The Location of Cultural Experience," *International Journal of Psycho-Analysis,* vol. 48, 1967, pp. 368–372; reprinted in idem, *Playing and Reality,* London, Tavistock, 1971, pp. 95–104.

8. D. W. Winnicott, "Transitional Objects and Transitional Phenomena," *International Journal of Psycho-Analysis,* vol. 34, 1953, pp. 89–97; reprinted in idem, op. cit., 1971, pp. 1–25, note 7 above.

9. The notion of fantasy (spelled "phantasy" to differentiate it from the earlier, more restricted use of "fantasy" by Freud) as the major material source for all mental processes was introduced by Isaacs in 1943 and derivative from the early work of Melanie Klein. See S. Isaacs, "The Nature and Function of Phantasy" (first published in 1943), in M. Klein, *Developments in Psycho-Analysis,* London, Hogarth Press, 1952.

10. M. Mahler, F. Pine, and A. Bergman, *The Psychological Birth of the Human Infant,* New York, Basic Books, 1975, pp. 223–224.

11. R. Josselson, "Ego Development in Adolescence," in J. Adelson (ed.), *Handbook of Adolescent Psychology,* New York, Wiley, 1980, pp. 188–210.

12. H. Hartmann, *Ego Psychology and the Problem of Adoption,* New York, International Universities Press, 1958.

13. F. Earls, W. Beardslee, and W. Garrison make the interesting point that the life context as it is acted out in communities may be more important than personal attributes as the primary determinant of competence in individuals. See their "Correlates and Predictors of Competence in Young Children," in E. J. Anthony and B. J. Cohler (eds.), *The Invulnerable Child,* New York, Guilford Press, 1987, pp. 70–83.

14. For a fuller description and analysis of these structures see F. A. J. Ianni, op. cit., 1983, note 2 above.

15. The internalization of external objects and object relations has been described by Otto Kernberg—in his *Object Relations Theory and Clinical Psychoanalysis,* New York, Jason Aronson, 1976, and also in his "Identification and Its Vicissitudes as Observed in Psychosis," *International Journal of Psycho-Analysis,* vol. 67, no. 147, 1986, pp. 147–149—as organized in two different forms. *Introjection* is the earliest and most primitive form, in which (a) the image of the object, (b) the image of self-object interaction, and (c) the affective ambiance are internalized as a unit.

In the earliest introjections the object-image (mother) and the self-image (infant) are fused (E. Jacobson, *The Self and the Object World,* International Universities Press, 1964), but with maturation and experience the individual comes to internalize an ever-growing complexity of information and affects about the object and the self. *Identification* is a more advanced form of introjection, in which "the perceptive and cognitive abilities of the child have increased to the point that it can recognize the role aspects of interpersonal interaction. Role implies the presence of a socially recognized function that is being carried out by the object or by both participants in the interaction'' (O. Kernberg, op. cit., 1976, p. 38). In Kernberg's 1986 reformulation he describes introjection as ''a symbiotic stage of development when self and object are not yet differentiated from each other'' and says that identification takes place ''when self and object representations have been differentiated from each other, that is, in the stage of separation-individuation''; he adds *identity formation* to the internalization process as ''the more general intrapsychic process of integration of libidinally and aggressively invested self-representations into a cohesive self'' (p. 147).

16. L. Vygotsky, *Thought and Language,* Cambridge, Mass., MIT Press, 1962. See also G. Bateson, *Steps to an Ecology of Mind,* New York, Valentine Books, 1971, pp. 309–337.

17. W. R. D. Fairbairn, ''Object Relationships and Dynamic Structure'' (first published in 1946), in *An Object-Relations Theory of the Personality,* New York, Basic Books, 1952, p. 145.

18. For a comprehensive review of some of the research which supports this point of view, see J. Wynn et al., *Communities and Adolescents: An Exploration of Reciprocal Supports,* Washington, D.C., Youth and America's Future: The William T. Grant Foundation Commission on Work, Family and Citizenship, May 1988.

19. F. A. J. Ianni, op. cit., 1983, note 2 above.

20. See S. F. Hamilton, ''Adolescents in Community Settings: What Is to Be Learned?'', *Theory and Research in Social Education,* vol. 9, 1981, pp. 23–38; idem, *The Interaction of Family, Community, and Work in the Socialization of Youth,* Washington, D.C., Youth and America's Future: The William T. Grant Foundation Commission on Work, Family and Citizenship, March 1988, p. 50.

21. For an excellent description and analysis of apprenticeship programs, see ibid.; idem, ''Work and Maturity: Occupational Socialization of Non-College Youth in the United States and West Germany,'' in R. G. Corwin (ed.), *Research in Sociology of Education and Socialization,* vol. 7, Greenwich, Conn., JAI Press, 1987.

22. Cf. J. Wynn et al., op. cit., 1988, note 18 above.

23. For an analysis of how and why such transitional processes work, see G. Rose, ''The Creativity of Everyday Life,'' in S. Grolnick and L. Barkin (eds.), *Between Reality and Fantasy: Transitional Objects and Phenomena,* New York, Jason Aronson, 1978; G. Rose, *The Power of Form: A Psychoanalytic Approach to Aesthetic Form,* New York, International Universities Press, 1980.

24. D. Levinson, *The Seasons of a Man's Life,* New York, Knopf, 1978, pp. 97–101.

25. A. Hebeisen, *Peer Program for Youth: A Group Interaction Plan to Develop Self-Esteem, Self-Understanding, and Communication Skills,* Minneapolis, Augsburg Publishing, 1973.

26. Personal communication from Monica Lamote of the National Crime Prevention Council. See also National Crime Prevention Council, *Making a Difference: Young People in Community Crime Prevention,* Washington, D.C., National Crime Prevention Council, 1985.

27. Cf. R. L. Calabrese and H. Schumer, "The Effects of Service Activities on Adolescent Alienation," *Adolescence,* vol. 21, 1986, pp. 675–687; F. M. Newman and R. A. Rutter, "A Profile of High School Community Service Programs," *Educational Leadership,* January 1986, pp. 65–71. In the same article, Newman and Rutter estimate that 27 percent of the country's public and private high schools have some type of community service program and that about 60 percent of the students involved are female.

28. Cf. W. T. Boyce, "Social Support, Family Relations, and Children," in S. Cohen and S. L. Syme (eds.), *Social Support and Health,* Orlando, Fla., Academic Press, 1985; B. E. Compas et al., "Relationship of Life Events and Social Support with Psychological Dysfunction Among Adolescents," *Journal of Youth and Adolescence,* vol. 15, 1986, pp. 205–221; I. L. Janis, "The Role of Social Support in Adherence to Stressful Decisions," *American Psychologist,* vol. 38, 1983, pp. 143–160; M. Pilisuk, "Delivery of Social Support: The Social Inoculation," *American Journal of Orthopsychiatry,* vol. 52, 1982, pp. 20–29; K. S. Rook, "Promoting Social Bonding," *American Psychologist,* vol. 40, 1984, pp. 1389–1406.

29. T. C. Antonucci, "Social Support: Theoretical Advance, Recent Findings and Pressing Issues," in I. G. Sarason and B. R. Sarason (eds.), *Social Support: Theory, Research and Applications,* Dordrecht, The Netherlands, Martinus Nijhoff, 1985. See also P. Brickman, "Models of Helping and Coping," *American Psychologist,* vol. 37, 1982, pp. 368–384.

30. See, for example, H. C. Boyle, *Community is Possible: Repairing America's Roots,* New York, Harper and Row, 1984; B. K. Bryant, "The Neighborhood Walk: Sources of Support in Middle Childhood," *Monographs of the Society for Research in Child Development,* vol. 50, 1985; U. Bronfenbrenner, P. Moen, and J. Gabarino, "Child, Family, and Community," in R. Parke (ed.), *Review of Child Development Research, vol. 7, The Family,* Chicago, University of Chicago Press, 1984; J. Scherer, *Contemporary Community: Sociological Illusion or Reality?,* London, Tavistock, 1972; W. J. Wilson, *The Truly Disadvantaged: The Inner City, The Underclass, and Public Policy,* Chicago, University of Chicago Press, 1986; P. Wireman, *Urban Neighborhoods, Networks,*

and Families: New Forms for Old Values, Lexington, Mass., D. C. Heath, 1984.

31. The William T. Grant Foundation's Commission on Work, Family and Citizenship has published a number of excellent and timely reports on the school-to-work transition in its Youth and America's Future series: *The Forgotten Half: Non-College Youth in America*, January 1988; I. Charner and B. S. Fraser, *Youth and Work: What We Know, What We Don't Know, What We Need to Know* (no date); S. F. Hamilton, *The Interaction of Family, Community, and Work in the Socialization of Youth*, March 1988; G. Magnum, *Youth Transition from Adolescence to the World of Work* (no date); and T. J. Smith, G. C. Walker, and R. A. Baker, *Youth and the Workplace: Second-Chance Programs and the Hard-to-Serve* (no date).

32. An excellent guide to partnership programs appears in S. D. Otterbourg, *School Partnerships Handbook: How to Set Up and Administer Programs with Business, Government, and Your Community*, Englewood Cliffs, N.J., Prentice-Hall, 1986.

33. Personal communication from Margaret T. Orr. Each of these programs, and a number of others, are more fully described in M. T. Orr, *Keeping Students in School*, San Francisco, Jossey-Bass, 1987.

34. Linkage developments here are particularly significant because so much of the treatment approach in juvenile delinquency has always been oriented toward finding the "guilty" institutional sector. The "broken family," the deviant peer group, failing schools, and unemployment—each has long been individually accused as the primary cause in delinquent careers. But, as I pointed out when we looked at deviance and delinquency in the various communities, an interactive social development perspective which looks at how all of these groups combine to produce and reinforce antisocial and delinquent behavior has slowly replaced these single-cause approaches. See, for example, R. Canter, "Family Correlates of Male and Female Delinquency," *Criminology*, vol. 20, 1982, pp. 149–168; J. McCord, "A Longitudinal View of the Relationship Between Parental Absence and Crime," in J. Gunn and D. Farrington (eds.), *Abnormal Offenders, Delinquency and the Criminal Justice System*, New York, Wiley, 1982; R. Chilton and G. Markel, "Family Disruption, Delinquent Conduct, and the Effect of Subclassification," *American Sociological Review*, vol. 37, 1972, pp. 93–99; T. Hirschi, *Causes of Delinquency*, Berkeley, University of California Press, 1969; S. Glueck and E. Glueck, *Unraveling Juvenile Delinquency*, Cambridge, Mass., Harvard University Press, 1950; M. Stern, J. Northman, and M. Van Slyck, "Father Absence and Adolescent 'Problem Behaviors': Alcohol Consumption, Drug Use, and Sexual Activity," *Adolescence*, vol. 13, 1984, pp. 301–312; T.

Thornberry, M. Moore, and R. L. Christson, "The Effect of Dropping Out of High School on Subsequent Criminal Behavior," *Criminology*, vol. 23, 1985, pp. 3–18; S. B. Zakaria, "Another Look at the Children of Divorce," *Principal*, vol. 62, 1982, pp. 34–38; and T. Thornberry and M. Farnsworth, "Unemployment and Criminal Involvement: An Investigation of Reciprocal Causal Structures," *American Sociological Review*, vol. 49, 1984, pp. 398–411.

35. R. Coates, A. Miller, and L. Ohlin, *Diversity in Youth Correction Systems*, Cambridge, Mass., Ballinger Press, 1978. See also J. A. Fagan, C. J. Rudman, and E. Hartstone, "Intervening with Violent Juvenile Offenders: A Community Reintegration Model," in R. Mathias, P. De-Muro, and R. A. Allinson (eds.), *Violent Juvenile Offenders: An Anthology*, San Francisco, National Council on Crime and Delinquency, 1984.

36. National Crime Prevention Council, *Preventing Crime in Urban Communities*, Washington, D.C., National Crime Prevention Council, 1986.

37. See J. G. Weiss et al., *Jurisdiction and the Elusive Status Offender: A Comparison of Involvement in Delinquent Behavior and Status Offenses*, National Institute for Juvenile Justice and Delinquency Prevention, Office of Juvenile Justice and Delinquency Prevention, Law Enforcement Assistance Administration, U.S. Department of Justice, Washington, D.C., U.S. Government Printing Office, 1980. For a comprehensive account of the evolution of the social development approach and for a statement of its current perspective, see T. P. Thornberry, "Toward an Interactional Theory of Delinquency," *Criminology*, vol. 25, 1987, pp. 863–891.

38. For fuller descriptions of these and other programs, see J. S. Wall et al., *Juvenile Delinquency Prevention: A Compendium of 36 Program Models*, National Institute for Juvenile Justice and Delinquency Prevention, Law Enforcement Assistance Administration, U.S. Department of Justice, Washington, D.C., U.S. Government Printing Office (GPO), 1981; and J. G. Weiss and D. Hawkins, *Preventing Delinquency*, Reports of the National Institute for Juvenile Justice and Delinquency Prevention, U.S. Department of Justice, Washington, D.C., GPO, 1981.

39. See L. A. Cremin, *Public Education*, New York, Basic Books, 1976; M. Fantini, *Regaining Excellence in Education*, Columbus, Ohio, Merrill, 1986; and F. A. J. Ianni, "School and Community," in D. Allen and E. Seifert (eds.), *The Teacher's Handbook*, Chicago, Scott, Foresman, 1971.

40. F. A. J. Ianni, "The Effective Community and Educational Reform: Implications for Instructional Design," in H. Sirois (ed.), *Instructional Design*, Albany, N.Y., New York Association for Supervision and Curriculum Development, 1988.

41. These programs and other home-school programs are fully described in

C. H. Collins, O. Moles, and M. Cross, *The Home-School Connection: Selected Partnership Programs in Large Cities,* Boston, The Institute for Responsive Education, 1982. See also C. Ascher, *Trends and Issues in Urban and Minority Education, 1987,* New York, ERIC Clearinghouse on Urban Education, 1987. See also S. D. Otterbourg, op. cit., 1986, note 32 above.

42. L. B. Schorr with D. Schorr, *Within Our Reach: Breaking the Cycle of Disadvantage,* New York, Doubleday (Anchor), 1988; The Edna McConnell Clark Foundation, *1987 Annual Report: October 1, 1986– September 30, 1987,* New York.

43. See *Teenage Pregnancy: The Problem That Hasn't Gone Away,* New York, The Alan Guttmacher Institute, 1981.

44. See *The Forgotten Half: Non-College Youth in America,* op. cit., January 1988, note 31 above.

45. There is also a growing trend among researchers and youth professionals to look critically at the relationship among youth service agencies. Lauren Resnick, for example, has pointed to real differences which exist between how we learn in school as contrasted to how we learn in the community; we insist that children work on their own and not share their answers in school and then expect that they will work as team members on the job. Joan Lipsitz, whose work has been instrumental in pointing to the importance of not dealing with adolescence as if it were the same for older and younger teens, questions how we can hope to improve schools without improving communities. See L. Resnick, "Learning in School and Out," *Educational Researcher,* December 1987; J. Lipsitz, "School Improvement and Out-of-School Learning: Making the Connection," paper presented at the First Biennial Meeting of the Society for Research on Adolescence, March 1986. Questions about the ability of any one institution (or even of linkage between any two, such as the school and the family) to provide for juvenile and adolescent developmental needs are beginning to appear on the agendas of youth-serving professional groups. For an excellent analysis of the need for linking the school with the community beyond the family, see S. B. Heath and M. McLaughlin, "A Child Resource Policy: Moving Beyond Dependence on School and Family," *Phi Delta Kappan,* April 1987, pp. 576–580. See also J. S. Coleman and T. Hoffer, *Public and Private High Schools: The Impact of Communities,* New York, Basic Books, 1987, chap. 8, pp. 211–243.

46. S. Freud, *Civilization and Its Discontents,* translated by Joan Riviere, Garden City, N.Y., Doubleday, 1958.

47. Personal communication from Robert A. Aldrich. For an excellent description of the type of data gathering and organization necessary to

move a community in this direction, see R. A. Aldrich, "Children and Youth in Cities: The Story of Seattle's Kidsplace," in R. Carlson and B. Newman (eds.), *Issues and Trends in Health,* St. Louis, C. V. Mosby, 1987, pp. 63–69.

48. P. Benson et al., op. cit., 1987, note 3 above.

Bibliography

ADELSON, J. (ed.). 1980. *Handbook of Adolescent Psychology*. New York, Wiley.

ALDRICH, R. A. 1987. "Children and Youth in Cities: The Story of Seattle's Kidsplace." In *Issues and Trends in Health*, edited by R. Carlson and B. Newman. St. Louis, C. V. Mosby.

ALEXANDER, K. L., and ECKLAND, B. K. 1980. "The 'Explorations in Equality of Opportunity' Sample of 1955 High School Sophomores." In *Research in the Sociology of Education*, vol. 1, edited by A. C. Kerckhoff, 31–58. Greenwich, Conn., JAI Press.

ANDRISANI, P. J. 1978. *Work Attitudes and Labor Market Experience: Evidence from the National Longitudinal Surveys*. New York, Praeger.

ANDRY, R. G. 1962. "Parental Affection and Delinquency." In *The Sociology of Crime and Delinquency*, edited by M. Wolfgang, L. Savitz, and N. Johnston, 342–352. New York, Wiley.

ANTHONY, E. J., and COHLER, B. J. 1987. *The Invulnerable Child*. New York, Guilford Press.

ANTONUCCI, T. C. 1985. "Social Support: Theoretical Advances, Recent Findings, and Pressing Issues." In *Social Support Theory: Research and Applications*, edited by I. G. and B. R. Sarason. Dordrecht, The Netherlands, Martinus Nijhoff.

ARIÈS, P. 1962. *Centuries of Childhood: A Social History of Family Life*. New York, Vintage Books.

———. 1966. *The World of Children*. London, Paul Hamlyn.

ASCHER, C. 1985. *Pregnant and Parenting Teens: Statistics, Characteristics, and School-based Support Services*. New York, ERIC Clearinghouse on Urban Education.

BAHR, S. J. 1979. "Family Determinants and Effects of Deviance." In *Contemporary Theories About the Family,* vol. 1, edited by R. Wesley et al. New York, Free Press.

BAUMRIND, D. 1975. "Early Socialization and Adolescent Competence." In *Adolescence in the Life-Cycle,* edited by S. E. Dragastin and G. H. Elder, Jr., 117–143. New York, Wiley.

BEALER, R. C.; WILLITS, F. K.; and MAIDA, P. R. 1971. "The Rebellious Youth Culture—A Myth." In *Adolescent Behavior and Society: A Book of Readings,* edited by R. E. Muus, 454–463. New York, Random House.

BENEDICT, R. 1948. "Continuities and Discontinuities in Cultural Conditioning." In *Personality in Nature, Society and Culture,* edited by C. Kluckholn and H. A. Murray. New York, Knopf.

BENGTSON, V. L., and TROLL, L. 1978. "Youth and Their Parents: Feedback and Intergenerational Influence on Socialization." In *Child Influences on Marital and Family Interaction: A Life-Span Perspective,* edited by R. M. Learner and G. B. Spanier, 215–240. New York, Academic Press.

BENSON, P.; WILLIAMS, D.; and JOHNSON, A. 1987. *The Quicksilver Years: The Hopes and Fears of Early Adolescence.* San Francisco, Harper and Row.

BERNARDI, B. 1985. *Age Class Systems: Social Institutions and Polities Based on Age.* Cambridge, England, Cambridge University Press.

BLOOM, B. 1985. *Developing Talent in Young People.* New York, Ballantine Books.

BLOS, P. 1979. *The Adolescent Passage: Developmental Issues.* New York, International Universities Press.

BLUM, R. H. 1974. *Students and Drugs.* San Francisco, Jossey-Bass.

BOTT, E. 1971. *Family and Social Network,* 2nd ed. London, Tavistock.

BOYER, E. 1983. *High School: A Report on Secondary Education in America.* New York, Harper and Row.

BOYLE, H. C. 1984. *Community Is Possible: Repairing America's Roots.* New York, Harper and Row.

BRENNAN, T.; HUIZINGA, D.; and ELLIOT, D. S. 1978. *The Social Psychology of Runaways.* Boston, D. C. Heath.

BRONFENBRENNER, U.; MOEN, P.; and GABARINO, J. 1984. "Child, Family, and Community." In *Review of Child Development Research: The Family,* edited by R. D. Parke. Chicago, University of Chicago Press.

BROOKS-GUNN, J., and PETERSEN, A. C. (eds.). 1983. *Girls at Puberty: Biological and Psychosocial Perspectives.* New York, Plenum Press.

BUDDE, R. *Education by Charter: Restructuring School Districts.* Andover,

Mass., Regional Laboratory of Educational Improvement of the Northeast and Islands, 1988.

CALHOUN, C. J., AND IANNI, F. A. J. 1976. *Anthropological Studies in Education*. The Hague, Mouton.

CARD, J., and WISE, L. 1981. "Teenage Mothers and Teenage Fathers: The Impact of Early Childbearing on the Parents' Personal and Professional Lives." In *Teenage Sexuality, Pregnancy and Childbearing*, edited by F. Furstenberg, Jr., R. Lincoln, and J. Menken. Philadelphia, University of Pennsylvania Press.

CLOWARD, R. A., and OHLIN, L. E. 1960. *Delinquency and Opportunity: A Theory of Delinquent Gangs*. Glencoe, Ill., Free Press.

COHEN, A. 1985. *The Symbolic Construction of Communities*. London, Tavistock.

COLE, M., and GRIFFIN, P. 1971. *The Cultural Context of Learning and Thinking*. New York, Basic Books.

COLEMAN, J. 1980. *The Nature of Adolescence*. London, Methuen.

COLEMAN, J. S. 1963. *The Adolescent Society: The Social Life of the Teenager and Its Impact on Education*. Glencoe, Ill., Free Press.

——. 1974. *Youth: Transition to Adulthood: Report of the Panel on Youth of the President's Science Advisory Committee*. Chicago, University of Chicago Press.

——, and HOFFER, T. 1987. *Public and Private High Schools: The Impact of Communities*. New York, Basic Books.

COMSTOCK, G., and FISHER, M. 1978. *Television and Human Behavior*. New York, Columbia University Press.

CONGER, J. 1984. *Adolescence and Youth: Psychological Development in a Changing World*. New York, Harper and Row.

CRAIN, R. L.; MAHARD, R. E.; and NAROT, R. E. 1982. *Making Desegregation Work: How Schools Create Social Climates*. Lexington, Mass., Ballinger Press.

CREMIN, L. A. 1976. *Public Education*. New York, Basic Books.

CZEIKZENTMIHALYI, M., and LARSON, R. 1984. *Being Adolescent: Conflict and Growth in the Teen-Age Years*. New York, Basic Books.

DOUVAN, E., and ADELSON, J. 1966. *The Adolescent Experience*. New York, Wiley.

DUSEK, J. B. 1981. *The Development of the Self-Concept During the Adolescent Years*. Chicago, University of Chicago Press for the Society for Research in Child Development.

ELKIN, D. 1988. *Miseducation: Preschoolers at Risk*. New York, Knopf.

EPSTEIN, J., and KARWEIT, K. (eds.). 1983. *Friends in School*. New York, Academic Press.

ERIKSON, E. H. 1950. *Childhood and Society.* New York, Norton.

——. 1968. *Identity: Youth and Crisis.* New York, Norton.

ERLENMEYER-KIMLING, L., and MILLER, N. E. (eds.). 1986. *Life-Span Research on the Prediction of Psychopathology.* Hillsdale, N.J., L. Erlbaum.

ESMAN, A. H. (ed.). 1975. *The Psychology of Adolescence.* New York, International Universities Press.

FITCHEN, J. M. 1981. *Poverty in Rural America: A Case Study.* Westview Special Studies in Contemporary Social Issues. Boulder, Colo., Westview Press.

FREUD, A. 1948. *The Ego and the Mechanisms of Defense,* translated by C. Baines. New York, International Universities Press.

FREUD, S. 1948. "Transformations of Puberty." In *Three Contributions to the Theory of Sex,* 4th ed., translated by A. Brill. New York, Dutton.

FROMM, M. G., and SMITH, B. L. (eds.). 1988. *The Facilitating Environment: Clinical Applications of Winnicott's Theory.* New York, International Universities Press.

FURSTENBERG, F., JR. 1981. "The Social Consequences of Teenage Parenthood." In *Teenage Sexuality, Pregnancy and Childbearing,* edited by F. Furstenberg, Jr., R. Lincoln, and J. Menken. Philadelphia, University of Pennsylvania Press.

GARELL, D. C. 1987. "Motivating the Adolescent: Special Needs and Approaches." In *Issues and Trends in Health,* edited by R. Carlson and B. Newman. St. Louis, C. V. Mosby.

GINSBERG, E.; BERLINER, H.; and OSTOW, M. 1988. *Young People at Risk: Is Prevention Possible?* Boulder, Colo., Westview Press.

GORDON, C., and GERGEN, K. (eds.). 1968. *The Self in Social Interaction.* New York, Wiley.

GOTTMAN, J. M. 1983. "How Children Become Friends." *Monographs of the Society for Research in Child Development,* vol. 48, series no. 201.

GOULD, R. 1965. "Suicide Problems in Children and Adolescents." In *The Psychology of Adolescence, 1975,* edited by A. Esman. New York, International Universities Press.

GREENBERGER, E., and STERNBERG, L. D. 1986. *When Teenagers Work: The Psychological and Social Costs of Adolescent Employment.* New York, Basic Books.

GREENSPAN, S. I., and POLLOCK, G. H. (eds.). 1988. *The Course of Life.* New York, International Universities Press.

GROLNICK, S., and BARKIN, I. (eds.). 1978. *Between Reality and Fantasy: Transitional Objects and Phenomena.* New York, Jason Aronson.

GROTEVANT, H., and COOPER, C. (eds.). 1983. *Adolescent Development in the Family*. San Francisco, Jossey-Bass.

HAIM, A. 1969. *Les Suicides d'Adolescents*. Paris, Payot.

HALL, G. S. 1904. *Adolescence: Its Psychology and Its Relation to Physiology, Anthropology, Sociology, Sex, Crime, Religion and Education*, 2 vols. New York, Appleton.

HAMILTON, S. 1988. *The Interaction of Family, Community and Work in the Socialization of Youth*. Washington, D.C., Youth and America's Future: The William T. Grant Foundation Commission on Work, Family and Citizenship.

HAWKINS, J. D., and WALL, J. S. 1980. *Alternative Education: Exploring the Delinquency Prevention Potential*. National Institute for Juvenile Justice and Delinquency Prevention, U.S. Department of Justice. Washington, D.C., U.S. Government Printing Office.

HENDIN, H. 1964. *Suicide in Scandinavia*. New York, Grune and Stratton.

HEWITT, R. 1986. *White Talk, Black Talk: Inter-Racial Friendship Amongst Adolescents*. Cambridge, England, Cambridge University Press.

HIBBS, E. D. (ed.). 1988. *Children and Families: Studies in Prevention and Intervention*. New York, International Universities Press.

HIRSCHI, T. 1969. *Causes of Delinquency*. Berkeley, University of California Press.

HOPKINS, J. R. 1983. *Adolescence: The Transitional Years*. New York, Academic Press.

IANNI, F. A. J. March 1974. "Attitudes Towards the Relationship Among Stress Relief, Advertising and Youthful Drug Abuse in Two Recent Field Studies." In The National Commission on Marijuana and Drug Abuse. *Drug Use in America*. Washington, D.C., U.S. Government Printing Office.

_____. June 1978. "Social Organization of the High School and School Violence." In DHEW. *School Crime and Disruption: Prevention Models*. U.S. Department of Health, Education and Welfare.

_____. 1983. *Home, School and Community in Adolescent Education*. ERIC Clearinghouse on Urban Education. New York, Teachers College, Columbia University.

_____, and REUSS-IANNI, E. 1979. *School Crime and the Social Order of the School*. IRCD Bulletin, vol. 14, no. 1. A publication of the Institute for Urban and Minority Education. New York, Teachers College, Columbia University.

INHELDER, B., and PIAGET, J. 1958. *The Growth of Logical Thinking*. New York, Basic Books.

JANUS, M. D. 1987. *Adolescent Runaways: Causes and Consequences*. Lexington, Mass., Lexington Books.

JESSOR, R., and JESSOR, S. L. 1977. *Problem Behavior and Psychosocial Development: A Longitudinal Study of Youth.* New York, Academic Press.

JOHNSON, R. E. 1979. *Juvenile Delinquency and Its Origins: An Integrated Theoretic Approach.* New York, Cambridge University Press.

JOSSELSON, R. 1980. "Ego Development in Adolescence." In *Handbook of Adolescent Psychology,* edited by J. Adelson. New York, Wiley.

KEITH, C. R. 1984. *The Aggressive Adolescent: Clinical Perspectives.* New York, Free Press.

KETT, J. F. 1977. *Rites of Passage.* New York, Basic Books.

KOHLBERG, L. 1969. "Stage and Sequence: The Cognitive Developmental Approach to Socialization." In *Handbook of Socialization Theory and Research,* edited by D. Goslin. Chicago, Rand McNally.

KONOPKA, G. 1976. *Young Girls: A Portrait of Adolescence.* Englewood Cliffs, N.J., Prentice-Hall.

LASCH, CHRISTOPHER. 1979. *Haven in a Heartless World.* New York, Basic Books.

LAX, R. F.; BACH, S.; and BURLAND, J. A. (eds.). 1986. *Self and Object Constancy: Clinical and Theoretical Perspectives.* New York, Guilford Press.

LEFKOWITZ, B. 1987. *Tough Change.* New York, Free Press.

LEVINE, M. D., and MCANARNEY, E. (eds.). 1988. *Early Adolescent Transitions.* Lexington, Mass., D. C. Heath.

LEWIS, M., and ROSENBLUM, L. (eds.). 1975. *Friendship and Peer Relations.* New York, Wiley.

MARCIA, J. E. 1980. "Identity in Adolescence." In *Handbook of Adolescent Psychology,* edited by J. Adelson. New York, Wiley.

MATTESON, D. R. 1975. *Adolescence Today: Sex Roles and the Search for Identity.* Homewood, Ill., Dorsey.

MEAD, M. 1928. *Coming of Age in Samoa.* New York, Morrow.

_____. 1952. "Adolescence in Primitive and Modern Society." In *Readings in Social Psychology,* rev. ed., edited by G. E. Swanson et al., pp. 531–538. New York, Henry Holt.

MISHNE, J. M. 1986. *Clinical Work with Adolescents.* New York, Free Press.

MUUS, R. E. 1982. *Theories of Adolescence,* 4th ed. New York, Random House.

OFFER, D. 1969. *The Psychological World of the Teenager: A Study of Normal Adolescent Boys.* New York, Basic Books.

_____; OSTROV, E.; and HOWARD, K. 1981. *The Adolescent: A Psychological Self-Portrait.* New York, Basic Books.

OPIE, I. A., and OPIE, P. 1959. *The Lore and Language of Schoolchildren.* Oxford, England, Oxford University Press.

ORR, M. T. 1987. *Keeping Students in School.* San Francisco, Jossey-Bass.

OTTERBOURG, S. D. 1986. *School Partnerships Handbook: How to Set Up and Administer Programs with Business, Government and Your Community.* Englewood Cliffs, N.J., Prentice-Hall.

PARSONS, T. 1965. "Youth in the Context of American Society." In *The Challenge of Youth,* edited by E. H. Erikson. New York, Doubleday.

_____, and BALES, R. F. 1955. *Family, Socialization, and Interaction Process.* Glencoe, Ill., Free Press.

PIAGET, J. 1965. *The Moral Judgment of the Child.* New York, Free Press.

_____, and INHELDER, B. 1969. *The Psychology of the Child.* New York, Basic Books.

POLK, K. 1975. "A Reassessment of Middle-Class Delinquency." In *Contemporary Adolescence: Readings,* 2nd ed., edited by H. D. Thornburg. Monterey, Brooks/Cole.

POUVAN, E., and ADELSON, J. 1966. *The Adolescent Experience.* New York, Wiley.

President's Science Advisory Committee. 1973. *Youth: Transition to Adulthood.* Washington, D.C., U.S. Government Printing Office.

PRUYSER, P. W. 1983. *The Play of the Imagination: Toward a Psychoanalysis of Culture.* New York, International Universities Press.

REISS, D.; OLIVERI, M. E.; and CURD, K. 1983. "Family Paradigms and Adolescent Social Behavior." In *Adolescent Development in the Family,* edited by H. D. Grotevant and C. R. Cooper. San Francisco, Jossey-Bass.

REUSS-IANNI, E. 1983. *Street Cops vs. Management Cops: The Two Cultures of Policing.* New Brunswick, N.J., Transaction Press.

RICHARDS, M., and LIGHT, P. 1986. *Children of Social Worlds.* Cambridge, Mass., Harvard University Press.

RIESMAN, DAVID. 1950. *The Lonely Crowd: A Study of the Changing American Character.* New Haven, Yale University Press.

ROBERTS, A. R. 1981. *Runaways and Non-Runaways in an American Suburb.* New York, John Jay Press.

ROSENBERG, M. 1965. *Society and the Adolescent Self-Image.* Princeton, N.J., Princeton University Press.

SCHONFELD, W. A. 1971. "Adolescent Development: Biological, Psychological and Sociological Determinants." In *Adolescent Psychiatry,* vol. 1, edited by S. Feinstein, P. Giovacchini, and A. Miller. New York, Basic Books.

SEBALD, HANS. 1968. *Adolescence: A Sociological Analysis*. New York, Appleton-Century-Crofts.

SELTZER, V. C. 1982. *Adolescent Social Development: Dynamic Functional Interaction*. Lexington, Mass., Ballinger Press.

SUTTLES, G. D. 1972. *The Social Construction of Communities*. Chicago, University of Chicago Press.

TEC, N. 1974. *Grass is Green in Suburbia*. Roslyn Heights, N.Y., Libra.

THORNBURG, H. D. (ed.). 1975. *Contemporary Adolescence: Readings*, 2nd ed., 87–100, 187–194, 384–390. Monterey, Brooks/Cole.

TURNER, J. C. 1987. *Rediscovering the Social Group: A Self-Categorization Theory*. Oxford, Basil Blackwell.

VARENNE, H. 1983. *American School Language*. New York, Irvington Publications.

WALL, J. S., et al. 1981. *Juvenile Delinquency Prevention: A Compendium of 36 Program Models*. National Institute for Juvenile Justice and Delinquency Prevention, Office of Juvenile Justice and Delinquency Prevention, Law Enforcement Assistance Administration, U.S. Department of Justice. Washington, D.C., U.S. Government Printing Office.

WEIS, J. G., et al. 1980. *Jurisdiction and the Elusive Status Offender: A Comparison of Involvement in Delinquent Behavior and Status Offenses*. National Institute for Juvenile Justice and Delinquency Prevention, Office of Juvenile Justice and Delinquency Prevention, Law Enforcement Assistance Administration, U.S. Department of Justice. Washington, D.C., U.S. Government Printing Office.

WEIS, J. G., and HAWKINS, J. D. 1981. *Preventing Delinquency*. Reports of the National Juvenile Justice Assessment Centers, National Institute for Juvenile Justice and Delinquency Prevention, Office of Juvenile Justice and Delinquency Prevention, U.S. Department of Justice. Washington, D.C., U.S. Government Printing Office.

WILSON, J. P. 1978. *The Rights of Adolescents in the Mental Health System*. Lexington, Mass., Lexington Books.

WINNICOTT, D. W. 1965. *The Maturational Process and the Facilitating Environment*. New York, International Universities Press.

———. 1971. *Playing and Reality*. London, Tavistock.

———. 1984. *Deprivation and Delinquency*. London and New York, Tavistock.

———. 1986. *Home is Where We Start From: Essays by a Psychoanalyst*, compiled and edited by C. Winnicott, R. Shepherd, and M. Davis. New York, Norton.

WIREMAN, P. 1984. *Urban Neighborhoods, Networks, and Families: New Forms for Old Values*. Lexington, Mass., D. C. Heath.

WOLFGANG, M., and FERRACUTI, F. 1982. *The Subculture of Violence: Toward an Integrated Theory of Criminology*. Beverly Hills, Russell Sage.

WYNN, J., et al. 1988. *Communities and Adolescents: An Exploration of Reciprocal Supports*. Washington, D.C., Youth and America's Future: The William T. Grant Foundation Commission on Work, Family and Citizenship.

YARDLEY, K., and HONESS, T. (eds.). 1987. *Self and Identity: Psychosocial Perspectives*. New York, Wiley.

YORK, P., and YORK, D. 1982. *Tough Love*. New York, Doubleday.

YOUNISS, J. 1980. *Parents and Peers in Social Development: A Sullivan-Piaget Perspective*. Chicago, University of Chicago Press.

———, and SMOLLAR, J. 1985. *Adolescent Relations with Mothers, Fathers, and Friends*. Chicago, University of Chicago Press.

Index

Abernathy, Virginia, 83
Ability grouping, 27, 109, 116, 119, 132, 134, 135
Abortion, 80, 81, 82
Accountability in Citizenship Training (ACT) (Jacksonville, Florida), 277
Acculturation, 287
Adolescence (Hall), 9
Adolescence, 1, 260, 265
  as age-grade, 8
  early, 243–245, 247
  late, 246–247
  middle, 245–246, 247
  perspectives on, 13–14
  portrait of, 279–280
  theories on, 9–10
  as transitional state, 244–245
Adolescent society, 11
Adolescents
  media portrayal of, 2
  social role of, 43
  variations in, 19–20, 23
Adopt-a-school program, 274
Adults, turning to, 86
Advocacy, 88, 89
Agency hoppers, 91
Aggression, 185

Alternative Schools Network (Chicago), 275
Apprenticeships, 182, 270
Argotown (pseudonym), 195, 200, 237, 238, 246, 248, 252, 266, 267
  description of, 193–194
Asian-Americans, 4, 76
Athletic (sports) programs, 53, 96–97, 98–100, 120–121
Autonomy, 64, 85, 267

Baby booms, 16
Back to basics movement, 116, 140, 299
Banfield, Edward, 175
Being together, 30, 84
Best friend relationships, 27, 35, 214
Big Brothers and Big Sisters, 270
Blended families, 76
Bloom, Benjamin, 137
Blos, Peter, 15
Bonding, 73
Boston Compact, 269
Burke, Edmond, 261

Career development, 140
Career education model, 182

Career Intern Program (Philadelphia), 274
Caring community, 259, 268
Caring team, 278
Centro de Cambio (San Francisco), 277
Centro de La Comunidad Unida Delinquency Prevention and Youth Outreach Program (Milwaukee), 277
CETA (Comprehensive Employment Training Act), 92
Chang, Amy (pseudonym), 128–129, 135, 240
Chinese, 43, 94, 113, 128–131, 144, 209–211
Church social activities, 97–98
Civilization and Its Discontents (Freud), 280
Clark, Burton, 141
Cliques, 115, 133, 134
Cohort size, 16–18
Coleman, James, 11–12, 56, 138, 253
Collective fantasy, 258
Communications, 17, 57, 58, 81
Communities
  diversity among, 13
  selection of, 4–5
Community Arbitration Project (Anne Arundel County, Maryland), 275
Community colleges, 140
Community consensus, importance of, 218
Community improvement projects, 182
Community organization, models of, 195–197
Community planning, comprehensive, 280
Community youth development model, 275

Competition, 27, 122, 123, 124, 127, 138
Compulsory education, 103, 141
Conformity, 39–40, 42–43
Contraception, 78
Control, 57, 58, 59, 61, 64
  societal, legislative takeover of, 184–185
Control theorists, 219
Cooperative Federation for Educational Experiences (Project COFFEE) (Massachusetts), 274
Cooperative learning, 138, 151
Cooperative teaching and learning team, 276
Corporate mind-set, 117, 119
Correction officers, 216
Correctional institutions, 212
  social relationship patterns in, 213–214
Counterculture, 12, 253
Courts, 213
Creativity, 245
Crews, 133, 134, 205
Crime, juvenile, 185, 191
Criminal justice sanction, 190
Criminal justice system, 195
  and community, 193
  complaints against, 197
  routes through, 188
  and social institutions, 189, 198
Criminal justice system programs, 275–276
Crisis Intervention Network (Philadelphia), 276
Cultural determinism, 289–290
Cultural deviance theory, 219
Cultural insularity, 34
Culture of poverty, 91, 175
Curriculum, relevance of, 150
Cypress City (pseudonym), 109, 136, 204, 250
  description of, 107–108

Daydreams, 167, 256–257
de Tocqueville, Alexis, 261
Delgado, Josie (pseudonym), 32–33,
    58–59, 60–61, 62, 69, 77, 112–
    114, 135, 169
Delinquency, 1, 186, 187, 198, 200,
    208
    theories on, 219
Delinquency prevention programs,
    220–221
Delinquents, views on, 218–219
Demographic trends, 16–18
Dependency, 103
Deviance, 187, 195, 200
    responses to, 202
Deviant groups, 205, 206, 208
Discipline, 57, 58, 59, 108, 124, 126,
    192
Disruptive local groups, 205
Disruptive students, 148
Diversion(ary) programs, 188, 212,
    230, 235
Divorce, 18, 76
Dorchester Youth Collaborative
    (Massachusetts), 276
Dropout programs, 274, 278
Dropout rates, 104, 280, 300
Dropouts, 143, 145, 154, 246
    return of, 151, 152
    special programs for, 148
    view of, 149
    warning signals of, 147, 148
Dropping out, 108, 300
    causes of, 152
    consequences of, 149, 151, 153
    contributing factors to, 146–147
    definition of, 146
    involuntary, 153
    reasons for, 149–150
Drug abuse, 1, 2, 192, 200, 202–
    204
Drug abuse prevention programs,
    203, 204
Drug culture, 201

Drug trade, 108, 204, 214
Drug use, reasons for, 210
Drug user, 202, 203, 205

East Harlem Youth Action Program,
    272
Educating Connection, 92
Education; *see also* School
    American, 104
    defining value of, 140
    extended, reasons for, 141
Educational Clinics (Washington
    State), 275
Educational mobility, 115, 119
Educational values, 129–130
Ego ideals, 264
Ego resilience, 236
Elkind, David, 246
Emancipation, early, 84
Employment; *see also* Jobs; Work
    description of, 155–156
    difficulty finding, 157–158
    part-time/summer, 155, 160
    views, 167–169
Employment networks, absence of,
    154
Employment programs, 177
    emphasis on school of, 178
    ideology behind, 181
    multiproblem approach of, 179
    opposition to, 162–163
Employment-training programs, 163
Environments, social; *see also* Insti-
    tutions, social
    changing, 65–66
    conflict among, 4, 7, 65, 88, 89,
    262
    congruence in, 127, 232, 283
    dispersal of, 163
    interaction of, 14–15, 20–21, 23,
    28, 29, 55, 266
    lack of alternative, 71
    relationships among, 105, 130–
    131, 142, 144

Epigenetic, or stage, theory, 9, 287
Erikson, Erik, 9, 12, 207, 227, 258
Escape plans, 43
Estrangement, 261
Ethnic conflict, 33
Ethnic consciousness, 94
Ethnic differentiation, 109, 111
Ethnic diversity, 25–26, 32, 46, 128
Ethnic homogeneity, 26
Ethnic politics, 93
Ethnicity, 17, 44, 114, 131, 134,
    200, 209, 213, 236, 240, 271
Expectations, 59–60, 130, 131, 137,
    262
  discrepancy in, 179–180
Extended family, 60, 62, 77

Facilitating environment, 259, 265,
    268
Fairbairn, W. R. D., 267
Families, 25, 27, 28, 36–37, 51–52,
    54, 181, 204
  activities with, 84–85
  alienation from, 207
  changing, 76, 83
  conflict within, 15
  continuity of, 55–56
  different relationships within, 56
  educational deficits of, 112
  emotional support within, 56
  intervening in, 91
  self-concept of, 63
  social changes in, effect of, 77–
    78
  socially isolated, 62
  strengthening of, 93
Family, 3, 4, 54, 102, 166, 257, 261,
    263, 264, 308
  as community, 60, 71
  community as, 59, 61
  impact on schooling of, 135–136
  traditional American, disappear-
    ance of, 75
Family analogue, 75

Family breakups, feelings about, 77
Family configurations, variety of,
    75–76
Family court, 188–189
Family Court Act, 189
Family experience, expanded, 62
Family Learning Center (Leslie,
    Michigan), 278
Family programs, 278
Family-centeredness, 27
Fantasies, 241, 244–250, 255–257,
    308, 310
  characteristics of, 243
  functions of, 242
Fathers, 85
  absence of, 76, 77
  adolescent, 81
  relationships with, 63–64, 65
Fidelity, 207, 208, 209
Focus group interviewing, 286–287
Fordham, Signithia, 111
Freedom, 57, 85
Frenchtown, 193–194
Freud, Sigmund, 134, 244, 280
Friedenberg, Edgar, 10
Friends, conflicts over, 36–37
Friendship groups, 46
Friendship patterns, 240
Friendships, 28, 35, 36
Future, concern with, 248–250

Gang culture, values in, 215–216
Gang members, 207–208
Gangs, 26, 32, 42, 133, 134, 206,
    211, 222, 278
  adult criminal, 209
  Chinese, 209–211
  in detention centers, 214–215
  fighting, 205, 207, 209
  younger, 41
GED (General Education Diploma),
    152–153
Geertz, Clifford, 264

Gender, 15–16, 42, 63, 64–65, 155, 246, 247, 256–257
  sexuality and, 37–39
Gender equity, campaign for, 19
Generation gap, 12
Gentrification, 33
Good enough environment, 51, 231, 266, 268
Gorer, Geoffrey, 252
Grange, 100
Green Valley (pseudonym), 70, 72–73, 76, 77, 79, 85, 87, 89–90, 98–101, 109, 128, 142, 160–166, 187, 191–192, 200, 222, 250, 267
  description of, 69
Group discussion-interviews, 6
Guardian Angels, 206
Guilford County Women's Resident Day Center (Greensboro, North Carolina), 276

Haim, A., 261
Hall, G. Stanley, 9
Hard drugs, 201
Health, concern with, 247–248
Health promotion programs, 248
High schools, 103, 104
  expectations for, 140
Hill-toppers, 194–195
Hispanic students, 112–114
Hoffer, Thomas, 138
Home is Where We Start From (Winnicott), 55
Home–school relationship, 143–145
Homebuilders (New York City), 278
Homework, 124–125, 137
Homicide rates, 186
How I Grew (McCarthy), 43
Husén, Torsten, 181

"I Have a Dream" Foundation, 269
Identification, 310–311

Identity, 10, 12, 43–44, 54, 65, 66, 73, 135, 235, 240, 250, 259, 261, 268
  achievement of, 227–228
  diversified, 241
  integration of, 243
Identity crisis, 227
Identity formation, 28, 231–232, 237, 257–258, 311
Immigration, 17
Incest, 74–75
Incorrigibility, 186
Individuation, 265, 266
  second, 288–289
Influence, 47
Initiation ritual, 258–259
Inmate culture, 216
Inner-city areas, 63, 65, 113, 201, 222, 235, 240, 242, 247, 248, 254, 256
Inroads (Chicago), 269
Institutional domains, 241
Institutions, social; *see also* Environments, social
  absence of, 173–174
  conflict among, 177, 211–212, 234, 235, 236
  failure of, 185
  interaction among, 189, 190, 220–222
  relationships among, 201
Interactionist inquiry, 20
Interviews, 5–6, 286
Introjection, 310–311
Invulnerable children, 53
Isolation, 69, 191

Jill (pseudonym), 70, 238–240, 241
Job future, absence of, 166
Job Readiness Program (Chicago), 274
Job readiness skills, 179
Job satisfaction, 170

Jobs; *see also* Employment; Work
  impacts of, 169–171
  importance of, 171
  low-paying, dead-end, 143, 145,
    149, 154, 160, 168
  subsidized public sector, 180–181
Job-training programs, 160–161
Jocks, 123–124
Johnson, Ginny (pseudonym), 224–
  226, 232, 240, 241
Juvenile Conference Committee
  (JCC), 189
Juvenile courts, 186, 190
Juvenile detention center, 213, 218
  alternative informal networks in,
  215
Juvenile justice services, 202
Juvenile justice system, as court of
  last resort, 191
Juvenile offender laws, 189

Kinship, 28, 61, 77, 174, 196, 213
Kohn, Melvin, 178

Labeling, 240
Labor market, 140, 141, 143, 144,
  152, 158, 171–172
  local, 160
Lang, Eugene, 269
Latchkey children, 83
Learning, factors of, 136–137
Learning centers, community's, rela-
  tionships of, 139
Learning environment, 129, 131, 136
Learning Web (Ithaca, New York),
  269
Levinson, Daniel, 271
Life cycle, stages in, 227
Life-style characteristics, 143, 144
Literacy, demands for, 141
Loss of love, 244, 245

Mahler, Margaret, 266
Maldonato, John (pseudonym), 41

Marriage, 82
Master identity, 237
McCarthy, Mary, 43
Media, 3, 45, 92
  influence of, 251–257
Mediating roles, 270–271
Megan, Bruce (pseudonym), 34–35,
  57, 60, 61, 114–115, 159
Mentoring, functions of, 87
Mentoring programs, 269–270
Mentors, 87, 101, 149, 270
Migrant workers, 101, 107, 108–109,
  166–167, 168, 188, 203–204
Minorities, 17–18, 81, 82, 94, 104,
  111, 113, 149, 154, 250, 271
Misbehavior, community attitudes to-
  ward, 186–187
Moral depravity, 186
Mortality rates, 185
Mothers, 85
  relationships with, 63
  unwed, 81, 82
Music, 251–252

Nature versus nurture debate, 10
Networks, 271, 273
New Futures School (Albuquerque,
  New Mexico), 278
New Lost Generation, 2
Newtown (pseudonym), 67–68, 72,
  76, 95, 115–116, 121, 142, 144,
  150, 160, 170, 188, 198–199,
  200, 224, 232–233, 237, 248,
  266
  description of, 66

Observations, description of, 5
Offer, Daniel, 19
Ogbu, John U., 111
Open schools, 116
Order, structure of, 126
Out-of-wedlock births, 82
Outsiders, 199, 200, 203

Parent Plus Project (Chicago), 276
Parental involvement, lack of, 113
Parenting, 76
    patterns of, 63
Parent-proof school, 113, 121
Parsons, Talcott, 11
Partnership Program, 274
Partnership Program (San Diego,
    California), 276
Peer counseling, 53
Peer group influence, 47, 50, 54
Peer groups, 2, 3, 11–12, 22–23, 27,
    41, 51, 55, 84–86, 131, 134,
    151, 158, 160, 169, 181, 184,
    202, 204, 205, 206, 221, 222,
    233, 234, 237, 257, 258, 261,
    263, 264
    differences in, 28–30, 46
    factions in, 31
    and family, interdependence of, 37
    feelings in common of, 29–30
    interaction within and between,
        25–26
    and local adult community, 45–46,
        50–52
    need to separate from, 43
    role of, 50
    as scapegoat, 50
    social needs of, 35
    subgroups within, 31
Peer interaction, conflictual, 25
Peer pressure, 48, 52, 201
Peer support groups, adult mediated,
    52, 53, 138
Peer tutoring, 53
Peer-based programs, 272, 278
Peers, concern for opinions of, 42
Person in need of supervision (PINS),
    189
Peterson, Anne, 19
Piaget, Jean, 134, 287
Police, 189, 192, 197, 201, 202
    discretion of, 186, 187

Policy Plan for Children and Youth
    (Seattle, Washington), 281
Political power, struggles over, 32
Politics of race, 199
Polk, Kenneth, 208
Popularity, 39
Positive Educational Experiences in
    Relationships (PEER) (Minne-
    apolis), 271
Positive Youth Action Team (Madi-
    son, Wisconsin), 272
Powerlessness, 250
Predictability, 127, 266
Pregnancy, 1, 38, 78–79, 81, 82,
    246, 280
    adult dual attitudes toward, 80
    deficits of, 80–81
    sociology of, 295
Pregnant teenagers, characteristics
    of, 82
Pressures to excel, 117, 119, 127,
    225
Primary Prevention School Program
    (Yale Child Study Center), 53
Primary social bonds, 217
Problem of the seventh grade, 127
Professionals, youth, disillusionment
    of, 178–179
Project City's Children (Minneapo-
    lis), 280
Project Community Pride, 189
Project Double Discovery (Columbia
    University), 269
Psychiatric wards, relationships in,
    216–217
Psychodynamic interviews, 6
Psychosocial moratorium, 227
Puberty, 8, 15, 288
Public schools, 138–139

Rainwater, Lee, 177
Ranchville (pseudonym), 108–109,
    111, 136, 146, 166, 168, 188,

Ranchville *cont.*
203–204, 236, 250, 254, 267, 270, 300
description of, 106–107
Reality testing, 242
Recapitulation, 9
Redl, Fritz, 236
Rejection, social, 37, 245
Rent-a-Kid Program (St. Paul, Minnesota), 270
Research methodology, 4–7, 285–286
Residential group home, 91
Resocialization, 190
Responsibility, 57
Rich's Academy (Atlanta), 274
Riesman, David, 11
Riverton (pseudonym), 133–135, 136, 139, 142, 170, 198, 244, 248
description of, 131–132
Rochester Brainpower Program, 274
Role identities, 237, 238, 241, 264
Role models, 12, 44, 62, 86, 218, 234, 251, 267, 270, 271
absence of, 149, 154
Roles, 43–44, 233, 240, 241, 246, 250, 264
Runaways, 73–75
Running away, 71–73
Rural areas, 69, 101, 113, 254
Rural family organizations, 100–101

Safe Schools Study, 126, 128
Sampson, Edward, 236
Say YES (Youth Enterprise System) (Los Angeles), 277
School, 3, 75, 92, 102, 233–234; *see also* Education
dissatisfaction with, 150
as part-time, 156–157
School achievement, elements related to, 137
School culture, 105

School–home connection, 136
School Mediators' Alternative Resolution Teams (SMART) (New York City), 271
School reform, 152, 299
School transitions, 127–128
School–work conflict, 158
School-based programs, 274, 277–278
Schooling
antagonism toward, 208
attitudes toward, 114, 137
disdain for, 112
view of, 119
Schools
differences among, 105
evaluation of, 142–143, 150
expectations for, 140
failure of, 144, 145
role of, 103–104
School-to-work transition programs, 273–274
School-with-work programs, 182–183
Second chance programs, 275
Second families, 76
Secondary Credit Exchange Program (Washington State), 275
Segregation, 33, 132, 134
Self
theories of, 309
truths of, 259
Self-awareness, 36, 37, 39, 43
Self-esteem, 114, 128, 131, 134, 138
approaches to, 241
Self-insight, 242
Self-sorting, 109, 112
Seminole County (pseudonym), 108, 110, 202
description of, 106
Senior citizens, 171
Sense of community, 138–139
Sensei, 86
Separation, 71, 243, 245, 265

Separation anxiety, 49
Separation-individuation, 308, 311
Settlement house, 90, 91
Sex roles, 43
Sexual abuse, 49, 74–75
Sexual fantasy, 242
Sexual identity, 83
Sexual maturation, 37, 38
Sexual revolution, 78, 81
Sexual teasing, 38
Sexuality, 15, 37–39, 78, 288
Sharing, 36, 138
Sheffield (pseudonym), 34–39, 42,
    44–47, 57–61, 64, 76, 77, 79,
    81, 83, 85, 87, 89, 95–98, 110,
    112, 114–123, 126–127, 135,
    139, 142, 144, 150, 158–160,
    168, 188–190, 195, 200, 221,
    232–233, 237, 248, 256, 266
  description of, 26–27
Single mothers, 280
Single-parent family, 75, 76, 77, 207
Situational identities, 236–238
Smyrna Beach (pseudonym), 108,
    111, 136, 160, 200, 203, 243,
    248
  description of, 106
Snap session, 42
Snowball sample, 5
Social agencies, 87–92, 95–98, 222
  community-based, 130: commu-
    nity-funded, 94–95; externally
    funded, 93–94; replacement of,
    176
  self-defined functions of, 92
Social agency culture, 89
Social categorization, 134
  characteristics of, 109–110
Social development approach, 220
Social differentiation, 110
Social integration, imperfect, 199
Social learning approach, 219
Social reality, child's perspective on,
    61

Social system, artificial, 199
Social trends, 18–19
Socialization, 10, 14, 56, 134, 135,
    177, 211, 220, 259, 262, 266,
    267, 308
  ineffective, 219, 222
Socioeconomic status, 17, 52, 76,
    104, 124, 137
Soft drugs, 201
Sorting, 109–110, 112, 114, 116,
    119, 121, 128, 130, 131–136,
    210, 222, 236, 240, 297
  result of, 111
Southside (pseudonym), 29, 32–34,
    36, 38, 39, 41, 42, 44, 46, 58,
    60, 62, 69, 72, 73, 76, 77, 79,
    83, 85, 87–93, 111, 112, 114,
    121, 127–130, 135, 139, 142–
    146, 157, 158, 168–170, 175,
    178, 179, 187–189, 201, 207,
    209–212, 216, 222, 228, 233,
    234, 236–238, 248, 256, 267,
    270
  description of, 24–26
Special education students, 148
Spruceville, 193
State Task Force on Youth Gang Vio-
    lence (California), 276
Status offenders, 184
Status offenses, 186, 187
Storm and stress, 9, 12, 19
Street family, 73
Structure, search for, 262
Subcultures, 208
Subsidized housing, 121–122, 199
Suburban areas, 63, 71, 201, 222,
    240, 249, 254, 256
Suicidal thoughts, 49
Suicide, 48, 128
  causes of, 49
  copycat, 3, 48
  family relationships and, 49
Suicide pacts, 2–3
Suicide rates, 48, 186

Sullivan, Mercer, 81
Supervision, absence of adult, 83–84
Surrogate families, 91

Teachers and administrators, 144
Teens on Patrol (Tampa, Florida),
    272
Television, 253, 256–257, 308
    influence of, 252
    viewing patterns for, 254–255
Territoriality, 33
Thefts, 188
Tracking (streaming), 110, 112, 133,
    135
Tran, Hoang Nhu, 3
Turner, Victor, 258
Tutoring programs, 269
Twelve Together (Detroit), 278

Underground economy, 175, 211
Unemployability, 172
Unemployment, 144, 153, 175, 181
    effects of, 141
    feelings about, 168
    impact of, 171–172

Valued Youth Partnership Program
    (San Antonio, Texas), 274
Values, 11, 12, 52, 59, 60, 78, 114,
    127, 259, 262
Van Gennep, Arnold, 259
Vandalism, 188, 191, 192, 208
Victor (pseudonym), 228–231, 233–
    237, 240, 241
Violence, 185, 187–188, 205
Vocational training, 142, 150, 163,
    182

Volunteer Corps (New York City),
    272

Walberg, Herbert, 136
Wharton Hill (pseudonym), 170,
    175–179, 188, 195–198, 201,
    207, 209, 211, 215, 220, 222,
    234, 236, 237, 243, 248, 256,
    267, 270
    description of, 172–174
Winnicott, D. W., 55, 244, 259, 265
Women's movement, 18
Work, 266–267; *see also* Employ-
    ment; Jobs
    fantasies about, 180
    meaning of, 154, 155, 166–167
    negative effects of, 159
    view of, 159
Work–family conflict, 159–160
Workplace, 75, 139
Work-study program, 161

Yankelovich, Daniel, 259
Youngs, David, 83
Youth, 8
Youth Action Program (East Har-
    lem), 269
Youth agenda, 281
Youth charter, 263–264, 266–268,
    279, 281–282
Youth culture, national, 12–13, 45,
    48, 78, 253
Youth programs, successful, 279
Youth Relations Deputy Program,
    202
Youth as Resources (Boston), 272
Youth services program, 195